MANIFEST DESIGN

MANIFEST DESIGN

*American Exceptionalism
and Empire*

REVISED EDITION

THOMAS R. HIETALA

Cornell University Press · Ithaca and London

First published 1985 by Cornell University Press
First printing, Cornell Paperbacks, 1990

Printed in the United States of America

Library of Congress Cataloging-in-Publication Data

Hietala, Thomas R., 1952–
    Manifest design.

    Bibliography: p.
    Includes index.
    1. United States—Territorial expansion.   2. United
States—History—1815–1861.   I. Title.
E179.5.H54   1985   973.5'8   84-45808
ISBN 0-8014-8846-X (pbk. : alk. paper)

Cornell University Press strives to use environmentally responsible
suppliers and materials to the fullest extent possible in the publishing
of its books. Such materials include vegetable-based, low-VOC inks
and acid-free papers that are recycled, totally chlorine-free, or partly
composed of nonwood fibers. For further information, visit our
website at www.cornellpress.cornell.edu.

Paperback printing   10   9   8   7   6   5   4   3   2   1

Contents

Preface to the Revised Edition

Stationed in northern Mexico with the United States Army in 1847, Samuel Ryan Curtis, a commander of Ohio volunteers, sensed "a strange fatality directing the counsels of the two nations, all tending to protract this unfortunate war." Mexican and American leaders had hoped to avoid hostilities, but the pride and miscalculation of one and the impatience and ambition of the other had led to bloodshed. In both countries people debated the causes and likely outcome of the war. Amid rampant confusion, one prediction seemed as good as another. "The town has been thrown into a great excitement in consequence of the reported approach of a woman who is represented to be a new 'Saint,'" Curtis reported from Camargo. "She was announced some hours before dark as approaching from Reinosa on foot. Thousands went out to meet her, and . . . it required some hours for her to travel the last mile." An "elderly woman" under "a black veil," she walked with "some hundred women," including two who shaded her with an umbrella. People fell at her feet and kissed her hands. "She said she had been dead eight days and was buried at San Jose near Reinosa," Curtis explained, and "had seen Jesus Christ three times." On more temporal matters she ventured a prophecy: "This war would continue for seven years, and at the end of that time the Americans would have possession . . . result[ing] in a benefit to the people of this Country." Curtis watched as local sentiment changed. "The so-called 'Saint' has rather declined in public esteem," he observed a few days later. "The multitude look for a miracle and no miracle is performed."

Mexican leaders also looked for a miracle to save themselves and their nation. Commander Anastasio Parrode rallied his troops after an initial setback. "Soldiers! Another time we shall conquer," he consoled them. "Such is the fate of war, a defeat today and glory tomorrow; that glory which shall be ours at the end of this holy struggle. The God of battles is trying our valour, but he has not abandoned us. We know how to conquer, and we know how to suffer." But Mexican forces suffered far more than they conquered. The armies mobilized for a showdown near Buena Vista in early 1847. "You are surrounded by twenty thousand men," General Santa Anna warned General Zachary Taylor, "and cannot, in any human probability, avoid suffering a rout and being cut to pieces with your troops. . . . I wish to save you from a catastrophe." But Taylor rebuffed Santa Anna, and American forces prevailed. United States troops occupied Vera Cruz and then marched on the capital. "Mexicans! Your fate is the fate of the nation!" Santa Anna exhorted his people. "Not the Americans but you will decide her destiny! Vera Cruz calls for vengeance!—follow me, and wash out the stain of her dishonour."[1]

Mexicans soon realized that their destiny could not compete with the Americans' "manifest destiny." Events revealed, however, that Mexico had no monopoly on false prophets. In the fall of 1845, President James K. Polk had dispatched John Slidell to reconcile Mexican leaders to the annexation of Texas and the purchase of California. "I have never at any time believed," Slidell wrote from New Orleans, "that we shall have war with Mexico." Polk strengthened the American squadron in the Gulf and ordered Taylor's army to the Rio Grande, moves Slidell hailed as "wise measures which may exercise a salutary influence upon the course of this Government." Polk expected the military pressure and the cash tendered for California to achieve his goals. "There

1. *Mexico under Fire: Being the Diary of Samuel Ryan Curtis*, ed. Joseph E. Chance (Fort Worth, 1994), 130–31, 133; Parrode's Proclamation, May 13, 1846; Santa Anna to Taylor, February 22, 1847; Santa Anna's Proclamation, March 31, 1847; Nathan Brooks, *A Complete History of the Mexican War* (reprint of 1849 ed.: Chicago, 1965), 152, 208, 320. President Mariano Paredes expressed similar sentiments on April 23, 1846, when he explained his order to the army to repel American forces on the northern frontier: "I . . . call upon the God of battles; He will preserve the valor of our troops, the unquestionable right to our territory, and the honor of those arms which are used only in defense of justice." *Origins of the Mexican War*, ed. Ward McAfee and J. Cordell Robinson, 2 vols. (Salisbury, N.C., 1982), 2:134.

will be no war with Mexico," he assured his brother. Hemmed in by rising anti-Americanism, Mexican officials refused to receive Slidell. "We can never get along well with them," Slidell informed the administration in early 1846, "until we have given them a good drubbing." Polk remained optimistic despite the failure of his diplomacy, noting in his diary that the war would be "speedily terminated." Thomas Ritchie, Polk's editorial voice, agreed, noting that Mexico had a high percentage of mixed races and relatively few Europeans. "The Mexican population can offer but a slight resistance to the North American race," Ritchie predicted after Congress declared war. "Its motley character and physical structure are the surest indications of defeat."[2]

The war lasted longer and cost more in lives, resources, and reputations than Polk and Ritchie expected. They were more accurate, however, in seeing the offensive against Mexico as a symbol of an evolving American empire. Expansion was not new in the 1840s, but this imperial surge was novel in its extent and urgency as the nation continued to remove eastern Indians to the West, annexed Texas, acquired Oregon south of 49°, and conquered and obtained New Mexico and California. To promote trade, the expansionists acquired ports on the Pacific, opened and enlarged foreign markets, and improved the navy. Presidents Tyler and Polk and their advisers employed many tactics— open diplomacy, intrigue by secret agents, economic leverage, intimidation, and offensive war—methods that raised predictable concerns in London, Paris, and Mexico City.

But these initiatives divided Washington as well. Charles J. Ingersoll of Pennsylvania defended the American conquest of the borderlands. "Do we not always civilize, humanize, and reclaim vanquished savages?" he queried in 1847. "And how much are the few straggling vagabonds of California, or the not much more numerous civilized half-breeds of New Mexico, superior to savages?" Caleb Smith, however, accused Polk and his partisans of baser motives. "The administration is a southern one," Smith complained. "Its partiality for southern men and southern interests has . . . excite[d] loud and open murmurs from many of its friends. . . . California is desired as a means of extending and perpet-

2. Slidell to Secretary of State James Buchanan, September 25, 1845, Buchanan Papers; Slidell Dispatch, February 17, 1846, William R. Manning, ed., *The Diplomatic Correspondence of the United States, Inter-American Affairs, 1831–1860*, 12 vols. (Washington, 1932–1939), 8:813; James Polk to William Polk, "Private," November 27, 1845, Polk Papers; Slidell Dispatch, March 17, 1846, *Diplomatic Correspondence*, 8:832; *The Diary of James K. Polk during His Presidency*, ed. Milo M. Quaife, 4 vols. (Chicago, 1910), 1:392, 411.

uating the power and influence of the South." The completion of "the iniquitous scheme of annexing Texas," he added, had "sharpened the appetite" of those wanting more "southern territory." Senator John Davis of Massachusetts defined those "southern interests." "I think I fully understand the views of the President on this question of enlarging our boundaries," he contended in 1847. "His sentiments, sympathies, and desires are those of a slaveholder, desirous of giving permanency and perpetuity to the institution."[3]

American settlers had eclipsed the Mexicans in Texas and, with ample aid from southern whites, had rebelled and won their independence. Other pioneers moved to Oregon, a territory open to Americans and British under a "joint occupation" agreement. A small band of Americans, many of them merchants, lived in Mexican California when war broke out in 1846. This dispersion of hardy migrants inspired observers to insist that pioneers and not politicians won the West. Editor John L. O'Sullivan, who coined the phrase "manifest destiny," articulated this vision of empire:

> Year upon year has the tide of our national increase rolled still further westward, making the desert to bloom in its progress, carrying with it the blessings of civil and religious liberty, and illuminating the night of barbarism with the light of education and science. During the whole time no instance of aggrandizement or lust for territory has stained our annals. No nation has been despoiled by us, no country laid desolate, no people overrun.[4]

The Shawnee, Sauk, Cherokee, and Seminole Indians could attest that the United States and its citizens had indeed "despoiled" and "overrun" other peoples. The conquest and occupation of the borderlands in 1846 was an obvious "instance of aggrandizement." But O'Sullivan and other Democrats did not fret about methods. They asserted a higher claim to new lands whether diplomats, soldiers, or settlers wrested them from rivals.

Pioneers played a role in expansion, but the historical record points to politicians and propagandists as the primary agents of empire. Racial, economic, social, and political factors coalesced to make territorial and commercial expansion enticing to American leaders. These

3. *Congressional Globe* (hereafter *CG*), 29 Congress, 2 session, Appendix 130 (January 19, 1847); *CG*, 29 Cong., 1 sess., App. 1118 (July 16, 1846); *CG*, 29 Cong., 2 sess., App. 420 (February 25, 1847).

4. New York *Morning News*, November 20, 1845.

forces gained momentum from 1842 to 1845 and climaxed with the acquisition of Texas and California.

The letters and journals of American soldiers in Mexico show that they carried more than muskets and munitions into battle. Lieutenant Napoleon Jackson Dana, a quartermaster in Taylor's Army, pondered prospects before the first skirmish of the war. "We will make them run to the tune of 'Yankee Doodle,' the black rascals," he predicted. "The best of them are robbers and murderers." After nine months in Mexico, Dana ridiculed reports by war correspondents that the Americans had been smitten by *las señoritas.* "As for ugliness, I have never seen any old Negro half so hideous and disgusting in appearance as very many of the wretched hags of this ill-famed race," he wrote to his wife, Sue. "The brown order of Mexican women as a race . . . are without exception the most revolting, forbidding, disgusting creatures in the world, not even excepting our own Indians." Writing from Puebla in 1847, Ralph Kirkham, an infantry officer, assessed the residents for his wife, Kate. "The lower classes . . . at least nineteen-twentieths of the whole population, are poor, miserable beings who are as ignorant and superstitious as it is possible to be," he maintained. "The majority of the Mexicans seem rather to vegetate than otherwise," though the "rascally priests" lived well. Kirkham thought Mexico City was no better. "I suppose there is no nation on earth where there is so much wickedness and vice of all kinds," he wrote from the capital. "There is little incentive to virtue here. . . . Instances are common of men selling their wives and sisters, and often their mothers and daughters."

Routinely described as torpid and venal, Mexicans seemed incapable of good government, sound economy, or true religion. After the initial American triumphs, Lieutenant William Henry predicted the victors would soon possess the Rio Grande Valley. "It certainly never was intended this lovely land, rich in every production . . . should remain in the hands of an ignorant and degenerate race," he reflected. "The finger of Fate points, if not to their eventual extinction, to the time when they will cease to be owners, and when the Anglo-American race will rule with republican simplicity and justice." Soldiers' opinions did not improve with greater familiarity. Franklin Smith, a captain of Mississippi volunteers, expected Mexican "laziness, cowardice, and ignorance" to "give way" to Yankee "industry, courage, and intelligence." "The Mexicans as a people are capable of any treachery, bribery, corruption, fraud, and robbery," Smith asserted. "There is and must be in every country . . . a civilized class that has pride of character—the men honourable—the women virtuous—but in Mexico this class must be smaller than in any other country called *civilized*."

Many soldiers contrasted Mexico's natural riches with its poor people. Cotton grew "quite plentifully" near the Rio Grande but was "not cultivated at all," Lieutenant George McClellan observed at Matamoros. Locals raised only "a little Indian corn" and seemed "the laziest people in existence." With "a rich and fertile country," they were "content to roll in the mud, eat their horrible beef and tortillas and dance all night at their fandangos." When American troops occupied the capital, Thomas Barclay of Pennsylvania anticipated a deluge of pioneers. "The Anglo-Saxon race, that land-loving people, are on the move," he warned. "In an incredible short time they have overrun an immense territory in the north. . . . And the same people who have driven before them the various Indian tribes and have in Texas come in contact with the Spanish race will soon hang like a wave over . . . Mexico. No embankments, no treaties can prevent the inundation." Barclay expected Mexico's defeat to discredit its military and Catholic clergy. "Other civilized countries strive to keep up with the spirit of the age," he suggested. "Those who rule Mexico endeavor to keep down every feeling of progress or improvement." To Barclay and his comrades, the war symbolized the inevitable triumph of civilization over savagery. "White" nations advanced; countries with Indian, African, Asian, or mixed majorities faced decline and probable extinction.[5]

The soldiers who whistled "Yankee Doodle," however, marched on Chapultepec in compliance with orders from the commander in chief and secretary of war. Their supplies and pay came from Congress. The images of caissons heading south to battle and covered wagons rolling westward have inspired generations of writers, painters, and lithographers, but such icons reflect romantic nationalism rather than the complex dynamics of aggrandizement. Expansionists assumed that the hand of God guided the nation's destiny, but skeptics pointed instead to the fidgety and grasping fingers of James Polk, Robert Walker, Lewis Cass, Stephen Douglas, and others. These leaders sought cheap secu-

5. *Monterrey Is Ours! The Mexican War Letters of Lieutenant Dana, 1845–1847*, ed. Robert H. Farrell (Lexington, 1990), 46, 180–81; *The Mexican War Journal and Letters of Ralph W. Kirkham*, ed. Robert Ryal Miller (College Station, 1991), 21; William S. Henry, *Campaign Sketches of the War with Mexico* (New York, 1849), 118; *The Mexican War Journal of Captain Franklin Smith*, ed. Joseph E. Chance (Jackson, 1991), 11, 89; *The Mexican War Diary of George B. McClellan*, ed. William Starr Myers (Princeton, 1917), 11–12; *Volunteers: The Mexican War Journals of Private Richard Coulter and Sergeant Thomas Barclay*, ed. Allan Peskin (Kent, 1991), 180–82.

rity and domestic harmony through territorial and commercial growth. Confident they could balance republicanism and empire, they viewed their critics as fools, even traitors.

Chapter 1 introduces the major themes of this study—that foreign policy in the 1840s was primarily a response to internal concerns and that Democrats (and Tyler Whigs) preferred new land and markets over extensive federal regulation and reform. Chapter 2 examines the disdain for African Americans among policy makers, politicians, and editors who hoped to annex Texas as a way to foil the abolitionists and counter the menace of a rising free-soil republic bordering the South. By the 1840s slavery was sectional, race prejudice national. Leaders who wanted Texas sought primarily to shield and expand the peculiar institution, not to extend the area of human freedom.

In the debate over annexation, exports, particularly cotton and grain, loomed large, and calculations about trade and territory are the subject of Chapter 3. Prosperity improved security; enhanced security promised even greater wealth. So political leaders and plebeians alike had a stake in acquiring lands, resources, ports, and markets controlled by other peoples and nations. The expansionists hoped to manipulate trade as a means to preempt Great Britain as the world's dominant military and commercial power.

Americans stood on the brink of the industrial revolution in the 1840s, and Chapter 4 examines the expansionists' fears about manufacturing, urbanization, congestion, and class conflict, and their expectations that new land and markets could prevent or alleviate the ills of modernization. These neo-Jeffersonians preferred farms and plantations to factories, villages to cities, and migration and mobility to concentration and stratification. White slavery, they warned, might replace black if Whigs, abolitionists, and industrialists had their way. Expansionists welcomed new inventions that could help conquer distance, but they looked askance at large mills, mines, factories, and a central bank, regarding them as inimical to individual opportunity and equality. More territory and trade were their bulwarks against labor strife, high taxes, and big government.

Chapter 5 explores the dilemma of desirable lands encumbered by undesirable peoples. James Gordon Bennett of the *New York Herald*, for example, wanted a white nation free of all blacks and their abolitionist allies. "When the white races of this country multiply as they will multiply to a certain extent, all the colored races will disappear," he predicted in 1844. "We have seen that problem already solved and determined in the case of the Indian races . . . the same thing will take place with regard to the African race." Representative Thomas Jefferson Henley cited Indian removal as a precedent for future policy in the West. "The same arguments now used against the acquisition of New Mexico and California could have been used with equal force against the conquest and purchase of all the territories we have derived from the Indians," he told the House in 1848. "The land of New England . . . was it not conquered from the Indian tribes? So with a large portion of the South." Jefferson and Jackson had found the answer—subjugate the natives, acquire their land by purchase or conquest, then move survivors to remote and poor areas of no interest to whites.[6]

The ideology of republican empire is the topic of Chapter 6. Denying any parallels between earlier empires and their own, expansionists insisted that democracy and dominion were complementary, not contradictory. Since leaders intended to transform cessions into states and their inhabitants (at least whites) into citizens, they scoffed at misgivings about governing a vast domain. "My confidence in the progress and duration of this Government," Lewis Cass assured senators in 1848, "is unshaken and unshakable." Like Cass, Stephen Douglas wanted to acquire Texas, all Oregon, and a large part of Mexico. "To me, our country and all its parts are one and indivisible," he proclaimed when war was declared in 1846. "I am as ready and willing to fight for 54° 40', as for the Rio del Norte. . . . I know no sections, no divisions."[7]

Maybe Douglas knew "no sections, no divisions," but many of his colleagues were becoming more conscious of regions and factions—largely because of the very policies he supported. The Democrats' initiatives, Chapter 7 contends, split the party and strained the Union. Polk and his advisers chose war to secure "all Texas" but then retreated from "all Oregon." The Democrats passed the Walker Tariff, but only

6. New York *Herald*, February 2, 1844; *CG*, 30 Cong., 1 sess., App. 511 (April 6, 1848). Whigs sometimes used racist appeals, too. "If we annex the land, we must take the population along with it," Florida's Edward Cabell warned in 1848. "And shall we, by an act of Congress, convert the black, white, red, mongrel, miserable population of Mexico . . . into free and enlightened American citizens, entitled to all the privileges which we enjoy?" Were all Mexico acquired, its people would be entitled to 112 seats in the House. He doubted that Americans wanted "one-half or one-third" of Congress "composed of these miserable, bigoted creatures." *CG*, 30 Cong., 1 sess., 429 (March 4, 1848).

7. *CG*, 30 Cong., 1 sess., App. 422 (March 17, 1848); *CG*, 29 Cong., 1 sess., App. 907 (May 13, 1846).

because the new senators from Texas backed it and Vice President George Dallas cast the tie-breaking vote. Whigs and Democrats approved bills to aid Taylor's troops, but then the administration transformed the muddled border dispute into a war of conquest. The prospect of vast new lands, riches, and patronage reduced Congress to a number of querulous factions. One insisted that slavery be entirely excluded from new cessions. Another demanded that Congress make no restrictions at all. A third favored sharing the spoils of war by extending the Missouri Compromise line to the Pacific, closing the area north of 36° 30' to slavery but permitting it below. Alarmed by the schisms, some Whigs opposed any new territory. When the Democrats nominated Cass for president and the Whigs chose Taylor, dissidents from both camps bolted to help create the Free Soil Party. George Julian, an Indiana Whig, called his party's proceedings "an exhibition of shameless political prostitution" and joined the free soilers. At the dissidents' convention, Ben Butler nominated Martin Van Buren for president. Van Buren's virtue and humility, Butler exclaimed, were reflected in the pride he took in the vegetables he raised on his modest farm. "Damn his cabbages and turnips!" Jacob Brinkerhoff of Ohio replied. "What does he say about the abolition of slavery in the District of Columbia?" The politics of the plow and log cabin seemed increasingly irrelevant to the emerging crisis of the late 1840s.[8]

Chapter 8 assesses manifest destiny and challenges popular misconceptions that have obscured the dynamics of empire. The expansionists insisted that their policies expressed the public will and complied with hallowed ideals, but critics demurred. "It is no longer pretended that our purpose is to repel invasion," George Ashmun, one of fourteen in the House who opposed the declaration of war against Mexico, protested three months later. "The mask is off; the veil is lifted; and we see in the clearest characters *invasion, conquest,* and *colonization* emblazoned upon our banners." Daniel P. King, another one of "the

---

8. George W. Julian, *Political Recollections, 1840–1872* (Chicago, 1884), 55; Oliver Dyer, *Great Senators of the United States Forty Years Ago* (New York, 1889), 101. James Russell Lowell gibed that Taylor "ain't exactly all a wig nor wholly your own hair." His views were a mystery: "He hez n't told you wut he is, an' so there ain't no knowin'/ But wut he may turn out to be the best there is agoin'." Democrat Charles Cathcart chided Whigs for nominating the hero of the war they had so often condemned. "The most Lilliputian edition of a blank book," he jeered, "would contain *all* the known sentiments of General Taylor upon the grave political measures which have divided the parties of this country." Lowell, *The Biglow Papers* (reprint of 1848 ed.: (Boston, 1892), 179–80; *CG*, 30 Cong., 1 sess., App. 826 (August 3, 1848).

immortal fourteen," contended in early 1847 that Polk had sought "not peace with Mexico, but a piece of Mexico."[9]

George Catlin, who did portraits of eminent whites during winters and painted and studied western Indians during summers, lamented that white traders, settlers, and diseases had decimated the Natives. "And no one but God knows where the voracity of the one is to stop, short of the acquisition of everything that is desirable to money-making man in the Indian's country," he sighed, "or when the mortal destruction of the other is to be arrested, whilst there is untried flesh for it to act upon, either within or beyond the Rocky Mountains." Frederick Douglass, a runaway slave turned abolitionist and editor, saw no reason for blacks to embrace the United States government. "Its Bill of Rights is to practise towards us a bill of wrongs," he complained in 1847. "Its self-evident truths are self-evident lies." The war upon Mexico was "disgraceful, cruel, and iniquitous," a sign of "Anglo Saxon cupidity and love of dominion." When the Democrats nominated Cass for president in 1848, Douglass denounced them for going "beyond all others in bowing the knee and prostrating themselves before the slave power." But the selection of Taylor distressed him even more. "The Whig party is the grave of all independence, self-respect and decency," Douglass objected. "In the face of all facts, they are at this moment attempting to make out a peace character for a war candidate, a slavery limitationist for a slavery propagandist, a friend of freedom of a vile slaveholder, and an honest man of a notorious robber." Douglass also chastised the rank and file for rejecting the Free Soil alternative. "As a people, you claim for yourselves a higher civilization—a purer morality—a deeper religious faith—a larger love of liberty, and a broader philanthropy, than any other nation on the globe," he scolded after the election. "To make your innocence apparent, you have now had a fair opportunity. . . . You have deliberately chosen slavery. . . . By your votes you have said that slavery is better than freedom—that war is better than peace, and that cruelty is better than humanity."[10]

9. *CG*, 29 Cong., 1 sess., App. 809 (July 27, 1846); *CG*, 29 Cong., 2 sess., App. 331 (February 4, 1847). Democrats called the dissenters "the ignoble fourteen" and equated them with the "blue light" Federalists of the War of 1812.

10. George Catlin, *Letters and Notes on the Manners, Customs, and Conditions of the North American Indians*, 3d ed., 2 vols. (London, 1842), 2:249–50, 255–56; Douglass to Thomas Van Rensselaer, May 18, 1847; "The War with Mexico," *North Star*, January 21, 1848; "Northern Whigs and Democrats," *North Star*, July 7, 1848; "The Blood of the Slave on the Skirts of the Northern People," *North Star*, November 17, 1848; *The Life and Writings of Frederick Douglass: Early Years, 1817–1849*, ed. Philip S. Foner (New York, 1950), 245, 292, 311–13, 344–45.

The politics and policies of the 1840s divided Americans then, and since its publication in 1985 this book has disturbed some readers who admire the agents of empire more than I do. Book reviews, I have learned, often say more about the reviewer than the author. A reply to the critics—particularly one who fumed that this book is really about the Vietnam War—would probably not change their opinions. In retrospect, I believe I might have done more with Mexican sources. I could have used American soldiers' memoirs more extensively to help define racial and religious beliefs at the time. But new documents would hardly mollify critics. The events of the 1840s and their legacy remain controversial, and no author can satisfy avid partisans of any particular nation, party, leader, or people. What mainly propelled United States expansion? I still think the evidence points to the fears and ambitions of a small corps of American political figures, not to threats from abroad or demands from pioneers. This perspective rankles because it is inconsistent with American exceptionalism—the belief that the nation's politics and diplomacy have been uniquely altruistic, open, and therefore beyond reproach.

But borders and biases affect viewpoints, as illustrated in the very naming of the war between the United States and Mexico. In the United States people have traditionally used the title of Justin Smith's nationalistic book of 1919 to label the conflict—*The Mexican War.* Recent scholars prefer the Mexican-American War. In Mexico, however, the nomenclature denotes a radically different interpretation— *Invasión de los Norte Americanos en México* (1890–1891), for instance, and, in 1998, *Las balas del invasor: la expansión territorial de los Estados Unidos costa de México* (The Invader's Bullets: United States Territorial Expansion at the Expense of Mexico). Pens and keyboards have replaced the muskets and artillery of 1847.

Since *Manifest Design* first appeared, the Cold War has ended. Mexican immigration across the Rio Grande, legal and illegal, has increased dramatically. The United States is far more dependent on oil imports from a region where millions of people hold this nation in utter contempt. American pilots patrol the no-fly zone over Iraq; ground and air forces operate in Afghanistan; peacekeepers prevent further ethnic cleansing in Bosnia. Americans watch the defense budget and federal deficit soar to finance the war on terrorism. After the Soviet Union's demise, the United States enjoyed a moderation in military spending and a new sense of security, but not for long. The horrendous losses of September 11, 2001, made Americans feel as vulnerable as ever, menaced by a fanatical and unfathomable enemy that draws no distinction between soldiers and civilians. The oceans provide no shield; borders seem badly patrolled and too porous. From coast to coast sleeper cells perhaps plot the next jihad. Doubts persist about the competence of intelligence and law enforcement agencies to counter the threat.

"Americans have thought of themselves as a people and a nation apart," the 1985 preface to this book observed. "But because of a strong desire to improve security, augment foreign trade, and acquire more resources, the United States . . . has frequently compromised its preference for isolation." Thomas Grattan, a British consul in the United States for much of the 1840s, noted that "the national epidermic texture is so fine"—Americans were extremely thin-skinned about criticism of their institutions and values.[11] Now, with homeland security and global cooperation against terrorism a top priority, Americans need to reconsider why foreigners often see the United States in ways so contrary to the national self-image. Whatever challenges lie ahead, Americans will improve their prospects for success if they learn from the past and take a more informed historical sensibility into the future.

Grinnell, Iowa

---

11. Thomas C. Grattan, *Civilized America*, 2d ed., 2 vols. (London, 1859), 2:126. The denial of empire, for example, remains sacrosanct in the national creed, as a July 15, 2002, episode of *Nightline* showed. The program reviewed recent United States foreign policy and the temptation of "going it alone" as the world's sole "super power." Former "great empires" had pursued self-interest in defiance of international opinion or law, but the United States was different. "If anything," Don Dahler assured viewers, "the United States in asserting its interests has been more benign than any of its predecessors." "Foreign critics" complained of a "contradiction between this country's proclaimed values and its actual policies," but Dahler did not say whether this was a new or recurring criticism. His closing assessment affirmed American exceptionalism: "The issue is not whether America has the economic and military clout to impose its will on the rest of the world, but whether in the long run it is prudent to do so. The United States has never engaged in empire building, nor does that seem now to be the intent of the Bush administration." Ted Koppel and Secretary of State Colin Powell then discussed the Middle East at length without a single word about oil. No "empire building" before, no oil diplomacy now—just (the program implied) noble principle combined with reasonable power to achieve multilateral, not national, interests.

Acknowledgments

After researching and writing the history of the Peloponnesian War, Thucydides observed that his account rested "partly on what I saw myself, partly on what others saw for me." Two millennia and four centuries have passed since Thucydides paid tribute to those who contributed to his work, but his insight on collaborative scholarship is timeless. I, too, have benefited considerably from "what others saw for me." Howard Lamar made me aware of the importance of considering the expansionist policies of the late Jacksonian period in terms of the larger context of Anglo-American contact with non-Anglo peoples and the growing preoccupation of antebellum Americans with the significance of the frontier in their national development. In addition to his suggesting a valuable thematic framework for the diplomacy of the 1840s, he cheerfully read and responded at length to several versions of this study. I am grateful for his many comments and kindnesses. Gaddis Smith, Michael Hunt, and John Coogan also read previous drafts of the manuscript, and they discerned significant themes in the research before I fully understood them myself. In many places, my ideas and theirs have become inseparable. More recently, James Wright and Michael Green offered valuable insights that found their way into the final draft. For particularly thorough and incisive criticism during the last stages of the work, Walter LaFeber deserves special thanks. Lawrence Malley of Cornell University Press patiently coordinated my efforts with others' throughout the publication process and suggested ways to bring the principal arguments into better focus. I appreciate his advice and encouragement. Through meticulous and perceptive editing, Christie Lerch saved me from some embarrassing errors and helped make the manuscript more cogent and readable. However brief and inadequate these acknowledgments may be, I hope my generous collaborators obtain some recompense in recognizing how frequently my analysis addresses the points they raised. Even when I have not followed their specific recommendations, their queries made me sharpen and clarify my own thinking.

Friendly criticism and personal support have also come from long-time friends and other scholars whom I met during my research and writing. Joan Challinor, Dermot Healy, Philip Nelson, and Robert Rydell enlivened and enriched my various research trips to Washington. James Essig, Charles Cheape, Michael Ermarth, and Michael Birkner have sustained me with a marvelous mixture of sound advice and good humor. Cheryl German helped me to correct some flaws in organization, leavened my writing style, and provided moral support. These and other friends such as B. J. Sullivan and David Abels understood that frequent solitude is indispensable to the researching and writing of history. They deserve to be thanked for their consideration.

I am grateful for financial support as well: grants from the Danforth Foundation, the A. Whitney Griswold Research Fund at Yale, and the Dartmouth Faculty Fellowship program have provided assistance for study, travel, research, and preparation of the manuscript. The staffs of the Library of Congress, the National Archives, the Sterling Library at Yale, and the Baker Library at Dartmouth aided my research whenever I sought their help—and I sought it often. Gail Patten typed various drafts of the work and answered countless questions about word processing. Finally, I thank my Dartmouth colleagues for providing so supportive an environment in which to teach and write history.

MANIFEST DESIGN

CHAPTER 1

Magnificent Distances, Magnificent Intentions

When Charles Dickens visited Washington in 1842, he called it "the City of Magnificent Intentions." The capital had not yet attained "the vast designs" of its architect Pierre Charles L'Enfant, for Dickens noticed "spacious avenues, that begin in nothing, and lead nowhere; streets, mile-long, that only want houses, roads, and inhabitants; public buildings that need but a public to be complete; and orna· ments of great thoroughfares, which only lack great thoroughfares to ornament."[1] To Dickens this haphazard collection of streets, squares, and public buildings hardly amounted to a viable city, much less the capital of a rising republic—an impression shared by many other European visitors. Unlike other capital cities such as London or Paris, Washington had little commerce or enterprise of its own, and its only business was government. There was not even much of that to invigo· rate the city most of the year. Stray cattle browsed on shrubs and flowers near the Senate chamber, while pigs shared Capitol Hill pathways with legislators, Supreme Court justices, and newspaper correspondents. Dust stirred by horses' hooves and carriage wheels often eclipsed the sun and contributed to the misery that residents suffered during Washington's infernal summers. Slaves in shackles

1. Charles Dickens, *American Notes and Pictures from Italy* (London, 1903), pp. 101–2. Washington had already been nicknamed "the City of Magnificent Distances," so Dickens merely substituted the word *intentions* for the word *distances*.

trudged through the city's streets, often headed for pens and auction blocks shadowed by the dome of the Capitol rotunda.

As the 1840s unfolded, Dickens's epithet for Washington proved prophetic. Not only had the intentions of city planners been magnificent in projecting thoroughfares not fully utilized until the twentieth century, but magnificent too were the intentions of policy makers who congregated in Washington during and shortly after Dickens's visit. They and their partisans came to "the City of Magnificent Intentions" determined to obtain a territorial and commercial empire for the United States.[2]

The administrations of John Tyler and James Polk acquired almost eight hundred million acres of land for the United States, annexing Texas in 1845, negotiating for Oregon south of the forty-ninth parallel in 1846, conquering and then acquiring by treaty California and New Mexico in 1848, and assuming jurisdiction over millions of acres of land in the Great Lakes region ceded by Native Americans who moved westward to the Great Plains. Never before had the nation obtained so much territory so quickly. In fewer than a thousand days, Tyler, Polk, and their supporters pushed the boundaries of the United States to the Rio Grande, the Pacific, and the forty-ninth parallel. In addition, they considered and sometimes pursued bold initiatives to obtain other commercial and territorial advantages beyond the continent in such places as Hawaii, China, Cuba, and Yucatán.

In both its means and its ends, this expansion is unique in United States history. Yet it is often depicted as merely a logical culmination of the nation's westward movement across the continent, an outward thrust occasioned by a public ideology embodied in the concept "manifest destiny." Expansionist ideas were "in the air" during the 1840s, and they presumably affected leaders who gathered in Washington at this time to transact the nation's business. There is no reason to be so indefinite, however, since it is possible to separate the amorphous ideas "in the air" from the particular ideas that actually motivated the expansionists. The American people as a whole may have shared their leaders' ideas, but the question of whether or not

2. Since the expansionists of the 1840s repeatedly used the term *empire* to describe their dynamic nation, the term is also used here. Empire meant to them a nation growing rapidly in territory, population, wealth, and military power. They did not regard the American empire as imperialistic, however, and they differentiated it from other empires based on colonialism and exploitation. The distinctions drawn by the expansionists between traditional empires and their republican empire are the focus of Chapter 6.

they did is less crucial to a comprehension of American expansion than identifying and examining the convictions of the public figures who attained the continental empire.

The pace and extent of territorial expansion during the mid-1840s intensified the decade's political polarization, since the issue of empire became entangled with party rivalry. As historians such as Lee Benson, Richard McCormick, Joel Silbey, and Thomas Alexander have noted, the United States by 1840 possessed a national political culture with a vigorous two-party system whose leadership and membership transcended both section and class. This "second American party system"—so labeled to distinguish it from the first party system composed of Federalists led by Hamilton and Adams and Republicans led by Jefferson and Madison—had taken shape during the 1830s, when a Whig opposition had emerged to challenge the ascendancy of the Democrats under Jackson and Van Buren. By 1840 the two parties had relatively well-defined positions on major issues and were evenly matched in strength in most states, and they played the dominant role in establishing the agenda and setting the tone for American political life during the late Jacksonian period.[3]

During the 1830s the Democrats and Whigs had feuded primarily over questions concerning the extent to which the power of the federal government should be used to direct or control regional and national development: disputes over banking, currency, land policy, credit, and internal improvements dominated the partisan strife of Jackson's and Van Buren's presidencies. On these issues the Whigs favored federal control and initiative, while the Democrats preferred laissez-faire and local initiative. Whigs supported a protective tariff to aid industry; Democrats leaned toward free trade. Whigs called for federal sponsorship of improvements in transportation and navigation; Democrats preferred that the states control such projects. Whigs defended the national bank, but the Democrats destroyed it. Whigs hoped to raise revenue through federal land sales, but Democrats wanted to reduce the price of public lands to encourage settlement and expansion. These disputes largely defined the differences between the parties, perhaps diverting attention away from foreign affairs during the 1830s.

3. Lee Benson, *The Concept of Jacksonian Democracy: New York as a Test Case* (Princeton, 1961); Richard P. McCormick, *The Second American Party System: Party Formation in the Jacksonian Era* (Chapel Hill, N.C., 1966); Joel H. Silbey, *The Shrine of Party: Congressional Voting Behavior, 1841–1852* (Pittsburgh, 1967); Thomas B. Alexander, *Sectional Stress and Party Strength: A Study of Roll-Call Voting Patterns in the United States House of Representatives, 1836–1860* (Nashville, 1967).

This preoccupation with economic policy in the early Jacksonian period has suggested to scholars that disparities in wealth and status were the chief determinants of political behavior at this time. More recently, however, historians such as Benson, Michael Holt, and Ronald Formisano have argued that ethnocultural factors rather than economic interests best explain mass partisanship and electoral behavior. Suspicious of the popular notion that the Democratic party was the haven of planters, artisans, and poor farmers, these "new" political historians join scholars such as Edward Pessen in warning against the deceptive nature of Jacksonian rhetoric. Just what the parties represented to their leaders and followers is a more complicated question than has generally been assumed.[4]

However one explains the origins and identities of the parties, it is clear that they largely defined the parameters of political choice during the Jacksonian period. Distinguishing sincere expressions of principles from the rhetorical flourishes so characteristic of antebellum political discourse poses special problems, since so much of the bitter debate of the time amounted to bunkum for partisan purposes. Benson and other scholars have convincingly shown that the concept of "Jacksonian democracy," for example, reveals more about the ability of Democratic leaders to manipulate images and symbols than it does about the actual historical character of the two parties: leading Democrats were seldom born in crude log cabins, nor were they any more the champions of the common man than their political rivals. Jackson and his followers adeptly portrayed their party and program as egalitarian and progressive and their opposition as aristocratic and reactionary, if not downright un-American, but such posturing is misleading, as the recent interpreters of Jacksonian America have shown. Nevertheless, the partisan invective of Democrats and Whigs was not meaningless. Perhaps the differences between the parties are

4. Michael F. Holt, *Forging a Majority: The Formation of the Republican Party in Pittsburgh, 1848–1860* (New Haven, 1969); Ronald P. Formisano, *The Birth of Mass Political Parties: Michigan, 1827–1861* (Princeton, 1971); Formisano, *The Transformation of Political Culture: Massachusetts Parties, 1790s–1840s* (New York, 1983); Edward Pessen, *Jacksonian America: Society, Personality, and Politics* (Homewood, Ill., 1969); Pessen, *Most Uncommon Jacksonians: The Radical Leaders of the Early Labor Movement* (New York, 1967). The classic description of Jacksonian democracy as a people's revolution is Arthur M. Schlesinger, Jr.'s *The Age of Jackson* (Boston, 1945). Since Benson's seminal study of New York, historians have studied virtually every major state in terms of the development of a new two-party system following the disappearance of the Virginia dynasty, the embattled term of John Quincy Adams, and Jackson's rise to prominence in the mid-1820s.

not the ones customarily assumed, but there were fundamental differences. The empire building of the 1840s provided an occasion for the enunciation of those sharp differences.[5]

There was a rough parity between the parties in most states by the early 1840s, and in the hotly contested elections political leaders could not resist the temptation to use foreign affairs for partisan advantage. Democrats at this time embraced territorial expansion as a means of redeeming their party from the damage suffered during the economic recession of Van Buren's troubled term, damage that had been dramatized by Harrison's triumph over Van Buren in 1840. Knowing that locofoco economic doctrine and Van Buren had both declined in popularity during the hard times and that there was no debating a depression, Democratic leaders needed to find a way of restoring the ascendancy that the party had enjoyed under Jackson. In 1844, led by Senator Robert J. Walker of Mississippi, they found a new standard in territorial and commercial expansion and a new standard-bearer in James K. Polk of Tennessee.

The political uncertainties of the early 1840s did not affect only the Democrats. The stability of the second-party system was strained by Harrison's unexpected death in 1841 and Tyler's accession to the presidency: the canoe had indeed tipped. Tyler's states' rights "Whiggery" often resembled the program of locofoco Democrats, and as Tyler served out his tumultous term Whigs wondered how he had ever been placed on their ticket in the first place. This squabbling among the Whigs understandably delighted the Democrats, who in 1843 and 1844 increasingly associated their party with aggressive territorial and commercial expansion. Their 1844 platform called for the "reannexation" of Texas and the "reoccupation" of Oregon, planks that demonstrated the party's appropriation of the idea of expansion for partisan advantage and for its abstract appeal. By the mid-1840s, then, a peculiar incongruity appeared in the two parties' domestic and foreign policies, with the Democrats insisting that the federal government act passively at home but aggressively in foreign

5. Expansionism was not just another political issue, however, like those concerning the tariff or internal improvements. It is important to define the political context of the 1840s, because so much of the available scholarship on the period deals with partisan politics. This study tries to add another dimension to the history by focusing on national leaders and their cultural and ideological context, rather than on the origins of partisan loyalty and mass voting behavior. In other words, the concern here is to discover why policy makers (predominantly the Jacksonian Democrats) acted as they did once in office and why the acquisition of a continental empire became so critical an issue to them.

relations, and the Whigs arguing for an assertive national government in domestic policy but a diminished profile in international
affairs. While the Whigs worried about consolidating and developing
the vast domain already in hand, the Democrats plotted to obtain
more land and trade. A relatively clear and consistent split on expansion characterized the parties during the late Jacksonian era, especially during and after the 1844 campaign.

Though nominal Whig John Tyler initiated the Texas annexation
scheme, annexation became more a Democratic than a Whig cause
during his term. After Polk's victory over Henry Clay in late 1844, the
partisan split over expansion became even more pronounced, with
the Democrats urging rapid expansion and the Whigs counseling
caution and consolidation. Democrats were not entirely in agreement
about expansion, and alignments among them shifted after 1846.
Southern Democrats, for example, demanded that Texas be annexed, but many were not equally committed to the acquisition of
all of Oregon. Northwestern Democrats were as enthusiastic about
Oregon as they were about Texas, however, and they chided their
southern colleagues for their timidity on the Oregon question. Sectional bias sometimes influenced the expansionist Democrats, especially after the introduction of the Wilmot Proviso, but it is nevertheless
true that party loyalties consistently transcended sectional ones. Democrats were enthusiastic about adding new territories to the Union,
and Whigs were apprehensive.

Democrats hoped to gain office through their championing of
territorial and commercial expansion, but political power was only
one of the advantages that they saw in the acquisition of new land
and markets. Their haste to obtain Texas, Oregon, and California
stemmed largely from their anxiety about certain trends that alarmed
them in the dynamic development of the United States during the late
Jacksonian period. The chapters that follow will demonstrate that
these anxieties were as influential in the expansion of the 1840s as
were the now familiar motives for expansion offered by previous
historians: a clearly conceived drive to acquire new land, ports, and
markets; an attempt to obtain more secure boundaries; a desire to
spread American ideals across the continent; and an expression of
confidence in the nation's progress. Expansionists occasionally relied
on such justifications, but other lesser-known motives were just as
crucial. Many expansionists feared the trend toward industrialization
and urbanization and cautioned against the probable consequences
of such modernization. In demanding abundant land for the Ameri-

can people, they repeatedly expressed conservative—even reactionary—Jeffersonian ideals regarding the sanctity of agriculture, the
volatility of self-government, and the perils to stability and harmony
posed by modernization. Racial problems also alarmed the expansionists, and their dislike of nonwhite peoples greatly affected their
policies.

Separating these specific fears and ambitions from the ideals and
actions that historians have customarily associated with "manifest
destiny" is a difficult task. Democrats frequently defended their expansionist policies in the loftiest of terms, calling for the vindication
of national honor, protection of pioneers on the frontiers, better
opportunities for the poor, and assistance to the benighted peoples
inhabiting the new lands. Much evidence from the period raises
doubts about these justifications, however. Contemporaries often
challenged the expansionists' rhetoric: radical Whigs and New England intellectuals, for example, repeatedly questioned the Democrats'
sincerity. Such skepticism was warranted. The demands for security,
prosperity, and the spread of democracy were not unique to the
1840s, nor were they alone sufficient to precipitate the decade's
unprecedented expansionist drive. The United States already had an
expansionist tradition by the early 1840s, but an additional impetus
was needed to provoke the imperial impulse of the Tyler-Polk years.
That impulse originated in several powerful neo-Jeffersonian anxieties and ambitions among Democrats, considerations usually omitted
from descriptions of manifest destiny ideology.

Attitudes toward expansion, then, can be used as another political
yardstick with which to measure the two major parties of the Jacksonian era. Many Democratic expansionists viewed the acquisition of
land and markets as essential to their program for sustaining the
unique character of American social and political life. The controversy over the annexation of Texas, the Oregon boundary dispute, and
the Mexican War became significant in the ongoing process of each
party's self-definition: as the Jacksonians heralded expansion as a
remedy for domestic problems, the Whigs expressed reservations,
fearing that rapid expansion might instead create an irrepressible
sectional crisis. When the Whigs warned against the perils of empire
building, the Democrats paired them with the hated British and
accused both of being hostile to the country's interests. In reconsider-
ing the political and diplomatic culture of the 1840s, then, "Jacksonian expansionism" may provide a more descriptive label for the
decade than "Jacksonian democracy."[6]

6. The label also fits the 1830s, when Jackson and Van Buren removed some

In an incisive study of Jacksonian politics and beliefs, Marvin Meyers has argued that the Democrats' "war" against the national bank in 1833-34 gave expression to "a matched set of attitudes, beliefs, projected actions: a half-formulated moral perspective involving emotional commitment" that he labels "the Jacksonian persuasion."[7] This persuasion involved basic political principles, but it also contained an influential emotional component. To take Meyers's analysis a step further, it seems reasonable to suggest that what the onslaught against the bank was to the 1830s, the sustained effort to acquire land and markets was to the 1840s. Though Meyers did not consider Indian removal and continental expansion in his work, his insights apply to the expansionist Democrats of the 1840s as well. Since the bank war and the Mexican War obviously grew out of fundamentally different issues, a comparison between them should not be overdrawn. But the Jacksonians saw in both struggles important opportunities to distance the United States from European influence, to promote greater economic freedom, and to preserve democracy. Jacksonian ideology and identity and the Democratic party's concern about domestic developments infused antebellum foreign relations—a feature of the period that has escaped the attention of scholars.

While political historians have debated the concept of Jacksonian democracy, historians of westward expansion such as Albert Weinberg, Norman Graebner, and Frederick Merk have challenged the validity of the concept of manifest destiny.[8] They have questioned the

seventy thousand Indians from the Southeast and relocated them in the trans-Mississippi West, opening vast areas of Georgia, Alabama, and Mississippi to white speculators and pioneers. Particularly noteworthy in this regard was Van Buren's admission in his autobiography that the first priority of Jackson's administration had been "the removal of the Indians from the vicinity of the white population and their settlement beyond the Mississippi." (The second and third priorities were "to put a stop to the abuses of the powers of the Federal Government in regard to internal improvements" and "to oppose as well the re-incorporation of the existing National Bank." Fourth was tariff reform.) Van Buren concluded that "certainly no other subject was of greater importance" than Indian removal. See "The Autobiography of Martin Van Buren," John C. Fitzpatrick, ed., *Annual Report of the American Historical Association for the Year 1918*, 2 vols. (Washington, 1920), 2:275–76.

7. *The Jacksonian Persuasion: Politics and Belief* (Stanford, 1957).

8. Albert K. Weinberg, *Manifest Destiny: A Study in Nationalist Expansionism in American History* (Baltimore, 1935); Norman A. Graebner, *Empire on the Pacific: A Study in American Continental Expansion* (New York, 1955); Frederick Merk, *Manifest Destiny and Mission in American History: A Reinterpretation* (New York, 1963); Merk, *Slavery and the Annexation of Texas* (New York, 1972). See also David M. Pletcher, *The Diplomacy of Annexation: Texas, Oregon, and the Mexican War* (Columbia, Mo., 1973); Glenn Price, *Origins of the War with Mexico: The Polk-Stockton Intrigue* (Austin, 1967).

relevance of the concept to the actual motives behind the expansionism of the 1840s and have indicated the flaws in the arguments that
stressed the ideal of mission in explaining the march to the Pacific.
Despite these effective reassessments of Jacksonian politics and policy, vital questions concerning the forces that impelled America toward territorial and commercial empire during the Tyler-Polk years
remain to be addressed. What follows is a hybrid inquiry that attempts to explain American foreign policy during the late Jacksonian
period in terms of the political and cultural context that gave it so
much of its direction and meaning. Inherent in the Jacksonian persuasion were fears and ambitions that lent themselves to an imperial
surge during the 1840s. If the Democrats of the early 1830s forged
their identity in destroying the national bank and all that it symbolized, their successors forged theirs in destroying Mexicans and creating a continental empire. The customary distinction between domestic
policy and foreign policy in the 1840s seems more a convenient
categorization by scholars than an accurate description of antebellum
reality. Jacksonian expansionism was the second front in a long-
standing war to preserve a vulnerable nation from enemies domestic
and foreign and to safeguard the American people from ominous
forces that threatened to subvert or subdue the Union.

CHAPTER 2

Texas, the Black Peril, and Alternatives to Abolitionism

The campaign to acquire Texas for the United States inaugurated a period of intense and unprecedented territorial expansion in American history. The United States annexed Texas in 1845, gained possession of Oregon south of the forty-ninth parallel in 1846, and then, with the termination of the Mexican War, acquired California and New Mexico in 1848. To many Americans then and since, the "manifest destiny" years stand out as a happy interregnum between more troubled times: the expansion during the mid-1840s followed the economic distress touched off by the Panic of 1837 and preceded the tumultuous sectional strife of the 1850s that climaxed in the Civil War. Unlike the periods before and after it, the nationalistic expansionism of the Tyler-Polk years seemed marked by a sense of optimism and self-assurance.

Yet much evidence suggests that the outward thrust during the 1840s represented a crisis of confidence. Expansionist policies developed in the shadow of the unwanted black. Enslaved and proscribed in the South, disdained and discriminated against in the North, and feared throughout the nation, the country's black population provided a powerful impetus behind territorial expansion in the 1840s. Many prominent politicians and publicists regarded the nation's black population as a menace to American security and promoted the annexation of Texas as a simple solution to a complex problem. Unwilling to accept a future that would include blacks, whether slave or free, as permanent inhabitants of the Republic, the expansionists viewed Texas as a potential outlet for their country's unwanted black population. The expansionists both encouraged and exploited an anti-Negro consensus to facilitate annexation. No explanation of the acquisition of Texas is complete without an analysis of how racial fears affected those leaders who sought security through expansion.

The preservation of slavery was a chief consideration among expansionists, as scholars who have studied the acquisition of Texas have stressed.[1] The concern with slavery—a divisive sectional issue—must also be seen as part of a far more pervasive national concern with determining the future of the black man in a predominantly white society. That question became particularly urgent by the early 1840s because of developments during the previous decade. Nat Turner's rebellion; the spread of radical abolitionism and the outbreak of racially inspired riots in the North; the emergence of the Liberty party; the failure of the federal and state governments to develop a program to colonize substantial numbers of manumitted blacks in Liberia—all of these combined to arouse apprehensions among white leaders who had searched unsuccessfully for a solution to the vexatious racial problem.

Troubled by this malaise of racial anxieties, both northern and southern advocates of annexation argued that Texas could provide the long-sought-for answer to the racial crisis. Though Texas, if it became a slave state, offered a wide field for the expansion of slavery in North America and presented the likelihood of more political power for the South, most northern Democrats enthusiastically supported annexation. Many of them disapproved of slavery in the abstract, but they were also horrified by the prospect of a hasty emancipation of over three million slaves who might migrate to the North. They embraced annexation as a means of easing the tension over slavery while simultaneously providing a method for the ultimate removal of the entire black population from the United States. Texas, they argued, would attract free blacks and slaves, and its location would facilitate the eventual exodus of all blacks to Central and South America. The Texas question, then, became inextricably linked to the perplexing "Negro question."

Like tobacco chewing, pentacostal politics, and exaggerated chival-

1. See Jesse Reeves, *American Diplomacy under Tyler and Polk* (Baltimore, 1907); Justin H. Smith, *The Annexation of Texas* (New York, 1911); Ephraim D. Adams, *British Interests and Activities in Texas, 1838–1846* (Baltimore, 1910); Frederick Merk, *Slavery and the Annexation of Texas* (New York, 1972).

ry toward women, racial prejudice was a prominent characteristic of
Jacksonian culture. A long procession of foreign travelers who toured
the United States during the 1830s were astounded by the hostility
toward nonwhite peoples that was expressed by citizens in the free
states. Expecting to find greater liberality toward blacks in areas
where slavery had been prohibited or abolished, observers from
overseas instead discovered that the absence of slavery seemed to
increase the barriers between the races. After visiting both sides of
the Mason-Dixon line, Alexis de Tocqueville noted that "in those
parts of the Union in which the Negroes are no longer slaves they
have in no wise drawn nearer to the whites. On the contrary, the
prejudice of race appears to be stronger in the states that have
abolished slavery than in those where it still exists; and nowhere is
it so intolerant as in those states where servitude has never been
known."[2] Law did not forbid contact between races in the North, but
custom did. Not even death equalized the races, for Tocqueville noticed that cemeteries too were often segregated. English traveler
Thomas Hamilton agreed with Tocqueville, pointing out that northern blacks were "subjected to the most grinding and humiliating of
all slaveries—that of universal and unconquerable prejudice." Hamilton related a personal anecdote to illustrate the racial animus he
noted. While passing through the Creek Nation in Alabama, Hamilton alighted from his stagecoach and shook hands with the Indians
and their black servants, "to the great scandal of the American passengers," he recalled. Several other foreign travelers noticed the rampant Negrophobia in America and expressed doubts about the nation's
ability to solve its racial problems without bitterness and bloodshed.[3]
Prospects appeared bleak: foreigners often anticipated internal insur-

2. Alexis de Tocqueville, *Democracy in America,* Philips Bradley, ed., 2 vols. (New
York, 1945), 1:359–60.
    3. Thomas Hamilton, *Men and Manners in America* (Edinburgh, 1843), pp. 55, 354,
374. See also Frederick Marryat, *Diary in America, with Remarks on Its Institutions,* 3 vols.
(London, 1839), 1:294, 3:78; John Robert Godley, *Letters from America,* 2 vols. (London,
1844), 1:216, 2:70–75; Tocqueville, *Democracy in America,* 1:349–69. Scholars have
confirmed these contemporary impressions of anti-Negro sentiment in the free
states. See Leon F. Litwack, *North of Slavery: The Negro in the Free States, 1790–1860*
(Chicago, 1961); Eugene H. Berwanger, *The Frontier against Slavery: Western Anti-Negro
Prejudice and the Slavery Extension Controversy* (Urbana, 1967); Lorman Ratner, *Powder
Keg: Northern Opposition to the Antislavery Movement, 1831–1840* (New York, 1968);
Leonard L. Richards, *Gentlemen of Property and Standing: Anti-Abolition Mobs in Jackson-
ian America* (New York, 1970); George M. Fredrickson, *The Black Image in the White
Mind: The Debate on Afro-American Character and Destiny, 1817–1914* (New York, 1971),
pp. 1–164.

rections, sectional divisions, and civil war as the probable consequences of racial strife in the United States.

Influential proponents of Texas annexation such as President John
Tyler and his adviser Abel Parker Upshur had earlier explored other
solutions to the racial dilemma. During the 1830s, Tyler, as a Virginia
senator, sought cooperation from the North on the racial problem
when he implored northern lawmakers to prohibit antislavery societies from using the federal postal service to disseminate their publications. In 1838, Virginians elected Tyler president of their state's
Colonization Society in hopes that he could accelerate the expatriation of blacks to Africa or Latin America. When Tyler addressed his
fellow colonizationists that year, he singled out the abolitionist movement as a dire threat to the South and described the menace in
alarming terms. "It invades our hearth, assails our domestic circles,
preaches up sedition, and encourages insurrection," he warned. He
condemned antislavery agitators, arguing that "philanthropy, when
separated from policy" is "the most dangerous agent in human affairs."
Tyler warned that radical abolitionism posed the gravest threat to the
Union's survival.[4]

Upshur, another public-spirited Virginia planter, shared the apprehensions of his friend and neighbor. In 1826, Upshur had piloted a
bill through the Virginia Assembly providing for state assistance in
the removal of free blacks to Liberia. When Tyler became president
of the state's Colonization Society, Upshur became one of the organization's several vice-presidents. During the 1830s, Upshur wrote extensively for public journals on race, slavery, and sectionalism. He
endorsed white supremacy, defended slavery as a positive good, and,
like Tyler, vilified abolitionists.[5]

Soon after succeeding Harrison as president in early 1841, Tyler
appointed Upshur secretary of the navy. In this role Upshur soon
demonstrated that his racial anxieties matched those of the new
president. In his first annual report to Congress in late 1841, Upshur
emphasized the danger to the country—especially the South—posed
by the presence of a large and concentrated black population that
could be manipulated by hostile foreign nations. Armed invasions by
European powers seemed to him a real possibility. Geographical

4. Lyon G. Tyler, *Letters and Times of the Tylers,* 3 vols. (Richmond, 1884–85),
1:567–70; Oliver Perry Chitwood, *John Tyler: Champion of the Old South* (New York,
1939), p. 154. See also Tyler's address to an antiabolition meeting in Virginia, August
22, 1835, in L. G. Tyler, *Letters and Times,* 1:574–79.

5. Claude H. Hall, *Abel Parker Upshur, Conservative Virginian, 1790–1844* (Madison,
1964), pp. 69–75.

isolation from Europe could no longer protect the United States, for technological innovations in naval armaments had narrowed the Atlantic Ocean. Upshur warned Congress that "a war between the United States and any considerable maritime power would not be conducted at this day as it would have been even twenty years ago." Any confrontation with a major European country "would be a war of incursions, aiming at revolution," since an enemy would avail itself of the "promising expedient" of "arraying what are supposed to be the hostile elements of our social system against one another." Unless American naval strength were substantially improved so as to prevent an invasion by sea, the enemy "would be armed with a four-fold power of annoyance." A foreign invasion combined with a domestic revolt by slaves and freedmen would be an "intolerably harassing and disastrous" kind of war. To protect the seaboard and the gulf, to promote trade, and to shield slavery from foreign interference, Upshur recommended an unprecedented peacetime buildup of the American navy.[6]

Such fears about American security—especially the impressions about the South's vulnerability—soon found expression in American foreign policy. Just when Tyler decided that Texas must be annexed remains unclear, but it is likely that the acquisition was already on his mind when he was summoned from his Virginia estate to succeed Harrison in April 1841. Tyler's course during his first two years in office—his vetoes of the national bank bills, his opposition to the distribution of proceeds from the sale of public lands, his anti-Clay patronage policy, and his preoccupation with Texas—alienated most Whigs from him. Philip Hone, a Whig merchant and politician from New York City, expressed the widespread disillusionment with Tyler when he reminisced about the alliterative ticket of "Tippecanoe and Tyler too": "There was rhyme, but no reason, in it," Hone complained. Tyler "was not a Whig in any sense," George W. Julian of Indiana suggested, since "the sole proof of his Whiggery was the apocryphal statement that he [had] wept when Clay failed to receive the nomination."[7] Tyler might or might not have wept his way into

6. *Report of the Secretary of the Navy, S. Doc.,* vol. 395, no. 1, 27 Cong., 2 sess. (December 4, 1841), pp. 380–81. On naval policy under Tyler, see Harold and Margaret Sprout, *The Rise of American Naval Power, 1776–1918* (Princeton, 1939), pp. 119–25.

7. *The Diary of Philip Hone, 1828–1851,* Bayard Tuckerman, ed., 2 vols. (New York, 1889), 2 (July 30, 1841): 85; George W. Julian, *Political Recollections, 1840 to 1872* (Chicago, 1884), pp. 12–13. In his political reminiscences Julian questioned Harrison's Whig credentials as well, calling him "an old fashioned State-Rights Democrat of the Jefferson school."

the White House, but his course once there certainly frustrated many Whigs. They learned to their chagrin that a former anti-Jacksonian did not necessarily make a Whig.

In the autumn of 1841, Tyler sent his friend Duff Green of Maryland to Great Britain as a confidential executive agent. Whether by accident or intention, Green proved indispensable in the development of the administration's annexation strategy. Bold, obtrusive, and pretentious, Green had been meddling in the back rooms of American politics for over two decades when Tyler recruited him into the annexation junto, a small but determined corps of expansionist Democrats, states' rights Whigs, and political appointees who shared Tyler's desire to acquire Texas. During the Missouri crisis of 1819-20, for example, Green had defended slavery there and had then participated in the Missouri Constitutional Convention that passed an amendment forbidding the migration of free blacks to the state. In the early 1820s, he established the first stagecoach line west of the Mississippi, received a profitable federal mail contract, conducted a lucrative law practice, and invested his earnings in St. Louis real estate. But speculating never fully satisfied Green's ambition. In 1823, he purchased the St. Louis *Inquirer* to promote Andrew Jackson for president, fearing that John Quincy Adams and his "federal party" were conspiring to form a northern antislavery coalition that would emancipate the slaves and prostrate the South. During the Jacksonian period Green excoriated abolitionists and defended the South and its "peculiar institution." In 1839, his memoirs note, he maneuvered to place Tyler on the Harrison Whig ticket because he believed that the presence of a states' rights Southerner on the slate was absolutely essential to protect the South's interests. Green's behind-the-scenes activities in London from 1841 until late 1843 revealed the same concerns that had driven him for twenty-five years: the perpetuation of slavery and the promotion of prosperity and security for the South.[8]

Green's ostensible purpose in London was to discuss a trade reciprocity agreement with the British. Tyler and his advisers hoped to persuade British officials to import more foodstuffs and staples from the United States, and they thought that an informal envoy such as

8. Despite Green's crucial role in the annexation of Texas (and his other political and diplomatic machinations for over two decades), no biography of him exists. His colorful and controversial career merits an in-depth study. The facts here are derived from his memoirs, *Facts and Suggestions, Biographical, Historical, Financial and Political* (New York, 1866); *Dictionary of American Biography;* and various letters and notes in the Duff Green Papers.

Green might be able to open the door to a less restrictive trade policy. Tyler also advised Green, however, to scrutinize attempts by Britain and France to obtain closer economic and political ties with the Texas republic, ties that would be inconsistent with interests of the United States. Green performed his duties zealously—so zealously that United States minister Edward Everett repeatedly complained to his superi-ors about Green's meddling in official diplomatic business. Green, however, assumed that he, not Everett (a Massachusetts Whig who had been appointed by Harrison), was to serve as the eyes and ears of the Tyler junto in London, and he behaved accordingly. When Prime Minister Robert Peel reprimanded Green and reminded him of the unofficial status of his mission, Green retorted, "I am one of the American people, who in the United States, direct and control the government itself."[9]

Exaggerated as Green's claim to political predominance was, he rightly recognized that the Tyler administration distrusted Everett and desired an alternative source of information in England. In fact, Everett had barely won Senate approval, a vote of 23 to 19 revealing widespread dissatisfaction with Harrison's nominee. Democratic sen-ators James Buchanan of Pennsylvania and William King of Alabama led the campaign against Everett. They suspected him of abolitionist leanings, which in their view made him unfit for such a sensitive post. The opposition wished instead to send a southern Democrat to Lon-don to monitor the conduct of the British ministry.[10] In lieu of an accredited envoy with proslavery principles, Green satisfied the wishes of proslavery Senate Democrats such as Buchanan, King, William Allen of Ohio, Ambrose Sevier of Arkansas, and John C. Calhoun of South Carolina, who assumed that a northern Whig would automati-cally truckle to the British.

Green arrived in London in December 1841, posing as a private

9. Green to Peel, March 29, 1843, Green Papers. For a typical Everett complaint about Green, see Everett to Caleb Cushing, August 2, 1842, Caleb Cushing Papers.

10. *Journal of the Executive Proceedings of the Senate,* 27 Cong., 1 sess., September 11, 1841 (Washington, 1887), 5:438. In August of 1841, Hone had noted, "If Mr. Everett's nomination is not confirmed it will be upon the ground that he is a Northern man, and, by the inference, an Abolitionist" (*Diary of Hone,* 2 [August 30, 1841]: 85). See also Benjamin Perley Poore, *Perley's Reminiscences of Sixty Years in the National Metropolis,* 2 vols. (Philadelphia, 1886), 1:274–75; Nathan Sargent, *Public Men and Events, from the Commencement of Mr. Monroe's Administration in 1817 to the Close of Mr. Fillmore's Adminis-tration in 1853,* 2 vols. (Philadelphia, 1875), 2:134–35. Thomas Colley Grattan, a British consul in the United States at this time, observed that Everett was "little more than a public nullity" in England (*Civilized America,* 2d ed., 2 vols. [London, 1859], 1:149).

citizen on personal business. To ascertain Britain's ambitions regarding Texas, he studied the chief newspapers and journals that spoke for the Peel government, attended or read the debates in Parliament, corresponded with American minister Lewis Cass in Paris, and established contact with foreign envoys in London, most important among them Chargé d'affaires Ashbel Smith of Texas. Green quickly learned that Smith shared his attitude toward slavery, his disdain for abolitionists, and his suspicions of British commercial ambitions, and also, like Green, desired the annexation of Texas to the United States.[11] Green also followed the proceedings of British antislavery societies, which were directing much of their fervor against the American South. Just what Green actually learned during his surveillance in Britain did not so much determine his course and its consequences as did the preconceptions he carried with him across the Atlantic. Green was an ardent anglophobe: everywhere he turned he saw Britain attempting to damage the South and to destroy the growing power of the United States.

Green believed that America's rising commercial power frightened British policy makers, who would stop at nothing to eliminate the mounting threat of American economic competition. Texas would be the decisive battleground between these two commercial rivals. Green reported to the administration that antislavery societies in Britain, acting in accordance with their government, sought to abolish slavery in Texas through a comprehensive program of manumissions combined with compensation to the slaveholders. British abolitionists would supply the revenue needed for compensation, receiving in

11. Smith regarded the abolitionists as "meddlesome, restless, unscrupulous traffickers in spurious humanitarianism." Smith sympathized with the South, and he believed that Britain's antislavery sentiments were based on commercial ambitions, not ideals. In 1843 he told Isaac Van Zandt, Texas chargé to the United States, "The independence of Texas and the existence of slavery in Texas is a question of life and death to the slaveholding states of the American Union." He recognized that "a free negro state [in Texas] would be an eternal festering thorn in the side of the United States on their most exposed flank." He attended meetings of English antislavery societies and condemned their principles and proceedings. Unlike Green, however, Smith denied that Britain's highest priority was to emancipate the slaves in Texas. For these quotations, see Smith to Van Zandt, January 25, 1843, in George P. Garrison, ed., "Diplomatic Correspondence of the Republic of Texas," *Annual Report of the American Historical Association for the Year 1908,* 2 vols. (Washington, 1911), 2:1106; Ashbel Smith, *Reminiscences of the Texas Republic* (reprint of 1876 ed.: Austin, 1967), pp. 50–53. See also Smith to Anson Jones, August 2, 1843, in Anson Jones, *Memoranda and Official Correspondence Relating to the Republic of Texas, Its History and Annexation* (reprint ed.: Chicago, 1966), pp. 236–37; and Smith to Jones, July 2 and 31, 1843, in Garrison, "Diplomatic Correspondence," 2:1099–1103, 1116–19.

return generous land grants in Texas. In the meantime the British
government would pressure Mexico to resolve the festering dispute
between that power and Texas, the object being Mexico's recognition
of the independence of its former colony. To placate Mexico and to
fulfill the British strategy of containing American westward expansion, Texas in return would agree not to seek or accept an offer of
annexation from the United States. Foreign secretary Lord Aberdeen
denied that Britain was making abolition a precondition for its diplomatic initiatives in Texas, and Minister Everett confirmed his denials,
but Green, Tyler, and Upshur remained skeptical.[12]

In early 1842, Green warned the administration that Britain actually sought to control Texas in order to render the world "dependent
on [Britain] for the supply of the raw material for the manufacture
of cotton." Britain could ensure its commercial dominance by persuading Texas to abolish slavery there as a precursor to its abolition
in the United States. Britain's "war upon slavery is a war on our
commerce and manufactures—through our domestic institutions,"
he cautioned. Green saw no benevolence behind British antislavery
sentiment. On the contrary, he emphasized to Tyler, the real purpose
of British policy was to make the products of the East Indies more
competitive in the world market and to obtain a monopoly over vital
raw materials and thereby "control the manufactures of other nations
and thus compel all nations to pay her tribute."[13]

12. On Upshur's anxieties, see Upshur to Everett, September 28, 1843, in William
R. Manning, ed., *The Diplomatic Correspondence of the United States, Inter-American Affairs,
1831–1860,* 12 vols. (Washington, D.C., 1932–39), 7:8–11. Everett brought one of
Green's letters to Aberdeen's attention and discussed the supposed abolition plot
with him. Aberdeen, according to Everett, "treated it as a notion too absurd and
unfounded to need serious contradiction." See Everett to Upshur, November 16,
1843, in ibid., p. 251. United States minister to Mexico Waddy Thompson also
assured Upshur that his fears were unwarranted. In early 1844 Thompson wrote, "I
have seen or heard nothing (although I have copies of all [British envoy] Captain
Elliot's correspondence with the Texan Gov[ernmen]t) to justify the suspicion that
G[reat] Britain has made the abolition of slavery in Texas the condition of her
interposition, however desirable that object may be with England" (Thompson to
Upshur, February 2, 1844, in ibid., 8:576–77). Useful scholarly appraisals of British
diplomacy in the New World during this period include Adams, *British Interests and
Activities in Texas;* Kenneth Bourne, *Britain and the Balance of Power in North America,
1815–1908* (Los Angeles, 1967), pp.75–169; and Wilbur D. Jones, *The American Problem in British Diplomacy, 1841–1861* (New York, 1974), pp. 13–54.

13. Green to Daniel Webster, January 24, 1842; Green to Tyler, January 24, 1842,
Green Papers. Secretary of State Webster did not share the junto's enthusiasm for
Texas, and he resigned in the spring of 1843. Green's assessment of British policy
in Texas appears in other important letters: see those to Nicholas Biddle, January
24, 1842; to Mrs. Duff (Lucretia) Green, August 16, 1842; and to Tyler, May 31, 1843,
Green Papers; also to John C. Calhoun, January 24 and August 2, 1842, in J. Franklin

Green elaborated on British designs in a long letter to his friend
and confidant, Senator John C. Calhoun. Green informed him that
the United States, Cuba, and Brazil were selling products such as
cotton and sugar at lower prices than those produced in India, and
consequently Britain was finding it "impossible to maintain her commercial and manufacturing superiority." Britain was attacking slavery
and the slave trade in hopes of increasing its competitors' costs in
producing raw materials. Ultimately, Green warned, Britain hoped
to "command the supply of raw material[s] and thus compel rival
manufacturing nations to pay her tribute while she in a great measure
controls the manufacture itself."[14] Britain pursued such desperate
measures because its leaders realized that their nation's abolition of
slavery in the Caribbean a decade earlier had been a terrible mistake.
"The effect of the abolition of slavery in the British West India
colonies has been to ruin the planter, to hand over his property to
the emancipated slave and to convert those islands into black colonies
of England," Green observed. Were England to succeed in its designs
on Texas, slavery would be imperiled in the United States. Moreover,
Britain would obtain an alternative supply of cotton, and the American South might soon be reduced to the condition of the British
colonies in the Caribbean.[15]

In early 1843, Green returned to the United States to confer directly with President Tyler and his advisers. By mid-May Green was back
in London, pleading for commercial concessions and condemning the
British government for continuing its efforts to maintain the independence of Texas. In letters to Tyler and Upshur Green repeated his
warnings that Britain was waging commercial warfare against the
United States through Texas and would not desist until that war was
eventually brought to American soil. Prime Minister Peel, Green
asserted, sought to incite "rebellion and servile war in the South by
purchasing and emancipating the slaves of Texas." Peel thought that
he could interfere in Texas and attack slavery with impunity because
he and other officials believed that the American people were badly
divided on both Texas and slavery. This impression arose from "the

Jameson, ed., "Correspondence of John C. Calhoun," *Annual Report of the American
Historical Association for the Year 1899,* 2 vols. (Washington, 1900), 2:841, 846; to
Upshur, November 3, 1843, in Manning, *Diplomatic Correspondence,* 12:313; and to the
New York *Herald,* September 18 and October 2, 1843.

14. Green to Calhoun, January 24, 1842, in Jameson, "Correspondence of Calhoun," 2:841.

15. Miscellaneous notes by Green, probably late 1842 or early 1843, Green Papers.

monomaniacal ravings" of John Quincy Adams "and the fanatical representations of the abolitionists." To disabuse English leaders of their erroneous notions, Green stepped up his attacks on abolitionists and argued strenuously that the vast majority of Americans desired that slavery be preserved in both Texas and the United States. In doing so he tried to convey an impression of American unity in the face of both internal and external threats to that unity. In late 1843, Green explained to Upshur that he had tried in his recent letters to newspapers in London to "identify the American abolitionists with the attempt of England to monopolize the trade and commerce of the world" and "to unite our people by the exposure of the hypocritical pretence of British philanthropy." Green hoped his letters would stigmatize the antislavery forces as puppets of the British government as well as arouse latent anglophobia in the United States. Renewed animosity toward Britain might assist in creating a national consensus behind annexation.[16]

Green obtained a valuable proannexation ally in James Gordon Bennett, the controversial editor of the New York *Herald,* the largest-selling newspaper in the United States during the 1840s. Green and Bennett met in London and discussed at length both international affairs and the state of American journalism. They also discussed their personal fortunes. Green told Bennett that although Bennett's "fortune was now made" from his having "established the most profitable newspaper in the country," he still lacked "position in society." Green offered to remedy that deficiency by making Bennett's paper "the channel of most valuable and interesting communications" from the Tyler administration—in other words, selective "leaks" to the *Herald* would enhance Bennett's status. In return, Bennett merely had to champion Texas annexation. He apparently agreed to these terms, for Green notified Upshur that the *Herald* would become "the most valuable auxiliary" in the annexation cause. To Calhoun, Green predicted that Bennett would return to the United States "prepared to take strong ground with the South on the tariff and on abolition." Green assured Calhoun that the *Herald* would "cooperate with us most efficiently" and suggested that his faction could henceforth "command it to the fullest extent."[17]

16. Green to Tyler, May 31, 1843; Green to Upshur, November 16, 1843, Green Papers.

17. Green to Upshur, August 3, 1843, in Manning, *Diplomatic Correspondence,* 12:297; Green to Calhoun, September 2, 1843, in Jameson, "Correspondence of Calhoun," 2:872. For a more positive assessment of Bennett's ability to scoop the news, see Chitwood, *John Tyler,* p. 276. David Brion Davis, in *The Slave Power Conspiracy and the*

Bennett complied with the junto's designs for reasons beyond a favor owed to a former employer or gratitude for confidential executive information. His impressions of blacks and abolitionists were similar to those of Tyler, Upshur, and Green. Ever since he had established the *Herald* in 1835, Bennett had defended slavery as being advantageous to blacks as well as whites. He agreed with Green's contention that "sympathy for the black man is but a pretence for plundering and oppressing the white," and he complained that American abolitionists were responsible for the British policy makers' perseverance in their efforts to make Texas a Free-Soil country hostile to the South. In addition to refuting the premises of antislavery agitators, Bennett bitterly assailed rival editors who urged abolition and racial harmony. Editor Benjamin Day of the New York *Sun* was so outraged by Bennett's attacks that he said in reply that Bennett's only chance of dying an "upright man" would be if he were found "hanging perpendicularly from a rope." After Moses Beach acquired the *Sun* in 1838, Bennett dismissed it as a "dirty, sneaking, drivelling, contemporary nigger paper." There were even physical encounters between contentious editors. While recuperating from a head wound inflicted by James Watson Webb of the New York *Courier and Enquirer,* Bennett speculated on Webb's motive: "The fellow, no doubt, wanted to let out the never failing supply of good humor and wit, which has created such a reputation for the *Herald,* and appropriate the contents to supply the emptiness of his own thick skull."[18] Such audacity usually delighted readers and sold newspapers. The administration welcomed Bennett's frequent salvos against its own foes—the abolitionists, the British government, and the opponents of annexation.

Bennett lived up to his pledge concerning Texas. During the intense debate on annexation in late 1844 and early 1845, a day seldom passed without the appearance in the *Herald* of an article or editorial favoring annexation. Green's arrangement with Bennett cost the junto virtually nothing, but it paid a substantial dividend. Since the cabinet consisted chiefly of Southerners, a pro-Texas northern newspaper was a useful asset to the partisans of annexation.

Paranoid Style (Baton Rouge, 1969), pp. 34, 90, observes that Bennett "played an important role in portraying the abolitionists as subversives and as tools of the British." See also Ratner, *Powder Keg,* pp. 37–38.

18. Green's comment that abolition was antiwhite appears in a September 18, 1843 letter to the New York *Herald* printed on October 12, 1843. Bennett endorsed the letter. Day's comments on Green, and Bennett's description of the *Sun,* are cited in Oliver Carlson, *The Man Who Made News: James Gordon Bennett* (New York, 1942), pp. 131, 183. Bennett's assessment of Webb's motives appears in I. C. Pray, *Memoirs of James Gordon Bennett and His Times* (New York, 1855), p. 205.

Green's reports from London greatly impressed Tyler and his advisers, and they searched for countermeasures to avert the alleged perils that British policy posed to the country. Upshur, now secretary of state, advised Everett to try to frustrate British efforts to strike at the United States through Texas. "The abolition of domestic slavery throughout the continent and islands of America is a leading object in the present policy of England," Upshur asserted in September 1843. Although the abolition of slavery in the British West Indies had been inimical to the interests of the United States, Upshur added, no compelling grounds for American intervention had existed in that case. Texas, however, was an entirely different matter because of its contiguity to the South. President Tyler found the abolitionist ideas of British leaders such as Lord Aberdeen and Lord Brougham especially distressing, Upshur continued, since their statements were "perfectly consistent with information received from other sources" indicating that British antislavery policy was "not limited to Texas alone."[19] That "other" source of information was, of course, Duff Green.

Upshur expressed his anxieties more explicitly in a confidential letter to Everett accompanying the official dispatch, demonstrating again the impact of Green's speculations about British policy. Britain's overall objective, according to Upshur, was "to revive the industry of her East and West India Colonies, to find new markets for her surplus manufactures, and to destroy, as far as possible, the rivalry and competition of the manufactures of the United States." If Britain accomplished emancipation in Texas, hasty abolition must soon follow in the United States, and this would endanger the very existence of the American Union.[20]

Abolition in the United States, Upshur wrote, would lead to the expulsion or extermination of blacks, since the free states would not accept a sudden influx of millions of former slaves and the southern states would not tolerate a large free black population. "It is impossible to calculate the amount of ruin and suffering which would follow the sudden emancipation of the slaves of the United States," Upshur

19. Upshur to Everett, September 28, 1843, in Manning, *Diplomatic Correspondence,* 7:6, 8–9.

20. Upshur to Everett, "Confidential," September 28, 1843, in Manning, *Diplomatic Correspondence,* 7:11–14. See also Upshur to William S. Murphy, United States chargé to Texas, August 8, 1843, in ibid., 13:45–49. Upshur told Murphy, "Few calamities could befall this country more to be deplored than the establishment of a predominant British influence and the abolition of domestic slavery in Texas."

stressed.[21] As a convenient haven for fugitive slaves, an independent, Free-Soil Texas would be a constant threat to the South. To protect the southern states from the ultimate consequences of abolition in Texas, Upshur advised Everett to confer with Ashbel Smith about relations between Britain and Texas and to discourage any accord between the two nations. Upshur hoped to persuade Texan officials to reject any plan of emancipation and permanent independence. He also urged Everett to monitor the British antislavery societies and to query Aberdeen in regard to his policy on Texas.

Tyler's own statements show that he also found Green's reports disturbing. In a message to Congress in 1844, he warned that if Mexico acknowledged the independence of Texas and if Texas in turn abolished slavery and pledged not to seek annexation to the United States, American security would be jeopardized. A reconciliation between Mexico and Texas "affecting the domestic institutions of Texas . . . would operate most injuriously upon the United States and might most seriously threaten the existence of this happy Union," Tyler stated.[22] He saw only one escape from the dangers of a powerful Free-Soil nation bordering the South: slavery had to be protected in both Texas and the United States through immediate annexation of Texas as a slave state.

Senator Calhoun, too, shared Green's anxieties, and during the summer of 1843 he reiterated what had become the junto's standard assessment of British policy. If Britain succeeded in emancipating the slaves in Texas, Calhoun wrote, the contagion of antislavery would spread to the South. The abolition of slavery in North America "would transfer the production of cotton, rice, and sugar . . . to [Britain's] colonial possessions, and would consummate the system of commercial monopoly, which she has been so long and systematically pursuing."[23] The commercial considerations alone disturbed Calhoun, but he was still more alarmed by the racial implications. After succeeding Upshur at the State Department in early 1844, Calhoun wrote to American diplomats abroad concerning the urgency of annexation. To Minister William King in Paris, for example, Calhoun wrote in late 1844 that abolition in Texas would promote Britain's "grand scheme

21. Upshur to Everett; September 28, 1843, in Manning, *Diplomatic Correspondence,* 7:12–14.

22. James D. Richardson, ed., *A Compilation of the Messages and Papers of the Presidents,* 10 vols. (New York, 1897), 5 (April 22, 1844): 2164–65.

23. Calhoun to Green, September 8, 1843, in Jameson, "Correspondence of Calhoun," 2:546. See also Calhoun to Green, April 2, 1842, in ibid., pp. 506–7.

of commercial monopoly" and would produce a racial war in the South "of the most deadly and desolating character; to be terminated in a large portion in the ascendency of the lowest and most savage of the races and a return to barbarism."[24] He feared that former slaves might take possession of Texas and parts of other southern states and establish an independent nation. On its most vulnerable frontier the United States might soon confront a continental Haiti.[25]

The junto utilized former president Andrew Jackson in its cause, soliciting proannexation letters from him and then publishing them in Democratic party newspapers and pamphlets. Distant from Washington and lacking any official capacity to influence events from the Hermitage, Jackson nevertheless commanded the allegiance of many Americans, including congressmen. Seventy-seven years old and sickly, a phlegmatic but aroused Jackson wrote in 1844 that a pro-British, autonomous Texas would make "our slaves in the great valley of the Mississippi worth nothing, because they would all run over to Texas and under British influence [be] liberated and lost to their owners." Britain might also incite the Indians concentrated west of the Mississippi to besiege the American frontier. The United States would then confront an unholy alliance of redcoats, Indians, and slaves. "I am gasping for breath while using my pen," Jackson complained, but, he said, he endured his pain and continued to write because "the perpetuation of our republican system, and . . . our glorious Union" were at stake.[26] Britain, in control of Canada and ascendant in Texas, could "raise a servile war, take New Orleans, arouse the Indians on our west to war, and . . . throw the whole west into flames that would cost oceans of blood and hundred[s] of millions of money to quench, and reclaim."[27] Memories of the Creek War and the Battle of New Orleans must have haunted Jackson as he calculated the price of failing to annex Texas.

24. Calhoun to William R. King, "Strictly confidential," December 13, 1844, in Jameson, "Correspondence of Calhoun," 2:632.

25. The presence of an independent black nation in the Caribbean greatly disturbed Tyler, Upshur, Calhoun, and other Southerners. In 1845, Tyler wrote to Calhoun, "The experiment which the blacks have made of governing themselves [in Haiti] has resulted in bloodshed and anarchy, and the most fertile Island in the world is almost converted into a waste" (Tyler to Calhoun, October 7, 1845, in Jameson, "Correspondence of Calhoun," 2:1058–59).

26. Jackson to William B. Lewis, April 8, 1844, Andrew Jackson Papers. For a more detailed Jackson letter on annexation, see the New York Herald, September 17, 1844.

27. Jackson to Amos Kendall, April 12, 1844, Jackson Papers. See also Jackson to Francis P. Blair, April 12, 1844, Jackson Papers.

Editor John B. Jones of the *Daily Madisonian,* the official organ of the Tyler administration, publicized these fears to a wider audience. From 1842 until mid-1844, Jones repeatedly denounced the critics of annexation and the abolitionists as fanatics and traitors. "To encourage this fatal principle" of abolitionism, he remarked, "is to prepare the way for the incursions of a foreign enemy." That enemy, Great Britain, had "proclaimed to the world that, in negotiating a treaty with Texas, the design is to procure the abolition of slavery in the United States." Jones attacked Congressman John Quincy Adams with particular severity, arguing that he and other abolitionist Whigs failed to recognize the complexity of slavery, "the weak point of our Union—that which exposes it to most danger from foreign and domestic foes." Jones found it incomprehensible that any American politician or publicist could refuse to sanction this institution that the administration considered a vital safeguard of prosperity and harmony. "It is to the *cotton crops of the South,* and the *kind of labor* employed in their production, that our country is indebted for the maintenance of peace with the only country from which we have anything to dread on the score of power," he contended.[28] Cotton and the slave labor that produced it guaranteed American security.[29]

Correspondence from Green aided Jones in his efforts to impugn abolitionists, critics of annexation, and the British government. In the fall of 1843, Jones published a letter from Green claiming that England based both its foreign and trade policies on the assumption that slavery would soon disappear in the United States. Britain, Green said, would respect American interests and modify its discriminatory trade policy only when its officials became convinced that slavery would endure in the South.[30] In early 1844, Jones printed another letter from Green reiterating that Britain sought to enrich its own "commercial and manufacturing interests" at the expense of those countries whose "domestic institutions" were under attack. Jones praised Green for having exposed the "fallacies and falsehoods which have been promulgated in England by the abolition missionaries from this country." More important, Jones said, Green was impressing upon British leaders that a confrontation over Texas would obliterate American divisions and restore national harmony. Jones thought this effort crucial, for he believed that Britain would forcefully resist

28. *Daily Madisonian,* January 20, 1842, September 24, 1843, October 19, 1843, and March 14, 1842.

29. Cotton as a critical factor in annexation is discussed in Chapter 3.

30. *Daily Madisonian,* October 19, 1843. The letter is dated September 18.

the junto's annexation efforts only if convinced that domestic divisions would prevent American commercial or military retaliation.[31]

The North's Stake in Annexation

Green offered the administration and its partisans powerful reasons to acquire Texas, but his arguments had limited appeal in the
North because they placed so much emphasis on the vital interests
of southern slaveholders. Although many northern Democrats sympathized with southern whites and accepted slavery as an economic
and social expedient sanctioned by both custom and law, Green
failed to provide the North with a clear and compelling reason why
the free states should support annexation. If it was to accomplish its
goal, the junto would have to marshal considerable support above the
Mason-Dixon line for annexation. That the junto eventually succeeded in bringing most northern Democrats into the proannexation fold
was largely the result of the prodigious labors of Senator Robert J.
Walker of Mississippi.

Walker's background, which combined experience of both northern and southern life, made him well suited to the task of enticing
northern Democrats into the annexation coalition. Born in Pennsylvania in 1801, Walker had attended the state university, read law, and
then entered politics, becoming at age twenty-two the chairman of
the Democratic Committee of Pennsylvania and a fervent partisan of
Jackson's presidential aspirations. In 1826, Walker moved to Mississippi, where he began to practice law. He helped organize and man-
age a land syndicate that acquired extensive territory obtained from
the Choctaws through the Treaty of Dancing Rabbit Creek in 1830,
and he used his profits to buy slaves and become a prominent planter.
After a decade's residence in Mississippi, Walker was elected to the
Senate, where he became a staunch defender of the South and a critic
of federal interference with slavery. In his first address to the Senate
in 1836, he pleaded against the receipt of antislavery petitions. The
following year he introduced a congressional resolution acknowledg-
ing the independence of Texas and journeyed there to urge its legislators to seek annexation to the United States. Walker possessed an
economic as well as political interest in Texas, since he and members
of his family were speculators in Texas land and script. Though
preoccupied with the South and its concerns during his Senate years,

31. *Daily Madisonian,* January 4, 1844.

Walker maintained close political and personal ties with Senator George M. Dallas, leader of a powerful Democratic faction in Pennsylvania. Walker had married into the prestigious and influential Bache family, and Dallas was his wife's uncle.[32]

In 1843, when local Democratic organizations across the country began to solicit information from potential candidates for president and vice-president in 1844, a Kentucky committee asked for Walker's ideas on his own political prospects and requested his views on Texas. He responded by denying any desire to be a candidate for national office in 1844, then proceeded with a twenty-six page appeal for immediate annexation. The reply struck a responsive chord throughout the nation, for several prominent papers such as the Washington *Globe* and Bennett's New York *Herald* printed the entire letter. Pamphlet copies of Walker's brief for annexation circulated by the millions.[33]

Walker recognized and shrewdly manipulated the racial anxieties shared by many Americans, defining annexation as a national concern by emphasizing racial problems throughout the nation rather than focusing on the slavery problem. Walker stressed that the presence of blacks throughout the country, not their enslavement in the South, most threatened the nation's well-being. To him the arguments of antislavery Northerners seemed irrelevant to the actual problem at hand, since blacks, and not just slaves, posed the difficulty. Walker cautioned the North that if abolitionists succeeded in preventing annexation they would eventually be able to emancipate the slaves within the United States, a move that would prove disastrous to both North and South. The rejection of Texas would represent the first fatal step down the road to abolition, racial violence, and civil war.

To convince the North to accept Texas as an alternative to radical abolitionism, Walker (and other proponents of annexation who uti-

32. See James P. Shenton, *Robert J. Walker, a Politician from Jackson to Lincoln* (New York, 1961); H. D. Jordan, "A Politician of Expansion: Robert J. Walker," *Mississippi Valley Historical Review,* 19 (1932): 362–81; William E. Dodd, *Robert J. Walker, Imperialist* (Chicago, 1914); "Robert J. Walker," *Democratic Review,* 16 (February, 1845): 157–62; Walker to Jackson, January 10, 1844, Jackson Papers; John W. Forney, *Anecdotes of Public Men,* 2 vols. (New York, 1873), 1:118–30.

33. Walker's biographer describes the letter as "a long, devious essay," but its devious quality alone does not explain its wide appeal (see Shenton, *Walker,* p. 38). The financing and distribution of Walker's letter is discussed in Frederick Merk, *Fruits of Propaganda in the Tyler Administration* (Cambridge, Mass., 1971), pp. 121–28, and in James Paul, *Rift in the Democracy* (Philadelphia, 1951), pp. 96–101.

lized his ideas) relied heavily on the controversial data of the Census of 1840.[34] This census was the first to gather statistics concerning serious mental and physical disorders among the population, a survey requested by humanitarian reformers seeking to improve treatment for the blind, deaf, dumb, and insane. Their humane intentions, however, inadvertently brought inhumane results. The census figures dramatically "proved" that the North's free blacks were far more susceptible to physical infirmities, mental illness, pauperism, and crime than their enslaved counterparts in the South: in other words, freedom degenerated blacks, whereas slavery uplifted them. In addition, the census indicated that geographical proximity to slavery benefited free blacks: in states like New Jersey and Pennsylvania, which bordered on slave states, blacks fared far better than those who resided in Maine and Massachusetts, states far removed from contact with slavery. Conclusions based on this data assisted the Tyler junto and the northern and southern Democrats who wanted Texas. With the disproportionate incidence of severe disabilities among free blacks— a free black was apparently eleven times more likely to be mentally defective than a slave, for instance—it was clear that liberty allowed blacks to follow their innate propensity toward crime, poverty, and physical decay. Bondage under a white master, on the other hand, prevented them from sinking to their natural level.

These startling census figures came under spirited attack from congressmen John Quincy Adams and Joshua Giddings, statistician and physician Edward Jarvis, and black physician James McCune Smith. Jarvis discovered, for example, that the federal census returns often claimed that black defectives were present in a town where the state census recorded not a single black inhabitant. Jarvis became suspicious when he noticed that Scarboro, Maine, for instance, held six insane blacks, according to the federal tally, yet state census data showed that the town had no black residents. In Rutland, New York, two blacks the town did not contain were deaf and dumb, if the federal census figures were credible. Other towns had blacks who were not only blind but also insane. In Worcester, Massachusetts, an

34. On the Census of 1840, see Albert Deutsch, "The First U.S. Census of the Insane (1840) and Its Use as Pro-Slavery Propaganda," *Bulletin of the History of Medicine*, 15 (1944): 469–82; Joseph E. Kuchta, Jr., "The Census of 1840, Slavery, and the Annexation of Texas" (Senior essay, Yale College, 1979). Other useful sources include Merk, *Slavery and the Annexation of Texas*, pp. 61–68, 85–92, 117–20; William Stanton, *The Leopard's Spots: Scientific Attitudes toward Race in America, 1815–1859* (Chicago, 1960), pp. 24–53; Fredrickson, *Black Image*, pp. 43–96.

astonishing 133 of 151 blacks were reported insane.[35] After extensive analysis, Jarvis in early 1844 decided that "no reliance whatever" could be placed on the census statistics. He remarked that the mental and physical disorders that seemed especially to victimize blacks in the North "exist there only in a state of abstraction, and, fortunately for humanity, where they are said to be present, there are no people to suffer from them." Though the sarcasm was justified, it alone could not correct the census.

Despite the obvious unreliability of the figures, Walker and other Negrophobes could not resist exploiting them. Walker questioned the judgment and patriotism of abolitionists who challenged the census and its compelling revelations, labeling them "Americans in name, but Englishmen in feelings and principles." The census proved that slavery was the best philanthropy for blacks. Not surprisingly, the abolitionists' attacks upon the census damned them twice in Walker's view. In his proannexation appeal he paired abolitionists and antiexpansionists and referred to antislavery agitation as the nation's "most dangerous" internal threat and a menace likely to precipitate the dissolution of the Union, "a calamity equal to a second fall of mankind."[36]

Walker warned Northerners that if Texas were spurned and the slaves of the South set free, three million blacks would cross the Mason-Dixon line and overwhelm the North "with an inundation of free black population that would be absolutely intolerable. . . .Much more wretched in condition, and debased in morals," free blacks were far more of a problem than slaves.[37] If slavery ended and liberated blacks drifted northward, "the poor-house and the jail, the asylums of the deaf and dumb, the blind, the idiot and insane, would be filled to overflowing, if, indeed, any asylum could be afforded to the millions of the negro race whom wretchedness and crime would drive to despair and madness." The North's eleemosynary institutions would be crushed by the black burden, necessitating heavy taxes upon white workers. As increasingly large numbers of exslaves

35. See Kuchta, "Census of 1840," pp. 10-15. The errors for Worcester alone changed the ratio of insane to normal blacks in Massachusetts from 1 in 129 to 1 in 43.

36. Robert J. Walker, "Letter of Mr. Walker, of Mississippi, Relative to the Annexation of Texas" (Washington, D.C., January 8, 1844). A facsimile of this letter is contained in Merk, *Fruits of Propaganda,* pp. 221-52. The citations are from the original pamphlet, pp. 11 and 25.

37. Ibid., pp. 13-14.

migrated to the free states, competition between white and black workers would intensify, provoking racial violence and "starvation and misery . . . among the white laboring population."[38]

Walker did not exaggerate the unwillingness of most northern whites to accept a large influx of manumitted blacks. Foreign travelers noted this animosity toward blacks in the free states and confirmed Walker's pessimism. Irish visitor John Robert Godley, for example, observed in 1842 that most Northerners opposed abolition "entirely from hatred to the blacks, and fear lest abolition in the South might be followed by a large immigration of negroes to the North, and a corresponding reduction of wages." Godley perceived that slavery was only part of a more fundamental dilemma concerning the future of the nation's black population. "The *bête noire* (literally) of Americans is a population of free blacks," he suggested. Whites were alarmed at the prospect of emancipation: "While the negroes are in a state of slavery they reckon upon being able to keep them under efficient control, . . . [but] they dread the combination and designs of a class to whose passions and energies emancipation has given a stimulus and scope."[39] Alexander Mackay, a perceptive and fair-minded English traveler, also recognized how racial apprehensions transcended sectional divisions in the mid-1840s. The "ultimate fate" of blacks in the United States would be "expulsion from the continent," Mackay predicted. "In nothing are the American people more determined than this, that no black community shall, for and by themselves, occupy any portion of the North American continent." Racial equality could never be attained. "One or the other must dominate," he concluded.[40]

Walker well knew which of the races "must dominate." Southern whites who faced a growing free black population and the ever-present danger of slave revolts, and northern whites who faced an increasing black presence concentrated in their urban centers, could counter the black peril by *reannexing* Texas to the United States.[41] The

38. Ibid., p. 14.

39. Godley, *Letters from America,* 2:186–87. For an assessment of Negrophobia in Philadelphia, see Joseph Sturge, *A Visit to the United States in 1841* (London, 1842) p. 40.

40. Alexander Mackay, *The Western World, or Travels in the United States in 1846–47,* 4th ed., 3 vols. (London, 1850), 2:140–41. Tocqueville was equally pessimistic (see *Democracy in America,* 1:370–73).

41. Walker purposely rekindled the controversy over the events of 1818–19 by using the term *reannex* to discredit John Quincy Adams for "giving away" Texas in the Transcontinental Treaty. Walker repeatedly equated abolitionism with Whig principles, one striking example being a propaganda piece he published in the fall

acquisition of Texas as a slave state was preferable to abolition; in the short term, annexation would safeguard slavery, but in the long term it would bring about gradual, peaceful emancipation because slavery was a self-destroying institution that declined in profitability as it exhausted the land. Ultimately the slave would not have to flee from his master—the master would abandon his slave. Texas, he admitted, offered a fertile field for extensive slave labor, and the number of slaves there would increase substantially after annexation. Yet Walker concluded that annexation would actually diffuse slavery in the United States and thereby benefit all sections: "It is clear that, as slavery advanced in Texas, it would recede from the states bordering on the free states of the North and West; and thus they would be released from actual contact with what they consider an evil, and also from all influx from those states of a large and constantly augmenting free black population."[42]

Walker tried to sell annexation to Northerners by appealing to both their interests and ideals. With annexation and the gravitation of slaves out of the areas bordering the North, the free states would distance themselves from an institution causing serious strains in social and political life. Of even greater significance to the free states, Walker promised that the acquisition of Texas would discourage the migration of free blacks to the North. Annexation would not only halt the intrusion of blacks into the free states; it would also soon reverse it, as the congenial climate and fine soil of Texas drew free blacks as well as masters and slaves southwestward toward the Gulf of Mexico. Walker portrayed Texas as a convenient and temporary rendezvous for the country's black people, pending the final exodus of the race to regions beyond the United States. Through this migration of population the security of whites would increase, for "as the number of free blacks augmented in the slaveholding states, they would be diffused gradually through Texas into Mexico, and Central and Southern America."[43] Since the countries below the Rio Grande were inhabited chiefly by "the colored races," freedmen from the United States could resettle there to attain legal and actual equality. They could never acquire that status in the United States.

---

of 1844 entitled "The South in Danger." Walker tried to impress upon Southerners that all Whigs were abolitionists and hostile to the South, as shown in the "surrender" of Texas in 1819 and the opposition to annexation in 1844.

42. Walker, "Letter of Mr. Walker," p. 14.

43. Ibid. Perhaps the shape of Texas, not merely its location, suggested its potential for funneling blacks into Latin America.

Walker's exposition presented cogent reasons for all sections of the country to support annexation. For the North and West, Walker juxtaposed two alternatives, leaving little doubt as to which was better: the free states could cooperate with the Tyler junto and bring Texas into the Union, thereby providing a refuge for slaves and free blacks, or they could reject annexation and suffer the intense labor competition, exhorbitant taxes, and recurrent racial violence that would result from black relocation to the North. Annexation would make the South more secure because it would disperse the region's concentrated slave population. Planters with exhausted estates could start anew in Texas. Even the slaves themselves stood to gain from annexation, Walker suggested. Prosperity on a new frontier would bring them a better life, and when Americans eventually opted for emancipation, blacks would find in Texas a passageway to freedom and equality where less of a stigma accompanied a nonwhite skin.[44]

The influence of Walker's arguments became evident during the nationwide debate over annexation. In this dispute, party transcended section as both northern and southern Democrats reiterated the views advanced by Walker. In mid-1844 Senator James Buchanan called for immediate annexation, declaring that the acquisition of Texas would soon "convert Maryland, Virginia, Kentucky, Missouri, and probably others of the more northern slave states into free states."[45] Editor John L. O'Sullivan of the *Democratic Review* also echoed Walker, pointing out, in an article on annexation, that southern whites justifiably feared their large black population and needed to disperse and diminish it, but emancipated blacks could not be dispersed in the North because Northern whites would not accept them. "Ohio has already closed her door against them by laws making it penal to introduce a free negro without indemnifying the state against the risk of his becoming a pauper," O'Sullivan observed, and Pennsylvania had "amended her Constitution so as to preclude the possibility of any but a white man becoming a citizen." Annexation was not a proslavery measure, O'Sullivan argued in response to abolitionist claims, since "in Maryland and Virginia and Kentucky, and the other

44. Ibid., pp. 13–14. Walker argued that if abolitionists sincerely desired what was best for the slaves, they would be "the warmest advocates of reannexation."

45. *Congressional Globe* (hereafter abbreviated *CG*), 28 Cong., 1 sess., App. 722 (June 8, 1844). Buchanan, like Walker, argued that annexation would be "the means of gradually drawing the slaves far to the South, to a climate more congenial to their natures." They would "finally pass off into Mexico, and there mingle with a race where no prejudice exists against their color."

states in which slavery is already on the decline, the opening of Texas must necessarily hasten its departure."[46] Texas, then, presented "the only well-grounded hope" for the "ultimate extinction" of slavery.[47] Senator Sidney Breese of Illinois saw the same advantages in annexation. "In the course of God's providence, and by the noiseless and unceasing operation of such causes as He has set in motion," Breese suggested to his Senate colleagues, "the whole black race will, at His own appointed time, find a refuge among a kindred population inhabiting the southern portion of this continent, where they may realize such liberty as they may be capable of appreciating." Annexation, he predicted, would facilitate the eventual extinction of slavery in the United States.[48]

Though primarily concerned with their own part of the country, southern Democrats also followed Walker in stressing the national implications of the Texas question. Senator George McDuffie of South Carolina said that free blacks in Philadelphia appeared to be "a libel upon the human race," a terrible "spectacle of human degradation and misery. . . .If we shall annex Texas," McDuffie assured his Senate colleagues, "it will operate as a safety-valve to let off the superabundant slave population from among us; and will, at the same time, improve their condition. They will be more happy, and we all shall be more secure."[49] Senator Sevier of Arkansas also feared the consequences of abolition and antiexpansionism: "Abolish slavery, and one race will exterminate the other; abolish slavery, and you turn the South into a desert, and destroy the commerce of the country."[50] "Slavery now exists in Texas, and surely, to add Texas to the United States would not change its real character, or in any way increase it," Alabama Congressman James Belser argued in the House in May 1844. "To acquire Texas would be to *diffuse* slavery, and to remove most of that population from Missouri, Kentucky, Maryland [and] Virginia."[51] Kentucky's John Tibbatts agreed that annexation would

46. "The Re-Annexation of Texas: In Its Influence on the Duration of Slavery," *Democratic Review*, 15 (July, 1844): 14–15. See also "The Texas Question," *Democratic Review*, 14 (April, 1844): 429, and "The Texas Question: A Letter from Alexander H. Everett," *Democratic Review*, 15 (September, 1844): 259–60.
47. "The Re-Annexation of Texas," p. 11. See also "The Texas Question," p. 429.
48. *CG*, 28 Cong., 1 sess., App. 543 (June 3, 1844). Bennett also believed that annexation would lead to the ultimate exodus of all blacks from the United States. See the New York *Herald*, February 2, March 10, and June 18, 1844.
49. *CG*, 28 Cong., 1 sess., App. 532 (May 23, 1844).
50. *CG*, 28 Cong., 1 sess., App. 559 (June 7, 1844).
51. *CG*, 28 Cong., 1 sess., App. 524–25 (May 21, 1844). Duff Green also endorsed the dispersion theory. See his remarks to a pro-Tyler meeting in New York City, reported in the New York *Herald*, April 26, 1844. Editor John Jones agreed. In the

make the black population "gradually recede from the North, which is uncongenial to their natures. They will be pushed and crowded on by the tide of emigration of the white races of Europe, now flooding this country with a hardy and industrious population." Blacks would advance in their pilgrimage until they became "blended with the mixed population of Mexico." As a result, the free states would "be cleared of a degraded and wretched population with which they are now infested, crowding their hospitals and jails, and with which their large cities will be overrun."[52] European immigrants, Tibbatts told his colleagues, would replace blacks on both sides of the Mason-Dixon line. The country would be better off without slaves and without free blacks.[53]

Tyler and his advisers, like Walker and these other proponents of annexation, did not think merely in terms of protecting slavery but were troubled by the broader issues of future race relations in the United States. Throughout 1843, Upshur had repeatedly stressed that an abolitionized Texas contiguous to the United States would disturb the entire Union, not just the South. The fact, he wrote to Everett, that whites and blacks had "from time immemorial" held the relationship of master and slave made it impossible for the two races ever to "live together as equals, in the same country and under the same government." The demise of slavery would necessitate that "one or the other of the races . . . leave the country, or be exterminated."[54]

Daily Madisonian of March 28, he observed that if Texas were annexed, "Delaware, Maryland, Virginia, North Carolina, Tennessee, Kentucky, and Missouri, (and at a later period others) would emerge into free states, and slavery would settle down to the distant South, where its duration would cease by the natural progress of events."

52. *CG,* 28 Cong., 1 sess., App. 450 (May 7, 1844).

53. Census statistics partly validated these arguments that slaves and free blacks were gradually being removed from the border states through natural causes. In Virginia, for instance, the black population declined from 520,000 to 502,000 between 1830 and 1840. In Maryland, the decline for the same period was from 156,000 blacks to 152,000. Only a slight increase occurred in Delaware, from 19,000 to 20,000 blacks. In the deep South the trend was the opposite. Mississippi's black population soared from 66,000 to 197,000 between 1830 and 1840, (and to 311,000 by 1850), for example, and Alabama's rose from 119,000 to 256,000 (and then to 427,000 by 1850). The comparable statistics for white population during the decade from 1830 to 1840 were Virginia, 701,000 to 748,000; Maryland 291,000 to 318,000; Delaware 58,000 to 59,000; Mississippi 70,000 to 179,000; Alabama 190,000 to 335,000. See United States Department of Commerce, Bureau of the Census, *Historical Statistics of the United States: Colonial Times to 1970,* 2 vols. (Washington, 1972), 1:24–36.

54. Upshur to Everett, September 28, 1843, in Manning, *Diplomatic Correspondence,* 7:12–13. See also Upshur to Murphy, August 8, 1843, in ibid., 12:48–49.

Calhoun, in 1844, had expressed similar pessimism. Sudden emancipation "would be followed by unforgiving hate between the two races, and end in a bloody and deadly struggle between them for the superiority. One or the other would have to be subjugated, extirpated, or expelled; and desolation would overspread their territories, as in Santo Domingo, from which it would take centuries to recover."[55] Green agreed that abolition would be as harmful to the North as to the South. "Abolition in the United States would involve the necessity of removal," Green asserted in reflecting upon the experience of the British West Indies. "The whites or the blacks must leave the country. They cannot live together on terms of equality. One race or the other must govern."[56] His forebodings about race relations partly stemmed from the Census of 1840. During a brief return to the United States in 1843, Green had acquired a statistical abstract of the census from the State Department. Those figures confirmed his grave misgivings about abolition.[57]

To many southern leaders, Texas appeared to be the only possible avenue for dispersing the nation's black population, especially the slaves. During the 1830s, the Jacksonian Democrats had championed the removal of eastern Indians to an isolated region west of the Arkansas-Missouri frontier as the best possible solution to the Indian problem. But by the mid-1840s, Southerners and proslavery sympathizers in the North were complaining that the Indian territory blocked the extension of slavery along the entire southwestern frontier.[58] As early as 1841, for example, Bureau of Indian Affairs commissioner Thomas Hartley Crawford noted that Southerners felt hemmed in by Native Americans. "The southwestern states complain of the congregation of so many Indians on their borders," Crawford told Congress. He assumed that whites in the Southwest were most concerned about the possibility of Indian attacks on frontier settlements and traders.[59]

55. Calhoun to King, August 12, 1844, reprinted in *CG,* 28 Cong., 2 sess., App. 7 (December 18, 1844).

56. "The United States and England," by "An American" [Duff Green], *Great Western Magazine* (September, 1842):62.

57. Green, *Facts and Suggestions,* p. 141.

58. Ronald N. Satz, *American Indian Policy in the Jacksonian Era* (Lincoln, Neb., 1975), pp. 218–19; James C. Malin, "Indian Policy and Westward Expansion," *Humanistic Studies of the University of Kansas,* vol. 2, no. 3 (Lawrence, 1921), pp. 27–28; Annie H. Abel, "Proposals for an Indian State, 1778–1878," in *Annual Report of the American Historical Association for the Year 1907,* 2 vols. (Washington, 1908), 1:89–102.

59. *Report of the Commissioner of Indian Affairs, S. Doc.,* vol. 395, no. 11, 27 Cong., 2 sess. (November 25, 1841), p. 253.

The threat of attack was a primary concern, but the Indian barrier to westward expansion also dismayed restless Southerners (and expansion-minded Northerners). If Texas became a Free-Soil, autonomous nation protected by Britain's military shield, an impenetrable barrier against the expansion of slavery and the dispersion of blacks would extend from the Rio Grande to the Missouri. Failure to acquire Texas, therefore, would place southern whites in grave danger.

During the Jacksonian period, Democrats looked to the far-western frontier as a dumping ground for unwanted Indians within the states and territories of the Union. Just as the United States had dispossessed Native peoples of their lands to provide new opportunities for white Americans, so would the nation facilitate the relocation of blacks in order to open land in the South for white farmers. Poor whites within the United States and destitute immigrants from Europe could experience geographical and social mobility in a competitive, fluid American society only so long as the federal and state governments made available ample resources for individual exploitation. Such impressions about economics and race lent sanction to the dispossession, decline, or utter extinction of nonwhite peoples at this time.[60]

Additional appeals to national racial anxieties and more political maneuvering might have secured annexation in 1844 had not the Tyler administration been leading the movement. By early 1844, Tyler had completely estranged the Whigs, but his political course had not gained him acceptance by the Democrats. A president without a party, Tyler submitted an annexation treaty to the Senate in April, when only six months remained before the presidential election. Political strategists from both parties, uncertain of the impact that annexation would have on the fall elections, were generally disposed to delay until after the contest. The uncertainties occasioned by Tyler's political course worked against immediate annexation.

Other factors impaired the junto. Tyler commanded little respect in Congress, and Secretary of State Calhoun possessed some implacable foes, among them Senator Thomas Hart Benton of Missouri, the leader of a crucial faction of pro-Van Buren Democrats. Benton dismissed as absurd the argument that England would abolitionize Texas if it were not acquired by the United States. He denied that American

60. The impact of racism on westward expansion during the 1840s is discussed more fully in Chapter 5.

slavery was in jeopardy, contending instead that the annexation gambit was a means to promote Tyler's deluded presidential ambitions and to enhance Calhoun's own prospects for that office.[61] Northern Whigs also rejected the junto's rationale, some suggesting that slaves who went to Texas might eventually migrate to Mexico but that their masters would accompany them. Those masters would organize additional slave states and seek admission to the Union, so Texas offered no remedy for the nation's racial problems. Several Whigs, North and South, repudiated annexation as a political ploy and a financiers' scheme for lucre. In the Senate Spencer Jarnagin of Tennessee called annexation "a desperate presidential speculation" promoted chiefly by "the gamblers and brokers of the bankrupt finances and fraudulent land grants of Texas." Ohio congressman Joshua Giddings declared the junto's handiwork an "unholy and nefarious plan."[62] All northern Whigs, most southern Whigs, and some northern Democrats refused to accept the idea that immediate annexation of Texas was vital to the United States.

Tyler's appointment of Calhoun to succeed Upshur as secretary of state proved to be a mistake.[63] The dark cloud of nullification still shadowed Calhoun, and his extremism bothered many men, including members of his own party. His course during 1844 validated the worst suspicions of those who doubted his judgment. In promoting annexation he had foolishly resorted to blatantly sectional, proslavery, and racist arguments that had a limited appeal outside the South. Expressing concern about slavery and the black peril in private correspondence and confidential instructions to American diplomats and in conversation was one matter, but to use pseudoscientific racism and a controversial census to extol the virtues of slavery and assert the duty of the national government to protect and promote it was quite another, especially when such justifications filled diplomatic

61. Thomas Hart Benton, *Thirty Years' View; Or, a History of the Working of the American Government for Thirty Years, from 1820 to 1850,* 2 vols. (New York, 1854–56), 2:583–624; *CG,* 28 Cong., 1 sess., App. 499, 609–11 (June 1 and 15, 1844).

62. *CG,* 28 Cong., 1 sess., App. 687 (June 6, 1844); *CG,* 28 Cong., 1 sess., App. 706 (May 21, 1844).

63. Calhoun had been offered the post after Tyler was compromised through an unauthorized commitment of it made in his behalf by Congressman Henry Wise. Without Tyler's knowledge, Wise told Calhoun's friend George McDuffie that Calhoun would be selected to head the State Department. Wise represented the district containing the Tyler and Upshur estates and was a friend of both men. Tyler might not have appointed Calhoun had it not been for Wise's indiscretion. See Henry A. Wise, *Seven Decades of the Union* (Philadelphia, 1881), pp. 221–25.

dispatches to European statesmen. In his explanation of American policy, Calhoun relied heavily on Green's denunciations of England— no coincidence, considering the two men's close political and person al ties. Green, Benton says in his memoirs, was "a person whose name was the synonym of subserviency" to Calhoun.[64] When Senator Benjamin Tappan of Ohio leaked several documents from Calhoun's diplomatic correspondence to the antislavery New York *Evening Post,* they created a sensation. The furor over Calhoun's dispatches halted the momentum toward annexation and delayed its consummation until early 1845.

Calhoun defended the administration's course by emphasizing to British minister Richard Pakenham that Britain's policy toward Texas imperiled the United States. Slavery and not freedom was the best condition for black people, Calhoun insisted, noting that the Census of 1840 revealed that a free black in the North was seven times more likely to be physically or mentally handicapped than his enslaved counterpart in the South. In Massachusetts, Calhoun explained, the blacks were "most wretched," since one of every twenty-one there was "in jails or houses of correction" and one of every thirteen was either deaf and dumb, blind, idiotic, criminal, or insane. Under the onus of liberty the black "invariably sunk into vice and pauperism, accompanied by the bodily and mental afflictions incident thereto . . . to a degree without example," Calhoun concluded.[65]

Even after the Senate rejected annexation in June, Calhoun contin ued to rely on Green's and Walker's arguments. To minister William King in Paris, Calhoun wrote in August that Britain had jeopardized its commercial supremacy by abolishing slavery within its empire. Since slaves were more productive than free blacks, England could maintain its commercial dominance only by fomenting antislavery in rival nations. Abolition in the United States, however, would harm both races, since "statistical facts, not to be shaken," proved the folly of emancipation in the free states. The alternative to slavery, Calhoun warned, would be "a deadly strife between the two races, to end in the subjection, expulsion, or extirpation of one or the other."[66]

Opponents of annexation and critics of Tyler and Calhoun (the two groups overlapped but were not identical) pounced upon the corre-

---

64. Benton, *Thirty Years' View,* 2:590.
65. Calhoun to Pakenham, April 18, 1844, in Manning, *Diplomatic Correspondence,* 7:20–21.
66. Calhoun to King, August 12, 1844, in *CG,* 28 Cong., 2 sess., App. 6–7.

spondence in order to discredit the junto and its claim that annexation was a truly national concern. John Quincy Adams was disgusted
with Calhoun for utilizing "the enormous blunders in the census."
Calhoun, Adams noted in his diary, had demonstrated a "total . . .
disregard of all moral principle" in his dispatches, a deficiency attrib-
utable only to an "absence of honesty or of mental sanity" in him.
Adams had a legitimate protest, for he had earlier told both Upshur
and Calhoun about the unreliability of the census data. Yet when
confronted with hard evidence of substantial errors, neither had
moved to correct them.[67] Calhoun, according to Adams, had retorted
that "where there were so many errors they balanced one another,
and led to the same conclusion as if they were all correct."[68] Giddings
had joined Adams in efforts to rectify the census, and he too chided
Calhoun for his reliance upon it. "The palpable errors are seized upon
as furnishing conclusive evidence that freedom was conducive to
insanity" in black people, Giddings noted, and he lamented to his
House colleagues that Calhoun had used his sensitive position "to
inform the British government of the sublime effects which slavery
and degradation has upon the human intellect, when the person is
of dark complexion."[69]

A few weeks after the publication of Calhoun's dispatches, a meeting of New York freedmen conducted by black physician James McCune
Smith petitioned Congress to "cause the census of 1840 to be reexamined, and, so far as is possible, corrected anew, in the Department of State, in order that the head of that department may have
facts upon which to found his arguments." This request, like the
earlier refutation by Jarvis, noted 116 towns in the North that held
no black residents whatsoever, although the federal census assigned
to them 36 blacks who were deaf and dumb, 38 who were blind, and
186 who suffered mental illness.[70] The junto's many blunders made

67. *Memoirs of John Quincy Adams, Comprising Portions of His Diary from 1795 to 1848,*
Charles Francis Adams, ed., 12 vols. (Philadelphia, 1874–77), 12 (May 18 and 27, and
June 21, 1844): 29, 36, 61–62.

68. Ibid., May 27, 1844, p. 29. Unlike Adams, editor John L. O'Sullivan supported
Calhoun on the census, noting that "a long and patient investigation, with every
desire to find fault, has produced but a few trifling errors." Calhoun had sustained
"in full the correctness of the census" (New York *Morning News,* February 10, 1845).
See also New York *Morning News,* March 14, 1845.

69. *CG,* 28 Cong., 1 sess., App. 708 (May 21, 1844).

70. Petition printed in the New York *Herald,* May 5, 1844. McCune noted that the
racist views expressed in Calhoun's letter to Pakenham had been taken almost
verbatim from Walker's letter.

the annexation measure even more distasteful to critics. "We have already more territory than we know what to do with, and more slavery within our borders than we choose to be answerable for before God and man," New York Whig Philip Hone confided to his diary.[71]

Proponents of annexation were as mortified by Calhoun's course as opponents, albeit for very different reasons. They recognized that his emphasis on slavery and the imperative needs of the South would make it difficult for free-state congressmen to support annexation. "The great majority" of Democrats, William King advised Buchanan in May 1844, would have resolutely declared for annexation had it not been for Calhoun's "ill-advised, unfortunate correspondence" that had "prevented them from doing so at once." Chairman Charles Ingersoll of the House Foreign Affairs Committee believed that Calhoun had "committed a great blunder by vindicating slavery in a letter to Pakenham." O'Sullivan observed in a letter to Walker that Tyler should have appointed Walker rather than Calhoun to head the State Department. William B. Lewis complained to his old friend Jackson of Calhoun's "great want of tact, as well as judgment." Massachusetts Democrat George Bancroft also deplored the turn of events. To Martin Van Buren he lamented, "What can be more sad than for a man to serve under John Tyler? What, unless it to be found an argument in defence of slavery on fictitious statistics, and address it to a British minister!"[72]

The Senate rejected the junto's handiwork. Only sixteen senators supported the treaty: ten southern Democrats, five northern Democrats, and one southern Whig. Thirty-five senators opposed the pact: twenty-eight of twenty-nine Whigs, six northern Democrats, and one southern Democrat.[73]

71. *Diary of Hone,* 2 (May 14, 1844):222.

72. King to Buchanan, May 10, 1844, James Buchanan Papers; Ingersoll memorandum of May 6, 1844, in William M. Meigs, *The Life of Charles Jared Ingersoll* (Philadelphia, 1897), p. 266; O'Sullivan to Walker, January 13, 1845, Robert J. Walker Papers; Lewis to Jackson, April 26, 1844, Jackson Papers; Bancroft to Van Buren, May 2, 1844, in "Van Buren–Bancroft Correspondence, 1830–1845," in Worthington C. Ford, ed., *Proceedings of the Massachusetts Historical Society* (Boston, 1908–09), 42:426. Additional complaints by O'Sullivan appear in the New York *Morning News,* December 17 and 26, 1844, and January 7 and 27, 1845.

73. *CG,* 28 Cong., 1 sess., 652 (June 8, 1844); Benton, *Thirty Years' View,* 2:619.

The Second Effort to Effect Annexation

This setback did not daunt the annexationists. Even before the Senate spurned the treaty on June 8, the expansionists had taken steps to ensure the ultimate triumph of annexation, perhaps anticipating that another major effort would be required. Ingersoll conferred with Walker and Henry Wise, Tyler's partisan and close friend, in early 1844 and promised that he would work to obtain a strong proannexation report from his House Foreign Affairs Committee. When a majority of the committee disapproved of Ingersoll's report, he withdrew it and published it in the Washington *Globe* on May 1. According to Ingersoll, over ten thousand copies of his statement circulated throughout the country. He and Calhoun also agreed at this time that should the Senate reject annexation, he would immediately introduce a joint resolution in the House for the acquisition of Texas. The junto welcomed Ingersoll's support, grateful to have a powerful Pennsylvania congressman behind them. A New York *Herald* reporter recognized the important alliance between the administration and Ingersoll, noting that he had been in "constant and confidential communication with the executive upon all matters pertaining to our relations with Texas and Mexico" and appeared to be "perfectly and correctly informed."[74]

The administraton and its partisans moved ahead on other fronts to acquire Texas. In late May, Walker and a faction of pro-Texas strategists took control of the Democratic convention in Baltimore and secured the nomination of dark horse candidate James K. Polk, an ardent expansionist, an intimate of Jackson, and friend of Texas president Sam Houston.[75] Because the front-runner for the nomination, Martin Van Buren, had declared against hasty annexation, he became anathema to Walker and his followers. They hoped that replacing Van Buren would first ensure a Democratic victory in the fall and then secure the triumph of annexation. Pennsylvania senator

74. Ingersoll memorandums, February 6 and May 6, 1844, in Meigs, *Life of Ingersoll*, pp. 261–62, 265–66; New York *Herald*, May 4, 1844. Ingersoll acknowledged, "My intercourse personal and official with Calhoun as Secretary of State has been intimate, and with Tyler quite kind—much more so than it was."

75. The chaotic proceedings at the convention are described in Charles G. Sellers, *James K. Polk, Continentalist, 1843–1846* (Princeton, 1966), pp. 85–100; Paul, *Rift in the Democracy*, pp. 144–68; Oscar D. Lambert, *Presidential Politics in the United States, 1841–1844* (Durham, N.C., 1936), pp. 150–56; Shenton, *Robert J. Walker*, pp. 142–49; and Glyndon G. Van Deusen, *The Jacksonian Era, 1828–1848* (New York, 1959), pp. 184–87.

George Dallas received the second spot on the ticket after New York senator Silas Wright, a Van Buren loyalist, rejected the nomination for vice-president. Following this unexpected series of events, Walker and New York delegate Benjamin Butler, former attorney-general in Jackson's administration, composed a party platform demanding "the reoccupation of Oregon and the reannexation of Texas at the earliest practicable period"—a plank designed to rally northern and southern Democrats behind the nominees and behind expansion.

By the summer of 1844, many Democratic expansionists regarded Tyler as an obstacle to the annexation of Texas. Relieved by Polk's nomination, they feared that Tyler's aspirations for a second term would jeopardize Polk's prospects and annexation. Tyler's followers had tacked the banner of annexation to his masthead, but many proponents of acquisition were unwilling to support it if the credit redounded to Tyler. In addition, an independent Tyler ticket might divert enough support from Polk to allow the triumph of Henry Clay and the antiexpansionist Whigs. Walker conferred with Tyler on July 10 and assured him that the Democrats would welcome his partisans into the party as equals if Tyler would retire from the presidential race.[76] The next day Walker counseled Polk that Tyler and his followers could be mollified if Polk and Jackson would publicly praise Tyler for promoting annexation and for opposing recharter of a national bank.[77]

Polk, for his part, believed that the sharp attacks by Francis P. Blair's Globe on Tyler were forcing him to seek a second term. Polk called upon Jackson to persuade Blair to stop criticizing the administration, hoping that Tyler would then bow out of the contest. Complying with this request, Jackson exhorted his former executive editor to support Polk and Dallas and to leave Tyler and Calhoun alone. Polk, Jackson, and Walker managed to persuade Tyler to withdraw from the presidential contest in late August.[78] With Van Buren shunted

76. Walker to Polk, July 10, 1844, James K. Polk Papers.
77. Walker to Polk, July 11, 1844, Polk Papers.
78. Polk to Jackson, "Confidential," July 23, 1844; Jackson to Blair, July 26, 1844; Tyler to Jackson, August 18, 1844, Jackson Papers; Walker to Polk, July 10, 1844, Polk Papers. Tyler told Jackson, "Your letter to Major Lewis was, as you requested, shown to me, [and] your views as to the proper course for me to pursue in the present emergency of public affairs has decided me to withdraw from the canvass." A detailed account of Tyler's withdrawal is contained in a letter he wrote to Alexander Gardiner, July 11, 1846, in L. G. Tyler, Letters and Times, 2:341–42. Calhoun was struck by the change in Blair. In late 1844 he wrote to his son-in-law, "The Globe has changed its tone, and the attacks from that quarter on me have abated" (Calhoun to Thomas G. Clemson, December 27, 1844, in Jameson, "Correspondence of Calhoun," 2:635).

aside, Blair muzzled, and Tyler removed from the race, annexation seemed more likely.

While putting their political house in order, the proponents of annexation proceeded on a number of other fronts. Walker supplied more propaganda to Democratic party leaders across the nation. In July, he informed Polk that he had recently sent fourteen thousand copies of his letter about Texas to North Carolina and Indiana, but "still the demand is unabated." At a private meeting in September, Walker, Tyler, and former Jackson adviser William B. Lewis decided that Andrew Donelson, the nephew, namesake, and ward of Old Hickory, should be dispatched to Texas as United States chargé. A wise choice it was, since Donelson could use his tie to Jackson and his own familiarity with Houston to gain the confidence and coopera-tion of the Texas government.[79] In mid-November, Donelson arrived in Texas and acquired a cabin next to Houston's. Now confident that the American Congress would approve annexation, Donelson urged Houston to forget the defeat of the 1844 treaty and to work toward obtaining Texas's consent for incorporation into the Union. When Anson Jones replaced Houston as president of Texas in December, Donelson redirected his efforts toward the new executive. By late December, Donelson was convinced that the expansionists would have another chance to annex Texas. The American Congress had reconvened in the meantime, and a resolution of annexation was pending. Donelson assured a now reticent Calhoun that "Texas will make no treaty with England until the decision of our government on the measure of annexation is known."[80]

79. Walker to Polk, July 10, 1844, Polk Papers; Lewis to Jackson, September 16, 1844, and Tyler to Jackson, September 17, 1844, Jackson Papers. Tennessee demo-crat J. George Harris wrote to Polk, "Gen[eral] Jackson has written [Houston] a most powerful and beseeching letter to await the result of the present [presidential] con-test. He will do it" (Harris to Polk, July 23, 1844, Polk Papers). William Lee wrote to Anson Jones, "Tyler selected Major Donelson as chargé to Texas, solely for the purpose of bringing Gen[eral] Jackson's influence to bear on Gen[eral] Houston, as he believed . . . Houston would oppose annexation" (Lee to Jones, October 25, 1845, in Jones, *Memoranda,* pp. 499–500).

80. Donelson to Jackson, December 28, 1844, Jackson Papers; Donelson to Cal-houn, December 24, 1844, Andrew Jackson Donelson Papers. Neither Houston nor Jones shared the junto's alarm about the fate of slavery in Texas. Both men pro-ceeded in late 1844 and early 1845 under the assumption that Texas would be best protected if good relations were maintained with England and France pending annexation. They thought that annexation might fail again in the United States or that the Texas people themselves might opt for independence rather than incorpora-tion. See Houston to the Texas Congress, December 4 and 9, 1844, in *The Writings of Sam Houston,* Amelia Williams and Eugene Barker, eds., 8 vols. (Austin, 1938–43), 4:393, 403; Anson Jones, *Memoranda,* pp. 43–46, 349, 430. Jones believed that Eng-

Though removed from the presidential contest, Tyler continued to pursue his own strategy for acquiring Texas, a course that dismayed the Democrats. Tyler wanted to cooperate with the Democrats, but not as a totally compliant puppet. He considered calling an extra session of Congress during the summer of 1844 to renew the legisla‑ tive battle for annexation. The idea alarmed Polk, who called on Donelson for help. Donelson contacted Jackson and urged him to convince Tyler not to summon Congress before the election, since the Whigs would use the session for electioneering that might harm the Democrats.[81] Jackson, in turn, succeeded in persuading Tyler, and Tyler gave up the idea of a special session.

Tyler, however, still would not surrender his ambitions for Texas. In September, he and Calhoun again called upon Duff Green to assist in annexation, appointing him consul at Galveston and bearer of dispatches to Mexico. But these official badges were intended to cover his actual purpose, which was to act as an executive agent to reconcile Mexico to annexation and to pressure Texan leaders to reject inde‑ pendence and an alliance with Britain. Green, his memoirs note, received verbal instructions from Calhoun "to aid in conducting the negotiation for the acquisition of Texas, New Mexico and California." Green could expect close cooperation from at least one American official in Mexico City, since Tyler had earlier appointed Green's son Benjamin secretary of the United States legation there. Bennett, in the *Herald,* was predictably enthusiastic about Duff Green's appointment, recalling that a few years earlier Green had traveled to Britain "and resided there for many months, sustaining with more or less dignity, success, and effect, the . . . position of American minister on his own hook." Green's journey to Texas, Bennett anticipated, would "raise a highly respectable dust in that direction."[82]

Green raised dust aplenty. He delegated the mundane chores of the Galveston consulate to an underling and proceeded to Mexico, where, he admitted, he and other Americans discussed fomenting "a

land's objective was "to build up a power independent of the United States, who could raise cotton enough to supply the world; of which power slavery would be a necessary element" (Jones, *Memoranda,* p. 82).

81. Polk to Donelson, "Private," August 27, 1844; Calhoun to Donelson, "Private and confidential," August 23, 1844, Donelson Papers.

82. Green, *Facts and Suggestions,* p. 85; "Statement of Colonel Benjamin E. Green, Secretary of Legation at Mexico in 1844," August 8, 1889, in L. G. Tyler, *Letters and Times,* 3:174–77; New York *Herald,* December 18, 1844. Letters to Calhoun from Green while he was en route to Mexico City are in Manning, *Diplomatic Correspondence,* 12:368–71.

movement in Texas which would enable the United States to inter-
pose, and thus obtain the concessions wanted."[83] What Green meant
was that he hoped to incite a war between Texas and Mexico that
could be used by the United States as a pretext for intervention. As
spoils for its participation in the war, the United States would immediately annex Texas, then claim New Mexico and California. Whether
Tyler and Calhoun had endorsed this scheme is uncertain, but the
impatient junto might have welcomed any opportunity to sneak Texas
into the Union.

After failing in Mexico, Green returned to Texas. There he encountered his old nemesis Britain, and he complained publicly of "the
combined influence of the British Minister and the President of Texas
acting in concert for the purpose of defeating the wishes of a majority
of the people of Texas and the United States" for annexation.[84] Green
urged the Texans to overthrow their government if its leaders continued to thwart annexation.[85] As the days slipped by, Green became
more desperate. He devised a fantastic plan that he tried to get Jones
to approve, asking permission to form a company of Indian warriors
under his direction to make war against Mexico. Composed of some
sixty thousand Indians from the United States, this force would invade, occupy, and retain Mexican territory as indemnity for the war.
Green hoped to pick up a few choice land grants himself. Jones,

83. Green, *Facts and Suggestions,* p. 85. Suspicions about Green's intentions appear
in a letter from Charles, prince of Solms, Braunfels, to Anson Jones, December 3,
1844, and British envoy Charles Elliott to Jones, January 14, 1845, in Jones, *Memoranda,* pp. 407, 413–14.

84. Green to the Houston *Telegraph,* January 2, 1845, reprinted in the New York
Herald, January 31, 1845.

85. Green was correct in noting Houston's ambivalence toward annexation. The
bitter dispute over annexation and the Senate's rejection of Tyler's treaty in mid-
1844 had shocked Houston. After Polk's election, however, Houston became more
receptive to annexation. See his letters to Issac Van Zandt, Texas chargé to the
United States, and to J. Pinckney Henderson, secretary of the Texas legation in
Washington, April 29 and May 17, 1844, in Garrison, "Diplomatic Correspondence,"
2:275, 282. Houston did not like the final terms of annexation offered by the United
States. He suggested to Donelson that "the salvation and future growth, prosperity
and safety of the U[nited] States depend upon the annexation of Texas to the Union.
The statesmen of the United States seem not to be impressed sufficiently with the
importance of Texas" (Houston to Donelson, April 3, 1845, Donelson Papers). Donelson confided to his wife Elizabeth, "Houston has disappointed me, and has not given
the [annexation] question the support I expected." He asked her to tell Jackson about
Houston's deplorable conduct (Donelson to Elizabeth Donelson, April 16, 1845,
Donelson Papers). Later, Donelson was more understanding of Houston's position
(see Donelson to Thomas Ritchie, May 28, 1845, Donelson Papers).

according to a Galveston correspondent for the New York *Herald,* gently but firmly refused to sanction this scheme, so Green had to settle for a less dramatic climax to the annexation crisis.[86]

In the presidential election, the Democrats behind Polk and Dallas fought a no-holds-barred campaign and defeated Henry Clay in November. The tariff, the bank issue, Texas, and relations with Britain were debated extensively during the campaign, but personalities were also a conspicuous factor. A Whig observer complained that the Democratic press maligned Clay so viciously that "one would come to the conclusion that he was more suitable as a candidate for the penitentiary than president of the United States."[87] Though the Democrats captured the White House by a very narrow margin, they interpreted the election as a clear mandate for annexation. Texas diplomats in Washington similarly viewed Polk's triumph as a vindication of the expansionists.[88]

After the election the annexationists stepped up their propaganda campaign. Jackson at this time admonished Donelson to use the words *reannex* and *reannexation* whenever referring to efforts to acquire Texas, so as to convey the impression that Texas, between the time of the Louisiana Purchase of 1803 and the Transcontinental Treaty of 1819, had belonged to the United States—a lost infant to be returned to its true parent. Yet Jackson may not have been entirely

86. New York *Herald,* March 23, 1845. Jones became increasingly annoyed with Green's meddling and demanded his recall. Donelson, however, was able to placate Jones. For other remarks on Green's scheme, see Ebenezer Allen, Texas secretary of state ad interim, to Donelson, January 4, 1845, in Garrison, "Diplomatic Correspondence," 2:332-33; John Tod, Texas naval officer, to Robert J. Walker, December 31, 1844, Walker Papers.

87. James T. Hathaway, "Incidents in the Campaign of 1844" (New Haven, 1905), p. 26.

88. Donelson wrote to Polk, "If you are elected I shall use the fact as decisive of the wish of the people of the United States to incorporate Texas immediately into our union, and shall calculate that the response to this wish on the part of the Government of Texas will be such as to shut out effectually all machinations of Great Britain and other powers to defeat it" (Donelson to Polk, November 6, 1844, Polk Papers). Henry Wise contended that "the question of the annexation of Texas controlled the presidential election" (*Seven Decades,* p. 230). For Texans' reactions to Polk's victory, see Charles Raymond, secretary of the Texas legation in Washington, to Anson Jones, December 4, 1844; Raymond to Ebenezer Allen, Texas secretary of state ad interim, January 27, 1845, in Garrison, "Diplomatic Correspondence," 2:323-24, 352; Raymond to Jones, November 26, 1844, in Anson Jones *Memoranda,* pp. 406-7. Even before the election, Isaac Van Zandt had written to Jones, "I have great confidence that Polk will be elected, if so, annexation will be certain, if Texas continues to desire it, which I trust she may" (Van Zandt to Jones, September 11, 1844, in Garrison, "Diplomatic Correspondence," 2:309).

convinced by his own argument, for the letter to his nephew clearly shows that he initially wrote the word *annexation* and only afterward squeezed in the prefix *re* to make his point. The expansionists also intensified their calumny against Adams, who had negotiated the 1819 treaty and had now emerged as an outspoken opponent of annexation. In a letter to editor Francis Blair, Jackson rejected as "sheer fabrication" Adams's protest that he had been reluctant to forfeit the tenuous American claim to Texas in 1819.[89] Ingersoll criticized Adams privately and in House speeches for "surrendering" Texas and for splitting Oregon with Britain when the United States had possessed a higher claim to both areas.[90] By continually agitating the Texas question, the Democrats attempted to show that Adams had slighted the South for over two decades.

Soon after the second session of the Twenty-Eighth Congress convened on December 2, 1844, expansionists introduced a joint resolution of annexation. Democrats Walker, Allen, and Daniel Dickinson of New York led the campaign in the Senate; Ingersoll and newcomer Stephen Douglas of Illinois provided leadership in the House. The proponents of annexation employed many different arguments to demonstrate the importance of Texas to the United States: fear of Britain, commercial advantages, desire for security, and protection for Americans living in Texas all emerged as reasons for annexation. Racial apprehensions resurfaced in the debate, with Texas again being portrayed by the Democrats as an escape from the black peril. Because of Calhoun's correspondence, however, expansionists probably tried to downplay racial themes at this time.

Congressman Robert Owen of Indiana observed in early 1845 that "the impression is becoming general" that the annexation of Texas "would speedily drain off a large portion of the slave population of the northern slave states; and aid in effecting, what modern abolitionism has retarded, the peaceful and gradual emancipation of slaves in Kentucky, Virginia, Maryland, Delaware, and then in other states. . . . If there be for the liberated African a path of deliverance and a place of refuge beyond, that path lies through Texas," he observed. In the Senate, Allen argued that annexation would transform Kentucky,

89. Jackson to Donelson, December 11, 1844, Donelson Papers; Jackson to Blair, February 28, 1845, Jackson Papers. Walker, of course, had also used the *reannexation* terminology in his speeches and writings. On the events of Monroe's presidency, Adams was right and Jackson wrong. See Adams, *Memoirs*, 5:67–69.

90. Ingersoll to Jackson, November 21, 1844, Jackson Papers; *CG*, 28 Cong., 2 sess., 85–87 (January 3, 1845).

Missouri, and Virginia into free states during his lifetime. He wanted Texas as "the great gangway" for slaves to use in leaving the country, since it was impossible for two different races "to occupy the same soil upon terms of equality." Allen "wanted the Negroes kept out of the state of Ohio," and he believed annexation would keep them out.[91]

Congressman Orlando Ficklin demonstrated that Illinois was no more hospitable to free blacks than Ohio was. "The free negro is more degraded, more addicted to crime, more stinted for food and raiment, and more miserable, in this country, than the slave," he noted. Fearing that emancipation would bring the substitution of white servitude for black, he advised his colleagues to protect slavery by annexing Texas. New York's Chesselden Ellis voiced similar concerns. "Confine the negro population within the limits of the present slave states, and you inevitably fix it upon them forever, or in time convert them into a continental Haiti," he warned other congressmen in early 1845. But if Texas were annexed, "a single generation" would not pass "before the states of Delaware, Maryland, Virginia, Kentucky, and Missouri join their sisters of the North in emancipation, then made safe by the drain of emigration. North Carolina and Tennessee must soon afterwards follow their example." Ellis predicted that the acquisition of Texas would hasten the "natural emigration" of blacks to "Mexico and the equator." Northern Democrats embraced this geographical determinism because it promised to disperse the slave population, open the border states to white labor, and remove the unwanted blacks from the North.[92]

Southern Democrats demanded Texas as the only available outlet for their black population. "Will the non-slaveholding states receive the emancipated blacks?" Senator Chester Ashley of Arkansas challenged in early 1845. He thought not: "Already most of the free states have severe laws against the introduction of free blacks among them. Many require security that they shall not become burdensome, and all are averse to submit to the greatest curse that could be inflicted

91. *CG*, 28 Cong., 2 sess., App. 100–1 (January 8, 1845); *CG*, 28 Cong., 2 sess., 343 (February 25, 1845).

92. *CG*, 28 Cong., 2 sess., 184 (January 23, 1845); *CG*, 28 Cong., 2 sess., App. 141 (January 25, 1845). Congressman Moses Norris of New Hampshire and Senator Daniel Dickinson of New York agreed. See *CG*, 28 Cong., 2 sess., App. 189–90, 324–25 (January 24 and February 22, 1845). O'Sullivan also reiterated his faith in dispersion and removal of blacks through annexation. See the New York *Morning News*, November 19, 28, and December 17, 1844, and February 1, 1845.

on them—the miserable, degraded, vagabond free blacks." Alabama senator William L. Yancey reminded Northerners that "the statistics of the various prisons and almshouses of the free states" showed that blacks, "though free to rise to the high estate of the white man . . . prefer[red] to revel in the brothel, until imprisoned in a jail or penitentiary." Surely the North could not deny that annexation was vital to the entire country.[93]

As the debate climaxed in late February 1845, Walker introduced a compromise bill of annexation that a majority of lawmakers found acceptable: the United States, through the president, could either offer Texas immediate admission as a state or could conduct further negotiations with Texas and Mexico and then submit any pact of annexation to the Senate or full Congress, as the president saw fit. In the mayhem of the Texas debate, preparations for Polk's inauguration, and Tyler's frantic efforts to achieve annexation during the final days of his term, Polk or one of his advisers probably assured skeptical northern senators that the incoming administration would pursue further negotiations to obtain Texas honorably and peacefully. Whatever means, fair or foul, were employed, the Senate passed the annexation resolution by 27 to 25 on February 27, every Democrat and three southern Whigs voting yea. In the House, 132 members supported the bill, and 76 opposed it, party affiliation and not sectional factors determining the vote.[94]

On March 3, his last full day in office, Tyler sent a messenger to Texas with a copy of the joint resolution, stipulating that the administration wanted immediate annexation without further negotiations. Shortly after his inauguration on March 4, Polk sent another messenger to Texas to affirm Tyler's previous offer.[95] The expansionists had triumphed: annexation now awaited the anticipated endorsement of Texas.

93. *CG*, 28 Cong., 2 sess., App. 287 (February 22, 1845); *CG*, 28 Cong., 2 sess., App. 89–90 (January 7, 1845).

94. For the Senate vote, see *CG*, 28 Cong., 2 sess., 362 (February 27, 1845); *Journal of the Senate*, 28 Cong., 2 sess., February 27, 1845 (Washington, 184[5]), p. 220. For the House vote, see *CG*, 28 Cong., 2 sess., 372 (February 28, 1845). The allegations about Polk's pledge to pursue further negotiations are discussed in Benton, *Thirty Years' View*, 2:635–37; Sargent, *Public Men and Events*, 2:261–63; Sellers, *Polk*, pp. 206–8. The three Senate Whigs who voted for annexation were John Henderson of Mississippi, Reverdy Johnson of Louisiana, and William Merrick of Maryland. The impact of annexation on the Democratic party is discussed in detail in Chapter 7.

95. Polk probably would have followed this course even if Tyler had not taken the initiative before him.

Elation spread among the Democrats. Polk associate J. George Harris informed Jackson that after the bill's passage "a national salute was commenced on Capitol Hill and the welkin rang with the roar of cannon for nearly half an hour. I never saw so many glad faces."[96] When Texas accepted annexation in July the Democrats were even more euphoric. A *Herald* reporter observed that Secretary of State Buchanan and Postmaster General Cave Johnson appeared "to be in ecstacies," executive editor Thomas Ritchie could "scarcely stand in his shoes," and Secretary of the Treasury Walker looked like "the happiest man this side of a Methodist revival."[97]

Walker was justifiably pleased. For it was he who had defined the Texas issue in terms that both northern and southern Democrats found compelling; it was he who had encouraged Jackson to join the annexation campaign and, perhaps unwittingly, to destroy Van Buren; it was he who had been the prime mover in Polk's nomination; it was he who had chiefly arranged Tyler's withdrawal from the 1844 campaign; and it was he who now received the acclaim afforded to leaders who offer simple remedies to complex problems and allay anxieties among the people.

Powerful Democrats recognized the magnitude of Walker's exertions. Dallas told Walker that his "comprehensive, clear, argumentative, and eloquent" letter on annexation had come " 'like manna in the way of starved people.' " After the election, vice-president-elect Dallas urged Polk to designate Walker their secretary of state. "[Walker's] letter on Texas flew like wild-fire through the whole country," Dallas reminded Polk, "and created for him a solid national reputation." "If the president-elect has a proper feeling of gratitude for services rendered," William King suggested to Buchanan in early 1845, "Walker will be able to command his position." O'Sullivan at this time honored Walker with a biographical sketch and tribute in the *Democratic Review,* contending that Walker's Texas letter had been "the principal cause of the revolution in public sentiment, which resulted in the nomination and election of James K. Polk to the presidency, as the avowed advocate of immediate annexation." And editor Thomas Ritchie, summoned by Polk to edit the Washington *Daily Union* in 1845, argued that Walker's tract had "constituted the textbook" of the Democratic strategists and had exerted a "prodigious influence" over public opinion.[98]

96. Harris to Jackson, February 28, 1845, Jackson Papers.
97. New York *Herald,* July 7, 1845.
98. Dallas to Walker, February 5, 1844, Walker Papers; Dallas to Polk, December 15, 1844, Polk Papers; King to Buchanan, January 28, 1845, Buchanan Papers;

Walker and Green were certainly instrumental in annexation, yet they could not have shaped events so decisively had there not been a national mood that made Americans so susceptible to their propaganda. The Tyler junto adeptly manipulated anxieties among the people, but they did not create them. As Walker, Green, and others well knew, those anxieties were not confined to the South, nor were they exclusively associated with the institution of slavery. The ominous presence of blacks throughout the country, not their enslavement in one part of it, made annexation a truly national concern to most expansionists. With colonization a dismal failure, with the census dramatizing the degeneration of free blacks in the North, with paranoia toward imminent racial strife present throughout the nation, Negrophobic Democrats embraced Texas as the great white hope. Whatever other attractions Texas presented to anxious American leaders, its promise as a solution to the nation's racial crisis was a principal factor behind the determination and urgency of the junto and its partisans.

The proponents of annexation believed Texas essential to the future security and prosperity of the United States. A permanently independent Texas conflicted with their imperial vision, for they feared that Texas might pursue its own commercial and territorial aggrandizement to the detriment of the United States. Not only might an independent Texas abolish slavery and provide a haven for fugitive slaves; it could also acquire the Californias, New Mexico, parts of Sonora and Chihuahua, and probably Oregon, and become a rival empire in North America.[99] Such fears were not unfounded. Texas president Sam Houston, in his valedictory in late 1844, had advised his fellow Texans to think of themselves as "an independent people." He warned that Texas must not go "begging again for admission into the United States." "If we remain an independent nation, our territory will be extensive—unlimited," he predicted. "The Pacific alone will bound the mighty march of our race and our empire."[100]

"Robert J. Walker," *Democratic Review*, 16 (February, 1845): 162; Washington *Daily Union*, November 22, 1845. Ritchie later contended that Walker's "celebrated letter [had] roused the whole country. It was as effective in setting forth the truth with its trumpet tones, as Paine's *Common Sense* was in arousing and convincing the American people at the commencement of their revolution" (Washington *Daily Union*, September 25, 1847).

99. See William C. Binkley, *The Expansionist Movement in Texas, 1836–1850* (Berkeley, 1925).

100. "Houston's Valedictory to the Texas Congress," December 9, 1844, in Houston, *Writings*, 4:403. See also Houston to William S. Murphy, May 6, 1844, in ibid., pp. 322–23.

Such imperial pronouncements alarmed the expansionists, since they assumed that Texas could attain its ambitions. Racially and culturally akin to the Americans, the Texans possessed the character that could transform their country into an imperial rival of the United States. Mexico, however, posed no such menace. For this reason a Free-Soil Mexico was acceptable to the expansionists, but a Free-Soil Texas was not. When Texas entered the Union in late 1845, then, two antagonistic imperial dreams were reconciled under one flag.

The events of 1844 and early 1845 baffled many contemporaries and subsequent students of the period. John Quincy Adams called the passage of the annexation resolution "the heaviest calamity that ever befell myself and my country," and he believed that it indicated "a signal triumph of the slave-representation in the Constitution of the United States." Ohio's Jacob Brinkerhoff, a Democrat growing in-creasingly wary of an apparent prosouthern tilt in his party, com-plained to his House colleagues that annexation was "a southern question; hatched and got up as a southern question, for the benefit of the South; for the strengthening of her institutions; for the promo-tion of her power; for her benefit; for the advancement of her influence." However the junto defined the measure, its sectional bias could not be mistaken. Using a mixed metaphor from the backwoods and the bard, Brinkerhoff suggested that "a skunk by any other name would smell as bad." Northern critics of annexation repeatedly stressed that it was a measure of the South, by the South, and for the South.[101]

Scholars have offered several reasons for the initial failure and final triumph of annexation. Jesse Reeves, in the first major study of Tyler's foreign policy, attributed the initial defeat of annexation to a northern reaction against the sectional and proslavery bias of the administration. But explaining the approval of annexation eight months later proved a more elusive task. Justin Smith, in 1911, assigned the success of annexation in early 1845 to Polk's election—a helpful but incomplete explanation. Frederick Merk, in a 1972 study on Texas annexation, suggested that the whip of party discipline snapped the northern Democrats into line behind annexation in early 1845. David Pletcher noted in 1973 that "opposition to a dishonorable war with Mexico" and northern distaste for the "expansion of slaveholding territory" largely led to the rejection of annexation in 1844. Yet those two factors were still present in 1845 when Congress passed the joint

101. Adams, *Memoirs*, 12 (February 27 and 28, 1845): 173; Brinkerhoff, *CG*, 28 Cong., 2 sess., 132 (January 13, 1845).

resolution. Pletcher agrees with his predecessors that the election of Polk settled the issue and that ties of "blood and business" then secured the union of Texas and the United States.[102]

Party discipline, sectional factors, personal animosities, and Polk's election are important factors in explaining the fate of Texas annexation in 1844 and 1845. Though the junto emphasized the South's interests in Texas, most Democrats did accept annexation as being vital to the entire country. The final approval of annexation reveals no significant sectional disagreement: thirteen northern senators and fourteen southern senators combined to provide the 27 to 25 margin of victory in the Senate; in the House, seventy-six free-state congressmen joined fifty-seven southern colleagues in support of annexation. In terms of party affiliation, Democrats overwhelmingly approved of annexation, and Whigs decisively opposed it. Party loyalty was stronger than sectional loyalty. Few Democrats agreed with Brinkerhoff.

The annexation of Texas appeared attractive because white racial biases transcended section, class, and, to an extent, party.[103] Elections often shift the reins of power from the hands of one group to those of another, but they do not change deep-seated cultural characteristics. In antebellum America, fear and hostility toward blacks was one of those characteristics. When Walker, Green, Calhoun, O'Sullivan, Bennett, and others defended slavery, they did so with the conviction that slavery actually prevented more problems than it created. If abolition ever occurred, only expatriation or the total elimination of blacks could protect whites both below and above the Mason-Dixon line. The advocates of annexation candidly proclaimed their pessimistic views. To them, racial prejudice was an ineradicable feature of American life.

Adams, Giddings, and Jarvis were unusual in their concern for blacks in the United States. They, far more than those who argued that slavery was the only safeguard for protecting blacks from themselves and the whites from blacks, represented an isolated and disdained minority on the racial question. The advocates of annexation

102. Reeves, *American Diplomacy under Tyler and Polk,* p. 137; Smith, *Annexation of Texas,* pp. 227, 343–48; Merk, *Slavery and the Annexation of Texas,* pp. 156–57; Pletcher, *Diplomacy of Annexation,* pp. 149, 204.

103. The Democrats were far more Negrophobic than the Whigs. The Jacksonians championed measures to proscribe blacks in the free states, and they fought occasional Whig efforts to repeal the discriminatory black codes. Demonstrating the racial animus of Democrats is one thing, but accounting for it is quite another. The correlation between party affiliation and racial attitudes deserves more scrutiny from historians.

not only condemned blacks; they also condemned what few prominent white sympathizers the blacks had. Unlike Negrophobes in both
sections, Adams, Giddings, and Jarvis believed blacks had a God-
given right to liberty. Moreover, they believed blacks had the capacity
to better themselves and their society if given the opportunity. Few
white Americans agreed.

The radical critics of the Tyler administration failed to attain two
of their chief objectives: Congress refused to investigate and correct
the Census of 1840, and Texas entered the Union as an additional
slave state in 1845. The dissidents lost both struggles for the same
reason. Whether enslaved or emancipated, blacks appeared to be a
nuisance and a threat to the nation's very existence: no major sectional disagreement existed on that point. To discredit and destroy abolitionism and to make their country more secure, the proponents of
annexation found the Census of 1840 and territorial expansion indispensable to their cause. The census strikingly illustrated the frailty of
blacks and the need to keep them in chains; Texas offered the only
means of quickly dispersing the country's unwanted black population
and eventually funneling it into Central America.

The intensity and extent of white racism throughout the nation
created a climate of fear that facilitated the addition of the lone star
of Texas to the flag of the United States. That climate helps explain
both the timing and the tactics of anxious leaders who viewed Texas
as a means of avoiding one of the gravest perils confronting the
nation during the late Jacksonian period. The expansionists did not
seek to emancipate the slave, but rather, through annexation, to
emancipate the United States from the blacks.

CHAPTER 3

Of Swords and Plowshares: Coercion through Commerce

During the 1840s, American leaders obtained vast territorial cessions west of the Mississippi, as "land hunger" found expression in national policy. But expansionism at this time meant far more than spreading new farms and plantations across the continent. American ambitions were global, not just continental, and commercial as well as territorial. Both the Tyler and Polk administrations sought to enhance the power of the United States through the manipulation of trade, and each sought to monopolize essential raw materials and to open additional overseas markets to the country's agrarian producers. A determined quest for export markets was a principal impetus behind the domestic and foreign policies of the 1840s. The intimate connection between anxiety about commodity surpluses and economic depression, on the one hand, and the search for more extensive opportunities for foreign trade, on the other, demonstrates the artificiality of the distinction often drawn by historians between domestic and foreign affairs. The reduction of the tariff, for example, was no less a foreign policy issue than was the Cushing expedition to China or the war against Mexico. As the United States extended its dominion to the Rio Grande and the Pacific, it also maneuvered to alter patterns of world trade so as to acquire a much larger share of it for American producers. In this struggle Britain's loss would be America's gain.

The Jacksonians represent the epitome of laissez-faire economics in American historiography, but that label is misleading in many ways. It would be more accurate to describe the Tyler and Polk administrations as practitioners of a unique brand of mercantilism. With the possible exception of Jefferson and Monroe, no other presidents can match the records of Tyler and Polk for bold initiatives in promoting the expansion of American trade before the Civil War. Nor had any of their predecessors recognized the coercive potential in holding a virtual monopoly over vital resources such as cotton and foodstuffs. As was often the case in the desire for new land, anxiety about American security and ambitions for economic ascendancy were the underlying motivations of the search for new markets.

Fears about the viability of the American economy contributed to the uneasiness of the 1840s. The prolonged recession following the Panic of 1837 caused hardship among many strata of the population, and the downturn alarmed many leaders who were bewildered by the vicissitudes of an expanding and dynamic economy. New York merchant and financier Philip Hone worried about the depressed condition of the economy, complaining at the beginning of 1843 that "the old year was marked by public calamity and individual misfortune." Prospects were not good: "Business is unprofitable, confidence impaired, stocks and other personal property of little value, taxes nearly doubled, rents reduced, tenants running away, debts wiped out by the bankrupt law, and Locofocoism triumphant."[1] Hone's complaints were those of a man of substantial means, yet people further down the economic ladder suffered far more than he. In typical partisan fashion, Hone (a Clay Whig) blamed the mess on Van Buren and Tyler.

Despite the deprivation and suffering caused by the recession, the expansionists of the 1840s concluded that abundance and surpluses, not scarcity, most menaced the economic well-being of the United States—a conviction that greatly influenced the policies of the Tyler and Polk administrations. To cope effectively with the fluctuating economic cycles of the late Jacksonian period, American leaders decided to acquire new territory and additional foreign markets. Their ultimate objective, beyond relieving the immediate economic distress of the nation, was to transform it into the world's preeminent commercial power.

The expansionists realized that replacing Britain as the leading commercial power of the world would be a difficult task requiring

1. *The Diary of Philip Hone, 1828–1851*, Bayard Tuckerman, ed., 2 vols. (New York, 1889), 2 (January 2, 1843): 169–70.

simultaneous battles on many fronts. As the campaign to overturn Britain's advantage in foreign trade developed, the means selected changed from year to year, but the general goal remained constant: the United States sought to penetrate closed or restricted markets around the world and then capture them at the expense of the European imperial powers. The tactics employed by the Tyler and Polk administrations included improving the American navy, making commercial accords with foreign powers, acquiring new territory on the North American continent, reducing tariffs, reforming the consular service, and acquiring a monopoly over the world cotton supply.

John Tyler and Abel Upshur were, generally, strict states' rights Jeffersonians, but they could set aside their constitutional scruples when they believed that deviations from strict construction and federal retrenchment would open new commercial opportunities for the United States. Both contended that the federal government had an obligation to protect and extend American trade around the globe. As secretary of the navy in 1841, for example, Upshur entreated Congress to increase naval expenditures by 50 percent, in order to double the size of the American squadron in the Pacific. "Commerce," he observed, "may be regarded as our principal interest because, to a great extent, it includes within it every other interest." The existing force of "some twenty ships in commission" were, he said, totally inadequate to safeguard "four thousand miles of exposed sea and lake coast, a foreign commerce scattered through the most distant seas, and a domestic trade exposed alike upon the ocean and our interior waters." Additional ships were the navy's greatest need, but Upshur also recommended establishing a naval base in Hawaii, tripling the size of the marine corps, and creating a training school for naval officers.[2]

A year later, Upshur expressed even greater anxiety about the navy's many deficiencies, grumbling that "for twenty years past, the navy has received from the government little more than a stepmother's care"—inexcusable negligence, in his view, since "a commerce, such as ours, *demands* the protection of an adequate naval force." He again recommended "a very large increase of the Pacific squadron," along with "a squadron of at least eighty guns" for the African coast. Rather than request a large appropriation for new ships during the lingering recession, however, Upshur advised that the ships already

2. *Report of the Secretary of the Navy, S. Doc.,* vol. 395, no. 1, 27 Cong., 2 sess. (December 4, 1841), pp. 379–81.

constructed be renovated and kept in service so as to make American naval power more conspicuous and "constantly in the tracks of our commerce."[3] Undoubtedly he regretted that he could not press for a substantial naval buildup, yet he felt compelled to ask Congress for an appropriation to recondition uncommissioned ships, and he repeated his call for "proper naval schools on shore."

Upshur's concern for protecting and promoting American trade was shared by Massachusetts congressman Caleb Cushing, a renegade Whig who supported Tyler and later drifted into the Democratic party. Cushing came from Newburyport, a coastal city at the mouth of the Merrimac River where his father had prospered as a merchant and importer during the late eighteenth century. By the close of the War of 1812, however, Jeffersonian restrictions on American commerce and the disruptions of the war itself had crippled the port, so Cushing pursued law and politics rather than a career in foreign trade.[4] After entering the House in 1835, Cushing championed military preparedness and the removal of foreign barriers to American trade. In 1842, for example, Cushing, as chairman of the House Foreign Affairs Committee, authored a much publicized report dealing with restrictions on American trade with Britain's colonies. He warned that Britain's "infliction of immense and still increasing injury" upon United States trade and navigation threatened to "place all our maritime resources" at that country's "mere discretion." He advised the Tyler administration to explore retaliatory restrictions on Britain until that power agreed to remove its "unequal, unjust, and injurious" prohibitions on American trade with the West Indies. On the House floor, Cushing accused Britain of "grasping ambition, of outreaching rapacity, and of wrong as wide as the all but boundless range of her empire." He urged Congress in 1842 to improve the navy, since it provided "military protection in war" and served as "the safeguard of the commerce of all parts of the country in peace and in war." So frequently did he revile Britain that his elder colleague John Quincy Adams complained, "Cushing thought that inflam-

3. *Report of the Secretary of the Navy, S. Doc.,* vol. 413, no. 1, 27 Cong., 3 sess. (vol. 1: December, 1842), pp. 538–45. Secretary of war John Bell agreed with Upshur. Because of the Europeans' great improvements in steam navigation, he warned Tyler in 1841, the United States would have to increase defenses "at an expense far exceeding anything heretofore deemed important or necessary to reasonable security" (Bell to Tyler, August 30, 1841, in Benjamin F. Cooling, ed., *The New American State Papers* [Wilmington, 1979], 2:175–79).

4. Claude M. Fuess, *The Life of Caleb Cushing,* 2 vols. (reprint ed.: Hamden, Conn., 1965), 1:9–36.

matory declamation against England upon all possible topics was the short cut to popularity, and he speechified accordingly." From 1841 to 1844 Cushing stood behind Tyler, and his support brought a close friendship with the harried president. The two men worked in tandem to protect and promote American trade around the world.[5]

Cushing paid particular attention to China after the Opium War. In late 1842, he reminded Tyler that England had recently forced China to open five ports to British ships and to cede in perpetuity a port at Hong Kong as indemnity for the war. Cushing doubted that Britain intended to exclude other countries from the China trade, but he did conclude that other nations would have to negotiate separate agreements with China to obtain similar privileges. He regarded the present as "an urgent occasion for dispatching an authorized agent to China with instructions to make commercial arrangements in behalf of the United States." The Chinese, Cushing assured Tyler, were "predisposed to deal kindly with us, the more so as we only can by the extent of our commerce act in counterpoise of . . . England and thus save the Chinese from that which would be extremely inconvenient for them, viz: the condition of being an exclusive monopoly in the hands of E[ngland]." Nor was China the only Asian market of concern to Cushing. He reported rumors that British gunboats would soon attempt to "compel the government of Japan to open its ports to the commerce of England." If Britain were to attain commercial dominance in China and Japan, seize Hawaii, and maintain its strong position on the Columbia River, it would then possess "a complete belt of fortresses environing the globe, to the imminent future peril,

---

5. *Colonial Trade—Great Britain,* House Foreign Affairs Committee, *H. Doc.,* vol. 409, no. 650, 27 Cong., 2 sess., pp. 19–20; *Congressional Globe* (hereafter cited as *CG*), 27 Cong., 1 sess., App. 421 (June 24, 1841); *CG,* 27 Cong., 2 sess., App. 928 (May 21, 1842); *Memoirs of John Quincy Adams,* Charles Francis Adams, ed., 12 vols. (Philadelphia, 1874–77), 11 (December 10, 1841):37; Tyler to Cushing, April 24, 1843, Caleb Cushing Papers. Tyler assured Cushing, "There is no office in my gift which is too high for your aspirations or your deserts." Tyler nominated Cushing for secretary of the treasury three times, but the Senate rejected him each time. Cushing's political course seemed too opportunistic to some. Democrat Thomas Hart Benton said of him, "He had deserted his party to join Mr. Tyler. He worked for him in and out of the House, and even deserted himself to support him" (*Thirty Years' View, or, A History of the Working of the American Government for Thirty Years, from 1820 to 1850,* 2 vols. [New York, 1854–56], 2:514). James Russell Lowell, in "The Biglow Papers," also criticized Cushing: "Gineral C. is a dreffle [dreadfully] smart man: He's been on all sides thet give places or pelf; But consistency still wuz a part of his plan,—He's been true to *one* party,—an' thet is himself." See *The Complete Poetical Works of James Russell Lowell,* Cambridge ed. (Boston, 1896), p. 188.

not only of our territorial possessions, but of all our vast commerce on the Pacific."[6]

Cushing urged hasty action to countermand Britain's present advantage in the Far East. He closed his letter to Tyler by pointing out that if an American envoy succeeded in negotiating concessions in China, he should then proceed to Japan to make similar arrangements there. Furthermore, China and Hawaii would welcome an American presence in East Asia as a counterbalance to Britain, and though Japan showed no receptivity to any foreign power, the rumor that Britain had designs there was enough to convince Cushing that the United States should stake its claim as well. Cushing emphasized to Tyler that "Congress could not fail to support you in these measures." What was good for the American economy would be good for the political prospects of the administration—of that Cushing had no doubt. Since the late 1830s, Cushing had anticipated an imminent struggle for commercial supremacy between England and the United States, and he hoped the implementation of his recommendations would enhance the competitive edge of his country not only in the Far East but around the world.

Tyler also hoped to increase foreign trade, recognizing during the prolonged recession the anomaly of economic hardship in the midst of abundance. In late 1842, in his second annual message to Congress, he defined the difference between foreign countries and his own: "While in some other nations steady and industrious labor can hardly find the means of subsistence, the greatest evil which we have to encounter is a surplus of production beyond the home demand, which seeks, and with difficulty finds, a partial market in other regions."[7] Distressed by recurring commodity gluts, Tyler directed the attention of Congress to trade with Asia. He admitted that American trade with China had fluctuated considerably over the past few decades, but he stressed that overall it had "more than doubled within the last ten years." He sensed that the time was auspicious for increasing that commerce, because "the opening of several new and important ports connected with parts of the [Chinese] Empire heretofore seldom visited by Europeans or Americans" would increase the demand for American products. He urged that an envoy be sent to China to secure access to those ports, as Cushing had advised. Tyler

6. Cushing to Tyler, December 27, 1842, Cushing Papers.
7. James D. Richardson, ed., *A Compilation of the Messages and Papers of the Presidents*, 10 vols. (New York, 1897), 5 (December 6, 1842):2047.

also requested that Congress "make appropriations for the compensation of a commissioner to reside in China to exercise a watchful care
over the concerns of American citizens."[8]

Tyler also reminded Congress of the special commercial ties between the United States and Hawaii. Because of its proximity to the
United States and "the intercourse which American vessels have with
it, such vessels constituting five-sixths of all which annually visit it,"
Hawaii seemed vital to United States merchants. Again heeding Cushing's advise, Tyler declared that his country desired "no peculiar
advantages, no exclusive control over the Hawaiian Government, but
is content with its independent existence and anxiously wishes for its
security and prosperity." Should any nation attempt "to take possession of the islands, colonize them, and subvert the native Government," such a move "could not but create dissatisfaction on the part
of the United States."[9] Tyler did not commit his country to guarantee
Hawaiian independence, but his words were meant to discourage any
European nation from threatening the preeminent commercial position of the United States in Hawaii. Tyler in effect was extending the
Monroe Doctrine to the island kingdom.[10]

Jealousy of Britain and expectations of a burgeoning trade with
Asia if Britain could be outflanked in the Far East significantly affected
American foreign policy after 1842. In March 1843, Tyler dispatched
a commissioner to Hawaii, the first diplomatic official sent there by
the United States. A few weeks later, the administration issued a
sharp protest when a British naval commander seized Hawaii in an
unauthorized act of preemptive imperialism.[11] The British foreign
ministry promptly disavowed the act and reaffirmed the autonomy
of the islands, but the damage was done. Already disturbed by British
meddling in Texas, Tyler and his advisers viewed this seizure as yet
another indication of Britain's campaign to hem in the United States.

8. Tyler's message on Hawaii, in Richardson, *Messages and Papers,* 5 (December 30,
1842):2067.

9. Ibid., p. 2065. See also the New York *Morning News,* December 30, 1844 and
April 15, 1845, for assessments of American commercial interests in Hawaii.

10. United States policy toward Hawaii during this important initial period is
discussed in Sylvester K. Stevens, *American Expansion in Hawaii, 1842–1898* (New
York, 1945), pp. 1–20.

11. *Daily Madisonian,* June 2, 1843; John Tyler to Daniel Webster, July 8, 1843, in
Lyon G. Tyler, *The Letters and Times of the Tylers,* 3 vols. (Richmond, 1884–85),
2:272–73. Important documents on the British presence in Hawaii appear in *British
and Foreign State Papers,* 169 vols. (London, 1841–1976), vol. 31, 1842–43 (1858):1023–
35.

While monitoring events in Hawaii, the administration continued its campaign to increase American exports to China. In April 1843, editor John Jones endorsed Cushing's idea that the United States was China's "natural ally." Jones suggested that histories of the American Revolution and the War of 1812 be translated into Chinese and made available to imperial officials so that they would recognize that China and the United States possessed a common enemy in Great Britain.[12] On May 8, Tyler appointed Cushing a special commissioner to China.[13] Jones hailed the selection, contending that Cushing had had "no superior in Congress" since entering the House in 1835.[14] In late July, Cushing and his entourage sailed for China with instructions to obtain most-favored-nation status for American merchants. En route to China, Cushing scouted the prospects for trade with Egypt, West Africa, India, and Ceylon and reported his findings to Upshur.[15]

Cushing concluded the Treaty of Wanghiya with Chinese officials on July 3, 1844, opening five ports to American traders and providing extraterritorial rights for American citizens in China. By the time news of the treaty reached the United States, however, Tyler had withdrawn from the presidential race, and his paper, the *Daily Madisonian,* had ceased publication. But Bennett of the New York *Herald* had now assumed the role of unofficial executive editor, and he lauded the junto's efforts to expand American trade. In late 1844, Bennett praised Cushing's diplomacy; England and the United States, he wrote, were locked in a fierce struggle "for naval supremacy and commercial greatness." Cushing's success in China, he asserted, would further disquiet the British, for the United States was making "rapid progress in the way to superior commercial importance."[16] Tyler, though he had surrendered his hopes for another term, did not slacken his efforts to improve commercial opportunities abroad. In early 1845, he communicated the China treaty to Congress and urged, "in view of the magnitude and importance" of American concerns, "actual and prospective, in China," that a permanent commissioner or minister be sent there. Britain and France had already sent resi-

12. *Daily Madisonian,* April 11, 1843.

13. The administration had first offered the China mission to Edward Everett. Eclipsed by Duff Green in London, Everett could have withdrawn from his post by accepting the offer, but he refused. Had Everett accepted the appointment from Tyler, Daniel Webster (who had just resigned as secretary of state) could have become American minister in London, an honorable exile for the unwanted secretary.

14. *Daily Madisonian,* May 8, 1843.

15. *The Cushing Reports,* Margaret D. Benetz, ed. (Salisbury, N.C., 1976).

16. New York *Herald,* November 24, 1844.

dent envoys to China, and that, to Tyler, necessitated similar action by the United States.[17]

In addition to attempting to expand exports to China, the administration also worked to improve commercial relations with the German states. At the same time that Cushing was concluding his negotiations with the Chinese in mid-1844, Tyler presented the Senate with a commercial pact recently arranged with the Germanic customs union, or *Zollverein*. Tyler stressed that the mutual tariff reductions contained in the pact rendered a valuable market of some twenty-eight million people more accessible to the producers and merchants of the United States. But this commercial treaty met the same fate as the Texas treaty, both setbacks constituting severe disappointments to the administration and its partisans. Jones, writing in the *Daily Madisonian* in late June, harshly rebuked the Senate for rejecting the commercial accord. *Zollverein* duties on American tobacco, rice, and lard would have been reduced and cotton admitted duty free in Germany in return for lower import taxes on some manufactured goods. Jones lamented that senators "refused to open a new and great mart for a number of the largest and most important staples of the country" solely because they wanted to deny Tyler any success in foreign relations. The Senate had slammed the door shut on almost thirty million customers badly needed by American agricultural producers.[18]

Editor Bennett had also strongly favored the *Zollverein* treaty. He predicted in the *Herald* that "in a short time the whole of Germany will be supplied with cotton . . . from this country instead of England." Approval of the pact would "cut off from England a most important branch of her trade and commerce" and improve the commercial position of the United States, serving as a means "to extend our manufactures—to increase our trade—to benefit the country generally—and at the same time give a permanent check to the progress of British monopoly and aggrandizement." The Senate's rejection of the treaty infuriated Bennett.[19]

17. Richardson, *Messages and Papers,* 5 (January 22, 1845):2211.

18. Tyler's message to the Senate on the *Zollverein* treaty, in Richardson, *Messages and Papers,* 5 (April 29, 1844):2167; *Daily Madisonian,* June 22, 25, and 27, 1844. The negotiator of the treaty, Henry Wheaton, wrote to Tyler from Berlin that the ratification and implementation of the treaty would secure "great advantages . . . to our staple articles of cotton, rice, tobacco, and lard in the markets of Germany." Such treaties, he suggested, provided "the most advantageous mode of effecting the desirable modification in our existing tariff " (Wheaton to Tyler, March 27, 1844, in L. G. Tyler, *Letters and Times,* 2:326).

19. New York *Herald,* March 24, June 15 and 18, 1844.

The Senate's intransigence only temporarily stifled the junto's campaign to overturn British commercial supremacy—it did not halt it. At issue for Tyler, Upshur, Cushing, and Jones was not merely increased trade with Asia or Europe. Their ultimate goal was to enhance American security by attaining control over the most vital trade of the globe. Although the junto and its supporters viewed the struggle to expand trade with China and the German states as important encounters in the commercial warfare with Britain, they regarded Texas, with its cotton industry, as the most crucial battleground. Consequently the administration focused its efforts on the acquisition of Texas and devoted only secondary attention to other policies designed to find new export markets abroad.

Executive agent Duff Green was instrumental in defining the high commercial stakes being contested between Britain and the United States in Texas. As was noted previously, Green believed that racial and economic considerations were intertwined in that struggle—that Britain sought to protect its commercial dominance by maintaining the independence of Texas as a rival to the United States and by fomenting abolitionism there as a preliminary to securing abolition in the American South.[20] In the opinion of Green and the cabinet he served, Britain's commercial pretentions were almost as dire a threat to the United States as were its abolitionist pretensions. Since British philanthropy simply cloaked the more sinister ambition among Britain's officials and merchants to gain control over the world's supply of essential raw materials such as cotton, the United States must act resolutely to deny England any inordinate influence over Texas.

Editor Jones had speculated on the significance of cotton in American foreign relations as early as 1842. In March he observed that the United States was the principal source "whence England derives the means by which she is enabled to furnish her cotton fabrics to the whole world, and should any interruption take place in the supply of these means, the effect upon her operatives and practical manufacturers would be disastrous in the highest degree." Though England at this time sought an amicable resolution of the northeastern border dispute and sent Lord Ashburton to the United States to settle the issue, Jones still contemplated the possibility of war and warned Britain of its consequences: "A war with the United States would stop nine-tenths, or at least a large majority of the looms of Britain, and would at once reduce millions of poor wretches who depend on their labor for a stinted subsistence from day to day, to actual starvation."[21]

20. See Chapter 2.
21. *Daily Madisonian*, March 14, 1842.

Another preliminary indication of the administration's ideas about cotton diplomacy was a House speech delivered in April of 1842 by Virginia congressman Henry Wise, a close friend and confidant of Tyler and Upshur.[22] Wise, according to editor John Forney of Pennsylvania, was "the undoubted dictator of the Tyler Administration," and Washington journalist Perley Poore described him as Tyler's "most influential adviser." Wise enjoyed easy access to Tyler, and knowledgeable observers such as Forney and Poore were generally correct in assuming that he spoke for the administration.[23] In his April speech, Wise, echoing Green, warned that Britain had in Texas "a rival to the United States in the production of cotton." The continuation of that rivalry between Texas and the United States was Britain's ulterior motive for supporting Texan autonomy. He suggested two alternatives for the American Congress: it could either annex Texas, or it could allow Texas "to conquer Mexico, and become our most dangerous and formidable rival." He obviously preferred annexation.

After the resolution of the northeastern boundary dispute in mid-1842, the junto turned its energies to Texas and paid greater attention to the commercial competition between Britain and the United States, and the role of cotton in that competition. As noted in Chapter 2, Green and other members of the junto were concerned not only with slavery but also with what they perceived as a plot by Britain to monopolize raw materials, especially cotton, by preventing the annexation of Texas to the United States. In May 1844, Green insisted that a permanent peace with Britain could be obtained only if annexation were secured. "Let Texas be annexed," he predicted, "and we command the cotton-growing district." Britain would then be forced "to cultivate peace and good will." Jones wrote in the *Daily Madisonian* that Britain's chief objective in North America was "to create a competitor and rival to our Southern states, by stimulating the cultivation of cotton in Texas." Senator Walker, in his important letter on annexation, also warned that Texas would become a "com-

22. Reported in the Washington *National Intelligencer,* April 15, 1842. The speech is reprinted in Frederick Merk, *Slavery and the Annexation of Texas* (New York, 1972), pp. 192–200.

23. John W. Forney, *Anecdotes of Public Men,* 2 vols. (New York, 1873), 1:144; Benjamin Perley Poore, *Perley's Reminiscences of Sixty Years in the National Metropolis,* 2 vols. (Philadelphia, 1886), 1:278. Editor Jones often praised Wise and suggested his intimate tie to the administration. See, for example, the *Daily Madisonian,* July 1, 1842, March 6 and June 15, 1843.

mercial dependency of England" and a "great rival in the cotton markets of the world" if it remained independent.[24] Jones agreed and developed Walker's view more fully in a revealing editorial, defining the dire consequences for the United States if annexation failed and Texas remained under the guardianship of England:

> Texas labor, stimulated and fostered by British capital, would soon raise as much cotton as does the United States—which, by treaty with England, would enter [England] duty free—while an increasing tariff [in England] on ours, would soon either exterminate cotton from our land or limit the market for its sale to our own country, when our manufactures would have to purchase at a price necessary to raise it on our worn out soil, while England would get it cheap from the rich lands of Texas. Our manufacturers could not, then, even with the present [American protective] tariff, compete with the British manufacturer.

Only the annexation of Texas, Jones repeated a month later, could "entirely preclude the attempt of England to raise up a cotton-growing nation in opposition to the United States" and prevent Texas's emerging as "a fatal rival."[25] The junto tried desperately to convince opponents of annexation that their course spelled calamity for the nation. The South might lose its cotton markets abroad, slavery would become superfluous as cotton prices plunged, northern manufacturers and export merchants would rapidly lose ground to their European competitors, and the higher tariffs that would be needed to afford domestic producers some protection against ruinous competition would result in higher prices for American consumers.

Trade-oriented Democrats adopted this perspective when pleading for annexation in 1844 and 1845. Annexation of Texas would, Senator Sevier of Arkansas told his colleagues, "enable us to monopolize, through the instrumentality of slave labor, the productions of cotton and sugar, and other southern productions, not only for the supply of our own markets, but the markets of the world." Another southwestern Democrat, Congressman James Bowlin of Missouri, maintained that "with Texas, we shall possess all the cotton-growing region of this country, which may be a salutary check on European policy, through the instrumentality of their looms." Many northern Demo-

24. Green to Senator Willie P. Mangum, *Daily Madisonian*, May 18, 1844; Jones, *Daily Madisonian*, December 13, 1843; Walker, "Letter of Mr. Walker, of Mississippi, Relative to the Annexation of Texas" (Washington, D.C., January 8, 1844), p. 16.
25. *Daily Madisonian*, April 11 and May 16, 1844.

crats agreed. Buchanan, for instance, told his fellow senators in mid-1844, "Annex Texas to the United States, and we shall have within the limits of our broad confederacy all the favored cotton-growing regions of the earth." Congressman Chesselden Ellis of New York agreed that annexation would bring "the monopoly of the cotton product of the world," and so did his colleague Moses Norris of New Hampshire, who said that "the control of all the most valuable cotton in the world" would result from the acquisition of Texas.[26] For many Democrats, then, Texas offered a golden opportunity to turn the tables on England. Not only could Britain's design to monopolize raw materials be thwarted, but the United States could instead attain such a monopoly and intimidate Europe with it.

Many expansionists suggested that a cotton monopoly could serve as an attractive alternative to maintaining an expensive and dangerous military establishment to counter British ambitions. Sevier contended in a Senate address that American control over the world cotton supply would "tend more successfully to insure our peace and security than a standing army," and Buchanan argued that Britain's imperative need for cotton meant that "an army of one hundred thousand men would not be so great a security for preserving the peace between the two nations as this dependence." Ellis told his House colleagues that a monopoly over cotton would be "a power more potent in our hands for the command of peace with foreign nations than any naval or military force we could array." House Foreign Affairs Committee chairman Ingersoll wrote to Andrew Jackson that "exclusive control of cotton" was "an all and sufficient reason by itself" why the United States must acquire Texas, even if Britain threatened war to prevent it.[27]

Angered by decades of British condescension toward all things American, the expansionists delighted in contemplating the consequences of a cotton embargo directed at Britain. A termination of cotton exports, Ellis predicted in early 1845, "would instantly paralyze an incalculable mass of capital and labor abroad, whose prostration would produce convulsions there, and endanger the stability and

26. Sevier, *CG*, 28 Cong., 1 sess., App. 557 (June 7, 1844); Bowlin, *CG*, 28 Cong., 2 sess., App. 95 (January 15, 1845); Buchanan, *CG*, 28 Cong., 1 sess., App. 721 (June 8, 1844); Ellis, *CG*, 28 Cong., 2 sess., App. 139 (January 25, 1845); Norris, *CG*, 28 Cong., 2 sess., App. 191–92 (January 24, 1845).

27. Sevier, *CG*, 28 Cong., 1 sess., App. 557 (June 7, 1844); Buchanan, *CG*, 28 Cong., 1 sess., 721 (June 8, 1844); Ellis, *CG*, 28 Cong., 2 sess., App. 139 (January 25, 1845); Ingersoll to Jackson, December 28, 1844, Jackson Papers.

security of the nation against which the blow should be aimed." As soon as Texas accepted annexation to the Union, editor O'Sullivan boasted, "the chance for the emancipation of England from her dependence upon the United States for cotton . . . will have passed away forever." Like Green, he thought that Britain recognized the ultimate consequences of such a reliance on the United States and was "nearly frantic" in its last-minute efforts to prevent annexation. Bennett, too, chortled in the *Herald,* in November of 1844, over Britain's supposed predicament. Once the United States acquired Texas and "possessed . . . the whole cotton fields of this western hemisphere," it would command "the means of engaging in a rivalry with England" that Britain would find "utterly impossible to maintain." Were the United States to cut all shipments of cotton to Britain, he claimed in January 1845, it would "curtail her resources, . . . throw the whole of her immense trade into our hands, perhaps producing lasting revolution in her industrial pursuits."[28] This concern with Texas and its commercial importance largely explains why Cushing's mission to China received less attention in late 1844 and early 1845 than it merited. Texas so preoccupied the expansionists that Cushing and China received short shrift in the press and in Congress.

Tyler said little at this time, not wanting his unpopularity to impede annexation. Another reason for his reticence might have been his fear that Britain would adopt drastic measures to prevent annexation if he revealed the commercial calculations behind his policy. England might take severe steps to deny a cotton monopoly to the United States but would probably acquiesce in annexation if the administration insisted that the security of slavery and the South was its chief concern.

After Texas entered the Union, however, Tyler explained that his primary purpose had been to control the world cotton supply, not to perpetuate slavery. Of most significance in acquiring Texas, he said, was "the value of the virtual monopoly of the cotton plant, . . . a monopoly [with] more potential in the affairs of the world than millions of armed men."[29] Long after leaving the White House Tyler

28. Ellis, *CG,* 28 Cong., 2 sess., App. 139 (January 25, 1845). (See also the remarks by Moses Norris of New Hampshire, *CG,* 28 Cong., 2 sess., 191–92 [January 24, 1845].) O'Sullivan, New York *Morning News,* June 14, 1845; Bennett, New York *Herald,* November 24, 1844; New York *Herald,* January 31, 1845.

29. Tyler to the Richmond *Enquirer,* September 1, 1847, quoted in L. G. Tyler, *Letters and Times,* 2:431. See also Tyler's notes on Texas annexation, in ibid., pp. 422–23.

had been subject to severe criticism from Free-Soilers and Conscience Whigs who pointed to the annexation of Texas as one of the most brazen of many acts by southern politicians that benefited their section of the country at the North's expense. Tyler denied these allegations, contending that his perspective on annexation had been national, not sectional. In a letter to Daniel Webster, he explained that it was often unwise in diplomacy "to disclose the whole policy" of an administration and that this had been "precisely the case" during the Texas crisis. Annexation, Tyler concluded, had been "vitally important" to the whole country, for "by securing the virtual monopoly of the cotton plant" the United States had acquired "a greater influence over the affairs of the world than would be found in armies however strong, or navies however numerous."[30]

To his former secretary of state John C. Calhoun, Tyler stressed in 1848 that he had pursued annexation in order to prevent England from obtaining "an absolute control over the trade of Texas under the stipulations of a commercial treaty." If Britain had succeeded in maintaining an independent Texas, only "a short time" would have elapsed before the British were "relieved . . . from all dependence upon us for the supply of cotton." Despite the "abuse" and "vituperation" heaped upon him, Tyler assured Calhoun that he did not regret his course, since "the result cannot but be advantageous to the country at large."[31] No wonder, then, that Tyler and other southern leaders placed so much trust in "King Cotton" sixteen years after annexation when the Civil War erupted in 1861. The Confederacy's faith in cotton partly originated in the Tyler administration's sustained campaign to annex Texas to the United States.

Tyler's reminiscences suggest that he may have deliberately allowed his subordinates Upshur and Calhoun to overstress the administration's concern about slavery in order to deceive Britain about the more important commercial considerations behind annexation. Upshur and Calhoun seemed obsessed with slavery; Tyler was worried about slavery too, but he may have been just as concerned about cotton. Five years after annexation Tyler still denied that his policy had been "narrow, local or bigoted." He confided to his son that "the monopoly of the cotton plant, . . . the great and important concern" in annexation, had been discussed in cabinet meetings

30. Tyler to Webster, April 17, 1850, John Tyler Papers.
31. Tyler to Calhoun, June 5, 1848, in J. Franklin Jameson, ed., "Correspondence of John C. Calhoun," in *Annual Report of the American Historical Association for the Year 1899*, 2 vols. (Washington, 1900): 2:1173-74.

between 1843 and 1845 but said that neither Upshur nor Calhoun had grasped the full significance of the issue: "That monopoly, now secured, places all other nations at our feet. An embargo of a single year would produce in Europe a greater amount of suffering than a fifty years' war. I doubt whether Great Britain could avoid convul- sions. And yet, with these results before him, Mr. Calhoun unceasing- ly talked of slavery and its abolition in connection with the subject. That idea seemed to possess him and Upshur *as a single idea.*"[32]

Tyler retired to Virginia in 1845, convinced that he had managed the nation's foreign affairs with considerable skill.[33] He had settled the northeastern boundary dispute and maintained peace with England; avoided war with Mexico while clearing the way for annexation; attempted but failed to acquire a part of California, including the port of San Francisco; tried and failed to settle the boundary in Oregon; and succeeded in negotiating commercial pacts with the German *Zollverein* and China, the former rejected by the Senate but the latter approved.[34] He regarded the acquisition of Texas as his crowning achievement. His defeats were in a sense as important as his tri- umphs, for they too showed the weight of commercial factors in his thinking—a trend that would continue under Polk. Tyler did not stand alone in his positive assessment of his foreign policy. Bennett asserted that Tyler had conducted the nation's foreign relations bet- ter than any president since Washington.[35]

Just a few months after Tyler left office, the halls of Congress and editorial rooms across the country again echoed with declarations about America's cotton monopoly and how it could be used against Britain. But now the object of contention was the Pacific Coast of North America. With Texas successfully incorporated into the Union in 1845, the expansionists believed that they could then acquire

32. John Tyler to Robert Tyler, April 17, 1850, in L. G. Tyler, *Letters and Times,* 2:483. Biographer Robert Seager, II, concludes that Tyler was less extreme in his proslavery views than Upshur and Calhoun. See *And Tyler Too: A Biography of John and Julia Gardiner Tyler* (New York, 1963), p. 215.

33. Tyler needed some consolation. On June 7, 1844, the *Daily Madisonian* came close to the mark when it complained, "President Tyler is abused worse than a pick-pocket."

34. For an overview of Tyler's policy objectives, see L. G. Tyler, *Letters and Times,* 2:434–41. See also John Tyler to Robert Tyler, December 11, 1845, in ibid., pp. 447–48; Duff Green, *Facts and Suggestions* (New York, 1866), p. 85; "Statement of Colonel Benjamin E. Green, Secretary of the Legation at Mexico in 1844," August 8, 1889, in L. G. Tyler, *Letters and Times,* 3:174–77; Adams, *Memoirs,* 11 (March 18, 25, and 27, 1843): 340, 346–47.

35. New York *Herald,* December 6, 1844.

California, as well as all of Oregon up to 54°40'. So in late 1845 and early 1846 the geographical region in dispute shifted, but the enemy—Britain—and a principal ambition—commercial supremacy in the Pacific and around the world—remained the same.

Aggressive Agrarianism and Commercial Expansion

The 1844 elections sent several hawkish and anglophobic Democrats to the Twenty-Ninth Congress. The transition to a more belligerent legislature in 1845 became apparent with the selection of a new Senate Foreign Relations Committee. Allen of Ohio was named chairman, and Sevier and Lewis Cass joined him as members. Allen and Cass headed a group of strident northwestern Democrats (including Douglas, Breese, and Orlando Ficklin of Illinois, and Edward Hannegan of Indiana) who believed that the party must adhere to the platform of 1844 and acquire every square inch of Oregon. A small coterie of southwestern Democrats also championed the acquisition of the entire territory. Though anglophobia and an exaggerated sense of frontier nationalism disposed these western legislators toward aggrandizement whatever the price, material factors also influenced them. It is no coincidence that the most productive agricultural states often sent the most pugnacious representatives to Washington. Worried about commodity surpluses and restricted markets abroad, they demanded the expansion of foreign trade to avoid depressed prices and economic stagnation at home.[36] Democrats from other states often shared their concerns and supported initiatives to increase American exports.

The new Treasury secretary, ex-Senator Walker, worried as much as anyone about the deleterious effects of limited foreign markets upon American staple producers. The nation's agricultural sector, he reported to Congress in late 1845, "must have the foreign market, or a large surplus, accompanied by great depression in price, must be the result. The states of Ohio, Indiana, and Illinois, if cultivated to their fullest extent, could, of themselves, raise more than sufficient food to supply the entire home market." Either Missouri or Kentucky could meet the domestic demand for hemp, Walker observed; Missis-

36. For analysis of the problem of surpluses in agriculture during these years, see Douglass C. North, *The Economic Growth of the United States, 1790–1860* (New York, 1960), pp. 143–46, 174–78, 413–16. Peter Temin, *The Jacksonian Economy* (New York, 1969), argues that the recession following the Panic of 1837 was less severe than is usually suggested by scholars.

sippi alone raised ample cotton to satisfy the home market; and Louisiana had nearly reached that point in sugar production. Florida, Louisiana, and Texas, he added, were on the verge of meeting the entire world's demand for sugar and molasses. Because farmers and planters sold their goods in a glutted home market, they received meager remuneration for their labor. Anticipating that a reduction of American duties on manufactured products would encourage reciprocal reductions by European nations on import taxes affecting agricultural staples, Walker implored Congress to reduce the protective duties in the Tariff of 1842. Congress responded with the less restrictive Walker Tariff of 1846, and Britain repealed its Corn Laws that same year. Walker heralded the more liberal trade policies of the United States and Britain, noting in late 1846 that "the home market can never be sufficient for our rapidly increasing agricultural products." The United States could absorb all domestic manufactured products and many imported goods besides, but foreign outlets were essential to farmers and planters.[37]

President Polk also considered additional markets essential to relieve distress among agrarians. "The home market alone is inadequate to enable them to dispose of the immense surplus of food and other articles which they are capable of producing, even at the most reduced prices," he informed Congress in 1846. "The United States can from their immense surplus supply not only the home demand, but the deficiencies of food required by the whole world."[38] Like Walker, Polk expected the recent tariff reductions to facilitate American exports. Territorial acquisitions would have the same effect.

Democratic expansionists repeatedly discussed the need for markets for domestic surpluses. A writer in the *Democratic Review* in 1844 complained that protective tariffs "enhance the natural concentration of wealth into the hands of the few, and . . . leave the masses impoverished." "The chief products of the United States being agricultural," he continued, "the quantity of goods either domestic or imported, which they can consume, depends altogether upon the foreign market for their surplus." Bowlin of Missouri pointed out to his House colleagues in early 1846 that the states of the Mississippi Valley alone were "more than sufficient to supply all the demands of Europe and

37. *Report of the Secretary of the Treasury, H. Doc.,* vol. 481, no. 6, 29 Cong., 1 sess. (December 3, 1845), pp. 1–20; *Report of the Secretary of the Treasury, H. Doc.,* vol. 498, no. 7, 29 Cong., 2 sess. (December 10, 1846), p. 10.

38. Polk's second annual message, in Richardson, *Messages and Papers,* 5 (December 8, 1846): 2351.

America." The United States should acquire all of Oregon, he advised, since "the ports of eastern Asia are as convenient to Oregon as the ports of Europe are to the eastern slope of our confederacy, with an infinitely better ocean for navigation." Eastern Asia could exchange tea, porcelain, silk, spices, ivory, and other products for American grain. Europe, however, afforded "a poor prospect of a market for our surplus." Oregon, then, represented "the natural outlet for the surplus productions of our country, and a direct inlet to that commerce which has enriched every country that has enjoyed the benefits of it."[39]

Mississippi senator Joseph Chalmers, appointed to fill the expansionist shoes of former senator Walker, said that the "vital interests" of Mississippi—"the great staple state of the Union"—were "inseparably united with free trade." Chalmers hoped the United States would gain control over all of North America, mainly for commercial reasons. Mississippi "wants the world for a market," he declared.[40] European trade policies, Congressman David Wilmot of Pennsylvania observed in early 1846, had always prevented extensive American exports to Europe. Asia, however, opened "a field for commercial enterprise, more vast and valuable" than all other regions, "a market both for our grain and staple manufacturers beyond our power to glut." The United States, he told the House, could either obtain all of Oregon and better access to Asia or could surrender Oregon and forfeit "commercial ascendency" to Britain. Douglas agreed: "The great point at issue" in the Oregon dispute, he said, was "the freedom of the Pacific Ocean, . . . the trade of China and of Japan, of the East Indies, and . . . maritime ascendency" in East Asia. Benton of Missouri also urged the Senate to acquire Oregon. "The trade of the East," he proclaimed, had always been "the richest jewel in the diadem of commerce."[41]

Few Whigs disagreed with the Democrats' assertion of the need for additional markets. The questions of the appropriate means to acquire those markets, however, and of whether conflict with Britain could be risked provoked controversy. Whigs, especially, feared the

39. "Free Trade," *Democratic Review*, 14 (March, 1844): 291–93; *CG*, 29 Cong., 1 sess., App. 80 (January 6, 1846). See also the speech by Congressman John Wentworth of Illinois, *CG*, 28 Cong., 1 sess., App. 91–92 (January 24, 1844).

40. *CG*, 29 Cong., 1 sess., App. 559 (March 24, 1846).

41. *CG*, 29 Cong., 1 sess., App. 186 (February 7, 1846); 259 (January 27, 1846); *CG*, 29 Cong., 1 sess., 916 (May 28, 1846). For similar views, see the New York *Herald*, October 8 and November 30, 1845, and "British Reviews on Oregon," *Democratic Review*, 17 (November, 1845): 331.

consequences of war with Britain, and many prominent southern Democrats such as Calhoun, King, and Louis McLane held similar views: all urged compromise on Oregon. A war for Oregon was acceptable to a noisy corps of extremists, but their rhetoric could not compensate for their actual weakness. Even the most optimistic observer had to admit that soldier for soldier, ship for ship, the United States lagged far behind Britain in military strength. America's standing army was miniscule, and despite recent innovations and expansion, its navy (at least when compared with England's) seemed more suited to a bathtub than the high seas. Yet these military realities did not daunt the "ultras" of the Democratic party, for they placed their faith in the power of cotton and grain.

Wise, now United States minister to Brazil, urged the Polk administration to stand firm against England on the Oregon question. Wise was willing to push Britain to the brink of war and beyond, if necessary—not an unusual stance for a man whose impetuosity was legend among his contemporaries. "Far more excitable than ordinary men," Wise possessed "a remarkably mercurial" temperament, according to Senator Henry Foote of Mississippi. "Upon the slightest examination of his well-formed cranium," Foote explained, a phrenologist would "pronounce his organ of combativeness to be developed in a manner very remarkable."[42] In late 1845, Wise assured the Polk administration that it need not fear any reprisal from England over Oregon. "Starvation in all Europe, troubles in the East India British possessions, and the brisk war now raging at the Parana, give G[rea]t Britain enough to do and her hands will be too full to touch us," he wrote to Buchanan. "We hold England by a cotton string."[43]

Allen's cranium must have resembled Wise's. On February 11, 1846, Allen concluded two exhausting days of oratory in the Senate on the Oregon dispute. With the "galleries . . . crowded almost to suffocation," he complained that the Webster-Ashburton Treaty of 1842 had been a shameful surrender to British arrogance.[44] Ashbur-

---

42. Henry S. Foote, *Casket of Reminiscences* (Washington, 1874), p. 364. Forney described Wise as "lean, tall, and cadaverous, with vehemence and tones not unlike John Randolph's, and a steel spring energy that, despite feeble health, never bent or broke" (Forney, *Anecdotes of Public Men,* 1:35). Hone called Wise "the most inflammable" among "the combustibles of the South" (*Diary,* 2 [June 15, 1841]:79).

43. Wise to Buchanan, December 24, 1845, James Buchanan Papers.

44. *CG,* 29 Cong., 1 sess., App. 838 (February 10 and 11, 1846). The setting of the speech is described in the Washington *Daily Union,* February 11, 1846. Several northern Democrats besides Allen resented the Webster-Ashburton Treaty. For a typical complaint, see David Henshaw to Polk, December 4, 1845, James K. Polk Papers.

ton, he said, had, "during a single campaign of six months in our capital, unaided by anything that belongs to an army, conquered for England, more of our territory, than all her armies could have conquered in a century."[45] Never again should the United States acquiesce to British ambitions in North America. With arms swinging like a frenzied windmill, Allen slammed his fists so forcefully into his Senate desk that gallery observers saw blood spurt from his crimson knuckles.[46] Allen took his politics seriously: the Senate custodian complained to a newspaper reporter that he frequently had to repair the senator's battered mahogany desk.[47] The United States could acquire all of Oregon, Allen thought, since Britain's global commitments and its reliance on American exports precluded any military move in Oregon.

Bennett of the *Herald* was also an ultra; in fact, he wanted Britain squeezed not only out of Oregon but out of North America altogether. It could be done without bloodshed, he argued, through the power of American cotton. "Not a gun need be fired—not a grain of gunpowder expended—no need of steamers and fleets and armies and munitions of war. The cotton bales will fight the battles of the country that produces them."[48] Bennett's hard-line stand on Oregon stemmed from his belief that Britain was "completely bound and manacled with the cotton cords" of the United States. "The trade of England with this country," he wrote, "is probably worth to that power twenty times as much as the whole value of that distant territory would be to it, and the supply of cotton, under the present British manufacturing system, is a lever with which we can successfully control the operations of England."[49]

Among the most enthusiastic proponents of commercial expansion were the New York Democrats in the House. They generally agreed that the United State could use its economic advantage to acquire all of Oregon. In early 1846, Congressman Stephen Strong told his peers that the nation that held Oregon between the forty-seventh parallel

45. *CG*, 29 Cong., 1 sess., App. 838 (February 10 and 11, 1846).
46. Mackay, *Western World*, 1:306–9. During a speech by Allen Senator John Fairfield of Maine wrote a letter to his wife and described the orator: "There is nothing in nature with which to compare him that I know of except the falls of Niagara" (Fairfield to Mrs. Anna Fairfield, February 4, 1846, in *The Letters of John Fairfield*, Arthur G. Staples, ed. (Lewiston, Maine, 1922), p. 385.
47. New York *Herald*, May 26, 1848.
48. New York *Herald*, July 10, 1845. See also the issues of July 27, July 30, and August 14, 1845.
49. New York *Herald*, November 14, 1845.

and 54° 40' and gained control over the northern half of California as well would "ultimately command the commerce of the world, and that at no very distant period." Colleague Samuel Gordon urged the House to take over the entire territory in defiance of Britain, whose "famishing millions live from hand to mouth, dependent on the cotton trade. Stop their looms, and you stop their daily bread." For Britain to go to war against the United States over Oregon "would be the most suicidal policy" Britain could pursue, since warfare abroad would precipitate revolution at home. If the United States halted cotton exports, Britain would face imminent chaos and eventual collapse. Britain would be absolutely helpless, because its salvation depended on "uninterrupted relations in commerce with the United States." It needed cotton far more than it needed Oregon.[50]

House Democrats suggested that Britain was doubly dependent upon the United States. By annexing Texas the United States had gained dominion over "nine-tenths of all the cotton-growing interests throughout the world," Mississippi's Jacob Thompson argued in early 1846, and Britain's reliance on that cotton supply provided "the bond . . . which required her to keep the peace."[51] In addition, he noted the growing support in Britain for lowering duties on imported American foodstuffs. The increased demand for American staples there would act as another inducement for the British government to acquiesce in the American claim to all of Oregon. Orlando Ficklin, like his Illinois colleagues John Wentworth and Stephen Douglas, also demanded all of Oregon. Ficklin stressed that both American cotton and American grain were crucial to Britain: "She wants our bread rather than our blood," he concluded. His colleagues also employed economic arguments to demonstrate their country's advantages in the struggle with Britain for Oregon.[52]

The Polk administration shared this faith in commercial intimidation. Polk told his advisers in early 1846 that "the reduction of our tariff would be a great object with Great Britain, and . . . to attain it that government might be willing to surrender her claim to the whole Oregon territory." Britain, Polk continued, "esteemed her commerce with the United States as of infinitely more value than she did the

50. *CG*, 29 Cong., 1 sess., 300 (February 3, 1846); *CG*, 29 Cong., 1 sess., App. 115 (January 14, 1846).

51. *CG*, 29 Cong., 1 sess., 296 (February 2, 1846).

52. Ficklin, *CG*, 29 Cong., 1 sess., 328 (February 6, 1846); Wentworth, *CG*, 28 Cong., 1 sess., App. 92 (January 24, 1844); Douglas, *CG*, 29 Cong., 1 sess., 259 (January 27, 1846).

Oregon territory."[53] Editor Ritchie placed the administration in the ranks of the All Oregon brigade in late 1845, insisting in the *Daily Union* that American cotton could force the British to back down on Oregon. "How can Great Britain continue to prosecute a desperate and continued war, which is destined to starve her own manufacturers?" he queried. Since Britain had lost Texas and had failed in efforts to promote the cultivation of high-grade cotton in India, the United States possessed "almost all the best lands in the world for the growth of cotton." America's monopoly of cotton, according to Ritchie, guaranteed the country "prosperity in peace and . . . power in war." Texas had been Britain's only opportunity to escape dependence on the United States, but American diplomacy had proved superior to Britain's. The movement for a more liberal trade policy in Britain, Ritchie wrote in early 1846, would soon make that nation dependent on the United States "not only for her cotton, but her meat and bread," which would further tip the scales in favor of the United States.[54]

Ritchie was not alone in his highly positive appraisals of American strength. Secretary of the navy George Bancroft also believed that a peaceful settlement of the Oregon dispute was more essential to Britain than to the United States. "If all Oregon were ceded to England today, she could not keep it. Her interest for an arrangement is greater than ours," he wrote to merchant William Sturgis in mid-1845. Following the resolution of the crisis a year later, Bancroft continued to emphasize England's weakness and America's strength. After his first two months as United States minister in London, he reported to Buchanan in February 1847 that "we can do without England better than England can do without us." The longer Bancroft stayed in Britain, the more assured he became of his nation's superiority. "America feeds England, furnishes to England raw materials, and so rapidly advances, that in capital [and] industrial skill she is independent and in enterprise and invention leads the way," he boasted to Secretary of War Marcy in 1847. Britain could not contest dominion with the United States in North America.[55] J. George Ram-

53. *The Diary of James K. Polk during His Presidency, 1845–1849,* Milo M. Quaife, ed., 4 vols. (Chicago, 1910), 1 (January 24, 1846): 191–92.

54. Washington *Daily Union,* September 24, 1845 and February 21, 1846. See also Ritchie's editorial on October 7, 1845.

55. Bancroft to Sturgis, August 25, 1845; Bancroft to Buchanan, February 3, 1847, in M. A. DeWolfe Howe, *The Life and Letters of George Bancroft,* 2 vols. (New York, 1908), 1:279, 2:10; Bancroft to Marcy, October 27, 1847, Robert J. Walker Papers.

sey, a Polk lieutenant in Tennessee, went even further in appraising America's strength. He told the president that since the United States held a virtual monopoly over the cotton-growing regions of the globe, it could "control the commerce of the world and secure thereby to the American Union inappreciable political and commercial advantages."[56]

As these last quotations reveal, a fascinating shift had occurred in the Democrats' assessment of the rivalry between the United States and Britain during 1845 and early 1846. Though still anxious about many domestic social and economic trends, they believed that the annexation of Texas had greatly enhanced American prospects for dominion in the Pacific. When Britain had appeared to be in control of Texas, the Democrats, as noted in Chapter 2, had warned that a permanent alliance between Texas and Britain would threaten the United States with commercial decay, increased sectional strife, economic ruin, slave insurrections, and foreign war. With slavery secured and the cotton market brought under American control by Texas's entry into the Union, however, the United States possessed a new weapon to use against Europe. The fate that would have been the Union's, without Texas, might now become the fate of Europe, especially Britain.

The frequent allusions in Congress and the press to commercial warfare with Britain attracted the attention of English visitors. Sarah Mytton Maury, who by her own estimate "travelled sixteen thousand miles in the United States" during a residence of nearly fifteen months in 1845 and 1846, wrote in her reminiscences that "the cotton planters of the United States possess a monopoly, bestowed upon them by nature, which places in their hands an immense controlling power, both in America and in England." Unlike most British visitors, Maury admired southern planters and defended slavery. Although she did not specify the origins of her ideas on the cotton monopoly and slavery, she mentioned that she had conversed with both Calhoun and Buchanan and that Charles Ingersoll had been her "almost constant companion" during most of her stay in Washington.[57]

A particularly well-informed English visitor, Alexander Mackay, American correspondent for the London *Morning Chronicle*, also recognized his country's commercial dependence on the United States. "As regards the supply of cotton, we are as much at the mercy of America

56. Ramsey to Polk, October 11, 1845, Polk Papers.
57. Sarah Mytton Maury, *The Statesmen of America in 1846* (London, 1847), pp. 432, 373, 313; *An Englishwoman in America* (London, 1848), pp. 234–45.

as if we were starving and to her alone we looked for food," he noted. "She need not withhold her wheat: America could starve us by with-holding her cotton." Mackay had often heard the cotton monopoly argument in Congress while covering the debate on Oregon. He had heard so much expansionist oratory there, in fact, that he offered his condolences to the American eagle, which was sent soaring over the continent several times daily by members of Congress, never being allowed a moment's rest from its frequent flights over North America.[58]

Not all American observers were certain that commercial consider-ations would keep Britain from fighting over Oregon. Most southern Democrats doubted the wisdom of challenging Britain on Oregon. Maryland's McLane, appointed United States minister to England in 1845, departed for London under the impression that Polk and Bu-chanan desired a reasonable compromise on the Oregon question. McLane, president of the Baltimore & Ohio Railroad, which carried flour to eastern ports for shipment to Europe, hoped to keep peace with Britain and to arrange trade concessions with its government.[59] When in late 1845 the Polk administration grew more belligerent toward Britain and claimed that the United States held an indisput-able right to all of Oregon, McLane became increasingly alarmed. He advised moderation and complained that the northwestern Demo-crats were using Oregon as a hobbyhorse for political purposes. In the spring of 1846, he became even more concerned with develop-ments in the United States, warning Secretary of State Buchanan that the American people would never support the administration if it went to war to acquire all of Oregon.[60] McLane feared that the administration had fallen under the sway of Cass, Allen, and Han-negan, and that extremists in both chambers of Congress were con-trolling American policy. He respected Britain's military power, and he cautioned the cabinet that in the event of war over Oregon the British would "make an exertion which they have never attempted since the battle of Waterloo."[61]

58. Mackay, *Western World,* 1:121, 294–300.
59. John A Munroe, *Louis McLane, Federalist and Jacksonian* (New Brunswick, N.J., 1973), pp. 489–537.
60. McLane to Buchanan, April 10, 1846, James Buchanan Papers. See also these letters: Louis McLane to Robert McLane, November 18, 1845, May 3 and July 3, 1846; McLane to C[harles] A[ugustus] D[avis], "Confidential," June 28, 1846, McLane Papers; McLane to Buchanan, February 3, 1846; McLane to Buchanan, "Private, unofficial and not for the file," March 17, 1846, Buchanan Papers.
61. McLane to Buchanan, "Private, unofficial and not for the file," March 17, 1846, Buchanan Papers.

Pleas for compromise also came from United States minister to France William King, the former senator from Alabama and a long-time friend of Buchanan's. King advised the administration in late 1845 that "we must not deceive ourselves with the idea that such is the condition of England, she dare not go to war with us." A war over Oregon would be popular in Britain, he observed, a nation never before "in a situation to wield a greater power for offensive warfare than at this very moment." If the United States pushed Britain into hostilities over Oregon, Britain's naval power could launch a devastating first strike against the Union. In early 1846, King emphasized the moderate tone in Britain and contrasted it with the conduct of extremists in Congress. "Swagger and boasting will not build ships, or put our forts in a state to protect our cities," he warned. Besides, Oregon was not the most crucial issue to be resolved between the two countries. "If Sir Robert Peel can succeed in carrying out his comprehensive plan for the moderation of duties," King explained to Buchanan, "it will open the best market in the world to the provisions of the United States and must I think cause our fire-eaters to pause upon the war question and dispose them to a reasonable compromise."[62] King agreed with McLane that congressional extremists were impeding a settlement and damaging the real interests of the United States. Most southern Democrats and virtually all Whigs agreed. Democrats with grand illusions about the Asian market demanded all of Oregon; others who viewed Europe, especially Britain, as a better market urged peace and negotiation of a more liberal commercial arrangement.

McLane's and King's concern about relations with Britain were shared by some powerful southern Democrats in the Senate such as Calhoun and George McDuffie of South Carolina, and William Haywood of North Carolina. Fearing that a war over Oregon would destroy southern planters and imperil slavery, Calhoun instead advised the Senate to follow a strategy of "a wise and masterly inactivity": the United States, he had earlier noted, could eventually obtain all of Oregon "by standing still and letting time and emigration settle the question."[63] Like Calhoun, McDuffie denied that Oregon was

62. King to Buchanan, November 28, 1845 and January 27, 1846, Buchanan Papers. See also King to Buchanan, February 28, March 28, and April 30, 1846. In his letter of April 30, King told Buchanan that "the war spirit of Cass, Allen, and company must not deter the President from making, if practicable, a fair compromise."

63. CG, 29 Cong., 1 sess., 505 (March 16, 1846); Calhoun to Pickens, May 6, 1845, in Jameson, "Correspondence of Calhoun," p. 653. See also Calhoun to John Y.

worth a war. As early as 1843, he had told the Senate that the
territory was not worth "a pinch of snuff." In an acrimonious exchange with Breese in 1846, he again stressed that "for purposes of
agriculture" most of Oregon "was not worth a fig."[64] Haywood also
urged compromise and suggested that western Democrats were exploiting the Oregon crisis for political advantage rather than trying
to find an honorable solution to the dangerous impasse.[65] These
southern Democrats angered the ultras. When the Fifty-four forty
flame failed to ignite the whole Congress in early 1846, Ficklin blamed
the South Carolinians led by Calhoun: "When her politicians take
snuff, the common people involuntarily sneeze all over the state."[66]

The Whigs in Congress opposed any course that might lead to war.
Trans-Atlantic commerce, they believed, was just as valuable to their
country as to Britain, and they doubted that the United States could
hold its own in a war with that power. (The Whigs did not subscribe
to the Democrats' myth that the Americans had already whipped the
British twice and could do so again. The Jacksonians had transformed
the Battle of New Orleans into a symbol of America's overall per-
formance during the War of 1812, and they regarded Jackson's stunning victory as a portent of future encounters. The Whigs prudently
questioned the validity of that position.)

The Whigs and southern Democrats stymied the All Oregon movement. On June 10, 1846, Polk reluctantly submitted to the Senate a
compromise proposal worked out in London by McLane and Aberdeen that divided the territory at the forty-ninth parallel. Polk reaffirmed
his preference for acquiring the entire territory, but he had realized
that he could not carry the Senate. Moreover, he was aware of special
military preparations undertaken by the British government, and the
treaty offered him an escape from the confrontation with Britain and
his own Congress. A few months earlier Polk had called upon Congress to improve the nation's defenses, warning that Britain was
"making unusual and extraordinary armaments and warlike prepara-

---

Mason, May 30, 1845, in ibid., pp. 660–61. Congressman Charles Cathcart of Indiana
repudiated this passive approach. "There is . . . something superlatively ridiculous
in this idea of masterly inactivity and bedchamber diplomacy," he complained to his
fellow congressmen in early 1846. "Why, run the one into the other, and a jury of
old women would declare you deranged" (*CG*, 29 Cong., 1 sess., 323 [February 6,
1846]).

64. *CG*, 27 Cong., 3 sess., 200 (January 25, 1843); *CG*, 29 Cong., 1 sess., 608 (April
4, 1846).

65. *CG*, 29 Cong., 1 sess., App. 377 (March 5, 1846).

66. *CG*, 29 Cong., 1 sess., App. 172 (February 6, 1846).

tions, naval and military, both at home and in her North American possessions."[67] With Congress unwilling to loosen the purse strings, however, Polk decided to dump the Oregon issue into the Senate's lap, disclaiming any responsibility for the final settlement. On June 18, the Senate approved the conciliatory pact by a decisive 41 to 14 margin, but northern ultras Allen, Cass, Hannegan, Breese, and Dickinson joined seven other northern Democrats in opposition. Only two southern Democrats—David Atchison of Missouri and James Westcott of Florida—voted with the northern ultras against the compromise.[68]

Polk fumed about his predicament and blamed it entirely on Congress. He confided to his friend Tennessee governor Aaron V. Brown that "the executive arm was greatly paralysed on the Oregon question, by the debates and proceedings in Congress, especially in the Senate."[69] Ritchie, in the *Daily Union,* echoed Polk's complaints but tried to emphasize the more positive aspects of the settlement. Despite the interference of the Senate, the administration had finally resolved the "long-vexed controversy upon terms far more advantageous to us than have ever before been offered by England." He emphasized how Polk had improved the country's commercial prospects: "The termination of our difficulties with England, and the acquisition of prominent ports on the Pacific, opens up to our vision a vast trade on that ocean, and an honorable and, we believe, a successful competition for the trade . . . of Asia."[70] Ritchie revealed a key consideration here. If commercial ascendancy over Britain was the chief goal of the United States, then the administration had acquired enough of Oregon to give American producers more than

67. On the administration's concern about England's preparations for war, see Polk, *Diary,* 1 (December 24, 1845): 143 and (February 23, 1846), 242–43; Buchanan to McLane, February 26, 1846, and McLane to Buchanan, "Private, unofficial and not for the file," March 17, 1846, Buchanan Papers; James K. Polk to William Polk, "Private," March 27, 1846, Polk Papers. The quoted material is from a message from Polk to the Senate, reprinted in Richardson, *Messages and Papers,* 5 (March 24, 1846): 2277.

68. *CG,* 29 Cong., 1 sess., 1224 (June 18, 1846). The other seven were Fairfield (Maine), Atherton and Jenness (New Hampshire), Cameron and Sturgeon (Pennsylvania), Bright (Indiana), and Semple (Illinois).

69. Polk to Brown, "Private," July 7, 1846, Polk Papers. See also Polk to McLane, "Private and Confidential," June 22, 1846, Polk Papers; Polk, *Diary,* 1 (June 6 and 17, 1846): 453–55, 475–77.

70. Washington *Daily Union,* June 20 and 23, 1846. Three months later Ritchie reiterated that Britain had "made a concession almost, if not altogether, without parallel in the annals of British diplomacy" (Washington *Daily Union,* September 25, 1846).

an even chance of capturing the Asian market from their rivals.

Polk's distress over the compromise stemmed more from political than commercial or strategic considerations. In acquiring the mouth and both banks of the Columbia River below the forty-ninth parallel, the administration had obtained a valuable concession from Britain. But the pledge of the 1844 platform remained sacrosanct to many northern Democrats, and Polk realized that his acceptance of the compromise, however grudging, would alienate the extreme expansionists in his party. That Polk could accept the compromise boundary as essentially meeting American commercial needs while lamenting the "surrender" of half the disputed territory simply demonstrates the extent to which the Oregon issue had become entangled in domestic politics. Polk wanted a unified party as well as land, ports, and markets. But with powerful factions of northern and southern Democrats at odds over Oregon, he could not have both.

California: Golden Gate to Asian Trade

The reaction against the "surrender" of Oregon might have been more severe had Polk not diverted the nation's attention to another campaign that promised even greater commercial benefits to the country. With the Oregon controversy approaching a climax, tensions between the United States and Mexico produced a skirmish between the nations' troops in the disputed territory near the Rio Grande River in late April of 1846. When Polk and his advisers received reports of the bloodshed on the Mexico-Texas frontier, they unanimously decided to recommend that Congress approve a declaration of war. In fact, the administration had decided even before news of the clash reached Washington that the United States had "ample cause" for war against Mexico.[71]

While the United States and England exchanged ratifications of the Oregon Treaty in mid-1846, the administration transformed a border skirmish on a distant frontier into a full-fledged war to coerce Mexico into relinquishing its northern provinces to the United States. Oregon was soon forgotten in the excitement of battle. During the summer of 1846 American military forces occupied New Mexico and California, and Polk decided that the borderlands would never be returned to Mexico.[72]

71. Polk, *Diary*, 1 (May 9, 1846):384–807. Only Bancroft hesitated to opt for war before an actual attack occurred.

72. Polk, *Diary*, 1 (May 30, 1846):438; ibid. (June 30, 1846):495–97; ibid., 2 (July 7, 1846):15–16. On January 13, 1847, Buchanan wrote to Larkin, "You are not to infer

The acquisition of California became to Polk what the annexation of Texas had been to Tyler. At the time of his inauguration, Polk had confided to Bancroft that the acquisition of California was one of four major goals he had defined for his single term.[73] That ambition was seldom out of his mind. In September 1845, for example, Polk had told his advisers that the acquisition of California and New Mexico would be worth as much as $40 million, "the amount of pecuniary consideration to be paid . . . of small importance." Suspicious that European powers had designs on California, Polk invoked the Monroe Doctrine and noted that "the people of the United States would not willingly permit California to pass into the possession of any new colony planted by Great Britain or any foreign monarchy." In warning the Europeans away from the Pacific Coast, Polk sought to protect "California and the fine bay of San Francisco as much . . . as Oregon."[74] How Polk knew the will of the American people in regards to California is not clear, but it was not unusual for him to assume that his own ambitions matched those of the electorate. In any case, between the lines lurked Polk's preoccupation with the Asian market, his anxieties about overproduction on the nation's farms and plantations, and his awareness that American producers had to expand their trade. Polk's exaggerated fear of Britain also influenced his approach to California.

To obtain additional leverage in the contest for California, the administration designated American consul Thomas Larkin a confidential agent in Monterey in October. Larkin, who had prospered as a merchant in the Pacific trade, was exuberant about California's commercial potential. Buchanan instructed him that "the future destiny of that country is a subject of anxious solicitude for the . . . United States. The interests of our commerce and our whale fisheries on the Pacific Ocean demand that you should exert the greatest vigilance in discovering and defeating any attempt, which may be made by for-

. . . that the president contemplates any contingency in which [the Californias] shall ever be surrendered to Mexico" (William R. Manning, ed., *The Diplomatic Correspondence of the United States, Inter-American Affairs, 1831–1860,* 12 vols. [Washington, D.C., 1932–39], 8:197). For the deliberations in the Polk cabinet on military maneuvers and territorial considerations, see Polk, *Diary,* 1 (May 14, 16, 20, 26, 30 and June 2, 5, 1846):400, 403–4, 411, 429, 438–39, 443–44, 449–50. The administration's military strategy is discussed in detail in K. Jack Bauer, *The Mexican War, 1846–1848* (New York, 1974), pp. 127–44, 164–200.

73. Charles G. Sellers, *James K. Polk, Continentalist, 1843–1846* (Princeton, 1966), p. 213.

74. Polk, *Diary,* 1 (September 16, 1845):34–35 and (October 4, 1845):71.

eign governments to acquire a control over that country."[75] Larkin did not need to be reminded of California's attractions. He regarded the port of San Francisco as "capable of great defenses" and able to hold "perhaps all the vessels in the world." To Bennett he extolled the ports of California and peremptorily stated in May 1846, "We must have it, others must not."[76] As further precautions, the administration dispatched Archibald Gillespie to the Pacific Coast as an executive agent and instructed explorer John C. Frémont of the Army Topographical Corps, already roaming through Mexico's northern provinces, to frustrate any British attempt to acquire California.[77]

After alerting Larkin and Frémont, the administration sent Louisiana's John Slidell to Mexico City to reopen diplomatic relations between the United States and Mexico. Slidell was to resolve the Texas-Mexico boundary dispute and obtain assurances from Mexico that it would pay American claims for loss of lives and property resulting from Mexico's frequent revolutions. The administration doubted that Mexico could pay these indemnities but hoped that the country's impoverished condition would force it to meet its debts by transferring California and New Mexico to the United States. "The possession of the bay and harbor of San Francisco . . . is all important to the United States," Buchanan advised Slidell. He stressed Polk's eagerness to acquire California and urged Slidell to exert his "best efforts" to convince Mexican officials to cede it to the United States. "Money would be no object when compared with the value of the acquisition," he concluded.[78]

Polk impressed the same idea upon Slidell. In a confidential letter in late 1845 he told him, "I do not desire that you shall feel yourself absolutely restricted to the maximum sum maintained in your instructions."[79] In other words, Polk wanted to protect his reputation

75. Buchanan to Larkin, October 17, 1845, in Manning, *Diplomatic Correspondence,* 8:169.

76. Larkin to Moses Yale Beach, May 28, 1845, and Larkin to Bennett, May 20, 1846, in George P. Hammond, ed., *The Larkin Papers: Personal, Business, and Official Correspondence of Thomas O. Larkin, Merchant and United States Consul in California,* 10 vols. (Berkeley, 1951–64), 3:201, 4:383.

77. Benton, *Thirty Years' View,* 2:688–93; Gillespie to Larkin, April 17, 1846, in Hammond, *Larkin Papers,* 4:290; Frémont, *Narratives of Exploration and Adventure,* Allan Nevins, ed. (New York, 1956), pp. 496-99.

78. Buchanan to Slidell, November 10, 1845, in Manning, *Diplomatic Correspondence,* 8:180–81.

79. Polk to Slidell, "Private and unofficial," December 17, 1845, Polk Papers. See also Polk to Slidell, "Confidential," November 10, 1845, Polk Papers.

for Jacksonian frugality in the public record, but in private he in essence gave Slidell a blank check with which to purchase California. But Mexico flatly refused to sell the province, so that made conquest necessary.[80] The news of the Mexican assault on American forces came as a great relief to Polk and his advisers, for it provided an opportune justification for a course they had already plotted.

Polk anticipated a short and decisive war that would add New Mexico and California to the United States, thereby depriving Britain of the best ports on the Pacific Coast. Secretary of War Marcy also believed that Mexico could be brought to terms quickly. In settling the conflict, Marcy noted, the United States would demand "a slice of upper California (including the harbors of Monterey and San Francisco) to satisfy the claims for our citizens and the government claim for the expenses of the war."[81] But two principal factors complicated the expansionists' optimistic calculations: Mexico proved more tenacious an antagonist than expected, and the introduction of the Wilmot Proviso in August precipitated a portentous rift between small but spirited factions of northern and southern Democrats.

The debate on the extension of slavery that commenced in mid-1846 soon eclipsed all other issues, but the Democrats did not lose sight of the importance of acquiring California and a land corridor from the Mississippi Valley to the Pacific Coast. Their observations on the California ports were remarkably reminiscent of earlier arguments in behalf of the commercial value of Oregon. Dreams of Asian commerce and ascendancy over Britain again animated the Democrats.

80. Polk based his strategy on a precedent set by Jefferson, who had asked Congress for secret funds in 1803 and 1806 to facilitate the purchase of Louisiana and the Floridas. Polk believed that a quick-fix payment of one or two million dollars to the general in charge in Mexico would secure the transfer of California to the United States. See Polk, *Diary,* 1(March 28–30, 1846):305–13; ibid. (April 3, 1846): 317; ibid., 2 (July 26, 30 and 31, 1846): 50, 56–57; ibid. (August 7, 8, and 10, 1846):70, 72–73, 75–78. Massachusetts Senator John Davis held the floor during the final half hour of the session and spoke until it expired, so the bill for two million dollars failed to pass. Polk was disappointed, to say the least. "Had the appropriation been passed I am confident I should have made an honorable peace by which we should have acquired California and such other territory as we desired, before the end of October," Polk observed on August 10. Polk apparently did not consider that what appeared "honorable" to him might not appear so to Mexican leaders. Polk discussed the need for a secret appropriation with many senators and noted in his diary that Allen, Benton, Cass, Calhoun, and McDuffie all agreed with him.

81. For Polk's expectations, see *Diary,* 1 (May 11, 1846):391–92; Polk to Gideon Pillow, May 16, 1846, and Polk to Pillow, "Private and Confidential," September 22, 1846; Polk to William H. Polk, "Private," July 14, 1846, Polk Papers. For Marcy's view, see his letter to Prosper M. Wetmore, June 13, 1846, William L. Marcy Papers.

In the House, southern Democrats such as John Harmanson of Louisiana recommended that the United States "stretch its arms to the Pacific, and control the commerce of that ocean." If "all obstacles to our intercourse with the world" were removed, he said in early 1847, "fifty years will not elapse ere the destinies of the human race will be in our hands." Congressman Samuel Inge of Alabama concurred, stressing that the United States must obtain California because "the safe and capacious harbors which dot her western shore invite to their bosoms the rich commerce of the East." James DeBow, of *DeBow's Commercial Review,* believed that the acquisition of California would especially enrich New Orleans. In early 1847 he observed that "the signs of the times" clearly indicated an imminent change in "the trade of Asia and the East Indies." Later that year he insisted that the United States demand a right of way across southern Mexico in any peace settlement. He predicted that an isthmian railroad or canal would facilitate commerce and communication between the Mississippi and Ohio Valleys, New Orleans, the Pacific Coast, and the Far East.[82] Commercial opportunities and all that they meant to the economy's viability beckoned the nation westward.

Trade-oriented northern Democrats viewed expansion to the Pacific in similar terms. Congressman John McClernand of Illinois spoke for many of his colleagues when he contended that the acquisition of California would bring "the mastery of the Pacific" to the United States because of improved access to East Asia's "inexhaustible markets." Editor Bennett favored permanent occupation of the borderlands, particularly "the whole of California and the splendid harbors on the coast." In mid-1846, he also recommended construction of a transcontinental railroad. These two steps would ensure American "pre-emption of all the markets in the Pacific. Our manufactures would find an unlimited market—our agricultural interests would be spurred on—our commerce increase." The *Democratic Review,* though no longer under O'Sullivan's direction, displayed its usual zeal for territorial and commercial expansion during the war, referring to California in 1847 as "a country affording harbors unsurpassed by any in the world, and capable of supplying to the marine of the United States the most valuable ports for repairing, refitting, and procuring supplies."[83] Though the expansionists often mentioned the

82. *CG,* 29 Cong., 2 sess., App. 360 (February 12, 1847); *CG,* 30 Cong., 1 sess., App. 435 (March 22, 1848); "Contests for the Trade of the Mississippi Valley," *DeBow's Commercial Review,* 3 (February, 1847):107; "Passage between the Two Oceans, by Ship Canal," *DeBow's Commercial Review,* 3 (June, 1847):497.

83. *CG,* 30 Cong., 1 sess., 913 (July 10, 1848); New York *Herald,* June 21, 1846; "California," *Democratic Review,* 20 (June, 1847):560.

agricultural potential of California, they saw the province primarily in commercial terms.

Polk and Walker viewed California as another vital asset in their efforts to assist agrarian producers and to attain global commercial supremacy. Its acquisition, like the passage of the Walker Tariff in 1846 and Britain's repeal of the Corn Laws, meant that American exports could be dramatically increased, protecting the predominantly agrarian economy from overproduction and depressed prices. Britain's abandonment of the Corn Laws in 1846 promised a double bonus to the Democrats: by opening a wider market for American staples the repeal would mean higher prices for American commodities, and, perhaps more important, it would facilitate the export of manufactured goods from Britain and thereby discourage the spread of industry in the United States.[84] In addition, Britain's growing dependence on American food imports would become another advantage for the United States. In late 1846, Walker proudly informed Congress of the benefits of the administration's liberal trade policy: "By freer interchange of commodities, the foreign market is opened to our agricultural products, our tonnage and commerce are rapidly augmenting, our exports enlarged and the price enhanced, exchanges are in our favor, and specie is flowing within our limits."[85] Still troubled at this time by the nation's "immense surplus of food and other articles," President Polk also hailed the less restricted commercial relationship with Britain. "By the simultaneous abandonment of the protective policy by Great Britain and the United States," he noted in his annual message to Congress in late 1846, "new and important markets have already been opened for our agricultural and other products, commerce and navigation have received a new impulse, [and] labor and trade have been released from the artificial trammels which have so long fettered them." With "a foreign as well as a home market . . . opened to them," agrarians were receiving "increased prices for their products."[86] This welcome development, like the acquisition of California's ports, would protect the Jeffersonian arcadia from the menace of manufacturing, economic distress, and monopoly.

Most of the anglophobic Democrats believed that freer trade be-

84. The Democrats' fears of industrialization and large-scale corporate enterprise are discussed in Chapter 4.

85. *Report of the Secretary of the Treasury, H. Doc.,* vol. 498, no. 7, 29 Cong., 2 sess. (December 10, 1846), p. 7.

86. Richardson, *Messages and Papers,* 5 (December 8, 1846):2351.

tween Britain and the United States would benefit both countries, but many also noted that the substantial rise in food imports by Britain further increased its dependence on its rival. The commercial expansionists could not have asked for more; they flaunted their humanitarianism by pointing out that America fed a hungry Europe, while they brandished the cotton or grain embargo weapon at foreign leaders who seemed inclined to resist the aggrandizement of the United States. Seldom had humanitarian and imperial pretensions coincided so neatly in American diplomacy.

The conquest of California, like the modernization of the navy, the annexation of Texas, the acquisition of Oregon, and the reduction of the tariff, was a measure intended to advance the commercial fortunes of the United States. Polk, for example, informed Congress in late 1847 that he desired to retain California as indemnity for the war: "The bay of San Francisco and other harbors along the Californian coast would afford shelter for our navy, for our numerous whaleships, and other merchant vessels employed in the Pacific Ocean." The California ports, he said, "would in a short period become the marts of an extensive and profitable commerce with China and other countries of the East." When Mexico ceded California and New Mexico in 1848, Polk reminded his countrymen of the cession's value. The two provinces "constitute of themselves a country large enough for a great empire, and their acquisition is second only in importance to that of Louisiana in 1803," Polk noted. He again emphasized the value of the California ports, which would "enable the United States to command the already valuable and rapidly increasing commerce of the Pacific." He predicted that "in this vast region, whose rich resources are soon to be developed by American energy and enterprise, great must be the augmentation of our commerce, and with it new and profitable demands for mechanic labor in all its branches and new and valuable markets for our manufactures and agricultural products." Here again Polk saw in the West a refuge for struggling laborers and farmers in the East.[87]

The administration also hoped to promote American trade through revisions in the consular service. In mid-1846, Congressman W. W. Campbell of New York introduced a bill for consular reform, but the House tabled the measure and instead called upon Buchanan to investigate and report on the system. Commercial expansionists recognized the need for an improved service. The consular agents'

87. Polk's third annual message, in ibid., 5 (December 7, 1847):2390 and Polk's message on the treaty with Mexico, ibid., 5 (July 6, 1848): 2438–39.

duties, editor Bennett believed, were "more important" to the nation than those of the diplomatic corps. He endorsed the bill's provision for regular salaries for agents so that the existing fees on trade could be eliminated, and he supported the stipulation that only United States citizens should serve as American consuls in foreign ports.[88] Editor Ritchie also urged a revamping of the system. He backed the provisions that prohibited consuls from engaging in private business and, like Bennett, called for compensation for them in the form of fixed salaries rather than levies on trade. These changes, Ritchie suggested, would help "to preserve the advantages we now enjoy, and to push our enterprise into new and profitable channels."[89]

In December of 1846, Buchanan submitted his report to the House.[90] Admitting that the existing consular system was "a very imperfect and inadequate" arrangement for promoting "the vast interests of our extended commerce," Buchanan recommended that consuls receive compensation "by salaries from the treasury—at least at the more important ports—and not by fees." This serious flaw in the system rendered the business of the consulate "subsidiary to" the private interests of the agent, who often engaged in personal trade to supplement his inadequate income. If these officials received a reasonable salary, however, they would then be obliged "to extend equal protection to all Americans engaged in foreign commerce." Buchanan further advised that American foreign commerce "ought not to be taxed with any consular fees." Since those fees increased the final cost of American products to foreign buyers, it made goods from the United States more expensive and therefore less competitive in overseas markets.

Ritchie publicized Buchanan's findings, imploring Congress to enact the suggested reforms. The *Herald* likewise urged Congress to modify the consular system, arguing that "no part of our government surely stands in greater need of a thorough reconstruction." Congress did not act during 1847, however, nor during 1848, and the system remained much the same as it had been since the late eighteenth century. Bennett repeated his pleas for consular reform to no avail in early 1849, complaining that the service was "positively a disgrace to the country."[91]

88. New York *Herald,* June 4, 21, and 29, 1846.
89. Washington *Daily Union,* June 23, 1846.
90. John Bassett Moore, ed., *The Works of James Buchanan,* 12 vols. (Philadelphia, 1908–11), 7 (December 12, 1846):155–66.
91. Washington *Daily Union,* December 22, 1846 and February 11 and March 4, 1847; New York *Herald,* January 8, 10, and 23, 1847; New York *Herald,* January 18, 1849.

Yet if the system remained "a disgrace to the country," the Polk administration was not to blame. It had repeatedly tried to modernize the consular service while pursuing other policies to secure additional markets for American farmers and merchants. Thurman Hunt, of *Hunt's Merchant Magazine*, appreciated these efforts. In late 1848 he praised the administration for "the change in the tariff, . . . the Mexican War, and the starting of mail steamers under the patronage of the government." Hunt encouraged Walker to write a commercial history of the administration and singled him out for particular commendation. "The commercial interest of the country is deeply indebted to your liberal and enlightened views, for a large share of its present and prospective prosperity," Hunt observed.[92]

For four years the Polk administration had labored to improve the country's commercial prospects. No one understood this sustained effort better than Walker, whose final report to Congress in 1848 amounted to a paean to the administration's achievements. Walker believed that the annexation of Texas, the resolution of the Oregon dispute, the reduction of the tariff, and the acquisition of California had transformed the United States into a dynamic commercial empire destined to dominate the Western Hemisphere and East Asia in the not-distant future. Another advantage secured by the administration was the Treaty of New Granada, approved in 1848, which granted the United States transit rights across Panama. "Our maritime frontier upon the Pacific," he wrote, "is now nearly equal to our Atlantic coast, with many excellent bays and harbors, admirably situated to command the trade of Asia and of the whole western coast of America." The United States, he suggested, had to reorient its traditional commercial perspective and look less toward Europe and more toward Asia. The East Asian markets could be monopolized by placing more steamships on the Pacific and by building a railroad across Central America. With these steps taken, the United States could "revolutionize" in its favor the world's trade and "more rapidly advance" its "greatness, wealth and power, than any event which has occurred since the adoption of the constitution." After taking leadership in Asian trade, the United States could then obtain, "in time, the command of the trade of the world."[93] Such a bald declaration of intent to make the world a commercial tributary of the United States

92. Hunt to Walker, December 28, 1848, Walker Papers.

93. *Report of the Secretary of the Treasury, H. Doc.*, vol. 538, no. 7, 30 Cong., 2 sess. (December 11, 1848), pp. 14–16.

made explicit in 1848 what had been implicit in American domestic
and foreign policy since 1841—the concerted campaign of two suc-
cessive administrations to restructure the world's commercial framework in a way that would shield the country from domestic depressions,
internal strife, and threats from abroad. The Democrats' anxieties
had not disappeared by the close of the Mexican War, but their
policies had, in their view, put the nation in a better position to deal
with both internal and external threats to the Union.

Every president from Washington to Van Buren had tried to expand United States trade, but wherever they turned they had encountered European empires jealously guarding their prerogatives and
privileges around the world. In attempting to obtain additional foreign markets for American producers, Tyler and Polk adhered to a
tradition that both preceded and succeeded them. The vast extent of
the lands acquired during the period should not obscure the vital
commercial component in American domestic and foreign policy at
this time. The leaders of the 1840s sought far more than just new
elbow room for restless Americans. Additional farms and plantations were useless unless they could be sustained by adequate export
markets.

Many scholars have noted the decisive impact of domestic factors
on late nineteenth-century American foreign policy. The boom-and-
bust cycle of the American economy, the discontent among farmers
and workers, and the fears of declining opportunity and mobility all
contributed to a conviction in this period that the acquisition of
Hawaii and the Philippines was necessary to safeguard American
prosperity and security.[94] The parallels between this period and the
1840s have not been clearly noted, however. In 1846, as in 1898,
expansionist administrations found moral justifications for their territorial and commercial designs. Although the Civil War and Reconstruction separated the imperialists of the 1840s from those of the
1890s, there was not much difference between them. The "new empire" of the 1890s was new in its geographical extent but hardly novel
in the purposes it was intended to serve. The chimera of the China
market was as instrumental in the expansionism of the late Jackson-

94. See, for example, William A. Williams, *The Contours of American History* (Cleve-
land, 1961), pp. 345-70, and *The Tragedy of American Diplomacy* (New York, 1962), pp.
18-50; Walter LaFeber, *The New Empire: An Interpretation of American Expansion, 1860–
1898* (Ithaca, 1963); Thomas McCormick, *China Market: America's Quest for Informal
Empire, 1893-1901* (Chicago, 1967); Marilyn B. Young, *The Rhetoric of Empire* (Cambridge, Mass., 1968).

ian period as it was in the closing decades of the nineteenth century. Caleb Cushing, for example, outlined the essential features of the Open Door policy in China over fifty years before John Hay wrote his celebrated diplomatic notes to foreign governments insisting that the United States must have access to the inexhaustible Far Eastern markets being contested by the world's imperial powers. In both cases, anxious policy makers feared that aggressive nations would circumscribe American trade and inflict economic hardship on the United States.

One of the most striking but neglected features of the expansionism of the 1840s was the belief among Democrats that the United States could monopolize vital raw materials and use them to lash rival empires into submission. Girded by this conviction, two administrations sought continental and commercial dominion for their nation. Humanitarian strains occasionally appeared in the arguments of the expansionists, who talked about the American mission to feed and clothe a hungry and naked world. But the diplomacy of the 1840s and the justifications for it starkly demonstrate that any sense of mission to alleviate misery around the world was seldom uppermost in the expansionists' minds. On the contrary, they regarded American productivity as an additional weapon in the nation's arsenal, an effective but less expensive weapon than a large standing army, a costly navy, or an elaborate diplomatic corps.

The drive for commercial monopolies and foreign markets, like the drive for territory and its resources, stemmed largely from the anxieties and ambitions of powerful Democrats during the 1840s. Fearful of domestic surpluses and the economic difficulties they caused, concerned about the power of Britain and its opposition to American expansion, and uneasy about European discrimination against American trade, the expansionists sought security in the acquisition of land, ports, and markets. Amid these dangers, however, were opportunities. American productivity might be transformed into a bulwark of national security if other nations could be made dependent on American agricultural products such as cotton and grain. Not only could improved access to additional markets guarantee ample rewards to American producers; it could also enhance the nation's competitive edge in the intensifying struggle for global commercial ascendancy and military superiority. Whether the expansionists' motives were primarily territorial or commercial is a moot point: they were both, and complementary rather than contradictory.[95] Land

95. Norman A. Graebner, in *Empire on the Pacific: A Study in American Continental*

hunger and a desire for ports and markets were two sides of the same imperial coin, two ways of safeguarding the predominantly agrarian society of the United States by compensating for Britain's commercial and military advantages. To the expansionists, the most decisive shift in the nation's favor occurred with the annexation of Texas and the acquisition of a purported cotton monopoly. The acquisition of the Columbia River country; the Walker Tariff; Britain's repeal of the Corn Laws; and the conquest of California also augured well for the empire's future. Neither accidental nor innocent, the expansion to the Pacific represented not manifest destiny, but manifest design.

Expansion (New York, 1955), explained the acquisitions of the 1840s largely in commercial terms. His focus on Oregon and California, however, precluded his giving the annexation of Texas and the cotton monopoly argument the attention they deserve. Moreover, Graebner's almost exclusive emphasis on commercial factors deprives the expansionism of the period of much of its complexity. He asserts, for example, that the coalition that carried Texas annexation "cared nothing for the extension of slavery"—an implausible argument that overlooks one of the most critical concerns of late Jacksonian-era Democrats. Though correct in noting that Polk and the Democrats were as commercially minded as the northeastern Whigs, Graebner says little about the relationship between the domestic economy and American foreign policy in the 1840s. The desire for Pacific ports was certainly an important aspect of mid-1840s expansionism, but other ambitions and anxieties besides maritime factors were also crucial.

CHAPTER 4

Jefferson *Redivivus:*
The Perils of Modernization

Mid-nineteenth-century Americans regarded themselves as a "go-ahead" people, and most foreign observers agreed with them. The typical Yankee who viewed the splendid falls at Niagara for the first time wondered how many waterwheels the torrent could turn, and even on the hurricane deck of a steamboat the restless American lurched back and forth in his rocking chair, the movement of the ship itself insufficient to satisfy his craving for constant motion. Americans and foreigners alike identified many traits characteristic of the "go-ahead" spirit in the United States: highly ingenious, inventive, and receptive to innovation, Americans devoted themselves to the practical and utilitarian rather than the theoretical and aesthetic as they eagerly applied machinery to the task of producing and distributing the nation's goods. Unlike other countries molded by a feudal past, the United States had no reactionary Luddites to do battle against the invading machines of the industrial revolution.

European visitors were struck by the rapid pace of change in the United States. Even during the Panic of 1837, for example, Frederick Marryat noticed "energy and enterprise" and "rapid improvement" all around him, leading him to conclude that "ten years in America is almost equal to a century in the old continent." To Charles Dickens, in 1842, the United States patent office seemed "an extraordinary example of American enterprise and ingenuity." Later that year Ireland's John Godley observed that "Americans 'go ahead' too fast to enjoy the blessings of sound sleep and good digestion": insomnia and heartburn had become national institutions. British traveler Alexander Mackay sensed particular significance in the fact that the railroad car carrying him in early 1846 resembled "a small church upon wheels." It contained a center aisle flanked with pewlike benches, an appropriate rolling shrine for a people "proverbially addicted to locomotion."[1] Wherever visitors ventured north of the Mason-Dixon line, the din of progress assaulted their senses: whirring steam engines, clattering looms, squeaking wheels. Americans were hammers, their ingenuity anvils, and their abundant resources iron to be forged by active and ambitious hands.

This image of a progressive and dynamic United States in perpetual motion during the Jacksonian era endures. Recent scholars who have studied antebellum thought and culture have generally agreed that both Americans and European visitors welcomed industrialization in the United States and regarded it as an additional frontier of opportunity that contributed to the young nation's unprecedented advancement. So long as American workshops remained in the wilderness— that is, in areas of sparse population and rural values—the reality of swift technological and economic change could be reconciled with the pastoral ideal of a New World Eden. With the exception of skeptical intellectuals such as Emerson, Thoreau, Hawthorne, and Irving, Americans accepted the industrial revolution and viewed modernization as still another example of their nation's progressive qualities.[2]

If acceptance of modernization was the rule, the exceptions are nevertheless noteworthy. Many of the Democratic expansionists of the 1840s, like the intellectuals mentioned above, expressed grave reservations about industrialization.[3] They believed that the industrial

1. Frederick Marryat, *A Diary in America: With Remarks on Its Institutions,* 3 vols. (London, 1839), 1:17–18; Charles Dickens, *American Notes and Pictures from Italy* (London, 1903), p. 107; John Robert Godley, *Letters from America,* 2 vols. (London, 1844), 2:98; Alexander Mackay, *The Western World, or Travels in the United States in 1846–47,* 4th ed., 3 vols. (London, 1850), 1:31, 2:239. See also Charles Lyell, *A Second Visit to North America,* 3rd ed., 2 vols. (London, 1855), 1:108.

2. See Leo Marx, *The Machine in the Garden: Technology and the Pastoral Ideal* (New York, 1964); John F. Kasson, *Civilizing the Machine: Technology and Republican Values in America* (New York, 1976); Marvin Fischer, *Workshops in the Wilderness: The European Response to American Industrialization* (New York, 1967); Max Berger, *The British Traveller in America, 1836–1860* (New York, 1943); Russel B. Nye, *Society and Culture in America, 1830–1860* (New York, 1974).

3. Jacksonian Democrats from the South especially criticized industrialization and all it entailed, perhaps because they feared that a prominent manufacturing sector would seek higher tariff duties that would primarily hurt southern cotton exports. Northern Democrats were more divided on industrialism: Stephen Douglas and George Dallas, for example, seemed more receptive to modernization (or at least some aspects of it) than Lewis Cass and Daniel Dickinson.

revolution threatening to engulf the United States posed a grave danger to what they most valued in their country: widespread owner-ship of property; agrarianism and a dispersed population; and geo-graphical and social mobility. To ward off the anticipated consequences of rapid modernization and to recreate an idealized Jeffersonian past, they sought to acquire new lands, to encourage agriculture, and to promote foreign trade. This was a conservative, even a reactionary, response to rapid change. It is misleading, then, to place technology and democracy in double harness in antebellum America. For it was more an apprehension about the technological revolution sweeping the Western world than an acceptance of it that influenced the expan-sionists of the 1840s. They hoped that new territory and additional markets could protect the country from the perils of industrialization and its inevitable concomitants such as urban congestion, uncertainty of employment, class stratification, labor agitation, and domestic strife.

The neo-Jeffersonians of the 1840s made territorial expansion a vital component of their program. To them, the acquisition of land seemed as indispensable to the welfare of the country as opposition to a national bank, resistance to corporate privilege, reduction of the tariff, or removal of barriers to foreign trade. Domestic and foreign policies were closely intertwined (if not inseparable) at this time, as the ideological heirs of Jefferson sought prosperity and security by encouraging agriculture and navigation while discouraging the growth of manufacturing and the concentration of capital. Despite significant differences, there was continuity in many of the principles and preju-dices held by the anti-Federalist and anti-Whig oppositions that ral-lied around Jefferson, Jackson, Tyler, and Polk. Expansionism became their antidote to the toxins of modernization. Jefferson had acquired an empire in Louisiana; Jackson had removed the eastern Indians and opened their rich agricultural lands to white entrepreneurs; Tyler had obtained Texas; and Polk had wrested the Spanish borderlands from Mexico. These leaders also sought greater commercial opportunities for American producers and merchants. The quest for land and markets during the 1840s was, in large part, a manifestation of old Jeffersonian fears about the impact of rapid modernization on Ameri-can society and government. To maintain republicanism and individ-ualistic entrepreneurship, the expansionists of the Tyler-Polk years obtained vast territorial cessions for additional farms and plantations and opened foreign markets that could absorb the products they produced.

The expansionists feared that rapid industrialization might transform the United States into a second Britain. Weakened by class
conflict and commercial dependence, Britain seemed to them a declining power in world affairs. For the American expansionists, Britain served an essential purpose: it provided a model of the inherent
dangers in a manufacturing society, a grim reminder of what the
United States must avoid in order to maintain its stability and security. The extent of Britain's internal difficulties so emboldened the
expansionists that they declared that the United States could defy
Britain with impunity. They claimed that Britain was so preoccupied
with domestic problems that it could not afford to contest commercial
or territorial dominion with the United States in the Western Hemisphere.

Like most Americans who toured the major cities of Europe during
the late Jacksonian period, editor James Gordon Bennett was appalled by the conditions he witnessed there. "England," he wrote in
the *Herald* in 1843, "is in a crisis, political, financial, and religious."
The United States, in contrast, was "the best and happiest country
for all classes and all tongues" because it had "none of the bloated
wealth or terrible misery that we see in this overcrowded land."[4]
Bennett went further, asserting that the working poor in Britain fared
worse than the slaves of the American South. "Weighed down to the
very earth by oppression and unequal laws, the poorer classes of that
country are in a condition, compared with which that of the slaves
of the South is perfect happiness," he remarked. According to Bennett and other proslavery northerners, slave labor on a southern
plantation was preferable to "free" labor in a mill or factory. Rapid
industrialization and the high costs of imperialism, he believed, were
destroying the European powers. After returning to the United States
in the autumn of 1843, Bennett told his readers that "the world is in
a strange position. Europe and America are in a transition state—the
one getting grey and gouty, and the other just beginning to cultivate
a pair of whiskers."[5]

John O'Sullivan also dramatized the plight of the English working
class when alerting his countrymen to the risks of modernization.
British law seemed "to favor accumulation, to promote monopoly,
and to place manual labor in dependence on capital." If precautions
were not taken to control the course of industrialization in the United

4. New York *Herald,* August 22, 1843.
5. New York *Herald,* September 23, 1844 and October 23, 1843.

States, it must sink to the level of Britain. After touring Lowell, Massachusetts, Nashua, New Hampshire, and other manufacturing cities in 1842, O'Sullivan warned Americans that "the principles of *white slavery* are gradually taking root in the very midst of us." Concentrated in the New England manufacturing towns were a growing "multitude of defective beings, with sallow complexions, emaciated forms, and stooping shoulders—with premature wrinkles and furtive glances," revealing "misery and degradation in language not to be mistaken."[6] His country, he feared, was slipping into the ravenous maw of industrialization. He accused the Whigs of trying to make the United States into a complex urban-industrial society through their program of a high protective tariff, centralized banking, stringent controls on sales of public land, and federal aid to expensive internal improvement projects. O'Sullivan opposed all these measures, since they tended to "favor and foster the factory system" in the United States. Like Bennett and other neo-Jeffersonians, he declared southern slaves to be healthier and happier than British workers. The United States could be spared the problems plaguing England only as long as farms and plantations remained the predominant sites of labor in the United States. But if the factory eclipsed the field as America's primary work place, then an oppressive system of white wage servitude would cripple the United States. In O'Sullivan's opinion, it was "almost a crime against society to divert human industry from the fields and the forests to iron forges and cotton factories" when the country possessed an "unlimited range of uncultivated or half-improved soil."[7]

Modernization could be forestalled, O'Sullivan thought, if the government acquired and made available to Americans an extensive territorial domain and also opened the markets of the world to the country's farmers and planters. But if the "agricultural and commercial interests" of the nation were not sustained "by throwing open the foreign markets to western produce, and by so doing raising the money value of the whole production relatively to that of manufacturing labor," the deplorable "condition of Lancashire with its starving operatives and lordly employers must soon and inevitably be that of New England."[8] In 1845, O'Sullivan implied that the textile industry

6. "White Slavery," *Democratic Review*, 11 (September, 1842):261, 270. See also the reviews of two books by C. Edwards Lester, *The Glory and Shame of England* and *The Condition and Fate of England, Democratic Review*, 10, 12 (January 1842, January 1843):89–94, 3–12.

7. "White Slavery," pp. 269–70.

8. "Free Trade," *Democratic Review*, 14 (March, 1844):296–97.

in the United States was fast approaching the condition of that of Great Britain. "Already is the corporate factory system beginning to produce in the United States that depth of distress which has long excited the horror of every observer of the condition of Lancashire," he warily observed. The mill owners of the Northeast ruled "with an iron hand, and cut down wages at their pleasure," until working conditions in New England approximated those in Old England. Industrialization, he warned, would ruin the nation unless the government supplied a counterbalance in the form of an extensive public domain. "Close to her population the safety-valve of the public lands," he predicted, and there was no guarantee that the manufacturing population "in Lowell, and Lynn, and Salem" would be spared those dreadful conditions "that now win our sympathy for the oppressed laborer of Britain."[9]

The United States was temporarily shielded from the worst evils of modernization because of its "sparse population" and its "wide-spreading domain," O'Sullivan maintained, but only the accessibility of cheap land protected the urban wage worker from poverty and degradation. Partly because of his fear of industrialization, O'Sullivan championed preemption legislation (permitting a settler to occupy government land before its survey and sale, the squatter then having the right to purchase it at the minimum price) and graduation legislation (providing a reduction in price for inferior lands long on the market). He also supported territorial acquisitions and free trade, believing that they would ensure that the United States possessed those vital prerequisites for a fluid and free society, a "sparse population" dispersed over a "wide-spreading domain."[10]

The two editors who spoke for the Tyler and Polk administrations—John B. Jones and Thomas Ritchie—frequently expressed anxiety over industrialization, revealing fears held by the presidents and their advisers as well. In late 1843, for example, Jones noted in the *Daily Madisonian* that "in the thickly settled parts of our non-slaveholding states, the condition of the poorer class of population is fast assimilating itself to that of the servile class in Europe. Already they are but hewers of wood and drawers of water to their wealthier

9. New York *Morning News*, October 24, 1845; "One of the Problems of the Age," *Democratic Review*, 14 (February, 1844):167. America's abundant land, O'Sullivan noted, postponed but did not eliminate "the fate that now imminently threatens England. When the land of refuge in the West is reclaimed and occupied, our laborers too may become the victims of machinery and of over-production" (ibid.).
10. "One of the Problems of the Age," p. 167.

brethren." Though the South's slaves might appear worse off than the North's free laborers, the situation of industrial workers was tan-tamount to "white slavery."[11] The Tylerites felt little or no repug-nance toward black servitude, but white servitude was another mat-ter. They admonished northern "philanthropists" to leave the slaveholders alone and to turn their attention instead to the plight of industrial workers in their own part of the country.

Ritchie had been preaching the Jeffersonian gospel for over forty years when Polk summoned him to Washington in 1845 to become executive editor.[12] Calling, in August of that year, for the reduction of import duties, Ritchie complained that the "enormous profits" from the protective tariff accrued to "the moneyed manufacturer who first skims the cream, and not [to] his toiling operatives." To make the economic system more equitable, Ritchie favored a tariff designed only to raise revenue, not to protect or encourage domestic manufacturing. In 1846, he expressed cautious optimism about the future, noting that "agriculture is, and for a century or two to come, will continue to be, the predominant branch of industry in the United States." Americans could maintain an agrarian republic for many decades because "the increasing population of the old states" pos-sessed a "strong tendency" to acquire "new homes in the West, rather than remain in the densely peopled parts of the country and employ themselves in manufactures."[13]

Yet Ritchie was not always so sanguine. He advocted territorial expansion because he regarded it as a guarantee against the dangers of industrialization, urbanization, and class polarization. American wage workers in the mid-1840s were better situated than their Euro-pean counterparts, Ritchie observed, only because "land is plenty, and the support by agriculture so easy and certain, that people will not work in the more confined, less healthy, and less independent atmosphere of a manufactory." Like other Jeffersonians, Ritchie as-sumed that workers preferred to toil in the field, not labor in the factory. He disputed the Whigs' contention that a protective tariff benefited both manufacturers and their workers. "The cheapness of good lands, and the facility with which a respectable and independent living is made by agriculture, keeps wages up, not the profits of the manufacturers," he observed in 1846.[14] Most Democrats, especially

11. Washington *Daily Madisonian,* October 30, 1843.
12. See Charles H. Ambler, *Thomas Ritchie, A Study in Virginia Politics* (Richmond, 1913).
13. Washington *Daily Union,* August 6, 1845, April 6, 1846.
14. Washington *Daily Union,* August 24, 1846.

those from the South and many from the West, agreed. In mid-1846, in response to the Polk administration's recommendation, Congress passed the reduced Walker Tariff in a largely partisan vote.[15]

The tariff of 1846 was intended to serve the same purposes as the annexation of Texas, the acquisition of Oregon, and the conquest of California. Most Democrats agreed that the protective tariff aided manufacturers, not workers. Certain that the profits of industry went into the pockets of corporate aristocrats who paid only bare subsistence wages to their laborers, critics of protectionism asserted that workers should be considered primarily as consumers, and as such their chief concern was to buy products at low prices. The best assistance for the "producing classes" was a lower tariff that would reduce the price of goods, whether imported or produced domestically. The Democrats' reduction of the tariff and their territorial and commercial initiatives were intended to prevent rapid industrialization and what might be termed the "Europeanization" of the United States. Preferring that most Americans work as farmers, the Jacksonians wanted to ensure that those who did labor in the factories received decent wages and paid reasonable prices for the goods they needed.

Many spokesmen for labor likewise viewed abundant land as a form of protection for industrial workers. George Henry Evans and his *Working Man's Advocate,* for instance, pleaded for a more liberal federal land policy that would enable workers to escape manufacturing for agriculture. As historian Roy Robbins has noted, early leaders of the American labor movement recognized "the difficulties of gaining the desired ends by organizing labor," so they instead "hit upon the idea of free land as a means of attracting the redundant population westward and consequently bringing about higher wages and better working conditions for laboring men in the eastern industrial areas." As an attractive alternative to the arduous task of unionization, legislation to encourage migration from the Northeast to the unsettled prairies of the West greatly appealed to humanitarian reformers. Even a staunch opponent of territorial expansion such as Horace Greeley urged that the government make federal lands more accessible to workers in order to mitigate the ills of industrialization. Alarmed by the unemployment and unrest in New York City following the Panic of 1837, Greeley urged Congress to promote settlement

15. Party discipline prevailed in every state except Pennsylvania. See Charles G. Sellers, *James K. Polk, Continentalist, 1843–1846* (Princeton, 1966), pp. 451–68; Joel H. Silbey, *The Shrine of Party: Congressional Voting Behavior in 1841–1852* (Pittsburgh, 1967), pp. 62–63, 71–73, 81–82.

in the West through land legislation.[16]

Europeans familiar with the baneful effects of widespread manufacturing warned Americans of its risks. Dickens, for example, emphasized the plight of the English working class and stressed the high price that society paid for industrial development. While touring the United States in 1842, Dickens reacted favorably to Lowell, Massachusetts, with its decent working conditions, healthy workers, and wholesome cultural and social life associated with the company boarding-houses. Yet Dickens also recognized Lowell's uniqueness, for it hardly represented American industry in general. Pittsburgh, with "a great quantity of smoke hanging about it," offended his aesthetic sensibilities, and on the whole Dickens remained suspicious of heavy industry. Shortly after Dickens set sail for England, a more pessimistic traveler, John Godley, toured America's industrial centers. He too expressed approval of Lowell but hedged his endorsement with the comment that "the experiment has been tried under eminently favourable circumstances." Americans were temporarily shielded from the worst effects of industrialization because most of their manufactured products came from Britain. "They ought to be only too happy to have our hotbeds of iniquity, at Manchester and Birmingham, to do their dirty work for them, while they revel in the free and happy life of the woodman and farmer," Godley suggested. Unfortunately for the United States, however, the Whigs were attempting to promote manufacturing and to transform the United States into an industrial power—a mistake, since "the evils which a widely-spread manufacturing system carries in its train spring from the operation of clearly-established and universal laws." The inexorable forces of industrial development, Godley concluded, would imperil the United States: population would concentrate in manufacturing areas, a permanent working class would form, wages would fall, factories would spread, and congestion would make effective policing of the lower classes impossible. The United States would find itself in the throes of a massive industrial revolution, wracked by terrible problems similar to Britain's.[17]

16. Roy M. Robbins, *Our Landed Heritage: The Public Domain, 1776–1970,* 2d ed. (Lincoln, Neb., 1976), pp. 98–104. Useful studies dealing with the general condition of American labor during the Jacksonian period are Norman Ware, *The Industrial Worker, 1840–1860: The Reaction of American Industrial Society to the Advance of the Industrial Revolution* (Boston, 1924); Arthur M. Schlesinger, Jr., *The Age of Jackson* (Boston, 1950), pp. 132–43 and passim; Edward Pessen, *Most Uncommon Jacksonians: The Radical Leaders of the Early Labor Movement* (New York, 1967); and Pessen, *Jacksonian America: Society, Personality, and Politics* (Homewood, Ill., 1969), pp. 114–21.

17. Dickens, *American Notes,* pp. 54–60, 134; Godley, *Letters from America,* 1:8, 2:27–29. Godley attributed "the gratifying conditions of the Lowell factories" to "temporary, and what may be called accidental causes" (ibid., 2:29).

Mackay admonished Americans not to rush blindly into industrialization and urged a policy of free trade. He advised them to till the
soil, since "the farmer can virtually manufacture, by means of his
plough, better and more cheaply than can the manufacturer with his
loom." Mackay apparently doubted that his counsel would prevail,
however, for he warned his fellow Britons that the United States
would soon threaten their industrial supremacy. Because of abundant
coal, ample water power, and extraordinary inventiveness, manufacturing in the United States was destined to reach "a colossal magnitude," and this achievement, along with the monopoly of cotton,
would pose a greater threat to England than all the world's armies
and navies combined. Another English observer told Duff Green in
1844 that the United States was fortunate in having an alternative to
mass industrialization. He suggested that Green remind Americans
of "the miseries entailed on human beings by fostering the growth
of a manufacturing population, such as exists in Lancashire—better
to cultivate the prairies of your western states, than to extend your
factories of Lowell." Nothing could be done to reverse the trend of
modernization in Britain: "Here the system has taken root, and with
our overgrown population we must submit to the evil that will inevitably some day arise out of having such large masses thrown out of
employment with no alternative but violence to get their food."
Green recognized Britain's plight, observing that it had "reached a
point where her population trenches upon the means of subsistence."
His sympathy was limited, though: he saw in Britain's problems great
advantages for the United States. What he witnessed in Europe made
him grateful for America's farms and plantations. Like other neo-
Jeffersonians, he hoped to encourage agriculture and foreign trade
while discouraging the spread of manufacturing.[18]

The Industrial Revolution and the Agrarian Counterrevolution: The Democrats Define Alternatives for America

The expansionists were more influenced by negative assessments
of industrialization and urbanization than by positive ones. Though
Americans relied on Britain for most manufactured products, the
expansionists did not believe it necessary for the United States to

18. Mackay, *Western World,* 1:105–15; 3:310; Melville Wilson to Green, April 3,
1844, Duff Green Papers; Green to Edward Everett, January 20, 1842, in Duff Green,
Facts and Suggestions (New York, 1866), p. 148.

develop its own industrial capacity in self-defense. They believed, as explained in Chapter 3, that since the British desperately needed American cotton and grain there was little likelihood that the British government would do anything to jeopardize trade with the United States. Faced with the prospect of domestic upheaval and revolution if trade with the United States were interrupted, Britain would not dare to cut off exports of manufactured products to America.

Many Democratic expansionists, especially Southerners and radical northern locofocos, preferred that the mines, mills, and factories remain in Europe.[19] They could not believe that the Whigs, who sought to stimulate domestic manufacturing, had the true interests of the country at heart. Only obeisance to northern capitalists or subservience to Britain could account for the Whigs' promotion of domestic manufacturing and their opposition to territorial expansion. Throughout the protracted debates on territorial acquisitions, federal land policy, and the tariff, the expansionists equated resistance to their program with treason against the nation. In their view, opposition to territorial extension and encouragement of domestic manufacturing were tantamount to giving aid and comfort to the enemy.

When urging the acquisition of Oregon in 1844, Senator Sevier of Arkansas suggested to his colleagues a common basis for the Whigs' resistance to expansion and their opposition to a more liberal land policy. The Whigs neither desired more land for the people nor wished to make what land there was more accessible to them: "Rather than see the land of the landholder reduced in value by emigration, they would see their poor but honest constituents [become] tenants at will and laborers for life upon the estate of some proud lord of the manor, or forced into the workshops of an exacting manufacturer, from the crumbs of whose table, or from the coffers of whose chest, this wretched class of mortality are to be daily fed." The Whigs, Sevier contended, wanted "no Oregons or new countries for emi-

19. The reactionary ideology of certain Democratic factions deserves more attention. Most studies of the Jacksonian era focus on Jackson's rise to prominence, his flamboyant style, and the dramatic events of his two terms, and often slight the significance of the locofoco world view. Indian removal, to cite just one example, had substantial social and economic ramifications, especially in the South. The voters of Mississippi, Alabama, and Georgia saw in Jackson an ardent expansionist who would open extensive Indian lands to white exploitation. The brutality of Indian removal and the refusal of the Jacksonians to recognize it suggest the extent to which the Democrats would go to provide opportunity and mobility to the average white American.

grants to go to" because migration diminished the political power of the Northeast. Their position, he said, was mistaken and potentially disastrous for the entire country. If all Americans shared "equal political rights, . . . equal privileges, and . . . an equal and proper proportion of the public burdens," if they enjoyed "independence, and ownership in the soil, room, air, and the means of a livelihood, and are not crowded, dependent, and starving," the United States would "never have either treason or rebellion to encounter and conquer."[20]

Congressman Alfred Stone of Ohio joined Sevier in the campaign for All Oregon and like him called for the immediate annexation of Texas. His reasoning was similar. He feared that the United States had reached the point where wages in several branches of industry had dropped below subsistence level. The protective tariff, restrictive land policies, and opposition to expansion all aided the privileged and exploited the masses. "Like causes will produce like results," Stone warned during the House debate on Texas in early 1845, when he compared the United States and Britain. Unless the American govern-ment reversed its policy of favoring manufacturing over agriculture and trade, within half a century the United States would become "like England, a nation of nabobs and paupers." Congressman William J. Brown of Indiana, a free-trade Democrat and an ardent expansionist, concurred in these views. "There is always less moral and political corruption in an agricultural country than in any other," he stressed in the House when promoting the hasty annexation of Texas at this time. Evils such as fraud, perjury, bribery, and corruption appeared "not in the wide-spread West" but only in "the great cities and manufacturing districts, where men are bought and sold in the politi-cal market as oxen in the stall."[21]

Particularly troubled by the social costs of modernization was Rob-ert Walker. During the 1840s, Walker, as a senator and as an adviser to Polk and Tyler, advanced several different policies designed to protect Americans from the perils of modernization. Among these were reductions in the tariff, graduation and preemption legislation, reciprocity treaties, commercial expansion, and, of course, territorial expansion. Walker hoped that the federal government would favor agriculture and guarantee its dominance in the American economy

20. *Congressional Globe* (hereafter abbreviated *CG*), 28 Cong., 1 sess., App. 309–10 (March 21, 1844).
21. *CG*, 28 Cong., 2 sess., App. 226 (January 24, 1845); *CG*, 28 Cong., 2 sess., App. 97 (January 14, 1845)

for many generations to come. In late 1845, for instance, Walker, as treasury secretary, noted that "when the number of manufactories is not great, the power of the system to regulate the wages of labor is inconsiderable; but as the profit of capital invested in manufactures is augmented by the protective tariff, there is a corresponding in-crease of power, until the control of such capital over the wages of labor becomes irresistible." He pointed out that "at least two-thirds of the taxes imposed by the present tariffs are paid, not into the treasury, but to the protected classes." By its tariff policy the govern-ment had arrayed itself with manufacturing against agriculture and trade, and, by augmenting the wealth and power of industrialists, it had nearly decided the struggle in favor of money over men, capital over labor. Workers might resist capital's growing power through walkouts, trade union activity, or "violence and bloodshed," as they had done in Europe, Walker warned. But there was a better way. To redress the balance between the two, Congress must rescind the protective tariff that artificially enriched the manufacturers and finan-ciers while it raised barriers against American exports and burdened consumers with inflated prices.[22]

Reducing the tariff was a step in the right direction, but in Walker's view it alone could not restore an equilibrium between industry and its workers. He also urged Congress to reduce the price of inferior federal lands that had not been sold at prevailing rates in order to accelerate the purchase and settlement of the public domain. Were Congress to lower the cost of these lands, "those who live by the wages of labor could purchase farms . . . and cultivate the soil for themselves and families, instead of working for others twelve hours a day in the manufactories," Walker stressed.[23] A lowering of the price of land "would enhance the wages of labor" by drawing work-ers away from the industrial centers of the Northeast and by creating a scarcity of workers there. Through the law of supply and demand, the migration of laborers from city to country would enhance the wages of those who chose to remain at their machines.

At this time, President Polk joined Walker in his plea to Congress to reduce both the tariff and the price of inferior public lands. Like many other Democrats, Polk held a romanticized agrarian ideal and feared that modernization might soon undermine the foundations of

22. *Report of the Secretary of the Treasury, H. Doc.,* vol. 481, no. 6, 29 Cong., 1 sess. (December 3, 1845), pp. 7–9.
23. Ibid., p. 16.

republican order. He referred to tariff reform as "the most important domestic measure" of his administration, since it would open additional markets to farmers and planters, and facilitate trade.[24] Polk, as his biographer Charles Sellers has noted, possessed "a morally admirable agrarian social philosophy that was by his time so anachronistic as to be reactionary."[25] Polk (and many other expansionists who traced their ideological lineage back to Jefferson and Jackson) thought that American democracy could survive only if the social order remained predominantly agrarian and political power rested in the hands of self-reliant yeomen, planters, and, to a lesser extent, artisans. The field, not the factory, nurtured virtue and promoted equality. There was no place for a national bank, spindles, or assembly lines in the Jeffersonian garden.

Another anxiety that the expansionists inherited from the Jeffersonian past involved a fear of large cities, the offspring of industrial growth. The spread of manufacturing invariably spawned urban concentration, which they regarded as a constant menace to social stability and harmony. Such fears were as old as the Republic itself, for Jefferson had suggested to James Madison as early as 1787 that the United States would enjoy domestic tranquility only so long as its people had ready access to vacant land and toiled chiefly in agriculture. But with depletion of the national domain, no outlet would exist for the country's superfluous population, and Americans would "get piled upon one another in large cities, as in Europe, and go to eating one another as they do there."[26] Jefferson, despite his reputation as a friend of revolution, showed little fondness for its usual agents, the masses of the metropolises. "The mobs of great cities add just so much to the support of pure government, as sores do to the strength of the human body," he had written in his most famous treatise.[27] To

24. Polk's second annual message, in James D. Richardson, ed., *A Compilation of the Messages and Papers of the Presidents*, 10 vols. (New York, 1897), 5 (December 2, 1845):2259–60; *The Diary of James K. Polk During His Presidency, 1845–49*, Milo M. Quaife, ed., 4 vols. (Chicago, 1910), 2 (July 3, 1846):10–11 and (July 29, 1846):55.

25. *James K. Polk, Continentalist*, p. v. See also Sellers, *James K. Polk, Jacksonian, 1795–1843* (Princeton, 1957), p. 7.

26. Quoted in Henry Nash Smith, *Virgin Land: The American West as Symbol and Myth* (Cambridge, Mass., 1950), p. 206. Nash observes that "the safety valve was an imaginative construction which masked poverty and industrial strife with the pleasing suggestion that a beneficent nature stronger than any human agency, the ancient resource of Americans, the power that had made the country rich and great, would solve the new problems of industrialism" (ibid., pp. 205–6).

27. Thomas Jefferson, *Notes on the State of Virginia*, William Peden, ed. (Chapel Hill, N.C., 1955), pp. 164–65. Jefferson advised, "While we have land to labour then, let us never wish to see our citizens occupied at a work-bench, or twirling a distaff."

avoid overcrowding and to maintain republican virtue, Jefferson had urged that domestic manufacturing be limited solely to industries that supplied finished products to the farmer. "For the general operations of manufacture, let our work-shops remain in Europe," he advised.

The vicissitudes of foreign trade caused by the wars of the French Revolution and the Napoleonic wars partly reconciled Jefferson to a mixed economy of agriculture, trade, and a substantial industrial sector.[28] Even before purchasing Louisiana and acquiring extensive Indian lands during his presidency, Jefferson had assured Americans in his inaugural address that they possessed "a chosen country, with room enough for our descendants to the thousandth and thousandth generation." The expansionists of the 1840s, however, feared that Jefferson had erred in his calculations—by about 999 generations. Less confident that the United States had land enough to cope with accelerating economic changes and rapid modernization, the neo-Jeffersonians advanced territorial expansion as a particularly effective means of holding off the dire consequences of industrialization and urbanization.

Several factors heightened anxiety about urbanization during the late Jacksonian period. The recession following the Panic of 1837 increased unemployment and discontent among workers, and this economic distress, often in conjunction with antiblack and antiaboli-tion sentiments, touched off a number of riots in northern cities such as Philadelphia, New York, and Cincinnati between 1837 and 1844.[29]

28. In 1816, Jefferson wrote, "We have experienced what we did not then [in 1785] believe, that there exists both profligacy and power enough to exclude us from the field of interchange with other nations: that to be independent for the comforts of life we must fabricate them ourselves. We must now place the manufacturer by the side of the agriculturalist." He added that "experience has taught me that manufac-tures are now as necessary to our independence as to our comfort" (Jefferson to Benjamin Austin, January 9, 1816, in *The Writings of Thomas Jefferson,* Paul Leicester Ford, ed., 10 vols. [New York, 1892–99]:10:10).

29. In describing the background of the 1837 riot in Alton, Illinois, in which abolitionist Elijah Lovejoy was murdered, Leonard Richards notes, "In March, 1837, the land boom failed, and the price of lead bought and stored by Alton entrepreneurs fell dramatically. In this time of general collapse, Lovejoy began his attack on slavery, and by late June the *Observer* was taking an open, clear-cut, unqualified stand for organized antislavery. . . . Thus the men of Alton, who were already suffering eco-nomic woes and had less confidence in the future than before, faced the terrifying prospect that their community might become a center for organized antislavery." The economic downturn alone, of course, did not cause the antiabolition riots. Richards's data suggests that 1835 and 1836 were the peak years of antiabolition violence. The Panic of 1837 greatly weakened the American Anti-Slavery Society, and its decline eased tensions between abolitionists and their opponents. In the early 1840s, the number of outbreaks dropped substantially. See Leonard L. Richards,

In addition, large numbers of Irish Catholic immigrants settled in northern urban areas in the early 1840s, and their growing presence aroused animosity among fearful nativists who believed that the newcomers would subvert republican government. Burning buildings and rampaging crowds offered striking reminders of the explosive potential in urban masses. Hard statistics caused concern as well. Census data from 1830 and 1840 showed a marked increase in the population of many principal cities such as New York, Boston, Philadelphia, Cincinnati, and Baltimore, and the accompanying rise in crime, prostitution, street violence, and disease intensified apprehensions about urban growth.[30] Such statistics caused Philip Hone some personal misgivings in early 1847: "Our good city of New York has already arrived at the state of society to be found in the large cities of Europe; overburdened with population, and where the two extremes of costly luxury in living, expensive establishments, and improvident waste are presented in daily and hourly contrast with squalid misery and hopeless destitution."[31] This polarization of rich and poor alarmed Americans; many Whigs such as Hone favored restrictions on immigration as the best means of halting the ominous trend, whereas Democrats usually opposed stricter immigration and naturalization laws and instead preferred territorial expansion as the best way to accommodate the population increase.

The Census of 1840, in particular, made the expansionists more sensitive to the problem of population growth and congestion. The statistics revealed a startling pattern in the increase of population: the American people were reproducing their number approximately once every twenty-three years. That domestic growth, in addition to the dramatic influx of impoverished immigrants from Europe, might soon place an intolerable strain on the nation's resources. A rapid rise in population necessitated a rapid extension of territory to support it, expansionists argued. Consequently they set out to find elbow room for future generations of Americans, natives and newcomers alike.

As early as 1842, Illinois senator Samuel McRoberts had relied on the recent census returns when he had urged Congress to take control

---

Gentlemen of Property and Standing: Anti-Abolition Mobs in Jacksonian America (New York, 1970), pp. 102–11, 157–61. Richards found no consistent correlation between party affiliation and antiabolition violence.

30. Pessen, *Jacksonian America*, pp. 59–72.

31. *The Diary of Philip Hone, 1828–1851*, Bayard Tuckerman, ed., 2 vols. (New York, 1889), 2 (January 29, 1847):293–94.

of the entire Oregon territory. Prior to the census, "It might have been thought that we had territory enough; and that, for some generations, we would not have use for more," he observed. But the two previous censuses had revealed "that we may calculate on our population being doubled every twenty-three or twenty-four years." "We have to act for those who are to succeed us," he advised. Other northwestern Democrats shared his concern. Congressman Andrew Kennedy of Indiana also believed that the federal government must acquire land for its steadily rising population. "Our people are spreading out with the aid of the American multiplication table," he told the House in early 1846. "Go to the West and see a young man with his mate of eighteen; after the lapse of thirty years, visit him again, and instead of two, you will find twenty-two. That is what I call the American multiplication table." To Kennedy, then, the simple arithmetic of population growth necessitated territorial acquisitions. Ohio congressman William Sawyer implored Congress to evict Britain from the entire continent at this time, stressing that the United States would soon require "every foot of territory" on the continent for its rapidly growing population. When editor O'Sullivan coined the phrase *manifest destiny* in mid-1845, he too discussed the relationship between population and territorial expansion. He looked to Texas, Oregon, and California as crucial outlets for the American population, destined to reach "two hundred and fifty millions (if not more)" within a century's time.[32]

The war against Mexico and the American conquest of its sparsely settled northern provinces renewed speculation on the connection between population and resources. Many expansionists viewed the borderlands as a providential bequest capable of absorbing the nation's excess population for decades to come. During the debate on the Mexican War, Senator Daniel Dickinson of New York excoriated the antiexpansionists, contending that the population of the United States would reach one hundred million by the turn of the century and that the country would need at least California and New Mexico to absorb that momentous increase.[33] Caleb Cushing observed in 1847 that Anglo-Americans were on the verge of surpassing their British rivals in population, wealth, and power. "The British Isles have already reached that fatal term in the history of nations when

32. *CG*, 27 Cong., 3 sess., 100 (December 30, 1842); *CG*, 29 Cong., 1 sess., 180 (January 10, 1846); *CG*, 29 Cong., 1 sess., App. 228 (February 3, 1846); "Annexation," *Democratic Review*, 17 (July, 1845):7; New York *Morning News*, December 27, 1845.
33. *CG*, 30 Cong., 1 sess., 157–58 (January 12, 1848).

their native land can no longer feed its sons," he suggested. In contrast, the United States was "still expanding with a rapidity and strength of possession which defies calculation."[34] The military triumphs over Mexico and the prospect of a large territorial indemnity boded well for the American empire, Cushing thought.

Cushing seemed optimistic, but most expansionists recognized that a booming population was a mixed blessing. An abundant population was one feature that distinguished a great empire, but congestion could provide enough combustible material to reduce a country to smoldering ruins within days. Perhaps the United States too would reach "that fatal term in the history of nations" when its territory could "no longer feed its sons." Proponents of commercial and territorial expansion during the 1840s assumed that the United States could escape Malthus's grim projections, but their confidence was premised on the perpetual availability of an extensive and cheap reserve of land. That reserve diverted workers from industrial centers to fertile fields and eased urban congestion; it guaranteed steady employment at remunerative wages for industrial workers; it safeguarded the country from labor violence and class conflict. Territorial expansion meant far more to the nation's welfare than meliorative legislation or philanthropic reforms, however well-intentioned or humane.

A neo-Jeffersonian propensity to define progress primarily in terms of an ever-expanding frontier distinguished the expansionists from their opponents. Few prominent expansionists participated in the many reform movements of the period, because they preferred instead to alleviate internal hardship by pushing the country's borders outward and by fostering settlement on the frontier. To a large extent, in fact, the expansionists refused to confront the realities of industrial and urban distress, for they seemed permanently wedded to a vision of a rural arcadia characterized by dispersed and largely autonomous farms and plantations. Indifferent or contemptuous toward reform or religious movements such as abolitionism, temperance, women's rights, pacifism, and Mormonism, the locofocos were downright hostile to any government intrusion into the private lives of the people. The Democrats' belief in territorial and commercial

34. *Niles' National Register*, 71–72 (August 7, 1847): 361. In mid-1846 a writer in the *Democratic Review* estimated that Britain contained 1.5 million paupers and suggested that "the manufacturing greatness of the British islands has outgrown their capacity to feed the operatives" ("Practical Annexation of England," *Democratic Review*, 19 [July, 1846]:5).

expansion as a panacea for the country's ills would later provide evidence for Frederick Jackson Turner's safety valve thesis.[35] A frontier obviated the need for an active government and made social reform unnecessary.

The domestic and foreign policies of the Tyler and Polk administrations can be seen as part of a comprehensive strategy aimed at protecting the internal security of the nation by promoting agriculture and softening the effects of rapid industrialization and urbanization. As noted earlier, Tyler sent Duff Green to London to negotiate a reduction of import duties on American staples. Although Green's chief concern in England turned from the tariff to Texas, he continued to urge a repeal of the Corn Laws and the importation of more American foodstuffs. In addition, Tyler sent Cushing to China to open its ports to more American products, and Henry Wheaton negotiated the *Zollverein* treaty with the German states for the same purpose. Persistent efforts to open foreign markets to farmers and planters continued under Polk. Both McLane and Bancroft worked to dismantle the trade barriers surrounding the British Empire, to break what Bancroft called "the paper chains that bind the oceans."[36] Minister to Prussia Andrew Jackson Donelson sought to persuade that country's leaders to import more American foodstuffs and staples, and William H. Polk negotiated in Italy and Sicily with the same goal.

The many Democrats who shared this anxiety about modernization and rapid growth believed that prices for food and staples had to be attractive enough to entice the vast majority of Americans into agriculture and that high prices could be maintained only by exporting a substantial portion of what was produced. If repeated domestic gluts occurred without a foreign outlet to absorb the surplus, agrarian

35. In his 1903 essay, "Contributions of the West to American Democracy," Turner wrote, "Whenever social conditions tended to crystallize in the East, whenever capital tended to press upon labor or political restraints to impede the freedom of the mass, there was this gate of escape to the free conditions of the frontier. These free lands promoted individualism, economic equality, freedom to rise, democracy. Men would not accept inferior wages and a permanent position of social subordination when this promised land of freedom and equality was theirs for the taking" (in his *Frontier in American History* [New York, 1920], p. 259).

36. Bancroft, in mid-1848, wrote to Caleb Cushing, "You know I formed an opinion about 1830, that the British colonial system under its character of commercial monopoly, could not last a quarter of a century more; and I was willing to attempt to contribute something towards hastening the period, when the few remaining paper chains that bind the oceans, are to be broken" (Bancroft to Cushing, June 23, 1848, Caleb Cushing Papers). See also Richard Rush to Cushing, June 16, 1842, in ibid.

producers might be forced to seek work in manufacturing. The desirable flow of the population to the country from the city would be
reversed, and the depression in agriculture might soon spread to
industry. Neither the field nor the factory could then provide economic security to the mass of Americans under such conditions:
disaster must follow.

To encourage exports and to assist agrarians, both the Tyler and
Polk administrations paid special attention to naval strategy and
improvements in the fleet. Navy secretary Abel Upshur warned Congress in 1842 that two-thirds of American trade, including much of
the country's cotton and grain exports, had to pass through the
Caribbean and the narrow Gulf of Florida—a vital commercial artery
that could be cut off by only two enemy steam frigates. "A commerce,
such as ours, *demands* the protection of an adequate naval force,"
Upshur stressed, recommending that American ships be kept in active
service and moved frequently in order to safeguard American trade.
Polk and his advisers agreed that a more powerful navy was needed.
In his first annual message, Polk requested "liberal appropriations"
for iron war steamers, since "the productions of the interior which
seek a market abroad are directly dependent on the safety and freedom of our commerce." Navy secretary George Bancroft applauded
the opening of the Annapolis naval school in 1845 in his report to
Congress that year, but he repeated Upshur's complaint when he
noted that "in comparison with other nations, our navy is poorly
supplied with sea going steamers." Convinced that trade would follow the flagship, the Tyler and Polk administrations repeatedly called
upon Congress to improve and expand the navy.[37] Like tariff reductions, then, naval appropriations can be viewed as a form of federal
assistance to farmers, planters, and merchants who needed foreign
markets. Tyler, Polk, and their advisers placed highest priority on
expanding American trade and treated defense of coastal areas as a
secondary concern. Here again, domestic economic considerations
significantly affected national "defense" policies.

37. On Tyler, see Richardson, *Messages and Papers,* 4(December 7, 1841):1941,
5(December 5, 1843):2122, and (February 23, 1844):2131-32. On Polk, see ibid.
(December 2, 1845):2262-63, and ibid. (December 7, 1847):2411-12. For Upshur's
and Bancroft's remarks, see *Report of the Secretary of the Navy, S. Doc.,* vol. 413, no. 1,
27 Cong., 3 sess. (December, 1842):539-41, and *Report of the Secretary of the Navy, S.
Doc.,* vol. 470, no. 1, 29 Cong., 1 sess. (December 1, 1845):649. On American naval
policy for this time period, see Harold and Margaret Sprout, *The Rise of American Naval
Power, 1776-1918* (Princeton, 1939), pp. 110-36.

All of these measures—a more liberal land policy, reduction of the tariff, acquisition of markets, and naval improvements—could not in themselves quell the expansionists' apprehensions. They believed territorial expansion to be absolutely essential to the country. Most incisive in analyzing the relationship between domestic order, prosperity, and expansion was the Jacksonian journal the *Democratic Review.* In the summer of 1846, O'Sullivan turned the editor's desk over to Thomas Kettell, a former finance editor for Bennett. But O'Sullivan's departure did not change the overall outlook of the *Review,* partly because he continued to write for it after Kettell assumed control.[38] A striking article on expansion and political principles appeared in the August 1846 issue, its substance and style suggesting that O'Sullivan was its author. The Whigs were trying to chain free men to "the steam engine and the loom," the writer complained, whereas the Democrats were struggling to protect them from wage servitude. The author preferred the Democrats' approach to the challenge of providing prosperity and security to the American people: "The general policy of the democracy is to favor the settlement of the land, spread the bounds of the future empire, and to favor, by freedom of intercourse and external commerce, the welfare of the settlers, . . . men of simple habits and strong hands, looking to mother-earth for their only capital, and to their own labor as the sole means of making it productive."[39] Neither Jefferson, Jackson, Polk, or Walker had ever expressed the Democratic creed more succinctly or more accurately than this. Particularly revealing was the assertion that one of the Democrats' three crucial policies was to "spread the bounds of the future empire." In other words, just as the federal government should encourage settlement of the public domain and promote free trade, so too should it acquire territory. To the Democrats the goal of territorial expansion was so critical that the means—whether purchase, forced removal, diplomacy, or conquest—were secondary. The *Democratic Review* reiterated its commitment to aggrandizement in 1847 when it observed, "Until every acre of the North American continent is occupied by citizens of the United States, the foundation of the future empire will not have been laid. The chief evil of Europe, that which oppresses England, and destroys Ireland, is the exclusion of the people from the soil."[40]

38. Landon Edward Fuller, "The *United States Magazine and Democratic Review,* 1837–1859, A Study of Its History, Contents and Significance," (Ph.D. dissertation, University of North Carolina, 1948), pp. 84–88.

39. "Legislative Embodyment of Public Opinion," *Democratic Review,* 19 (August, 1846):86.

40. "New Territory versus No Territory," *Democratic Review,* 21 (October, 1847):291.

Throughout the 1840s, O'Sullivan and Kettell urged the government to make abundant land available to the American people so that
the country could avoid the ills debilitating Europe. This became a
standard argument in behalf of expansion. Speaking in support of the
annexation of Texas in early 1845, Brown of Indiana told his fellow
lawmakers that he could "show that white slavery, as it exists in the
manufacturing districts at the North, would be greatly diminished by
opening a wide field for emigration to those who are now bound
down by toil in the steam and grease-scented manufactures of the
North." On the prairies of the West the workers could "become
owners of the soil, and be freemen indeed." Daniel Dickinson stressed
the importance of expansion in 1845 by contrasting the plight of the
Old World with the promise of the new. The struggle between England and the United States over Oregon, he told the Senate, represented "not a mere struggle for . . . distant territory" but also "a
contest between two great systems—between monarchy and freedom, . . . between the mines and manufactures of Europe and the
fertile fields of the distant West."[41] Fearful of wage servitude in the
North, Democrats such as Brown and Dickinson warned that England
sought to contain American expansion in order to foment domestic
disturbances in the United States. Without an extensive domain accessible to all Americans, industrialization and urbanization might
weaken the United States just as they had weakened Britain.

Despite the rhetorical excesses of partisan Democrats who tried to
blame the Whigs for the nation's economic problems, a fundamental
difference did exist between the parties on the question of the relationship between capital, labor, and government. Democrats rejected
any notion of a concert of interest between employers and employees
and dismissed the Whig argument that a protective tariff benefited
all classes. To assist workers and to protect the Jeffersonian ideal of
a predominantly agrarian society, the expansionists advocated a revenue tariff, open foreign markets, and territorial additions.

Jacksonian stalwart, Senator Cass of Michigan, argued in 1847 that
the Mexican War provided the United States with a golden opportunity to obtain ample land for its growing population. As minister to
France from 1837 to 1842, Cass had witnessed severe hardship there
as well as in England. "In Europe, one of the social evils is concentration," he observed. "Men are brought too much and kept too much
in contact. There is no room for expansion. Minds of the highest

41. *CG*, 28 Cong., 2 sess., App. 98 (January 14, 1845); *CG*, 29 Cong., 1 sess., App.
327 (February 25, 1846).

order are pressed down by adverse circumstances, without the power of free exertion." The Old World was in decline because it suffered "the evils of a dense population, with scanty means of subsistence, and with no hope of advancement." Hoping to avoid similar conditions in the United States, Cass advised Congress to acquire ample territory for future generations. "I trust we are far removed from all this; but to remove us further yet, we want almost unlimited power of expansion," he declared. "That is our safety valve."[42] Cass had earlier backed the annexation of Texas and had marched in the vanguard of the fifty-four forty corps, but the acquisitions of 1845 and 1846 had not satisfied his territorial ambitions. He called upon the Senate to approve the military appropriations necessary to enable the United States to acquire a large territorial indemnity from Mexico. At this time he advocated that Mexico surrender all its land north of the Sierra Madre Mountains to the United States. Within a year Cass was trying to convince his colleagues to annex all Mexico.

Calhoun's reaction to the war has confused many scholars of American expansion. In February 1847, Calhoun called for the United States to stop its active prosecution of the war and recommended instead that American forces be withdrawn to a "defensive line" running along the Rio Grande to the thirty-second parallel and then west to the Gulf of California and the Pacific. John Fuller, the most noted scholar of the "All Mexico" movement, has contended that "it was pro-slavery Calhoun who stood out as the leading anti-imperialist in Congress and perhaps in the country." In the same vein, Frederick Merk concluded that Calhoun, "outstanding in stature among Southern Democrats, opposed taking much, if any, Mexican territory." John Schroeder, in his excellent study of the opposition to the Mexican War, found Calhoun's position on territorial expansion and the method by which he arrived at it problematic as well. And in a recent incisive look at Calhoun and the war, Ernest M. Lander suggested that Calhoun, "for the sake of unity within his home state," sanctioned "an imperialist grab that he knew was fraught with danger for his region." Calhoun supported expansion, Lander concluded, because of political pressures in South Carolina.[43] But economic and racial

42. *CG,* 29 Cong., 2 sess., 367–68 (February 10, 1847).
43. John Douglas Pitts Fuller, *The Movement for the Acquisition of All Mexico, 1846–1848* (Baltimore, 1936), p. 101; Frederick Merk, *Manifest Destiny and Mission in American History: A Reinterpretation* (New York, 1963), p. 152; *History of the Westward Movement* (New York, 1978), pp. 368–69; John H. Schroeder, *Mr. Polk's War: American Opposition and Dissent, 1846–1848* (Madison, 1973); Ernest McPherson Lander, Jr., *Reluctant Imperialists: Calhoun, the South Carolinians, and the Mexican War* (Baton Rouge, 1980), pp. 68–79, 175.

concerns were as important to Calhoun as political ones, and he was hardly a "leading anti-imperialist." He wanted new territory but only insofar as white Americans could occupy and dominate it to the exclusion of its nonwhite inhabitants. As Calhoun's racism grew stronger, his imperialism waned in proportion. His repugnance toward nonwhite peoples best explains his opposition to the All Mexico movement.

In an address to the Senate in early 1847, Calhoun had in fact emphasized his agreement with Democrats who desired a large territorial indemnity from Mexico. "What we want is space for our growing population," he told an overcrowded chamber when supporting the permanent acquisition of California and New Mexico. Drawing again upon the Census of 1840, Calhoun reminded his colleagues that the nation's population was doubling every twenty-three years and predicted, "For this rapidly growing population, all the territory we now possess, and even that which we might acquire, would, in the course of a few generations, be needed." The country needed territory for its "growing population," but Calhoun qualified his statement by adding, "What we ought to avoid, is the addition of other population, of a character not suited to our institutions." And he concluded, "It is better for our people and institutions, that our population should not be too much compressed."[44]

Calhoun also expressed his fears of overcrowding in letters to his daughter Anna, who was living in Brussels with her husband Thomas G. Clemson, American chargé there from 1844 to 1848. Anna reported the widespread poverty and oppression in Europe to her father and contrasted the bleak situation there with the brighter prospects at home. Calhoun agreed that a young, rapidly advancing country was preferable to an older, less dynamic one and said that he himself would like to live on the American frontier. "So strongly do I feel the charms of a growing and improving country, that I would be much disposed to place myself on the very verge of the advancing population and growth of our country, were I to follow my inclination," he wrote to her in late 1846. He cautioned his daughter, several months later, against assuming that the United States was immune to the perils plaguing Europe. "We are for the present far better off," he admitted, "but it may be doubted whether we are not treading the path, that will lead in the end to a similar or worse state."[45] Calhoun

44. *CG*, 29 Cong., 2 sess., App. 325 (February 9, 1847).
45. Calhoun to Anna Clemson, November 21, 1846, and June 10, 1847, in J. Franklin Jameson, ed., "Correspondence of John C. Calhoun," *Annual Report of the American Historical Association for the Year 1899* (Washington, 1900), 2:712, 730-31.

worried that the indebtedness incurred during the war would serve as justification for the reimposition of a higher tariff, and he also feared that the Whigs would gain control of the government in 1848. Neither prospect pleased him. Contemplating the future deeply disturbed Calhoun, for it might bring an oppressive tariff; impoverishment of planters, farmers, and workers; and the rise of a manufacturing aristocracy. He dreaded consolidation and congestion and saw in territorial expansion a way to mitigate the ills of modernization.

Other Democrats followed the lead of Cass and Calhoun. Congressman Thomas Turner of Illinois accused the Whig party of trying to shackle workers through its policies on the tariff, land sales, banking, and expansion. "Extension and expansion are preeminently democratic, but the anti-war Whigs prefer the government of corporations," he complained in 1848. Since only abundant land had protected Americans from degradation in the past, the Whigs should not resist further acquisitions. "The great West has found an outlet for our people, and thus has frustrated their designs," he asserted. "But circumscribe our limits, give corporations the controlling influence, and white slavery will be substituted for black. . . . Wherever corporations rule, the great mass of the people are enslaved," Turner observed. He implored Congress to protect the population by seizing a vast territorial indemnity from Mexico.[46]

During 1847 and 1848, Europe slipped toward the brink of revolution, and Americans there reported the ominous developments to the Polk administration. These reports dramatized the inescapable consequences of exclusionary landownership and industrialization—congestion, exploitation of workers, poverty among farmers, class divisions, and social disorder—all conditions that might be introduced into the United States by the growth of manufacturing and constraints on expansion. In early 1847, Bancroft informed Buchanan that "in Ireland the number of officials employed in distributing charity, is larger than our usual army; and the moneys required by the misery of the pauper population of that wretched island from the national revenues of Great Britain, will sweep away every trace of the economy of past years, and will amount to a larger sum than all our expenditures for the Mexican War." In October, he again noted that

46. *CG*, 30 Cong., 1 sess., App. 512 (April 6, 1848). Senator Henry Johnson of Louisiana noted, "Our increase of territory has diluted our population. It has cheapened the price of land; this has invited [our population] to the pursuits of agriculture; and, in all ages, agriculture has been friendly to the promotion of peace, frugality, and virtue" (*CG*, 30 Cong., 1 sess., App. 379 [March 16, 1848]).

the condition of Britain was "sad beyond measure in all that relates to the labouring classes." Bancroft reassured the administration that England and France were so preoccupied with internal problems that they dared not interfere in American affairs. Europe could not contest American expansion beyond the Rio Grande; the United States could take what it wanted from Mexico without fear of reprisals from Europe.[47]

Minister Andrew Jackson Donelson in Berlin watched in horror in early 1848 as Prussian troops used artillery in the city streets to smash barricades and exterminate dissidents. Donelson's own dwelling was placed under heavy guard, since he resided in a building shared with members of the Prussian government. He notified Buchanan in February that German emigration to the United States was increasing substantially because of the strife in Central Europe. The continent seemed in the depths of despair, "thousands dying for want—its millions without a conception of that personal independence on which our system rests—its territorial divisions, nationalized by the accident of brute force, with but little regard to homogeneousness of character and interests or to the principles of political equality." With all of Europe about to burst into flames, he was relieved to be merely a sojourner in a troubled land.[48]

When Bennett returned to Europe for eighteen months in 1846–47 to obtain correspondents to improve the *Herald*'s coverage of international news, he scrutinized social and political conditions there and relayed his impressions to American readers. Bennett found the plight of the Old World deplorable, but he viewed the suffering in Europe chiefly in terms of how it could be exploited by the United States. In Europe's countless distresses Bennett saw substantial advantages for his own country. The United States, he suggested, could expand across the continent with impunity because both England and France were too distracted to interfere in North America. "Each country is too much occupied with its own domestic difficulties—each is too anxious for peace and commerce with the United States—each de-

---

47. Bancroft to Buchanan, February 3 and October 18, 1847; Bancroft to Polk, January 19, May 14, and November 18, 1847, in M. A. DeWolfe Howe, *The Life and Letters of George Bancroft,* 2 vols. (New York, 1908), 2:9, 23–24, 7–8, 17–18, 28. See also Bancroft to William H. Prescott, March 3, 1847, Bancroft to William Cullen Bryant, November 3, 1847, and Bancroft to Buchanan, March 24, 1848, in ibid., pp. 15, 26–27, 33.

48. Donelson to Buchanan, February 26, March 4, and April 1, 1848, Andrew Jackson Donelson Papers. See also Donelson to A. J. Donelson, Jr., March 28, 1848, and Donelson to Buchanan, June 4, 1848, in ibid.

pends too much on being fed by our corn, and clothed by our cotton," he boasted in early 1847.[49] They were so dependent, he asserted a few months later, that they were "tied hand and foot, bound to the stake of peace and starvation, from which they cannot get away."[50] To Bennett, traditional military considerations were not applicable at this time: overpopulation, bad harvests, class conflict, and social upheaval in Europe were liabilities for which no quantity of ships or soldiers could compensate.

These missives from Europe served as poignant reminders of what could happen if the United States were corrupted by the forces of modernization. By the mid-1840s, few American expansionists believed that their nation was likely to suffer a sustained assault from abroad. Rather, the United States encountered its greatest dangers at home. Internal discord and divisions posed a more serious threat than foreign military forces. The acquisition of New Mexico and California, like that of Texas, served primarily to alleviate either actual or anticipated domestic ills. To the expansionists of the late Jacksonian period, the nation's domestic problems and European policy in North America were closely related. Britain did not have to invade the United States to imperil its security: containing American expansion and limiting its commerce could undermine the nation's welfare. Whatever the risks, the expansionists believed extensive acquisitions were needed to foster democracy, opportunity, and geographical and social mobility. America had to be saved from the excrescences of Federalism and Whiggism, or it would repeat the errors of the European countries. The United States, established as a self-conscious repudiation of European social and political mores, must not surrender its national purpose by adopting Old World ways.

President Polk, a career politician and not a penetrating thinker, rarely pondered the long-range significance of his policies. He tended to evaluate events in terms of their impact on partisan politics. But in his final annual message in late 1848 he speculated about the importance of the territory acquired during his presidency. His administration, he estimated, had obtained almost 1.2 million square miles of land for the United States, increasing the national domain by some 50 percent. Looking back over the course of American development, Polk wondered "whether if our present population had been confined within the limits of the original thirteen states the

49. New York *Herald,* March 1 and May 19, 1847.
50. New York *Herald,* June 6, 1847.

tendencies to centralization and consolidation would not have been such" as to alter fundamentally the character of American society and politics.[51] His impression was that territorial expansion had provided an "additional guaranty for the preservation of the union itself," an observation that indicated how closely intertwined empire and republicanism had become for the neo-Jeffersonians. American history seemed to validate the view that expansion fostered liberty and mobility. But old republican certitudes had become new uncertainties during the Mexican War. By late 1848, the Democrats were badly divided on the territorial question; many recognized that expansion had drawbacks, too. That split among the Jacksonians signified an important shift in American politics and precipitated the series of events that eventually climaxed in civil war in 1861.

Continentalism and Jeffersonianism: The Struggle for the Far West

The sectional consciousness spurred by the Wilmot Proviso demonstrated the intensity of two different fears, one becoming increasingly important in the North and the other of long-term concern to the South. If slavery were permitted to spread into New Mexico and California, then many northern Democrats feared that industrialization and concentration would increase in their section, since white workers would refuse to migrate to an area where slaves and freedmen would degrade white labor. Southern Democrats (and many southern Whigs), on the other hand, worried that any restriction on the extension of slavery into the Southwest would confine their rapidly growing black population to the slave states themselves. As southern whites without slaves headed west in search of opportunity, planters and their families would be left behind in the midst of a disproportionately large number of blacks. Disturbed by these respective apprehensions, certain leaders from each section became convinced that the other was conspiring to obtain absolute control over new lands for its exclusive benefit. Men such as Polk, Walker, Cass, Buchanan, and Douglas continued to regard expansion as a panacea for the nation's ills, but other Democrats, both northern and southern, became increasingly skeptical. Polk's campaign of conquest in 1846, so soon after the annexation of Texas, placed lawmakers from the free states in a predicament. Should slavery be permitted to

51. Richardson, *Message and Papers,* 5 (December 5, 1848):2493–94.

expand across the entire continent to the Pacific? Wilmot of Pennsylvania did not think so.

On a sizzling hot August night in 1846, Wilmot proposed to add to a war appropriation bill an amendment providing that "as an express and fundamental condition to the acquisition of any territory from the Republic of Mexico . . . neither slavery nor involuntary servitude shall ever exist in any part of said territory, except for crime, whereof the party shall first be duly convicted."[52] By this time it was apparent that Polk would demand a large territorial indemnity from Mexico, and Wilmot wanted Congress to determine the status of that territory before it became an integral part of the Union. His interjection of the issue of the extension of slavery into the debate on the war contributed to the mounting frustration on Capitol Hill: the debate over the Walker Tariff had been intense and acrimonious; tempers had flared during the protracted discussion of the Oregon question; the border skirmish with Mexico had become an offensive war; Polk had just vetoed a popular Rivers and Harbors bill; and Washington was prostrated by the infernal weather. "Preachers here never talk of the heat of the place below," observed a New York *Herald* reporter. "The good people of this city would think it an insult to their understanding to be told of any place more insufferably hot than Washington."[53] Wilmot's gambit raised the temperature a few more degrees, at least in the halls of Congress.

Wilmot had steadfastly marched to the administration's drum during the first session of the Twenty-Ninth Congress. He had supported the claim to all of Oregon; he had endorsed budget increases for the navy; he had sustained Polk's veto of internal improvement legislation; he had violated the instructions of his state legislature by voting for the Walker Tariff (the only member of the Pennsylvania delegation to do so); and he had heartily endorsed the declaration of war against Mexico. His introduction of the Free-Soil amendment represented his first deviation from the administration's program. But in announcing his opposition to the extension of slavery, Wilmot labored to minimize the differences between himself and other Demo-

52. *CG,* 29 Cong., 1 sess., 1217 (August 8, 1846).
53. New York *Herald,* August 18, 1846. Senator John Fairfield of Maine complained about the mood of the "sorry-looking set of fellows" at his boarding house at this time. "Our faces when we meet at breakfast are as long as a turnpike, and as solemn as a tombstone," he noted (Fairfield to Virginia E. Dickinson, August 2, 1846, in John R. Dickinson, ed., *Speeches, Correspondence, etc. of the Late Daniel S. Dickinson of New York,* 2 vols. [New York, 1867], 2:384).

crats. In his August 8 speech, he reaffirmed his commitment to territorial expansion, reminding House members that he had enthusiastically supported the annexation of Texas as a slave state in 1845.
Slavery had already existed there, and he had been willing to admit
the state on that basis. Slavery had been forbidden by Mexican law
in New Mexico and California, however, and Wilmot wanted that
prohibition sustained.[54] But Congress adjourned on August 10 without approving the proviso or the appropriation bill.

After Congress adjourned, Wilmot came under attack for his controversial amendment. Six months after presenting the proviso, Wilmot again addressed his peers to clarify his position and to dispel the
misapprehensions surrounding the measure. "I make no war upon
the South," he protested in early 1847. "I have no squeamish sensi-
tiveness on the subject of slavery—no morbid sympathy for the
slave." In calling for an exclusion on slavery's expansion, he sought
to preserve for whites "a fair country, a rich inheritance, where the
sons of toil, of my own race and own color, can live without the
disgrace which association with negro slavery brings upon free labor."[55]
Wilmot denied that he was an abolitionist and denied as well that his
proviso violated previous views expressed by Southerners themselves
on the extension of slavery. To accentuate this point he turned the
clock back three years to the time of the Texas crisis and recalled:
"Walker told you, when he was urging the annexation of Texas, (and
I admit the force of his argument), annex Texas, and you open a
frontier of two thousand miles bordering on Mexico, where this slave
and black population, as it shall increase and press upon the country,
can pass off, and become mingled up with the mixed races of Mexico
and South America."[56] Walker had pledged in 1844 that slavery
would not extend west of the Rio Grande if the United States acquired
Texas as a reservoir for the nation's black population. Now, in early
1847, the administration in which Walker was the most influential
adviser favored unrestricted access to new territories for slaveholders
and free laborers alike, at least in the area below 36° 30'. Wilmot and
a number of northern Democrats who formed the Free-Soil faction
in 1846 could not accept that: the South must abide by Walker's
promise, and Texas, not California, must serve as the final repository
for the country's unwanted black population.

54. Several other Free-Soil Democrats supported exclusion on this basis. See, for
instance, the important statement by Barnburner John Dix of New York, CG, 29
Cong., 2 sess., 542–43 (March 1, 1847).
55. CG, 29 Cong., 2 sess., 354, App. 317 (February 8, 1847)
56. CG, 29 Cong., 2 sess., 355 (February 8, 1847).

Wilmot's maneuver was ingenious, a master stroke that has not yet been placed in its proper context by historians. Charles Buxton Going attributed the proviso to Wilmot's revulsion toward slavery. "Wil-mot, finding that he could not follow both the President and his own principles, chose the latter," he concluded. Other historians, in seek-ing the origins of the Free-Soil movement, have also neglected the long-term impact of the Texas crisis.[57] The accepted interpretations of Wilmot's conduct are not entirely compatible with his political course, nor do they comply with Wilmot's own candid explanation of his motives and objectives. He did not oppose slavery in the abstract. He had supported the administration and had not accused it of subservience to the South. His purpose was simply to keep blacks out of the far West.

Wilmot's strategy was little short of brilliant. Calling to account the southern Democrats and their northern cohorts who had been the most spirited expansionists during the previous three years, he placed them at a disadvantage by reminding the public of their propaganda pledges of 1844 and 1845. He offered them a choice: they could reaffirm their commitment to the Rio Grande as the final barrier to the westward expansion of slavery, or they could confess that Walker's pamphlet and the speeches and editorials on gradual emancipation and removal that it had inspired were mere ruses to secure Texas for more sordid reasons. If the expansionists admitted that the slave-drain theory had only been a subterfuge, they would have to ac-knowledge that a resolution of the nation's racial crisis was no closer now than three years earlier. Moreover, if slavery were now sanc-tioned beyond the Rio Grande, Wilmot and others could blame several prominent Democrats for deliberate deception, among them cabinet members Walker, Buchanan, and Dallas; senators Allen, Breese, and Dickinson; and editors O'Sullivan and Bennett. Wilmot had re-trieved the Texas annexation propaganda brush from the Democratic closet and had painted the southern Democrats and northern dough-faces into a tight corner with it. He left them no means of escape.

Rumors in Washington during the summer of 1846 suggested that the Polk administration would accept only a partial exclusion on the

57. Charles Buxton Going, *David Wilmot, Free-Soiler* (New York, 1924), p. 143; Glyndon G. Van Deusen, *The Jacksonian Era, 1828–1848* (New York, 1959), p. 242; Chaplain W. Morrison, *Democratic Politics and Sectionalism: The Wilmot Proviso Controversy* (Chapel Hill, N.C., 1967), p. 181n; Joseph G. Rayback, *Free Soil: The Election of 1848* (Lexington, Ky., 1970), pp. 23–26; David Potter, *The Impending Crisis, 1848–1861* (New York, 1976), pp. 22–27; Merk, *History of the Westward Movement,* p. 370.

extension of slavery into the borderlands. Wilmot's and other Free-Soilers' suspicions were confirmed in early 1847, when Ritchie complained that the proviso was "calculated to divide our councils, to paralyze our exertions, and to animate the enemy by the prospect of our own divisions."[58] Wilmot certainly must not have appreciated the inference that he was a traitor, but he probably appreciated even less Ritchie's recommending that the Missouri Compromise line be drawn to the Pacific. The veil had been lifted: Polk, Walker, Buchanan, and virtually every southern Democrat in Congress (and probably southern Whigs as well) would demand that slavery be allowed to expand into California. Perhaps they would demand that the entire Southwest cession be open to masters and their slaves.

Since 1842, radical antislavery Whigs such as Joshua Giddings, John Quincy Adams, and Salmon Chase had been insisting that southerners dominated the Democratic party for their own selfish ends.[59] Ritchie's statement on the proviso seemed to validate that charge. The Free-Soil revolt, then, emerged as a logical response to what might be termed "the great betrayal." The outrage felt by Wilmot and others originated in the Texas question, not in the disputes over the tariff, Oregon, patronage, or internal improvements. Wilmot sought to transform Walker's 1844 promise into law: slavery and a black population must not be permitted to sully the Pacific Coast.

Congressman Preston King of New York, a close friend of Wilmot's, best explained why a Free-Soil West was so important to the North. King reintroduced the proviso during the first week of 1847 and warned his free-state colleagues that "if slavery is not excluded by law, the presence of the slave will exclude the laboring white man." Paying homage to the substance and spirit of the Northwest Ordinance of 1787, he praised the founding fathers for having saved the states of the old Northwest "from the evils of slavery and a black

---

58. Washington *Daily Union,* January 11, 1847.

59. Scott Alan Schoen, "Antislavery Whig Politics: Joshua Reed Giddings, John Quincy Adams and the Tactics of Sectional Protest in the 1840s" (Senior essay, Yale College, 1980). Eric Foner analyzes the idea of a slave power conspiracy in *Free Soil, Free Labor, Free Men: The Ideology of the Republican Party before the Civil War* (New York, 1970), pp. 73–102. In early 1842, Salmon Chase wrote to Giddings, "It will not do to compromise anymore. The principle must be established and acquiesced in that the government is a non-slaveholding government—that the nation is a non-slaveholding nation—that slavery is a custom of state law—local—not to be extended or favored, but to be confined within the states which admit and sanction it." Chase to Giddings, February 15, 1842, Giddings Papers. Chase was instrumental in the formation of Ohio's Liberty Party in 1841–42.

population." Like Wilmot, King argued that Texas had been annexed to provide a refuge for free blacks and slaves until their exodus out of the country. He did not want blacks, either slave or free, to enter the borderlands. Free labor must not be relegated to "a condition of social equality with the labor of the black slave," he declared. New states had to be protected from the blight of slave labor and its companion evil, a sizable free black population.[60]

The opposition of Wilmot, King, Brinkerhoff, and other Free-Soilers to slavery was not based chiefly on humanitarian grounds. Rather, they deemed blacks to be ineradicably inferior and wished to minimize or eliminate contact between the races. In this context, antislavery meant anti-Negro. Those who pushed for a Free-Soil West sought a Pacific paradise without blacks, a final frontier where whites could be entirely spared from a black presence through timely legislation. Frontiersmen on the shores of the Pacific agreed. The provisional government of Oregon as early as 1844 had passed an antislavery bill and in addition had warned free blacks to leave the Oregon territory within two years or face expulsion. Even before Wilmot introduced the proviso, northern lawmakers, with near unanimity, had voted to ban slavery from the Pacific Northwest by including an exclusion amendment in the bill organizing the Oregon Territory. And in 1848 and after, Congress extended the Northwest Ordinance of 1787 to Oregon and moved to discourage the migration of free blacks there by prohibiting land grants to them. The Free-Soil movement sought to circumscribe blacks, whether slave or free, in order to discourage racial heterogeneity in California and Oregon. Already burdened with Native Americans and mixed-blood Mexicans, the western territories should be closed to blacks.[61]

Southern Democrats conveniently forgot Walker's propaganda. Walker, for his part, remained conspicuously silent during the slavery extension controversy, perhaps realizing that his specious promises and devious politicking had finally brought his party to an impasse. Senator Arthur Bagby of Alabama expressed a common southern

---

60. *CG*, 29 Cong., 2 sess., 114 (January 5, 1847).

61. New York *Herald*, August 3 and 9, 1846; *CG*, 30 Cong., 1 sess., 1079 (August 12, 1848); Thomas Hart Benton, *Thirty Years' View; or, A History of the Working of the American Government for Thirty Years, from 1820 to 1850*, 2 vols. (New York: 1854–56), 2:711–15; *CG*, 31 Cong., 1 sess., 1090–93 (May 28, 1850); *United States Statutes at Large*, 9:497; 10:308; Eugene Berwanger, *The Frontier against Slavery: Western Anti-Negro Prejudice and the Slavery Extension Controversy* (Urbana, 1967), pp. 78–82; Leon Litwack, *North of Slavery: The Negro in the Free States, 1790–1860* (Chicago, 1961), pp. 46–49.

view when he condemned the proviso and insisted that he would "never consent that territory, acquired by common blood and common treasure, shall be open and free for the citizens of one portion of the Union, with their property, while the citizens of another portion of the Union and their property are to be excluded from it." An increasingly anxious Calhoun also lashed out against the Free-Soil movement. Regarding the proviso as a frontal assault upon the concept of confederated government, he resolved to open the western territory to slavery or lead the South out of the Union. The North, Calhoun complained in late 1846, was scheming "that the South shall do all the fighting and pay all the expense, and they [are] to have all the conquered territory." After Polk submitted the Trist Treaty to the Senate in early 1848, Calhoun remained adamant that either the proviso or the confederation must be surrendered. "The slave question will soon come up, and be the subject of deep agitation," he observed. "The South will be in the crisis of its fate. If it yields now, all will be lost."[62]

An impassioned appeal for the rejection of the proviso came from Democratic congressman William Giles of Maryland. An officer of the American Colonization Society for over thirty years and a member of his state's commission for removing free blacks to Liberia for over two decades, Giles resorted to the earlier tactics of proslavery expansionists who had appealed to northern Negrophobia to promote southern expansion. Claiming in early 1847 "to be as much the friend of the black man as any abolitionist of the North," he warned that emancipation would only usher blacks into "crime, and misery, and degradation" while imperiling the safety of both the North and South. He raised again the fear that if slavery were confined to its existing limits, whites without slaves would migrate to the West and leave behind a shrinking white population surrounded by a predominantly black population. That, he said, would be unacceptable to the South, a development almost as dangerous as immediate abolition. Dispersion of the South's black population was essential: "Diffuse it, and it is innocuous," he observed. "Create a large disproportion between the white and black population, and you make it a mighty weapon of evil."[63] Here again was the siren song directed at northern Negrophobes.

62. Bagby, *CG,* 29 Cong., 2 sess., App. 399 (February 15, 1847); Calhoun to Anna Clemson, December 27, 1846; Calhoun to Andrew P. Calhoun, February 28, 1848, in Jameson, "Correspondence of Calhoun," 2:715–16, 744. Congressman James C. Dobbin of North Carolina also stressed during the debate in the House that the South was entitled to share the spoils (*CG,* 29 Cong., 2 sess., 383–86 [February 11, 1847]).
63. *CG,* 29 Cong., 2 sess., 387–88 (February 11, 1847).

Slavery's extension westward, Giles stressed, would not deprive the North of an outlet for its own superfluous laboring population. To convince Northerners of this, Giles returned to Walker's gradual abolition and removal scheme. Noting that Maryland possessed "an open door to the North" and "an open door to the South," Giles contended that masters were taking their slaves to more fertile cotton-growing regions, "therefore gradually . . . passing off to the South a portion of this population." Through this process the black population would "gradually travel down to the extreme southwest," where it could "mingle with the mixed population of Mexico, and meet there a homogeneous race." Much the gainer by this development, Maryland would "take her rank amid the free states of the North." Since the free states did not want former slaves, Maryland's Colonization Society in the meantime was attempting to make Liberia "as attractive to the black man, as our shores are to the oppressed white man of Europe." The vacancies left by departing slaves and free blacks could be filled by white workers from the North and immigrants from Europe. If parts of California and New Mexico were permitted to become slave soil, then whites in the South would be protected from the black peril, and the border states would eventually become free by "the slow process of causes beyond human agency, and above all human legislation."[64]

Much of what Giles said reflected wishful thinking. But there were indications in the mid-1840s that the more northern of the slave states were being slowly transformed by an influx of laborers from the free states and Europe.[65] British consul Thomas Grattan observed that "many settlers from New York and New England are gradually obtaining a footing in the upper districts of Virginia, doing the field work themselves, and causing a sensible diminution in the Negro population, which is largely disposed of to Georgia, Louisiana, and Texas." Irish traveler Godley attributed the continuation of slavery in Virginia, Maryland, North Carolina, Tennessee, Kentucky, and the District of Columbia to "feeling" rather than "self-interest." He emphasized that New York farmers had settled and succeeded on depleted land in Virginia, and he predicted that slavery would shift southward by the pressure of free labor competition. Other visitors offered similar views.[66] So there was some basis for Giles's observations. But

64. Ibid.
65. See Chapter 2, n. 53, for census statistics on black and white population in 1830 and 1840.
66. Thomas C. Grattan, *Civilized America*, 2 vols. (London, 1859), 2:249; Godley, *Letters from America*, 2:203-13. See also Mackay, *Western World*, 2:137; Lyell, *Second Visit*, 1:273-76.

his argument seemed absurd to Free-Soilers and antislavery Whigs. The process was too sluggish and too uncertain. Moreover, prosouthern administrations could prolong the life of slavery through selective acquisitions, as Tyler and Polk had done. Free-Soilers wanted an absolute guarantee of exclusion, seeing no room for further compromise.

Prominent expansionists tried to reconcile Free-Soil extremists with proslavery extremists. Expresident Tyler hoped that Northerners would be patient. "Climate should be left to determine the question of slavery as it will most assuredly," he wrote in early 1847. "It has already abolished it as far as Delaware, and if left to work out its results, will at no distant day produce similar effects on Delaware, Maryland and Virginia."[67] Buchanan urged Northerners to compromise. Abolitionists had "arrested the natural progress of emancipation and done great injury to the slaves themselves," he argued. The Missouri Compromise line of 1820 had earlier "saved the Union from threatened convulsion," and its extension to the Pacific now would "secure the like happy result." The *Herald* opposed the proviso and contended that the acquisition of California would soon transform many slave states into free states.[68] Reminiscent of 1844, such arguments were far less effective in 1847 and 1848. The southern Democrats and northern doughfaces had simply reneged on too many promises.

As the expansionists wished, Mexico ceded California and New Mexico to the United States in 1848. The immediate sectional confrontation over the acquisitions persisted until 1850, when the compromise of that year papered over deepening cracks between North and South. Like most accords reached under considerable duress, this one displeased so many influential leaders in each section that its implementation and enforcement created unprecedented problems. The crisis over Kansas from 1854 through 1856 shattered the precarious truce of 1850, and after 1852 the American party system was a shambles.[69]

67. Tyler to Alexander Gardiner, March 2, 1847, John Tyler Papers. Tyler understood Calhoun's concern but doubted that the Wilmot Proviso "speaks forth the settled policy of the non-slaveholding states." Tyler preferred a vigorous prosecution of the war and a guarantee that the South would share any territorial cession from Mexico.
68. Buchanan to the Committee of Berks County Democrats, August 25, 1847, James Buchanan Papers; New York *Herald,* September 17, 1846. See also Buchanan to William L. Yancey, May 18, 1848, Buchanan Papers.
69. Michael F. Holt, *The Political Crisis of the 1850s* (New York, 1978), pp. 101–38.

The country's unprecedented expansion in 1845 and 1846 and the simultaneous reintroduction of the slavery extension question disturbed the already fragile balance of power sustaining the confederation of states. The war against Mexico brought ample spoils to the victor, but by early 1847 the leaders of the victorious nation were deeply divided about how those spoils should be apportioned. After the introduction of the proviso, Northerners spoke more frequently of the containment of slavery or even its abolition; Southerners discussed and considered more seriously the option of secession. Increasingly in 1847 and 1848, sectional considerations began to undermine the regularity of party behavior.

Perhaps the antiproviso Democrats were too caught up in the war and the acquisition of a continental empire to realize how anachronistic their Jeffersonian principles had become. They could not understand the opposition to expansion, since it promised so much for so little. Whigs such as Daniel Webster, Philip Hone, and Horace Greeley argued that the consequences of expansion might eventually prove more detrimental than the consequences of containment. The expansionists, however, doubted that anything could menace the country more than the development of countless factories, burgeoning cities, a congested and volatile population, economic recession, and a decline in geographical and social mobility. In the tradition of the sage of Monticello, the expansionists of the 1840s sought to exploit European distractions for American advantage, to extend the nation's territory and trade, to enrich its citizens, and to protect them from the perils of modernization—if not for the thousandth and thousandth generation, at least for their own and perhaps the next.

CHAPTER 5

Continentalism and the Color Line

Many American historians in the twentieth century, especially those who wrote during the two decades following World War II, explained the expansion of the United States during the 1840s in terms of "manifest destiny" or "mission," concepts that the Jacksonian Democrats themselves had occasionally employed to sanction their policies. In this still influential perspective stressing the nation's geographical predestination and its duty to less fortunate peoples everywhere, the expansion of the United States is described not so much in terms of what territorial acquisitions would do for the country but what the country would do for those new territories.

The expansionists relied on other self-serving beliefs to explain and justify territorial acquisitions. They perpetuated the convenient myth of a vacant continent, invoking an image of North America as an uninhabited, howling wilderness that the new, chosen people had transformed from savagery to civilization during their predestined march to the Pacific. Others recognized that the continent was not empty and that Indians and Mexicans had occupied much of it prior to American ascendancy but stressed that the United States, in seeking to expand, sought only what was best for these dispossessed races. Unlike the exploitative Spanish who had first encountered nonwhite natives in the trans-Mississippi West, Americans in the nineteenth century came to indigenous peoples as missionaries, not conquistadores.

Historians writing during the Cold War era who studied the Tyler-Polk years may have accepted this flattering interpretation of American expansion because the tensions within their own historical setting suggested parallels to the 1840s.[1] Just as the United States sought to shield the free world from Communist aggression and to promote American values around the globe in the atomic age, so too had American leaders a century before launched a noble crusade to uplift and regenerate peoples living under oppression and poverty in the New World and the old. In the 1940s and after, a grasping and dangerous enemy, the Soviet Union, threatened the world order desired by American leaders; a century earlier, another powerful and hostile foe, Britain, had seemed determined to thwart the territorial and commercial designs of the United States. Characteristic of many policy makers during other periods as well, American leaders in both the late Jacksonian era and the Cold War era pursued their goals with the self-assurance that their motives and methods were beyond reproach. There are, however, two sides to the missionary impulse that has so often marked United States foreign policy: actions purported to be benevolent and generous often became chauvinistic and condescending, and the ostensible beneficiaries frequently became victims instead. A policy's actual effects often betrayed the rhetoric that surrounded it.

Expansionists occasionally expressed concern for nonwhite peoples. But interpretations of American territorial expansion that emphasize a humane commitment to Indians or Mexicans as a principal or even a significant motive for the acquisition of a continental empire in the 1840s cannot stand up to the abundant evidence to the contrary. Preoccupied with attaining racial homogeneity in the United States, the expansionists looked forward to the time when blacks, Indians, and Mexicans would completely disappear from the continent and whites would take sole possession of it.

With the exception of a few extremists whose desire for territory was so great that they could ignore racial considerations to the point where all acquisitions appeared justified, the expansionists generally contemplated in their calculations not only the land that would be

1. See, for example, Ray Allen Billington, *The Far Western Frontier, 1830–1860* (New York, 1956); Frederick Merk, *Manifest Destiny and Mission in American History: A Reinterpretation* (New York, 1963); William H. Goetzmann, *When the Eagle Screamed: The Romantic Horizon in American Diplomacy, 1800–1860* (New York, 1966); Goetzmann, *Exploration and Empire: The Explorer and the Scientist in the Winning of the American West* (New York, 1966).

acquired but also the quantity and quality of the population inhabiting it. Expansionists wanted regions such as Texas, Oregon, or California, where Anglo-Americans already predominated or where their migration would soon eclipse the native inhabitants, whether Indians or Mexicans. But when a more concentrated nonwhite population inhabited an area, as in Mexico below the Rio Grande or in Cuba, enthusiasm waned because of fears about amalgamation and racial conflict. In other words, the fact that the continent was not empty posed a serious dilemma for the expansionists. White racism could act as either a stimulus or a deterrent to the country's extension, depending on the size of an area, the racial composition of its inhabitants, and the density of its population. In the short run the expansionist Democrats sought to acquire land that could be dominated rapidly by Anglo-Americans; what happened to the native inhabitants was a secondary consideration. In the long run, however, most expansionists envisioned an American empire coextensive with the entire continent. Eventually the peoples of pure European lineage would become integral members of that empire, but nonwhites would be excluded from it.

By the 1840s, seven generations of Anglo-Americans had coexisted uncomfortably with Indians and blacks in the New World. From the very beginning of contact, whites had assumed that Indian lands and black labor were to be exploited for both individual and national benefit. During the late eighteenth and first half of the nineteenth century, the systematic dispossession of the natives proceeded apace with the expansion of the cotton kingdom and the fastening of chattel slavery upon the states below the Mason-Dixon line. The dipossession of the five civilized tribes during the 1830s, for example, converted millions of acres of rich southern soil to cotton cultivation. The expansion of slavery and the decline of the Indian drew upon and contributed to a racist ideology justifying subordination, dispossession, or even elimination of nonwhite peoples. Indians, especially, became the popular prototype of the inferior breed, and whites then projected their negative images of Indians onto other non-Anglo populations that were in the way of American expansion. Contact between English colonists and Native Americans, and the images whites formed of Indians, exerted a powerful and persistent impact on the dialectic of white America's encounter with nonwhite peoples during the late eighteenth and early nineteenth centuries.[2]

2. See Robert F. Berkhofer, Jr., *The White Man's Indian: Images of the American Indian from Columbus to the Present* (New York, 1978); Reginald Horsman, *Race and Manifest Destiny: The Origins of American Racial Anglo-Saxonism* (Cambridge, Mass., 1981).

Protestant missionaries often initiated the most determined assaults upon Native American culture, but their assumptions of superiority were shared by government leaders and the general population
as well. Robert Berkhofer has noted how missionaries firmly believed
that "any right-thinking savage should be able to recognize the superiority of Christian civilization when shown him." Not only should
Indians accept Christianity; they should also accept the English language, the white man's government, his approach to the natural
environment, and his social and cultural mores. Missionaries, in short,
tried to make Indian men and women into farmers, artisans, and
homemakers, mirror images of the supposedly more advanced whites.[3]
It was an ambitious project, this radical effort to convert Indians to
white culture, but initially missionaries were not disposed to doubt
their prospects for success.[4] To them conversion must have seemed
as inevitable as it was desirable.

Yet even when missionaries succeeded in converting the Indian to
white ways, the Indian usually failed: acculturation did not bring him
equality in white society. Still disdained by most whites because of
his race, the Christian Indian now encountered hostility and ridicule
from his unconverted tribesmen who adhered to tradition.[5] The Indian might shed his religion, but he could not shed his race; a converted
native was still more "Indian" than "white."

Because of the difficulties inherent in rapid acculturation, the resistance of both whites and Indians to complete assimilation, and the
impatience of the missionaries, the mission program largely failed.
As one might expect, the once confident clergymen (and officials who
supported their efforts) blamed the Indians and not themselves for
this failure. It is unfair to expect early nineteenth-century white Americans to have approached the Indians with the cultural relativity of
twentieth-century anthropologists, and it is important to point out
that the parochialism and ethnocentrism of most agents of conversion and acculturation were shared by most of their contemporaries.

3. Robert F. Berkhofer, Jr., *Salvation and the Savage: An Analysis of Protestant Missions
and the American Indian Response, 1787–1862* (New York, 1976), pp. 1–14, and passim.
The quotation is on p. 14.
4. Government officials shared the missionaries' optimism. From Jefferson to
Jackson, leaders agreed that advanced civilization and Christianity were two sides of
the same coin. Church spokesmen and federal officials sometimes disagreed on
whether conversion must precede acculturation or vice versa, but generally they
believed that the Indians would not attain a progressive society until they accepted
both the white man's religion and his culture.
5. Berkhofer, *Salvation and the Savage*, p. 123.

Nevertheless, pervasive white bigotry placed the Indians in a hopeless situation, for white contact and its often disintegrating effects frequently undermined tribal life without substituting a viable alternative. Whether noble or ignoble, the Indian could not escape the white man's image of him as a savage.[6] Just as the unfavorable stereotype of the black in the nineteenth century excused his enslavement in the South and his proscription throughout most of the country, the prevailing image of the Indian became a useful justification for his subjugation and dispossession.

From the winning of independence to the late Jacksonian period, white Americans invoked a negative image of Indians to assuage their own insecurities about their culture. Constantly taunted by Europeans for their lack of art, literature, and refinement, Americans found solace in contrasting their culture to that of the original inhabitants of the New World forests. When held up to the Indian tribes rather than the European nations, the United States appeared to be on the high road to advanced civilization. Already convinced that their political institutions were unequaled in Europe, Americans anticipated that their culture, too, would eventually match or even surpass its counterparts abroad. To measure their progress Americans could use the seemingly unregenerate Indians as a standard for comparison. According to Roy Harvey Pearce, the natives became a useful symbol of savagery for white culture, a reminder of the inferior condition of primitive man and an indication of how far Anglo-Americans had come in transcending the limitations of the wilderness to create a progressive and prosperous society.[7]

No one expressed this faith in American advancement on a primitive continent more fervently than Andrew Jackson. Defending his policy of Indian removal in 1830, he offered a widely held view when he asked if any American "would prefer a country covered with forests and ranged by a few thousand savages" over the United States, now "embellished with all the improvements which art can

6. A positive stereotype ("the noble savage") can be as detrimental as a negative one, for it places high expectations on a group to live up to an unrealistic standard. Berkhofer doubts whether the reality of Indian history can ever be told, in view of the persistence of erroneous images and ideology surrounding the natives. His pessimism is justified, for myths and misconceptions about Native Americans seem to have a more persistent hold on the American mind than the troubling complexities of historical actuality. Only in the last two decades have scholars and the informed public begun to sort out the misconceptions from the reality.

7. Roy Harvey Pearce, *The Savages of America: A Study of the Indian and the Idea of Civilization*, rev. ed. (Baltimore, 1965).

devise or industry execute, occupied by more than 12,000,000 happy
people, and filled with all the blessings of liberty, civilization, and
religion."[8] Since the territorial expansion of the United States had
become synonymous with the advancement of civilization—and since
Americans had increasingly tended to attribute their democratic institutions, mobility, and much of their unique culture to the existence
of a vast frontier—the Indians and Mexicans were bound to suffer.
If Americans regarded each removal of a tribe as an achievement
comparable to the creation of an English novel or a German sympho-
ny; if the admission of a new state symbolized progressive civilization
no less than a French painting; if stumps and cultivated fields represented American substitutes for learned societies—then Americans
would become increasingly disposed to conceptualize their advance
and to validate their superiority in terms of territorial acquisitions,
the despoliation of resources, and the extension of the country's
boundaries. Many Democrats held this perspective by the mid-1840s,
and consequently they regarded nonwhites who held desirable land
as obstacles to progress rather than worthy beneficiaries of humane
assistance.

Foreign visitors during the Jacksonian era questioned the philanthropic pretensions behind American Indian policy. Alexis de Tocqueville, for example, witnessed a phase of Choctaw removal when
he passed through Memphis during his tour in 1831. The inhumanity
of removal appalled him, but he doubted the Indians had any choice
other than to seek refuge from white intrusion by migrating westward. Since the United States was "the most grasping nation on the
globe," the Indians had been "half convinced and half compelled"
to believe that their survival depended on relocation. Yet Tocqueville
predicted that removal offered no permanent remedy for the Indians'
problems, for eventually whites would want the lands in the West as
well. In order to endure and flourish, the natives would have had to
"destroy the Europeans or become their equals," but this they could
not do. The Indians were "doomed to perish." Even if American

8. James D. Richardson, ed., Messages and Papers of the Presidents, 10 vols. (New York,
1897), 3 (December 6, 1830):1084–85. Jackson insisted in this second annual message
that the national government treated Indians more generously than it treated its own
citizens. He asserted that "rightly considered, the policy of the General Government
toward the red man is not only liberal, but generous. He is unwilling to submit to
the laws of the States and mingle with their population. To save him from this
alternative, or perhaps utter annihilation, the General Government kindly offers him
a new home, and proposes to pay the whole expense of his removal and settlement."

expressions of regret for the Indians' sufferings were sincere, there was no denying the fundamental disparity between the benevolent rhetoric and the cruel reality of removal. "It is impossible to destroy men with more respect for the laws of humanity," he observed.[9]

More caustic in his comments on the treatment of Indians in America was Frederick Marryat, who toured the United States during the forced removal of the Cherokees over the Trail of Tears in 1838–39. Marryat regarded Cherokee removal as a singularly striking indication of America's brutal expansionism and self-conscious aspirations for empire. While meandering through upstate New York he became annoyed with crude villages bearing the names of Syracuse, Utica, Troy, and Rome. To Marryat this seemed a foolish mockery. "Why do not the Americans take the Indian names?" he queried. "They need not be so very scrupulous about it; they have robbed the Indians of everything else." Moving on from the Seneca reservation in New York to the Upper Mississippi River frontier, Marryat reached Fort Snelling and recorded a Sioux's remarks about the contrast between the treatment afforded his tribe by the British and the Americans: "The rifles and blankets which [the British] gave us, according to promise, were of good quality; not like the American goods; their rifles are bad, and their blankets are thin."[10] Marryat saw little to commend in the precepts and prejudices of boisterous Americans. He found their promises to nonwhite peoples to be as thin as their blankets.

Thomas Grattan likewise commented upon the Indians' suffering. Unlike Marryat, however, Grattan excused the Americans of responsibility for the natives' hardships. He pointed out that Indians had "altogether failed to bear out the fantastic imaginings of poets and romance writers." Primitive but not noble, the Indian in America showed "neither the energy of savage life nor the capability of refinement." The Indians remaining in the United States did "inspire a sort of compassionate curiosity in the observer," but only to the point where the witness of their condition hoped that "they may quietly become extinct, and escape the fate of a violent extermination."

9. Alexis de Tocqueville, *Democracy in America,* Phillips Bradley, ed., 2 vols. (New York, 1945), 1:341–55. On Choctaw removal, see Arthur H. DeRosier, Jr., *The Removal of the Choctaw Indians* (Knoxville, 1970); Ronald N. Satz, *American Indian Policy in the Jacksonian Era* (Lincoln, Neb., 1975), pp. 64–96. See also Grant Forman, *Advancing the Frontier, 1830–1860* (Norman, Okla., 1933).

10. Frederick Marryat, *A Diary in America, with Remarks on Its Institutions,* 3 vols. (London, 1839), 1:154, 2:115, 1:111–36.

Grattan believed that Indians would have fared better had whites enslaved them. But Americans had discovered "that the Indians were as unfit for slavery" as they were "unworthy of freedom," so there was no incentive to encourage reproduction among them and no guilt or sympathy that might have aided them had they once been productive slaves of white masters. Using a comparison that appeared often in ruminations about Indians, Grattan noted that when in contact with white civilization, they perished "as the forest trees which have been girdled and let to rot; and do not even fall with a crash like them, when they are finally struck down by the woodman's axe." Anticipating, like Tocqueville, the fate of the Indians between the western frontier and the Pacific, he too predicted that their future held only "despair and extermination."[11]

By the mid-1840s, the Jacksonians sensed the immanence of a major eclipse or complete extinction of the Indians on the continent. They did so with little regret, placing highest priority on removing whatever Indians still remained in the East, while also making the new territories acquired west of the Mississippi safe for migration and settlement by white Americans. Since the Native Americans had already demonstrated a perverse reluctance to accept Christianity or a progressive civilization, they appeared doomed to extinction. With the acquisition of Texas, Oregon, New Mexico, and California, the expansionists no longer viewed the Great Plains as a "Great American Desert" holding no attractions for whites. Even if the plains themselves were not yet coveted by Americans, pioneers demanded routes to Oregon and California, and western agitation for unmolested migration westward in the 1840s began to put pressure on those Indians that had been relocated in the Indian territory, as well as on the original inhabitants of the region. The panacea of the previous decade, removal of Indians to a "permanent" western Indian reserve, became simply a self-serving expedient for the expansionists of the Tyler-Polk years. The Jacksonian Democrats knew that the western states and territories and the pioneers themselves would demand that Indian lands be turned over to the United States for use by white settlers—for when the Indians were promised land "forever," it meant

11. *Civilized America,* 2 vols. (London, 1859), 2:131–39. Twentieth-century scholars often repeated this imagery. Note, for instance, Thomas A. Bailey's revealing comment about the direction of American policy after the War of 1812: Americans "turned their backs confidently on the Old World, and concentrated on the task of felling trees and Indians and of rounding out their natural boundaries" (*A Diplomatic History of the American People,* 8th ed. [New York, 1969], p. 163).

not for all time but only for as long as the territory remained unap-
pealing to whites. The acquisition of Oregon and California altered
perceptions of the vast area between the Pacific Coast and the Missou-
ri-Arkansas frontier. By the mid-1840s, white leaders were already
considering the establishment of a series of small reservations that
would confine the western Indians to a greatly diminished sphere and
open up much of their lands to extensive white penetration and
exploitation.[12]

In the early 1840s, federal Indian policy reflected what had become
by then a characteristic blend of expressions of benevolence for the
Indians' welfare coupled with explanations and speculations about
the demands that white America must inevitably place upon them.
As was typical of Indian affairs throughout the nineteenth century,
white frontiersmen and their spokesmen in Congress and the press
were far more impatient and grasping than eastern bureaucrats and
reformers, and as usual the hard-liners proved to be more perceptive
and realistic in emphasizing that the interests of white Americans
must always be placed before those of the natives.

Commissioner of Indian affairs Thomas Hartley Crawford, a Pennsylvania Democrat who had been appointed by Martin Van Buren in
1838, exemplified the curious inconsistencies in federal policy during
the late Jacksonian period. He insisted that somehow the federal
government could find a means to satisfy white demands for territory, trading privileges, and safe passage through tribal lands while it
also protected Indians from white intrusions and the corrosive effects
of contact with degraded frontiersmen. Despite occasional misgivings, he also reaffirmed the government's program for civilizing the
tribesmen. A sincere man of divided loyalties, Crawford sought what
was best for both the United States and its Indian wards, but he never
fully comprehended the discrepancy between federal intentions and
federal actions. In 1841, for example, he called upon Congress to
create an additional Indian territory in southern Minnesota, a project
he deemed "judicious, in reference as well to our own citizens as the
Indians." It would be difficult, he warned, to find space in the southern Indian territory "for all the tribes yet to be removed" from the

---

12. United States Indian policy during the 1840s is discussed at length in Satz,
American Indian Policy in the Jacksonian Era; Robert A. Trennert, Jr., *Alternatives to
Extinction: Federal Indian Policy and the Beginnings of the Reservation System, 1845–1851*
(Philadelphia, 1975). Less informative is Francis P. Prucha, "American Indian Policy
in the 1840s," in John G. Clark, ed., *The Frontier Challenge: Responses to the Trans-
Mississippi West* (Lawrence, Kansas, 1971), pp. 81–110.

East. Concerned with American security as well as the welfare of the Indians, he hoped that "a dense white population" would soon inhabit the central plains, and this population, "interposed between the two [Indian] settlements," would pacify the plains and alleviate the anxieties of frontier whites. In the meantime, Crawford noted, federal efforts to acculturate those Indians already relocated during the 1830s were succeeding. The Cherokees, Choctaws, and Chickasaws, he observed, "promise soon . . . to be distinguishable from our citizens only by their color." To hasten cultural change among the natives, Crawford urged that schools teaching agriculture and mechanical arts be further encouraged among them.[13]

Crawford reassured Congress in 1842 that the Tyler administration would continue to remove Indians from Ohio, Michigan, Iowa, and Florida. The Wyandots, Sacs, Foxes, Chippewa, and Seminoles were being relocated to the Indian territory, away from white settlement. Crawford believed that this removal was beneficial to whites and red men alike and that it alone offered a final solution to the Indian problem. "We have transplanted, or will transplant them to land chosen by ourselves; and I trust the day will never come, when they shall be asked to go further towards the setting sun," Crawford noted. He welcomed the transfer of Indian lands to the United States and epecially lauded the recent cessions in central Ohio, a region "heretofore comparatively a waste in the centre of culture and advancing improvement." Through white settlement this area would soon contribute to "the general productiveness and wealth of the country."[14]

Crawford often wondered how long it would take before "those who are now savage shall . . . become civilized." Despite the Indians' "natural indolence and pride, and a long course of unbroken traditionary customs," however, he insisted that conversion to Christianity, temperance, and instruction in mechanical arts would prepare them to live among whites and to participate in the mainstream of

13. *Report of the Commissioner of Indian Affairs, S. Doc.,* vol. 395, no. 11, 27 Cong., 2 sess. (November 25, 1841), pp. 253, 263–64. Crawford might have admitted that frontiersmen were never satisfied with just controlling Indians in their vicinity. Control was usually a preliminary to ultimate removal or extermination. On the military threat posed by the Indians west of Missouri and Arkansas, see also Secretary of war John N. Bell to Speaker of the House John White, August 28, 1841, in *The New American State Papers,* Benjamin Franklin Cooling, ed. (Wilmington, 1979), 2:168–70, and Caleb Cushing's remarks in the *Congressional Globe,* (hereafter abbreviated *CG),* 27 Cong., 2 sess., App. 830 (August 3, 1842).

14. *Report of the Commissioner of Indian Affairs, S. Doc.,* vol. 413, no. 10, 27 Cong., 3 sess. (November 16, 1842), pp. 377–88. The quotations are on pp. 377 and 379.

American life.[15] Despite his own ambivalence and discouragement, he refused to blame the natives exclusively for their plight. "If their progress is slow," he asserted in his final report to Congress in 1844, "so has it been with us and with masses of men in all nations and ages." But few Americans at this time shared Crawford's impression of Indians' being "in no respect inferior to our own race, except in being less fortunately circumstanced."[16] During the expansionist surge of the next four years, even that small and sympathetic minority dwindled as the United States attained its continental empire.

The aggressive expansionism of the mid-1840s greatly complicated federal Indian policy. From the time when Jefferson had first proposed removal and gradual acculturation, after the purchase of the Louisiana Territory in 1803, up to the time of the removal of the five civilized tribes in the 1830s, American policy makers had concentrated on relocating the eastern Indians to the Great Plains. With the termination of the Seminole War in 1842 and the removal of additional tribes during the early 1840s, Americans considered the Indian problem east of the Mississippi largely solved; only a few scattered remnants of weakened tribes still resided within the states. As politicians and publicists turned their attention toward Oregon, Texas, New Mexico, and California, however, they increasingly stressed the dangers presented by natives west of the Mississippi. Expansionists hoped the government would control the Indians of the plains and confine them to fixed habitations so that pioneers could travel westward without incident. In addition, as the appeal of the West increased in the East, so did demands for dispossession of the nonwhite inhabitants holding the land. The expansionists primarily wanted to substitute Anglo-American pioneers for Indians and people of mixed blood in the West, and to make the Pacific Coast and the Great Plains integral parts of the United States as quickly as possible.

Among the most forceful proponents of the acquisition of Oregon in the early 1840s was Illinois senator Samuel McRoberts. In late 1842, he reminded his colleagues that the British had used their strategic position in Canada before and during the War of 1812 to

15. *Report of the Commissioner of Indian Affairs, S. Doc.,* vol. 449, no. 9, 28 Cong., 2 sess. (November 25, 1844), p. 313; *Report of the Commissioner of Indian Affairs, S. Doc.,* vol. 413, p. 382; *Report of the Commissioner of Indian Affairs, S. Doc.,* vol. 431, no. 9, 28 Cong., 1 sess. (November 25, 1843), pp. 270–71.

16. *Report of the Commissioner of Indian Affairs, S. Doc.,* vol. 449, p. 315. President Tyler at this time also reaffirmed the government's commitment to removal "of all the tribes residing within the limits of the . . . states" and to the improvement of "the arts of civilized life" among the Indians (Tyler's fourth annual message, in Richardson, *Messages and Papers,* 5 [December 3, 1844]:2201).

incite Indians in the Northwest against American frontiersmen and warned that Britain might now be able to use this strategy again with the tribes that had been moved to the West. The government's removal policy had placed "a numerous Indian population" along the western border "from Iowa to the line of Texas." Although the relocated Indians were presently at peace with the United States, as "the shattered fragments of a hundred hostile tribes . . . composed of the very elements of war," they posed a perpetual menace to the United States. "Being on the frontier, they are liable to be influenced by those who have been, and again may become, inimical to us," he warned. Congress could avert this threat by giving military protection to Americans en route to Oregon, for if Oregon were settled rapidly by white pioneers the territory would provide a buffer between the British in Canada and the Indians in the West. This achieved, McRoberts predicted, there could never be another unholy alliance between the two. He admitted that he could never rest easy while Indians lived in proximity to vulnerable whites. "The natural element of the Indian is war," he contended. "He is taught it from his mother's lips in the wigwam, and sees it practised and cherished as the highest virtue of his tribe. We must counteract as far as possible this dangerous propensity of his being." Congressman William Sawyer of Ohio similarly maintained that Britain's influence over Indians had brought "the most damnable atrocities committed upon our people." Like McRoberts, he wanted Britain removed from Oregon and the entire North American continent.[17]

Senator Lewis Linn of Missouri agreed. He, too, urged Congress to furnish military escorts to emigrants bound for Oregon, and to stimulate further migration there he proposed free homesteads for Americans who would settle in the territory. "We have raised a barrier against our own onward march westward, by the Indian tribes planted on our territorial borders," he complained in 1843. "They are there open to a foreign subsidy, for impeding our accession to our ocean limits." Linn denied that "masterly inactivity," as counseled by Senators Calhoun and George McDuffie of South Carolina, would ensure American ascendancy over "these treacherous and dangerous neighbors." The hasty acquisition and occupation of Oregon was essential to prevent any possible cooperation between Indians and the British.[18]

17. CG, 27 Cong., 3 sess., App. 91 (December 30, 1842); CG, 29 Cong., 1 sess., 228 (February 3, 1846).

18. CG, 27 Cong., 3 sess., App. 80 (January 9, 1843). Contrary to Linn's assumption, the United States had no "ocean limits" on the Pacific in 1843.

Virulently anti-Indian and anti-British, Indiana senator Edward Hannegan championed the acquisition of all of Oregon during the mid-1840s. In 1844 he reminded senators that the architects of Indian removal during Jackson's presidency had considered it essential to separate the relocated natives from foreign powers, especially Britain. To contain American expansion, the British, he warned, might attempt to turn "the knives of fifty thousand Indian warriors" against pioneers on the overland trails and frontiersmen settled in remote areas.[19] Determined to prevent any coalition between the British and the Indians, Hannegan joined the other northwestern Democrats in the ranks of the Fifty-four forties.

The expansionists also feared the Indian tribes that roamed over the southwestern borderlands between the settled parts of the United States, Texas, and Mexico.[20] They sought to end this threat by acquiring Texas and New Mexico, a move that would bring the marauding tribesmen under the jurisdiction of the United States. Pleading in 1844 for the immediate annexation of Texas, Andrew Jackson admonished Americans to "look at the Indians we have located on our western border, near to Texas." Like McRoberts, Jackson feared British intervention. Were Texas to become a pawn of England, New Orleans would be endangered, slaves in the South would flee to Texas, and British agents could incite Indians to harass the American frontier and the caravans crossing the overland trails. The United States must acquire Texas, "peaceably if we can, but forcibly if we must," Jackson declared.[21]

Undoubtedly Jackson viewed the annexation crisis as another manifestation of British and Indian treachery, treachery that he himself had three times punished—in the Creek campaign of 1814, at the Battle of New Orleans, and in the 1818 raid into Florida. He was not alone in his belief that he had previously saved the United States from English animus and was, by promoting annexation, selflessly doing so again. Congressman Charles Ingersoll of Pennsylvania, himself a war hawk a generation earlier, praised Jackson in 1844 for his earlier achievements: "The Treaty of Ghent would have been ignominious, it would have been but a truce and that disgraceful but for your

19. *CG*, 28 Cong., 1 sess., App. 245 (February 23, 1844).
20. See *Report of the Commissioner of Indian Affairs, S. Doc.*, vol. 431, p. 265, and *Report of the Commissioner of Indian Affairs, S. Doc.*, vol. 449, p. 307.
21. Jackson to W. B. Lewis, April 8, 1844, Andrew Jackson Papers. See also Jackson to Kendall, April 12, 1844, and Jackson to Francis P. Blair, April 12, 1844, Jackson Papers; Jackson's letter on Texas annexation, August 28, 1844, James K. Polk Papers.

glorious victories in the South."[22] Democrats such as Jackson, Linn, Hannegan, and Ingersoll detected vestiges of the past in the present, and little provocation was needed to motivate them to point an angry, accusing finger at Britain. During the 1840s Democrats catalogued with ritualistic regularity the grievances of the United States against England over the past seven decades and often blamed the country's racial, economic, and diplomatic problems on the British. Anglophobic Jacksonians expected—perhaps even hoped—to find a British agent lurking behind every teepee on the plains.

After the annexation of Texas in 1845, expansionists continued to voice concern about the Indian menace in the Southwest. Chargé Andrew Jackson Donelson reported from Texas in mid-1845 that Mexico could not enforce its distant and feeble authority over Indians who ranged through the disputed territory between the Nueces and Rio Grande rivers. Mexico, he wrote to Buchanan, had failed to colonize the borderland areas, and the sparse population there was "at the mercy of the Indians who without fear of her authority murder her citizens and pillage their property." The Mexican government during the past two decades had demonstrated its "utter inability" to control the Indians of the southern plains. "To arrest the growing mischiefs resulting from the superiority of these Indians," he advised, "the United States in self-defence must make the Rio Grande the boundary."[23] Here, then, was another reason for the Polk administration to insist that Mexico surrender its borderland territory. Since Mexico could not control the wild Comanches and Apaches in the area, the United States would have to assume sovereignty there.

The Polk administration accepted Donelson's advice. Editor Thomas Ritchie, for example, reiterated Donelson's view when he declared in the summer of 1845 that "Mexico has never been able to control the Indians, or to enforce any regular authority over the territory that lies between the Nueces and the Rio Grande." Ritchie suggested that the United States could justifiably occupy any or all of the disputed area. In November, Buchanan instructed envoy John Slidell that amicable relations could be restored between the two countries if Mexico agreed to a boundary running along the Rio Grande: the disputed territory must be ceded to the United States. Buchanan went further, confiding to Slidell that the administration also hoped to acquire New

22. Ingersoll to Jackson, February 14, 1844, Jackson Papers.
23. Donelson to Buchanan, July 11, 1845, in William R. Manning, ed., *The Diplomatic Correspondence of the United States, Inter-American Affairs, 1831–1860*, 12 vols. (Washington, D.C., 1929–39)12:451.

Mexico in any resolution of the border controversy. "Mexico would part with a remote and disturbed province, the possession of which can never be advantageous to her; and she would be relieved from the trouble and expense of defending its inhabitants against the Indians," he explained. Those dangerous border tribes could be con-trolled only by a superior power that could "restrain the savage tribes within their limits and prevent them from making hostile incursions into Mexico."[24] The principal consideration of Polk and his advisers, however, was not the Indians' attacks on Mexicans but those on American traders and pioneers traversing the overland trails. Buchan-an tried to find ways of making territorial concessions palatable to the Mexican government, but his desire for safe commerce and un-molested migration took precedence over any sense of mission to Mexicans or Indians.

When General Stephen W. Kearny and his troops occupied New Mexico in the summer of 1846, he tried to win the favor of the Spanish-speaking population there by promising that the United States would provide protection against the hostile Indians roaming the region. His forces proving inadequate for so demanding a task, how-ever, he failed to keep his pledge. But his assurance that his soldiers could control the borderland's Indians indicated that Americans thought they could accomplish what the Spanish and the Mexicans had never been able to achieve.[25]

Some officials in Washington were less sanguine than Kearny. Commissioner of Indian affairs William Medill, in late 1846, acknowl-edged that controlling the southwestern tribes would be difficult, since they were "of a roving and unstable disposition, and . . . proba-bly among the most barbarous and least civilized portions of the Indian race." A year later he advised Congress to send a punitive expedition against the Comanches because of their attacks upon United States supply trains using the Santa Fe trail.[26] With the acquisi-tion of Texas and the conquest of the borderlands, Medill faced the

24. Washington *Daily Union*, August 9, 1845; Buchanan to Slidell, November 10, 1845, in Manning, *Diplomatic Correspondence*, 8:179. See also Washington *Daily Union*, August 11 and 15, 1845.

25. See "Kearny's Proclamation of August 22, 1846," in *H. Doc.*, vol. 520, no. 60, 30 Cong., 1 sess., 170–71 (December, 1847); *The Original Journals of Henry Smith Turner, with Stephen Watts Kearny to New Mexico and California,* Dwight L. Clarke, ed. (Norman, Okla., 1966), pp. 66–67.

26. *Report of the Commissioner of Indian Affairs, S. Doc.*, vol. 493, no. 11, 29 Cong., 2 sess. (vol. 1: November 30, 1846), p. 225; *Report of the Commissioner of Indian Affairs, S. Doc.*, vol. 503, no. 23, 30 Cong., 1 sess. (November 30, 1847), pp. 743–44. See also the Washington *Daily Union*, July 12, 27, 29, and 30, 1847.

challenge of exerting control over some of the most belligerent tribes in North America. Medill complained of his difficulties to Senator William Allen in September 1846, observing that though the unbearable heat had rendered Washington a virtual ghost town during recent weeks, he was captive in the infernal city because of the war and the mounting responsibilities of his department. It had been a long, hot summer for Medill.[27]

Subjugating the western tribes proved to be much harder than expected and was not accomplished in the Southwest until the 1880s. Even though the many difficulties of gaining unquestioned dominance over these Indians were unforeseen by the expansionists of the 1840s, the subjugation of the nomadic tribes of the Great Plains occurred much more rapidly than had the defeat and removal of the eastern Indians—a striking manifestation of the growing determination and power of the United States to consolidate the entire continental empire. Early indications of that ambition to destroy the Indians as a threat to American ascendancy between the Mississippi and the Pacific appeared simultaneously with the acquisition of Oregon and California during Polk's term. The desire to civilize and christianize the natives still formed a part of United States relations with the Indians, but the material desires of white Americans were certainly paramount in Polk's mind when he reviewed his administration's Indian policy in his final annual message to Congress in late 1848.

Polk reported that his administration had negotiated eight major treaties with various tribes, acquiring over 18.5 million acres of land for about $1.8 million. These treaties contained provisions "for settling in the country west of the Mississippi the tribes which occupied this large extent of the public domain. . . . The title to all the Indian lands within the several states of our Union, with the exception of a few small reservations, is now extinguished," Polk announced. "A vast region" had been "opened for settlement and cultivation."[28] Polk had virtually completed the process of removal so persistently pursued by Jackson and Van Buren. But Jackson's earlier approach seemed too paternalistic to Polk. In the removal treaties concluded during the mid-1840s, the Indians themselves rather than the national government were made responsible for the actual process of relocation.[29] Polk had gone a step beyond Jackson, relieving the federal

27. Medill to Allen, "Private," September 1, 1846, William Allen Papers.
28. Richardson, *Messages and Papers,* 5 (December 5, 1848):2501.
29. Polk learned from the earlier miscalculations of Jackson, Cass, and others. The costs of removal during the 1830s had far exceeded the executive's projections. Medill, in his 1848 report, noted, "These treaties [of cession] were all made without

government of all obligation to the Indians while they migrated to the West. In his valedictory in 1848, Polk said little about the federal government's programs to assist the natives. Achievement, by his standards, was measured in territory obtained from the Indians. All else was secondary.

Medill's final report on Indian affairs in 1848 addressed some of the issues that Polk ignored, but overall his assessment amounted to little more than a strained apologia for white cupidity and greed. Medill chastised critics of federal Indian policy and complained of the "misrepresentation and unjust national reproach" surrounding it. To him the dispossession of natives was inevitable. "Apathy, barbarism, and heathenism must give way to energy, civilization, and christianity," he asserted. During the long process of Indian decline there had been, in his opinion, "much less of oppression and injustice than has generally been represented and believed." Whites could not have preserved the Indians, for they were their own worst enemies. "The inequality of [the Indian's] position in all that secures dignity and respect is too glaring, and the contest he has to make with the superior race with which he is brought into contact, in all the avenues to success and prosperity in life, is too unequal to hope for a better result," Medill observed. "The rapid decline and disappearance" of the Indian population had resulted not from "wilful neglect, or . . . deliberate oppression and wrong" but rather from "natural and unavoidable causes, easily understood and appreciated."[30]

Medill hoped the government would continue to remove Indians from the white frontier, encourage agriculture among them, discourage their consumption of alcohol, and promote schools to teach them trade skills. Everything else depended upon the Indians' own initiative. To stimulate hard labor among the tribesmen, Medill recommended cutting their annuities, in order to force them to earn their living through disciplined toil. Federal policy, he predicted, would prepare them "to compete with a white population, and to sustain themselves under any probable circumstances of contact or connexion with it."[31] He supplied no evidence to support his optimism, and past experience should have suggested a gloomier forecast.

---

granting a single reservation, without assuming a dollar of any Indian indebtedness, and where removal was necessary, they provided for its being accomplished by the Indians themselves" (Report of the Commissioner of Indian Affairs, H. Doc., vol. 537, no. 1, 30 Cong., 2 sess. [November 30, 1848], p. 398). See also the New York Herald, December 5, 1848.

30. Ibid., pp. 385–86.

31. Ibid., p. 387.

The territorial acquisitions of the 1840s could not be turned to account unless the United States encouraged settlement and gained undisputed dominion over their native populations. In mid-1847, confidential executive agent Thomas Larkin, in Monterey, advised the Polk administration to send more troops to California. "Nothing but strong and efficient measures to put down the depredations of the Indians (who are wild) is wanted to cause the farming interest to advance rapidly," he told Buchanan. Since the American conquest of 1846, he reported, California's commerce had trebled in value, and he expected agriculture to prosper similarly if the Indians could be subjugated. In mid-1848, Secretary of war William Marcy recommended protecting California with six or seven military posts and fifteen to eighteen hundred troops, Oregon with three or four posts and one thousand troops, New Mexico with three or four posts and twelve hundred troops, and the lower Rio Grande valley with fifteen hundred strategically placed troops. But with federal funds badly depleted by the war, Congress failed to provide appropriations for such a large army of occupation, leaving settlers in Oregon to suffer what Ritchie called "the outrages of blood-thirsty savages." At this time Medill advised that the Pawnee and Sioux tribes be confined north of the Platte River; American pioneers would then have "a wide and safe passage" to Oregon and California.[32] Even without Marcy's military buildup, however, the Indians' ascendancy in California and Oregon quickly ended, since gold and fertile soil soon drew many thousands of Americans westward. Pioneers, not diplomats, acquired the land as they decimated and displaced the Indians of the Pacific Coast.

Medill, Marcy, Buchanan, and other officials had refused to recognize that the federal government, as constituted in the 1840s, could not meet its obligations to Indians sheltered behind the thin tissue of treaties and proclamations of good intent. However humane and sincere certain whites were in their concern for Indians, they could not reconcile the desires of the natives with the demands of the whites. The national government faced a dilemma: treaties obligated federal leaders to honor the country's commitments to the Indians, but state governments, citizens, and distant pioneers demanded in-

32. Larkin to Buchanan, August 25, 1847, in George P. Hammond, ed., *The Larkin Papers: Personal, Business, and Official Correspondence of Thomas Oliver Larkin . . .* , 10 vols. (Berkeley, 1951–64), 6:291–92; Marcy to Polk, July 31, 1848, in Cooling, *New American State Papers*, 2:201–2; Washington *Daily Union*, June 2, 1848; *Report of the Commissioner of Indian Affairs, H. Doc.*, vol. 537, p. 390.

stead that the government respond to their own immediate needs. White philanthropists and policy makers were unable to grasp the intricacies of white expansion and native decline. This inability of even the most informed observers to recognize the inherent defects in American Indian policy appears in the recommendations made by Thomas McKenney in his autobiography, published in 1846.[33]

McKenney approved of American territorial expansion, but he also sincerely advocated humane treatment of Indians and was prepared to go further than most of his contemporaries to give them a secure place within the Union. From 1816 to 1830, as superintendent of Indian trade and head of the Indian Bureau, McKenney had acquired as much experience in Indian affairs as anyone during the Jacksonian era. His knowledge of natives was unsurpassed. His reputation renders his detached advice on Indian policy during the 1840s all the more fascinating, since like others before him he proved unable to reconcile his benevolent sentiments with the hard realities of relentless white expansion.[34] His program to save the Indian was not only unrealistic about the needs of the Indians; it was also oblivious to the prejudices of most whites.

McKenney was among a group of men of letters, including George Bancroft and John O'Sullivan, who detected the hand of God in the expansion of white Americans across the continent.[35] Providential favor, however, did not excuse Americans from all obligations to Indians. McKenney supported the previous federal efforts to civilize the Indians but regretted that the "great mass" of them still remained "one exhibition of human degradation and human misery." The problem, he maintained, was that neither church nor state had yet been able to devise a way "to reform and civilize the Indians, *as a race.*" It was important to continue the various civilizing methods that were already in use, but McKenney also advised that the western Indian reserve be made an official federal territory and be prepared for statehood. All citizenship rights should be extended to the Indi-

33. Thomas L. McKenney, *Memoirs, Official and Personal,* 2 vols. (New York, 1846). For scholarly works on McKenney, see Herman J. Viola, *Thomas L. McKenney: Architect of America's Early Indian Policy, 1816–1830* (Chicago, 1974); Robert M. Kvasnicka and Herman J. Viola, eds., *The Commissioners of Indian Affairs, 1824–1977* (Lincoln, Neb., 1979), pp. 1–7; Richard Drinnon, *Facing West: The Metaphysics of Indian-Hating and Empire-Building* (New York, 1980), pp. 165–90.

34. See Drinnon, *Facing West,* p. 178.

35. During the Jacksonian period the cry for a distinctly American literature was accompanied by a cry for a distinctly American history. The nationalistic history of the Jacksonian era is discussed by Fred Somkin, *Unquiet Eagle: Memory and Desire in the Idea of American Freedom, 1815–1860* (Ithaca, 1967), Chapter 5.

ans. "There is no difference between us, save only in the color, and in our superior advantages," he asserted. The need to make amends for past injustices inflicted by whites upon Indians, as well as the Indians' own inherent capacity for improvement, were the justifica- tions for his recommendations. "Our fears and our passions are at rest," he concluded. He hoped that white demands for Indian lands had ceased.[36]

Whether McKenney had any means of ascertaining the wishes of Indians—or for believing that whites would accept his solution—is unclear. The notion that a "savage" confederation of Indians could be granted full civil rights and representation in Congress was, given the racial prejudices of the day, unrealistic if not absurd. White Americans would not allow a separate but equal territory on the continent for Indians or blacks, and the prospect for the eventual acculturation and assimilation of Indians and blacks was not promis- ing either. No prominent Jacksonian Democrat shared McKenney's generous impression that the races of mankind were innately equal and distinguished from one another by characteristics acquired through adaptation to different environmental and historical circumstances. For all his experience and knowledge, McKenney could not fathom the complexities of prejudice and politics and their impact on policies during the 1840s.

Yet prominent Americans continued to contend that in the newly acquired western territories the federal government could and would protect and assist the Indians. Senator Sevier of Arkansas, a member of the Committee on Indian Affairs, argued in 1844 that the United States would "civilize, educate, and christianize" the Indians in the West and "save and preserve them from falling by the bloody hand of each other, and make them, as we have other tribes, what they should be, under the favor of Providence, better images of their Creator." Ingersoll, in 1847, similarly proposed that the United States always sought to "civilize, humanize, and reclaim vanquished sav- ages." He described the mixed inhabitants of the borderlands in terms usually applied to American Indians: "slothful, superstitious, brutish people, sprinkled over great spaces," badly in need of enlight- enment and regeneration. The Indians apparently needed only pro- tection from other Indians, not whites. The natives' primitive instincts, rather than white behavior or flaws in federal policy, were at fault.[37]

36. *Memoirs*, 2:60–69, 79–81, 126–27. The idea of making the Indian reserve a formal federal territory was not new in the 1840s.

37. *CG*, 28 Cong., 1 sess., App. 309 (March 21, 1844); *CG*, 29 Cong., 2 sess., App. 130 (January 19, 1847).

Senator John Dix of New York, on the other hand, avoided the pretenses of altruistic mission and, in 1848, predicted a darker future for the western Indians. California's and New Mexico's Indians "must there, as everywhere else, give way before the advancing wave of civilization, either to be overwhelmed by it, or to be driven upon perpetually contracting areas, where, from a diminution of their accustomed sources of subsistence, they must ultimately become ex-tinct by force of an inevitable law," he told his colleagues. Senator Benton, in 1846, had also emphasized the predominance of racial factors in recent history. As the United States consolidated its conti-nental empire and encountered China and its people during its west-ward surge, white "moral and intellectual superiority" would determine the course of events, as had been true in the case of contact with Indians. "The White race will take the ascendant, elevating what is susceptible of improvement—wearing out what is not," Benton de-clared. "The Red race has disappeared from the Atlantic coast: the tribes that resisted civilization, met extinction."[38] To most expansion-ists, the "wearing out" of unimproved races was an indisputable fact of history at this time. The annals of United States Indian policy could offer little solace to the western Indians. Unable to save themselves, they could not count on the government to save them either.

The "Savage" Mexicans

To the expansionists, comparisons between Indians and Mexicans seemed logical because both peoples appeared to be inferior to Anglo-Americans and both posed obstacles to the acquisition and consolida-tion of a continental empire. Moreover, in the view of racially con-scious Protestant Americans, miscegenation and Catholicism in Mexico had prevented the Mexicans from forming a progressive society or a democratic government. As Gene M. Brack has shown, between 1821 and 1846 many influential Mexicans altered their views of the United States as they became aware of these racist and ethnocentric biases, moving from initial respect or ambivalence to animosity that culminated in widespread anti-Americanism among much of the pop-ulation, and, in 1846, in a willingness to go to war. Brack notes that "it did not take long for Mexicans to discern the similarity of Ameri-can attitudes toward blacks, Indians, and Mexicans. The Americans,

38. *CG*, 30 Cong., 1 sess., App. 181 (January 26, 1848); *CG*, 29 Cong., 1 sess., 918 (May 28, 1846).

they knew, justified the despoliation of Indians by insisting that the
Anglo-Saxon race could make better use of their lands. Americans
used precisely the same argument in justifying their craving for Mexican territory."[39] During the war American public figures projected
their negative images of Indians and blacks onto Mexicans; they
disparaged Mexico and sanctioned the conquest of its territory in a
litany of contemptuous outbursts.

Anti-Mexican prejudices were widespread in the United States, but
not universal. Some Whigs understood why Mexico still criticized the
United States for the role American adventurers had played in the
Texas revolution, and they had warned the Democrats from 1844 to
mid-1846 that Mexico would view the annexation of Texas by the
United States as a culmination of a decade-long conspiracy to rob
Mexico of its strategic province. The Democrats, however, scoffed at
such warnings and dismissed Mexico's diplomatic protests against
annexation as mere rodomontade from a vicious and deluded people.
The pervasiveness of racist and ethnocentric biases among the Democrats prevented them from dealing with Mexico as a nation worthy
of the respect that the United States demanded in its own foreign
relations.

Illinois congressman Orlando Ficklin denounced the religion, government, and character of the Mexicans when urging the annexation
of Texas in early 1845. "A corrupt priesthood, with an affiliated
moneyed aristocracy" had "waged unceasing war upon the liberties
of the people" of Mexico, he told his House colleagues. Lest his
audience assume that he sympathized with those oppressed masses,
however, he quickly added that "rapine, plunder, and the spoils of
conquest" seemed to be "the only sentiment that animates the bosom
of her people." A Negrophobe, who hoped (as noted in Chapter 2)
that Texas would become the repository for the unwanted blacks in
the United States, Ficklin described Mexico's heterogeneous population as "barbarous and cruel," a "sordid and treacherous people"
who were "destitute of noble impulses."[40] In other words, Mexicans
resembled blacks and Indians in the United States and should be
treated accordingly.

The Polk administration treated Mexico and its people with condescension and scorn. Prior to the outbreak of war in mid-1846, Polk

39. *Mexico Views Manifest Destiny, 1821–1846: An Essay on the Origins of the Mexican
War* (Albuquerque, 1975), p. 170.
40. *CG,* 28 Cong., 2 sess., 183 (January 23, 1845).

pursued a diplomatic approach to Mexico that would have outraged Americans had a similar policy been directed by a foreign power toward the United States. Inspired by the precedent set by Jefferson's 1803 request for a secret appropriation to purchase the Louisiana Territory from France, Polk in early 1846 decided to solicit secret funds from Congress that could be paid to Mexican officials as induce-ment to cede all Mexican territory north of the thirty-second parallel to the United States.[41] Polk confided to his cabinet and Senators Benton, Allen, Cass, and Calhoun that a million-dollar appropriation would give him all the leverage he needed to settle the crisis with Mexico.[42] Polk thought he could bribe Mexican leaders to cede the disputed area between the Nueces and Rio Grande rivers, and per-haps to hand over California and New Mexico besides. Preoccupied with securing their own power in a revolution-ridden country, Mexi-can officials would exchange territory for money they could use to protect their own ascendance at home. So reasoned Polk.

The administration's assumption that the Mexicans would not fight—and its outraged assertion, when the Mexicans did fight, that their attack was treacherous and unprovoked—reflected an underlying conviction that the Mexicans were an inferior people.[43] On the day Polk asked Congress to declare war against Mexico, Ritchie ran a particularly strident editorial that insisted that his nation was entirely

41. *The Diary of James K. Polk during His Presidency, 1845–1849,* Milo M. Quaife, ed., 4 vols. (Chicago, 1910), 1 (March 28, 1846):305–10.

42. *Ibid.* (March 28–31, April 3, 1846):305–10, 315–17.

43. See James K. Polk to William Polk, "Private," November 27, 1845, Polk Papers; Marcy to Prosper M. Wetmore, July 6, 1845, William Marcy Papers; Washington *Daily Union,* August 1, 1845; August 18, 27, and 28, 1845; Polk's war message to Congress, in Richardson, *Messages and Papers,* 5 (May 11, 1846):2291–92. O'Sullivan also ridiculed Mexico's protests against United States policy: "Let its bark be treated with contempt, and its little bite, if it should attempt it, [be] quietly brushed aside with a single stroke of the paw, without hurting it anymore than cannot be helped" (New York *Morning News,* August 16, 1845). Polk and his advisers had realized prior to hearing about the skirmish on the Rio Grande that war would be necessary to attain the administration's territorial objectives. Polk, however, believed he could control events, take the initiative, and wage war against Mexico when it suited the United States. He preferred to buy off Mexico, not fight it. For a different view that argues that Polk, through his executive agents in Texas, deliberately tried to provoke war with Mexico, see Glenn W. Price, *Origins of the War with Mexico: The Polk-Stockton Intrigue* (Austin, 1967). Price's argument is an elaboration of an earlier view by Richard R. Stenberg, "The Failure of Polk's Mexican War Intrigue of 1845," *Pacific Historical Review,* 4 (March, 1935):39–68, and " Polk and Frémont, 1845–1846," *Pacific Historical Review,* 7 (1938):211–27. Chargé Donelson, however, saw no evidence of any plot to use Texas to incite war with Mexico (see Donelson to Buchanan, June 2, July 2, and July 11, 1845, in Manning, *Diplomatic Correspondence,* 12:423–24, 444–45, 450).

right, its antagonist entirely wrong. "The foreign foe dishonors and desecrates American soil by his footsteps, and has made it red with American blood," he cried.[44] With Mexico so clearly at fault, the United States would be justified in demanding whatever terms it wanted.

After Congress had declared war and American troops had invaded Mexico, negative images of Mexico permeated the Democratic press and the debate over the origins of the war. Ritchie expected Mexico to seek a hasty reconciliation with the United States. Mexico could offer only "a slight resistance to the North American race," he noted during the first week of the war. "Its motley character, and physical structure are the surest indication of defeat—for out of seven millions of souls four millions are Indians, and of the remaining three millions, but twelve hundred thousand are whites." In June, Bennett, writing in the *Herald,* attributed "the imbecility and degradation of the Mexican people" to "the amalgamation of races" there and predicted an early triumph for the United States. He observed that "the idea of amalgamation has been always abhorrent to the Anglo-Saxon race on this continent." As Americans had moved westward, they had wisely "kept aloof from the inferior races, and . . . barbarism [had] receded before the face of civilization." Bennett expected that Anglo-Americans would similarly displace Mexico's mixed population. As "the tide of emigration" from the United States swept over Mexico, the "imbecile" inhabitants were "as sure to melt away at the approach of Anglo-Saxon energy and enterprise as snow before a southern sun." The fate of the Mexicans, Bennett predicted, would be "similar to that of the Indians of this country—the race, before a century rolls over us, will become extinct."[45]

Contrary to American expectations, Mexico did not capitulate quickly even after a series of significant defeats. This stubborn resistance incensed the expansionists, who searched for some explanation for the enemy's protracted opposition. In the meantime they stepped up their verbal assaults on Mexico. Congressman Richard Brodhead of Pennsylvania spoke for many Democrats in early 1847 when he complained that General Santa Anna had retained power in Mexico and sustained the war "by telling the people that this is a war upon their race and their religion; that we wish to drive them from the land

44. Washington *Daily Union,* May 11, 1846. For Polk's war message, see Richardson, *Messages and Papers,* 5:2287-93.
45. Washington *Daily Union,* May 15, 1846; New York *Herald,* June 5, 1846.

which contains the graves of their ancestors, and destroy their Government, and make them slaves. The people, particularly those of mixed blood, are ignorant, and they believe it," he grumbled.[46] His contention that the United States did not wish to dispossess the Mexicans of their land was not very convincing, since his disavowal of territorial ambitions was drowned out by a simultaneous chorus of cries for a large territorial indemnity. Like the eastern Indians, the Mexicans in the borderlands would have to forfeit "the land which contains the graves of their ancestors." There was no resisting manifest destiny.

Ingersoll, in early 1847, cited the Mexicans' alleged inferiority when he defended the administration's establishment of interim governments in New Mexico and California. Those provinces, he contended, were sparsely inhabited by inferior races, and their occupation and possession by Americans would benefit the degraded natives as well as the United States and its people. New York congressman Samuel Gordon agreed that a "perfidious and mixed race—a community of pirates and robbers," inhabited the borderlands. The United States was obligated "to civilize, Christianize, and moralize" them and to "teach them what they so much stand in need of—a knowledge of humanity, industry, and justice; to their own great advantage, and to the advantage of all nations that have any intercourse or correspondence with them." No kinder to the enemy, Senator Fairfield of Maine described Mexicans as "a rascally, perfidious race." "No reliance can be placed in their most solemn compacts," he complained to his wife in early 1847. "They are little better than a band of pirates and robbers."[47] The repetition of the same pejorative labels reflected the pervasiveness of the ethnocentrism.

Like other expansionists at this time, Edward Hannegan wanted territory, but he also wanted to segregate the Mexican population from Anglo-Americans who would settle in the borderlands. "Mexico and the United States are peopled by two distinct and utterly unhomogeneous races," he noted in a Senate speech in 1847. "In no reasonable period could we amalgamate." The Mexicans appeared "utterly unfit for the blessings and the restraints of rational liberty, because they cannot comprehend the distinction between regulated freedom, and that unbridled licentiousness which consults only the

46. *CG*, 29 Cong., 2 sess., App. 330 (February 9, 1847).
47. *CG*, 29 Cong., 2 sess., App. 130 (January 19, 1847); *CG*, 29 Cong., 2 sess., 391 (February 11, 1847); John Fairfield to Mrs. Anna Fairfield, January 10, 1847, in *The Letters of John Fairfield*, Arthur G. Staples, ed. (Lewiston, Maine, 1922), p. 437.

evil passions of the human heart."[48] Such a people, resembling "our own savage tribes," could never become equal participants in American politics or society.

The Democrats underestimated the Mexicans' hostility and their determination to contest the "inevitable" expansion of the United States. Polk, for example, miscalculated the enemy's resolve when, two months into the war, he advised his brother not to return home from Italy to join the army in Mexico because the fighting would be over before he could reach New York.[49] To the chagrin of the administration and the detriment of the Democratic party, however, Mexico fought on into 1848 before capitulating to the United States. The expansionists had counted on the Mexican people to greet the American forces as liberators but realized that Americans were instead regarded as conquerors. After six months of intense fighting in northern Mexico, Slidell notified Polk that American troops were encountering fierce resistance from the Mexicans. "There would seem to be more hostility towards us on the part of the population of the Northeastern provinces of Mexico than was anticipated," he admitted.[50] Slidell and other Democrats apparently assumed that the Mexicans were not aware of the racism and ethnocentrism in the United States, or perhaps the Democratic expansionists refused to recognize the magnitude of their own prejudices and were therefore astonished to learn that the Mexicans saw them differently than they saw themselves.

Polk, Buchanan, and Marcy all regarded Mexico's reliance on guerrilla warfare as further proof of the Mexicans' debased natures. Polk angrily reported to Congress in 1847 that "the Mexican people generally became hostile to the United States, and availed themselves of every opportunity to commit the most savage excesses upon our troops. Large numbers of the population took up arms, and, engaging in guerrilla warfare, robbed and murdered in the most cruel manner individual soldiers or small parties whom accident or other causes had separated from the main body of our army; bands of guerrilleros and robbers infested the roads, harassed our trains, and whenever it was in their power cut off our supplies." In the same vein, Buchanan claimed that the United States had been forbearing in its invasion and occupation of Mexico, having paid fair prices for Mexican goods

48. *CG,* 29 Cong., 2 sess., 516 (February 26, 1847).
49. Polk to William H. Polk, "Private," July 14, 1846, Polk Papers. See also Polk to Gideon Pillow, May 16, 1846, Polk Papers.
50. Slidell to Polk, November 4, 1846, Polk Papers.

while respecting property rights and assisting stricken soldiers. Yet
Mexico had responded with vicious warfare and insulting peace terms.
Brigadier General Caleb Cushing, then a commander of volunteers
in Mexico, echoed the administration's bitterness. Mexico, he wrote
to Buchanan, must be vanquished "by the unflinching application of
physical force." Marcy complained that "the guerrilla system which
has been resorted to is hardly recognized as a legitimate mode of
warfare" and advised General Winfield Scott to retaliate "with the
utmost allowable severity." To punish the Mexican people for assisting the guerrillas, Marcy recommended that the burden of sustaining
American forces in Mexico "be thrown, to the utmost extent, upon
the people of that country."[51]

By late 1846, it was clear that the United States would expand at
Mexico's expense. The question during the remainder of the war was
how much territory would be acquired, and whether or not slavery
would be permitted to spread west of Texas. The issue of the size of
the territorial indemnity divided the Democrats, since the coveted
land of Mexico also contained a population repugnant to most Americans. The dilemma was to strike a happy balance between the desire
for Mexico's land and resources and the demand that masses of
nonwhite people be excluded from the Union. After exhaustive deliberation the conflict was resolved, although the compromise did not
satisfy the more extreme proponents of expansion who entertained
the notion of acquiring all of Mexico for the United States.

The predicament resulting from the competing pressures of racism
and ethnocentrism and a desire to possess Mexico's abundant resources was explored in depth in the *Democratic Review* during the
closing months of 1847. In response to a small but spirited group of
expansionists in Congress who called for the acquisition of all of
Mexico, a writer for the *Review* pointed out that "the difficulties of

51. Polk's third annual message, in Richardson, *Messages and Papers*, 5 (December
7, 1847):2397; Buchanan to Nicholas Trist, October 6, 1847; Cushing to Buchanan,
October 31, 1847, Buchanan Papers; Marcy to Scott, October 6, 1847, Marcy Papers.
Polk agreed that "it is now manifest that the war must be prosecuted with increased
forces and increased energy. We must levy contributions and quarter on the enemy"
(*Diary*, 3 [October 5, 1847]:186). See also the Washington *Daily Union*, October 1 and
5, 1847. In California, the Mexicans' tactics also enraged Americans. From Los
Angeles, confidential agent Archibald Gillespie wrote to his associate Thomas Larkin
in Monterey, "I would make every one of these rascally Californians pay most dearly
for every drop of American blood they have spilt, through their treachery and want
of faith. Had they waged an honest open war from the commencement, I would then
have some sympathy for them, but as it is I feel myself surrounded by assassins, and
I would deal with them accordingly" (Gillespie to Larkin, March 5, 1847, in Hammond, *Larkin Papers*, 6:37).

Mexico have grown out of the fact that [the Mexicans] possess vast natural wealth, which they do not appreciate nor exert themselves to develop." "It is not in the nature of things," he argued, "that a race of enterprising adventurers should permit rich mines and valuable lands to remain unoccupied, merely because they are within the limits of a government whose people are too imbecile to turn them to advantage."[52] Despite the lure of Mexico's resources, though, many moderate expansionists resisted the idea of acquiring the entire country. "The annexation of the country to the United States would be a calamity," a writer in the *Review* cautioned in August 1847. The addition of five million "ignorant and indolent half-civilized Indians" along with a million and a half "free negroes and mulattoes, the remnants of the British slave trade, would scarcely be a desirable incumbrance, even with the great natural wealth of Mexico."[53] The riches of Mexico, however plentiful and enticing, could not compensate for the perils of incorporating its nonwhite peoples into the United States.

Moderate expansionists who opposed the All Mexico movement suggested that the United States might ultimately absorb most or all of Mexico safely if it acquired sparsely settled areas immediately but deferred the incorporation of densely inhabited areas until American migration substantially altered the composition of their populations. Rather than attempt to uplift all of the colored peoples below the Rio Grande at once, the proponents of gradual acquisition preferred to whitewash Mexico piece by piece through migration from the United States. An article in the *Democratic Review* suggested that "the admirable climate, fertile fields, and boundless mineral resources of Mexico" had been recognized by American soldiers and that this knowledge was now circulating rapidly among Americans. Enterprising troops would form the vanguard of American settlement in Mexico, and civilian pioneers would soon follow. "Had Mexico been settled by a vigorous race of Europeans . . . that would have turned its advantages to account, developed its wealth, increased its commerce and multiplied its settlements, she would not now be in danger of losing her lands by emigration from the North," the *Review* concluded.[54]

52. "Occupation of Mexico," *Democratic Review*, 21 (November, 1847):389. Congressman Thomas Jefferson Henley of Indiana also contended that Americans would find the rich resources of Mexico irresistible and would eventually acquire them, with or without Mexico's consent (*CG*, 30 Cong., 1 sess., App. 251 [January 26, 1848]).

53. "Mexico—The Church, and Peace," *Democratic Review*, 21 (August, 1847):101.

54. "New Territory versus No Territory," *Democratic Review*, 21 (October, 1847):291; "Occupation of Mexico," ibid. (November, 1847):389. The *Review* advised that the United States obtain Mexico "piece by piece" as it became "Anglo-Saxonized."

A similar cautiousness appeared in Ritchie's editorials. He too found Mexico's land attractive, but he found its inhabitants very unattractive. In the fall of 1847 he described New Mexico's and California's peoples as being "immersed in ignorance—destitute of talent, of enterprise, and of all generous ambition." As Americans settled the borderlands, however, he expected the original residents there to become "more improved, more refined, and more active." They would also become "reconciled to their lot, and live in peace with us." He did not endorse the acquisition of densely populated areas south of the Rio Grande, however, fearing that such areas would prove less amenable to rapid American colonization.[55]

Speculations about Mexico's future often resembled ruminations about the Indians' future. The *Democratic Review* anticipated that "a strong infusion of the American race would impart energy and industry gradually to the indolent Mexicans, and give them such a consistency as a people, as would enable them to hold and occupy their territories in perfect independence."[56] As white Americans gradually gained predominance in Mexico and the indigenous population improved, the United States could then consider adding the country to the Union. Offering a similar view was the enigmatic Bennett. "In the end," he wrote in October 1847, the United States would "be obliged . . . to seize and annex the whole country." Such a remark seemed to identify Bennett with the All Mexico faction, but he carefully qualified his statement. "The admission into the union, on an equality with the other states, of any Mexican state in whose population Mexican blood preponderates, must be after years of patient probation," he counseled. "Once the fiat goes forth for the subjugation of the whole country," he predicted, "our citizens will pour into it in such numbers that very few years will elapse before they have the preponderance." Congress could then admit new states "as each qualifies for that privilege by a sufficient admixture of our own blood."[57] Bennett expected the nonwhite Mexican population to recede and then disappear in the face of competition from white Americans.

After the acquisition of Texas and Oregon and the occupation and anticipated acquisition of California and New Mexico, many Democrats hesitated to obtain more territory. After 1846, the divisive effects

55. Washington *Daily Union*, September 16, 1847.
56. "Occupation of Mexico," vol. 21, p. 388.
57. New York *Herald*, October 28, 1847.

of the Wilmot Proviso, mounting animosity among northern Democrats toward the Polk administration, and fears of adding Mexico's
nonwhite peoples to the Union diminished ardor for expansion.
Extremists such as Walker, Cass, Allen, Douglas, and Hannegan still
pressed for more territory in 1847 and 1848, but their agitation for
all Mexico was a pis aller, not a popular or prominent movement, as
some scholars have maintained.[58] To some expansionists, the occupation and annexation of all of Mexico seemed preferable to an interminable guerrilla war with an enemy that refused to make war yet
refused to make peace. But by this time only a radical contingent in
Congress and the press wanted to acquire Mexican territory heavily
encumbered with nonwhite peoples.

During the Senate debates on the war and the issue of territorial
indemnity, Calhoun insisted that the color line be drawn at the Rio
Grande River and that the United States not extend its jurisdiction
south of it. The racial composition of the population below the Rio
Grande, he warned, precluded American expansion there. The vast
area north of the river, however, could be held by the United States,
since it was "almost literally an uninhabited country." California and
New Mexico, under the nominal control of Mexico, stood as "an
uninhabited and barren waste" and would remain so "for generations" unless occupied by Americans. Mexico could never retain
control over the borderlands, and Americans alone could "people it
with an industrious and civilized race."[59] Because Mexicans were
neither industrious nor civilized, they could never become American
citizens.

The day after Calhoun's important statement, Cass resumed the
Senate's discussion of an indemnity and of the character of Mexico's
population, and clarified his own position. In comments demonstrating the similarity between the views of southern white supremacists
and northern Negrophobes, Cass said that Calhoun had "submitted
many sound observations respecting the diversity of character, of
races, and of institutions,. . . which exist between us and Mexico, and
he deprecates, with equal zeal and justice, the union of the Mexican
people and ours." Cass agreed that such a union "would be a deplorable amalgamation. . . . We do not want the people of Mexico, either
as citizens or subjects," he stressed. "All we want is a portion of

58. For a different view, see John Douglas Pitts Fuller, *The Movement for the
Acquisition of All Mexico, 1846–1848* (Baltimore, 1936), and Billington, *Far Western
Frontier,* p. 191.
59. *CG,* 29 Cong., 2 sess., App. 325–26 (February 9, 1847).

territory, which they nominally hold, generally uninhabited, or, where inhabited at all, sparsely so, and with a population which would soon recede, or identify itself with ours."[60] Like the Indians east of the Mississippi whom Cass, as Jackson's secretary of war from 1831 to 1837, had helped to remove, the Mexicans would have to acculturate or acquiesce in their own extinction.

As the war continued into 1848, the agitation by the All Mexico faction again brought Calhoun to the fore to denounce any scheme to acquire well-populated territory. The United States, Calhoun proclaimed, had never "incorporated into the Union any but the Caucasian race. To incorporate Mexico would be the first departure of the kind; for more than half of its population are pure Indians, and by far the larger portion of the residue mixed blood," he protested. "Ours is the government of the white man," Calhoun continued, urging Congress not to commit "the fatal error of placing the colored race on an equality with the white."[61] Rejecting any notion of natural rights, Calhoun instead stressed racial determinism. Even those more amenable to obtaining land below the Rio Grande shared Calhoun's view that the Mexican population was incapable of self-government, some even suggesting that Mexico's nonwhite peoples be removed to isolated reservations to make room for white pioneers.[62]

Immediately after Calhoun had addressed the Senate, Ritchie tried to dispel the rumors concerning Polk's intentions. Ritchie observed that Calhoun seemed "alarmed at the prospect of annexing the whole of Mexico to the United States, with a population of seven or eight millions of people, who are unfit to participate in the benefits of our free institutions." Such apprehensions lacked foundation, Ritchie wrote; Polk "particularly disclaimed such a scheme" and instead heartily

60. *CG,* 29 Cong., 2 sess., App. 191 (February 10, 1847).

61. *CG,* 30 Cong., 1 sess., App. 51 (January 4, 1848). Calhoun had also expressed this view as secretary of state in 1844 when he wrote to William King, "It is our policy to increase, by growing and spreading out into unoccupied regions, assimilating all we incorporate: in a word, to increase by accretion, and not, through conquest, by the addition of masses held together by the cohesion of force" (August 12, 1844, *CG,* 28 Cong., 2 sess., App. 6 [December 18, 1844]).

62. In early 1848, for example, Senate Foreign Relations Committee chairman Sevier advised that the United States occupy all of Mexico by extending American naturalization laws to whites there and removing the vast nonwhite population to reservations. Maryland Congressman Robert McLane advocated that the United States take formal possession of Mexico north of Tampico, then incorporate all of Mexico into the commercial system of the United States. The "aboriginal" population could be relocated to remote areas (see *CG,* 30 Cong., 1 sess., App. 261–62 [January 4, 1848], *CG,* 30 Cong., 1 sess., 202 [January 13, 1848]).

desired "to maintain the nationality of Mexico." The administration shared Calhoun's fears of racial amalgamation, but it rejected his suggestion of withdrawing American troops from Mexico to a "defensive line" along the Rio Grande and the thirty-second parallel.[63] The rift between Calhoun and the administration developed because of disagreements over military strategy, not because of differences over the issues of race and expansion.

Calhoun was not alone in drawing a crucial distinction between the acquisition of sparsely and densely settled regions. Envoy Donelson, in letters to Polk in 1846 and 1847, warned him not to demand any territory from Mexico south of a line drawn from the Rio Grande west to Monterey in California. The addition of any land containing large numbers of nonwhite peoples, he feared, would create insurmountable problems for the nation. "Nothing can be gained by a war with Mexico," Donelson had warned in 1846. Though there was "no danger" in eventually acquiring California by peaceful means, "because in five years four-fifths of its population will be emigrants from the Union," Donelson added that the acquisition of any well-populated Mexican territory would be problematic because the Mexicans were "not fit for incorporation into our Union." A year later he reiterated his concern. "The Mexican climate and soil are as inferior to ours as are her people," he advised. "We cannot engraft . . . either our government or our labor" upon them.[64]

Still suspicious that Polk and his advisers disagreed with him, Donelson in early 1848 again wrote to the president, denouncing those who favored acquiring all of Mexico. "We can no more amalgamate with her people than with negroes," he warned Polk. After the war and the cession of the northern provinces to the United States, Donelson remained apprehensive about the racial and sectional difficulties exacerbated by the new acquisitions. After the Democratic defeat in the 1848 election, he confided to Buchanan that the conquest of Mexico's northern provinces had "nothing in it but distraction to the Democratic party" and predicted that the problems of expansion and slavery would plague the Union "for the next 100 years." Polk had obtained a vast but divisive western empire and a new slavery extension controversy, and had split his party. The triumph of the Whigs showed that in gaining the borderlands, the Democrats had lost New York and Pennsylvania.[65] Donelson's premonitions were correct. Bu-

63. Washington *Daily Union,* January 4, 1848. See also ibid., January 7, 1848.
64. Donelson to Polk, May 23, 1846, and May 11, 1847, Polk Papers.
65. Donelson to Polk, March 13, 1848, Polk Papers; Donelson to Buchanan, "Private," December 14, 1848, Buchanan Papers.

chanan's own presidential difficulties a decade later, especially during the Kansas crisis, demonstrated the difficulty of reconciling white expansionism with racism and slavery, and of appeasing the South without alienating growing numbers of Free-Soilers in the North.

Buchanan frequently shifted his position on how extensive a territorial indemnity the United States should demand from Mexico. But his opinion on the character of the enemy's population remained consistent. In the spring of 1847, Buchanan explained to General James Shields, a commander of Illinois volunteers in Mexico, "You desire to annex the country on this side of the Sierra Madre Mountains to the United States. This would not be in accordance with public opinion in our country. . . . How should we govern the mongrel race which inhabits it?" Buchanan asked. The acquisition of Upper and Lower California was desirable, though, since they were "comparatively uninhabited and will therefore be almost exclusively colonised by our own people."[66] Racial considerations, however, could sometimes be overshadowed by political calculations. Buchanan badly wanted the presidency in 1848, and he was willing to support the acquisition of territory below the Rio Grande if it seemed a politically expedient course. Later in 1847, Buchanan switched to the Sierra Madre line he had earlier opposed, a move that irked Polk and Walker.[67]

The debate over expansionism during the war revealed that the blade of prejudice cut both ways. American feelings of superiority over other peoples provided a self-serving sanction for taking territory from them, but these same feelings also inhibited expansion by making areas more densely populated by nonwhite peoples less attractive to the Democrats. The acquisition of California and New Mexico proved a satisfactory solution to the dilemma of balancing imperialism with racism. Ritchie expressed the sentiments of all but the most extreme expansionists when he hailed the Trist Treaty in early 1848. "Fortunately for us, we obtain that very portion of the country which is the sparsest in population," he noted. "Our own population, swelled as it will be by the emigration from Germany and other countries of Europe, will so rapidly pour into the new territory,

66. Buchanan to Shields, "Confidential," April 23, 1847, Buchanan Papers.
67. Polk and Walker had consistently advocated a larger territorial indemnity than Buchanan had, and their differences produced some spirited exchanges in cabinet meetings. "Buchanan is an able man," Polk noted in his diary near the close of his term, "but is in small matters without judgment and sometimes acts like an old maid" (*Diary*, 4 [February 27, 1849]:355).

as to control the actual settlers, and overcome their moral degradation." He suggested that the inhabitants of the borderlands could
soon become "equal members of our great confederacy." But a month
later he retreated from his tolerant position. Referring to Senator
Daniel Webster's critical comments on the native population of the
new territories, Ritchie replied, "He ridicules the Mexican population
already there—and we agree with him that they are not such as we
admire; but how long can this miserable and sparse population stand
up before the hardy and enterprising . . . American people?" "What
we desire to obtain from Mexico is more of territory and less of
population," Ritchie continued, "but we have no objection to the
acquisition of a few of her people along with the soil which we get."[68]

In the Polk administration, missionary idealism was conspicuously
absent. If any benefits were to come to the inhabitants of the new
acquisitions, they would be more incidental than intentional. Blacks
and Indians within the United States encountered harassment, proscription, removal, and enslavement, and there was little prospect
that nonwhite peoples in the new territories would fare any better.
The national government had not been willing to protect a Cherokee
in Georgia or a free black seaman in Charleston, so it seemed improb-
able, whatever the rhetoric, that federal authority could protect nonwhites in the distant West.

Regardless of their disagreement over how many acres and how
many nonwhite people the United States should acquire, most expansionists believed that the fate of Mexicans, like that of Indians, was
not a matter of government policy but rather a matter of racial
destiny beyond human control: Anglo-Saxons were preordained to
rule the continent. A writer in the *Democratic Review* in early 1847
predicted that the experience of the borderland's population would
repeat that of the Indians who had been removed since the War of
1812. "The Mexican race now see, in the fate of the aborigines of the
north, their own inevitable destiny," the author noted. "They must
amalgamate and be lost, in the superior vigor of the Anglo-Saxon
race, or they must utterly perish."[69] Of like mind was Senator Dickinson of New York. A majority of the Mexican population belonged to
"the fated aboriginal races" that could "neither uphold government
or be restrained by it." Such races must "perish under, if they do not
recede before, the influences of civilization." Dickinson argued that

68. Washington *Daily Union*, February 28 and March 30, 1848.
69. "The War," *Democratic Review*, 20 (February, 1847):100.

all of Mexico might ultimately fall into American hands because of the inevitable demise of nonwhite races everywhere. "Like their doomed brethren, who were once spread over the several states of the Union, they are destined, by laws above human agency, to give way to a stronger race from this continent or another," he predicted.[70]

Indiana congressman Thomas Turner explicitly compared Indian removal to the situation facing the indigenous populations of New Mexico and California in 1848. Conceding that inhabitants of the two provinces "would prefer to keep their territory," Turner asked if it was "not equally true that the Indian tribes would have preferred to keep their territory? . . .I witnessed myself the removal of the Pottawatomies, the Winnebagoes, and the Sioux," he recalled. Regardless of how much it would "wound the pride of Mexico to yield to us California and New Mexico, it will not wring their hearts as it did the hearts of those savages when they turned their eyes for the last time upon their council fires and the graves of their fathers." Like Dickinson, Turner emphasized the inevitability of racial competition and exonerated the United States of blame for the eclipse of the "savages."[71]

Senator Sam Houston's views were similar. Speaking at Tammany Hall in early 1848, Houston pointed out that "from the first moment" the pilgrims had landed at Jamestown and Plymouth they had gone on "trading with the Indians, and cheating them out of their lands." He continued, "Now the Mexicans are no better than Indians, and I see no reason why we should not go on in the same course now, and take their land." A "mandate from God" accounted for the success of the American army in Mexico, Houston asserted, and he defined the prospect of the American people in grandiose terms: "The Anglo-Saxon race" would "pervade the whole southern extremity of this vast continent, and the people whom God has placed here in this land, spread, prevail, and pervade throughout the whole rich empire of this great hemisphere." To Houston, American destiny was hemispheric, not merely continental. Nothing could save the hemisphere's indigenous peoples from the "go-ahead" Anglo-Saxon hordes.[72]

70. *CG*, 30 Cong., 1 sess., 158 (January 12, 1848).

71. *CG*, 30 Cong., 1 sess., App. 511 (April 6, 1848).

72. *The Writings of Sam Houston, 1813–1863*, Amelia W. Williams and Eugene C. Barker, eds., 8 vols. (Austin, 1938–43), 5 (February 22, 1848):34–35. "Be it for fame, profit or sport," Thomas Larkin suggested to Bennett in mid-1846, "the Anglo-Saxon is ever the same . . . ever going ahead, ever seeking and g[r]asping some thing he has not" (Larkin to Bennett, May 30, 1846, in Hammond, *Larkin Papers,* 4:403).

Renascent Negrophobia: Antiblack Prejudice
and the Free-Soil Debate

The debates over Indian policy, the Oregon controversy, and the Mexican War generated considerable speculation concerning the bleak prospects for Native Americans and mixed-blood Mexicans on the continent, but the protracted dispute over the Wilmot Proviso reignited the powerful fears about the country's largest and most menacing minority—the blacks. If Robert J. Walker and other propagandists for the acquisition of Texas had expected annexation to ease the Negrophobia in the country, the bitter wrangling over the proviso proved them badly mistaken. Differences among Democrats on the proviso did not signify any basic disagreement over blacks and the problems they posed. Rather, the divisions precipitated by the Free-Soil movement stemmed largely from different expectations about how the adoption of the proviso would affect the North and South—whether closing the Far West to slaves (and free blacks) would benefit or harm whites, especially in states bordering the South. Distinct echoes of the Texas annexation debate sounded again in the battle over the proviso, an indication of the enduring influence of Walker's previous analysis of the connection between westward expansion and the country's racial crisis and a further reminder of the intensity of antiblack feeling in most parts of the nation. Democrats agreed on the desirability of obtaining vast territorial cessions, but they disagreed on where, when, and how the color line should be drawn west of the Mississippi.

Even before the outbreak of the Mexican War in mid-1846 and the conquest of the borderlands later that year, Congressman William Wick had proclaimed, "I do not want any mixed races in our Union, nor men of any color except white, unless they be slaves." Disturbed by the proviso agitation in early 1847, Wick lamented the entire gamut of complications presented by unwanted blacks. "We have our antipathies in Indiana, but they are not local antipathies," he told his House colleagues. Like other whites living in proximity to the slave states, his constituents detested "abolitionism, free-niggerism, and slavery." To keep themselves as free as possible from "the nuisance of a free negro population," his constituents wanted an outlet for "the emigration of free negroes to the South." The presence of nonwhites in the borderlands bothered Wick, but he especially feared blacks in the settled East. He hoped to direct them westward, pending their final exodus out of the country. If the proviso became law, he warned, blacks would enter the North instead of moving beyond the Rio Grande.[73]

Congressman Preston King of New York, on the other hand, urged that a slavery exclusion provision be applied to the borderlands. "The presence of the slave will exclude the laboring white man," he maintained. "Any representative of free white men and women" who would "place free white labor upon a condition of social equality with the labor of the black slave," he continued, would prove himself "false and recreant to his race and to his constituency."[74]

Samuel Gordon agreed with his New York colleague that slavery's harmful effects reached beyond the slave states themselves. Mere proximity to slavery damaged nonslave areas. "Facts proved that in cases where free states were in contact with slave states, the former, and not the latter, suffered," he observed. Because of the proximity of Ohio and Kentucky, for instance, "it was Ohio that suffered, [by] becoming the receptacle of all the free and manumitted negroes, and runaway niggers, who were a curse to any community." Gordon, like King and Wilmot, wished to preserve the West as a refuge for free white laborers from the East.[75]

Congressman Brodhead of Pennsylvania, however, countered that passage of the proviso would actually imperil the North. Having earlier advocated the annexation of Texas, he based his antiproviso stance on similar grounds. Brodhead accused the Free-Soilers of abolitionist leanings and condemned their effort to interfere with slavery by absolutely restricting its expansion. "To free the negroes of the southern states at once would be the greatest calamity which could happen to the whites, as well as the blacks," he asserted in early 1847. If slavery were confined to its present limits, "thousands and tens of thousands" of blacks "would go to the free states, particularly to Pennsylvania," he warned in imitation of Walker. The state's "jails and almshouses would not hold the poor and vicious, and the poor [white] laboring free men and women would be without employment, for the blacks would work cheaper and live on less." Both racial bias and economic factors, then, necessitated measures to prevent a massive influx of blacks into the North. Blacks should be directed toward the Gulf and the Pacific, Brodhead advised, since they were "a nuisance, whether slave or free."[76]

73. CG, 29 Cong., 1 sess., App. 201 (January 30, 1846); CG, 29 Cong., 2 sess., App. 159–60 (February 2, 1847).

74. CG, 29 Cong., 2 sess., 114 (January 5, 1847).

75. CG, 29 Cong., 2 sess., 84 (December 24, 1846); CG, 29 Cong., 2 sess., App. 54 (December 24, 1846).

76. CG, 29 Cong., 2 sess., App. 331 (February 9, 1847).

Even after several futile attempts by Free-Soilers to enact the proviso, Ohio congressman William Sawyer continued to insist that slavery's westward expansion was as vital to the North as the South. "Most of the free negroes in the state of Ohio [are] the most despicable of all creatures," whose situation was "tenfold worse than that of the slaves in the slave states," he asserted in 1848. In the event of emancipation, he warned, the banks of the Ohio River "would be lined with men with muskets on their shoulders to keep off the emancipated slaves which the slave states might attempt to throw in among them." He pledged that he would join his constituents in forming armed columns a mile deep to repel any black invasion of Ohio. Disappointed by the failure of colonization in Africa, Sawyer nevertheless repeated his belief that expatriation remained the "best plan" for solving the racial problem.[77] Although California was no Liberia, it seemed to many northern Negrophobes a better repository for blacks than the free states. Ideally, they would have preferred California to be free of all nonwhite peoples, but since mixed-blood Mexicans and Indians already lived there, no compelling reason existed for closing the distant province to the nation's blacks.

Sawyer did not exaggerate the prejudice in southern and western Ohio. During the summer of 1846, some 387 exslaves who had been liberated and given several thousand dollars by John Randolph to start a new life tried to establish a black community in Mercer county. Before the blacks actually entered Ohio, whites there had accepted payment for real estate and construction costs, but when the blacks arrived to occupy their land the whites repulsed them. According to Samuel Hendry, the liberal editor of the Ashtabula *Sentinel,* the prospective black settlers "found the people of the county assembled at the place of landing ready to meet them in hostile array, and they were prevented by force from entering upon the lands they had purchased." The blacks were compelled to disperse, and they then settled in various parts of the state.[78]

Less racially tolerant than Hendry, Bennett exemplified the curious

77. *CG,* 30 Cong., 1 sess., App. 727–28 (June 22, 1848). Sawyer exhorted southern masters to retain their liberated slaves: "If they would have slaves, let them keep them to themselves; and not when they had worn out a negro's strength manumit him, that Ohio might open her arms and make herself the asylum of all the broken-down negroes in the slaves states" (*CG,* 29 Cong., 2 sess., 91 [December 28, 1846]).

78. Ashtabula *Sentinel,* August 3, 1846. Sawyer's version of the conflict is presented in *CG,* 29 Cong., 2 sess., App. 84 (December 28, 1846), and in *CG,* 30 Cong., 1 sess., App. 726–27 (June 22, 1848). The area to be settled by the blacks was within Sawyer's legislative district.

mixture of concern, remorse, and hatred that often characterized speculations about nonwhite peoples during the late Jacksonian period. Admitting that Indians had been "most wretchedly compensated for the losses they sustained" through white encroachments, Bennett suggested in 1846 that Americans would "have reason to repent" that their treatment of Indians had not been more humane. The day was not far distant when the Indians would have "melted away from the face of the earth."[79] Though contrite about United States Indian policy, Bennett saw no alternative to the Native Americans' rapid decline and final destruction: they were destined to become only memories of a tragic but inescapable past. The Indians' fate influenced Bennett's ideas about other nonwhites, for he predicted that blacks, too, would become extinct. "They do not, when thrown on their own resources, possess the faculties or powers which are necessary to secure to them a high condition of social happiness and prosperity," he argued. Only slavery protected them from ruin. Pairing and condemning the Free-Soilers and abolitionists in 1847, Bennett insisted that blacks and whites in the South were "in a proper and natural position towards each other" and "could not exist in any other relation together." If slavery were allowed to expand into the borderlands, Bennett explained in a reaffirmation of Walker's slave drain theory, it would "tend to diminish slavery in the old slave states, by drawing off the surplus negro population to the newly acquired and fertile territory, and scattering them among the new inhabitants."[80] This dispersion of blacks, however—like the removal of Indians or the displacement of Mexicans—was only a temporary expedient, since "all other races . . . must bow and fade" before "the great work of subjugation and conquest to be achieved by the Anglo-Saxon race" in North America.[81]

Two principal objectives guided the expansionists during the 1840s. They sought to acquire land in order to augment the nation's wealth, power, and security, and they also tried to ensure racial and cultural homogeneity within their expanding empire. At times, as in the additions of Texas, Oregon, and California, their demand for territory could be accommodated with their desire for ethnic and racial purity. At other times, though, as in the All Mexico movement or proposals to acquire Cuba or Yucatán, the two impulses clashed and

79. New York *Herald*, October 6, 1846.
80. New York *Herald*, May 13, 1845, November 28, 1847, September 17, 1846.
81. New York *Herald*, July 4, 1845.

inhibited them. By the late 1840s, the longing of white politicians and publicists for domestic tranquility and racial homogeneity diminished ardor for a constantly expanding empire. Anxieties had not vanished; they had merely changed form, as more Americans began to realize that expansion had drawbacks as well as benefits. The United States had obtained a dysfunctional empire: expansionism alone was not necessarily detrimental to the country; slavery by itself might have been handled successfully. But together they were explosive, and they precipitated the sectional showdown that led to the Civil War.[82]

During the 1840s, little was said or done that would have convinced Indians, blacks, or Mexicans that they could expect any benefits from American expansion. As the expansionists melded simplistic ideas of race, culture, and nationality into a single self-serving concept of empire, enlightenment ideals faded and disappeared. It was not clear to observers at the time whether biology, culture, religion, language, or government made the United States great, but successful expansion at the expense of nonwhite peoples seemed to validate the American sense of superiority. With the rise of scientific racism in the 1830s and 1840s, Americans tended to emphasize race more, and history, environment, and culture less in explaining the differences among peoples and nations.[83] Indians appeared to be a doomed aboriginal race, Mexicans seemed incapable of material progress or self-government, and blacks were a menace whether slave or free.

Explaining the events of the Jacksonian era was simple for Caleb Cushing. "*Race* is the key to much that seems obscure in the history of nations," he wrote in the *Democratic Review* in 1846. "Throughout the world, the spectacle is everywhere the same, of the whiter race ruling the less white, through all gradations of color."[84] Like so many of his contemporaries, Cushing classified various nations and their peoples along a spectrum ranging from inferior to superior, savage to civilized, based largely on their racial compositions. Though he and

82. On the dysfunctional empire, see William A. Williams, *The Contours of American History* (New York, 1973), pp. 276–300; Lloyd C. Gardner, Walter LaFeber, and Thomas McCormick, *Creation of the American Empire* (Chicago, 1973), pp. 157–84.

83. On scientific racism and growing racial consciousness, see George M. Fredrickson, *The Black Image in the White Mind: The Debate on Afro-American Character and Destiny, 1817–1914* (New York, 1971); William Stanton, *The Leopard's Spots: Scientific Attitudes toward Race in America, 1815–1859* (Chicago, 1960); Reginald Horsman, "Scientific Racism and the American Indian in the Mid-Nineteenth Century," *American Quarterly,* 27 (May, 1975):152–68; *Race and Manifest Destiny* (Cambridge, Mass., 1981); Berkhofer, *White Man's Indian.*

84. "Mexico," *Democratic Review,* 18 (June, 1846):434.

other expansionists remained anglophobic during the 1840s, white imperialism, whether British or Yankee, made more sense to them than it had before. Indian removal, the perpetuation of slavery, the capitulation of China to Western gunboats, the victories of the United States over Mexico, and the easy conquest of the borderlands fit in neatly with the course of history in the mid–nineteenth century. Wherever whites ventured, they dominated indigenous peoples.

The United States, then, was no exception to the development of Western imperialism but rather an integral part of it. Racism, commercial ambitions, nationalism, and, to a lesser extent, missionary fervor characterized the United States as much as any other nation of the mid–nineteenth century. Generally associated with the 1890s, the "cult of Anglo-Saxonism" was very much a part of the 1840s.

Expansionists believed that race was a fundamental determinant in human history. Their frequent maligning of nonwhite peoples and their repeated predictions of their demise and extinction were essential components of manifest destiny. The racial thought of the time regarded inequality as an inescapable scientific fact and excused the nation's expansion as an unavoidable historical process. The expansionists viewed territorial acquisitions primarily in terms of their own fears and ambitions, not those of "lesser" peoples cluttering the rich continent. Often oblivious to the discrepancies between their occasionally benevolent rhetoric and their persistently brutal treatment of nonwhites, the expansionists refused to accept responsibility for the consequences of their actions. Manifest destiny, or rather manifest design, offered nothing to nonwhite peoples who faced the restless Anglo-Saxon but inevitable decline, expulsion, or final extinction.

CHAPTER 6

American Exceptionalism, American Empire

Acquiring an empire is one matter; consolidating and governing it quite another. The problem of ruling a continental empire presented a particular challenge to the Democratic expansionists of the 1840s, since the very concept of empire clashed with the theory of republican government. Empires traditionally entailed militarism, colonialism, and exploitation—practices that were anathema to self-determination and self-government, the basic features of the American system. To justify the aggrandizement of the United States, expansionists had to convince themselves and, if possible, their adversaries, that their nation could expand indefinitely without resorting to undemocratic tactics characteristic of imperial rule. The expansionists of the late Jacksonian era syncretized an elaborate ideology of republican empire, promising not only that the institutions of democratic government within the nation would be unharmed by expansion but also that democratic values would be honored in the administration of acquired regions as well.

The expansionists went so far as to contend that territorial expansion would actually promote democracy within the nation. So enthusiastic were they in justifying territorial expansion that they came close to concluding that most if not all of the good things in the American past were the result of previous acquisitions of land. A sprawling domain did not endanger liberty; it protected it. This was not a new notion in the 1840s, though, since two of the founding fathers, Alexander Hamilton and James Madison, had reached a similar conclusion even before the Constitution was approved. Using the past to serve the present, the expansionists of the 1840s relied on many of the founders' arguments to sanction territorial acquisitions. By doing so they attempted to link themselves to the first generation of venerated leaders and to show that liberty and empire were complementary legacies of the American past.

When proselytizing for the Constitution's adoption in 1787, Hamilton had contended that Montesquieu's argument that a democratic form of government and an extensive territorial domain were incompatible did not apply to the novel concept of a federated union outlined in the new national charter. Hamilton pointed out in *The Federalist* that Montesquieu himself had conceded that a "confederate republic" composed of separate states that retained certain crucial powers for themselves while delegating others to a national government provided a system that combined the advantages of both a large monarchy and a small democracy. The new Constitution, according to Hamilton, "so far from implying an abolition of the state governments, makes them constituent parts of the national sovereignty, by allowing them a direct representation in the Senate, and leaves in their possession certain exclusive and very important portions of sovereign power." This distinct separation of powers outlined in the Constitution would allow the United States to meet Montesquieu's chief requirement for a strong republican confederation: local initiative would not be obliterated by a despotic central authority.

On a related issue, Hamilton denied that it was feasible to subdivide the thirteen states into a number of small republics, as some critics of the Constitution recommended. Nor did he sympathize with skeptics who wished to fragment the larger states into smaller units. The suggestion of splitting up New York, Pennsylvania, Virginia, and North Carolina he dismissed as "an infatuated policy, . . . a desperate expedient" that would serve no useful purpose. The people of the United States must not be constrained by Montesquieu's theories, which were, in Hamilton's opinion, irrelevant to the exigencies of the 1780s. If Americans blindly obeyed an obsolete political theory unsuitable to their particular needs and ambitions, they would face the alternative of "taking refuge at once in the arms of monarchy, or of splitting . . . into an infinity of little, jealous, clashing, tumultuous commonwealths, the wretched nurseries of unceasing discord and the miserable objects of universal pity or contempt."[1] To Hamilton there

1. Clinton Rossiter, ed., *The Federalist Papers* (New York, 1961), no. 9, pp. 71–76.

existed only one prudent course: the Articles of Confederation must be scrapped for the new federal charter, in order to ensure stability and strength to the fledgling nation.

James Madison, father of the Constitution and patriarch of the new American empire, joined Hamilton in refuting what Madison called "an objection that may be drawn from the great extent of country which the union embraces." For Madison, one of the principal misconceptions behind opposition to the Constitution was the conviction that self-government and extensive territorial dominion were incompatible. He too used *The Federalist* to expose the fundamental flaws in that position. Distinguishing between a democracy where the people themselves congregated to transact public business and a republic where people delegated responsibility to elected representatives, Madison emphasized that the Constitution created a republican government, not a democratic one. "A small compass of territory" had proved unnecessary for a republic, since representatives from all thirteen of the original colonies had successfully assembled to make policy at the outbreak of the Revolution. The relative success of the national assembly from 1775 to 1787 convinced Madison that the thirteen colonies were sufficiently compact to form one central confederation under the Constitution.

Madison did not stop there. He added that the Constitution reserved many vital powers to the individual states, so that a great deal of governance would be performed close to home under the scrutiny of vigilant citizens. Madison expected that improvements in roads, navigation, canals, and travel accommodations fostered by private enterprise would integrate the various states into a cohesive federation under the Constitution. Conceding that states on the periphery of the Union would initially encounter some inconvenience in sending their representatives to the national capital, he hastily added that those states were also the most vulnerable to foreign attack. Urgently in need of the military protection a strong government could provide, those distant states would gladly accept the minor annoyances of isolation in return for security against Indians and Europeans. Like Hamilton, Madison urged Americans to avoid "a blind veneration for antiquity, for custom, or for names." The dead hand of abstraction should not thwart the Constitution and the expansive republic it envisioned. He desired to make all Americans "fellow-citizens of one great, respectable, and flourishing empire."[2]

2. Ibid., no. 14, pp. 99–105. Madison's political theories and his concept of republican empire are discussed by Walter LaFeber, "Foreign Policies of a New

Hamilton, Madison, and the Federalists triumphed. The Constitution became the law of the land, yet its adoption alone could not
shield the United States from the contempt or depredations of foreign
governments. The new charter in itself did not elevate the nation to
the status of a respected power. Economic development and territorial expansion, along with geographical isolation and a century of
relative peace in Europe, eventually shielded Americans from the
slings and arrows of other nations and allowed the United States to
attain the greatness that Hamilton and Madison had sought for the
republic.[3] In fact, arguments formulated by Hamilton and Madison
became American gospel during most of the first half of the nineteenth century. Except for New England Federalists and most Whigs,
who preferred a more compact, integrated republic, Americans placed
Montesquieu's theories on a high shelf and turned their attention to
enlarging the United States. By the time Texas, Oregon, and California were acquired in the 1840s, territorial expansion had become a
national habit. Two generations of American leaders had by then
developed an exceptionalist imperial ideology to justify the nation's
territorial and commercial aggrandizement. As Indian tribes ceded
their lands and European powers surrendered their colonies contiguous to the United States, leaders such as Benjamin Franklin, Thomas
Jefferson, James Monroe, John Quincy Adams, and Andrew Jackson
contributed in various ways to an evolving nationalistic ethos that
bestowed upon the country a proscriptive right to territory on the
North American continent claimed or inhabited by Indians or European colonists.[4]

Nation: Franklin, Madison, and the 'Dream of a New Land to Fulfill with People in
Self-Control,' 1750-1804," in William A. Williams, ed., *From Colony to Empire: Essays
in the History of American Foreign Relations* (New York, 1972), pp. 22-37. LaFeber
emphasizes the importance of *Federalist* no. 10, but no. 14 is just as significant a
treatise on the relationship between liberty and expansion. See also Drew McCoy,
The Elusive Republic: Political Economy in Jeffersonian America (Chapel Hill, N.C., 1980).
   3. The powers granted to the federal government by the Constitution undoubtedly
facilitated the development and expansion of the United States. As treasury secretary
and chief adviser to Washington, Hamilton used whatever federal powers were at
his disposal to promote rapid economic growth, economic diversification, internal
security, and international prestige. Disagreements over the extent of those central
powers largely produced the rift between Hamilton and the Madisonian opposition.
   4. See Gerald Stourzh, *Benjamin Franklin and American Foreign Policy,* 2d ed. (Chicago, 1969); Bernard W. Sheehan, *Seeds of Extinction: Jeffersonian Philanthropy and the
American Indian* (Chapel Hill, N.C., 1973); Walter LaFeber, ed., *John Quincy Adams and
American Continental Empire* (Chicago, 1965); Michael P. Rogin, *Fathers and Children:
Andrew Jackson and the Subjugation of the American Indian* (New York, 1975); Albert K.
Weinberg, *Manifest Destiny: A Study of Nationalist Expansionism in American History* (Balti-
more, 1935); Henry Nash Smith, *Virgin Land: The American West as Symbol and Myth*

The expansionists of the Tyler-Polk years inherited this imperial ideology and twisted and stretched it to make it suitable to their own time and purposes. They borrowed extensively from their predecessors, but they also added important concepts of their own to sanction the acquisition of a continental empire. Hamilton had contended that a large confederation of states under a strong national government was both possible and preferable to a small, divided confederation. The expansionists of the 1840s went a step further and proposed that an expanding empire was actually indispensable to the stability and security of the United States.

The expansionists argued that the United States could become a powerful continental empire without incurring the usual imperial burdens of colonialism and militarism. Not all empires need be imperial. While defending their own nation's aggrandizement in idealistic terms, they condemned the European empires, especially Britain, for their rapacity and oppression. The expansionist Democrats asserted that the United States could expand rapidly without falling prey to the practices that often undermined traditional empires. In attacking European aggrandizement and differentiating it from their own, Americans drew upon their strong sense of exceptionalism and combined it with an increasingly strident and chauvinistic definition of their national destiny. To sanction the acquisitions of the 1840s, the Democrats developed three critical concepts: they emphasized the vulnerability of America's rivals, a vulnerability that provided proof of the decadence of Old World empires; they contended that Anglo-Americans possessed an innate genius for self-rule that made it possible to

---

(Cambridge, Mass., 1950); Robert F. Berkhofer, Jr., *The White Man's Indian: Images of the American Indian from Columbus to the Present* (New York, 1979); Richard W. Van Alstyne, *The Rising American Empire* (New York, 1960); Richard Drinnon, *Facing West: The Metaphysics of Indian-Hating and Empire-Building* (New York, 1980). That these policy makers mentioned here each contributed to an exceptionalist ideology justifying expansion should not be construed to mean that they held a common political or social philosophy or even agreed with one another on specific territorial acquisitions. John Quincy Adams and Andrew Jackson are a case in point. Adams, as Monroe's secretary of state, strenuously defended Jackson's military incursion into East Florida in 1818, and both Adams and Jackson desired to obtain the Floridas from Spain. Later, in the 1820s and 1830s, Adams and Jackson diverged on Indian removal, Jackson being far more anxious and eager to remove the eastern Indians and Adams being less compulsive and more concerned with the means as well as the ends of removal. Adams and Jackson were completely at odds over Texas annexation in 1844–45, Adams viewing it as "the heaviest calamity" in American history and Jackson supporting it as absolutely vital to national security. The expansionists of the 1840s used whatever previous theorists suited their needs—including Adams, much to his chagrin.

reconcile individual liberty with empire; and they placed faith in advances in communication and transportation that rendered obsolete former limitations of time and distance. American political institutions, the railroad, the rotary press, and the telegraph could bind the entire continent together in a unified yet diverse empire.

The American Empire: A Greater Britain

Though the Jacksonian Democrats both feared and hated England, they thought that the Whigs overestimated Britain's capabilities; the British lion's growl was far worse than its bite. Many expansionists thought that England was weakened by its sprawling global empire. Deep domestic divisions among the various classes within Britain and the disaffection of distant colonial subjects made it difficult for the British government to control its own domain, let alone intervene effectively in American affairs.

When pressing for all of Oregon in early 1844, for example, Senator Buchanan rejected the notion that Britain would go to war with the United States over the territory. Britain had to "weigh well her position before she would destroy our friendly relations," he proposed, since war "would light the torch of civil war" in Ireland and would deprive Britain of cotton from the United States. Buchanan insisted that because of the already exhausting expenses of administering a heterogeneous empire, Britain could neither afford to lose its cotton supply or to support a costly foreign war. Senator Allen of Ohio agreed that the United States could push its claim to the whole territory without fear of reprisal. "Great Britain has many guns," Allen admitted in early 1846, but Britain also found it necessary "to scatter them around the world, for the defense of many colonies— colonies always threatened by rival nations [and] threatened with colonial revolt." He argued that Britain's prosperity and stability depended in large part on its commerce with its colonies, and this reliance impaired Britain's autonomy and diminished its strength. A war in Europe or a major crisis in North America would threaten Britain with the possible loss of its colonies and "would contract the circle of her commerce, unsettle her public and private credit, close her factories, turn out yet more of her laborers to starve, and, by bankruptcy and famine, provoke civil revolution."[5]

5. *Congressional Globe* (hereafter abbreviated *CG*), 28 Cong., 1 sess., 372 (March 2, 1844); *CG*, 29 Cong., 1 sess., App. 840 (February 10 and 11, 1846).

Like Buchanan and Allen, editor Bennett derived a grim satisfaction from the purported feebleness of the British Empire. Ireland, Bennett asserted, was "crying aloud for deliverance" from British rule, Scotland was eager to assert its independence, and Canada was "prepared at any favorable moment to throw off the yoke of foreign tyranny." After touring Europe in 1843, Bennett reported that Britain faced a "political, financial, and religious" crisis. Giant Gulliver though it was, Britain was bound by the stakes of its imperial problems and the ligatures of American cotton. He did not stand alone in this view. With virtual unanimity, Democratic expansionists asserted that colonialism debilitated England and gave the United States an advantage over its Anglo-Saxon rival. Illinois Democrats Stephen Douglas and Orlando Ficklin observed, for example, that Canada provided the United States with an especially convenient hostage in its relations with Britain. Expansionists repeatedly stressed that war over Oregon would result in the transfer of Canada to the United States.[6]

Besides the ever-present danger of revolt in its colonies, Britain faced the danger of insurrection at home. Expansionists contended that the United States could manipulate the British working class by controlling the flow of vital commodities such as cotton and grain to Britain. Editor John O'Sullivan, for example, noted in late 1845 that British industry was "almost entirely dependent" on American cotton because Texas had decided to join the Union. That dependence meant that an American cotton embargo would plunge the British manufacturing system into depression and would produce widespread unemployment and unrest among workers. To prevent such an upheaval, O'Sullivan suggested, Britain would acquiesce to American demands concerning Oregon.[7]

After Texas entered the Union, expansionists concluded that little latitude remained for Britain to act decisively in North America. When the Oregon dispute reached a climax in 1846, expansionists became more aggressive in their demands for the entire territory. Congressman John Chipman of Michigan spoke for many of his northwestern Democratic colleagues when he denounced legislators who favored compromise on Oregon. Boasting that Michigan militia alone could conquer Canada in ninety days if war broke out, Chipman assured lawmakers that England dared not challenge the United

6. New York *Herald*, March 3, 1846; *CG*, 29 Cong., 1 sess., 126 (January 2, 1846); ibid., 29 Cong., 1 sess., App. 174 (February 6, 1846).
7. New York *Morning News*, November 19, 1845. See also November 7, 1845.

States. Were war to suspend British trade with the United States and bring England's industrial machinery to a grinding halt, the "starving millions would rise in infuriated masses and overwhelm their bloated aristocracy." Another All Oregon enthusiast, Congressman James Faran of Ohio, also indicated that colonial unrest and domestic dissension impaired Britain. "A war would be too momentous in its results for her to risk it," he concluded. Thomas Ritchie could not believe that Britain had initiated a major military buildup in late 1845. Such a course seemed incomprehensible in view of the internal difficulties plaguing England, "yet Providence sometimes maddens those whom it means to destroy," he noted.[8] Dependence on American cotton and grain; disaffection among Scottish, Welsh, and Irish subjects; imminent class conflict in the manufacturing centers; and European imperial rivalry—all reduced the power of England and increased the leverage of the United States in disputes with that nation.

The expansionists failed to demonstrate that British officials shared this perception that global empire actually weakened England's position in international affairs. In fact, the Whigs, and many southern Democrats, doubted that whatever advantages the United States possessed could compensate for Britain's naval superiority. When the British government sent reinforcements to Canada and augmented its Pacific squadron in early 1846, most Democrats prudently decided that the Oregon territory could be honorably divided with England. Though the United States chose compromise over confrontation with Britain, many anglophobes regretted the retreat from 54°40'. Their calculations about American strength and British weakness and their assumptions about the superiority of their new empire over an older type of empire were never put to the ultimate test.[9]

Americans who traveled extensively abroad or resided in Europe during the 1840s sensed that the Old World was on the brink of a major upheaval. After eighteen months in Europe in 1846–47, Bennett assured his readers that the Europeans could not challenge the prerogatives of the United States in North America: overpopulation, poor harvests, frequent famines, and internal discontent preoccupied

8. *CG,* 29 Cong., 1 sess., 207–8 (January 4, 1846); ibid., App. 615 (April 14, 1846); Washington *Daily Union,* December 22, 1845.

9. Many of the same Democrats who condemned the Oregon compromise had also condemned the Webster-Ashburton Treaty of 1842. In both cases they argued that the United States had surrendered its rightful territory to the British and suggested that Britain should have to fight for such gains rather than win them dishonorably at the negotiating table.

European leaders, who were now too distracted to affect events in the New World. With Europe in such straits, no limitations could be placed on the future "power, progress, or preponderance" of the United States. Bancroft, sent to London as American minister in late 1846, viewed England's problems in terms similar to Bennett's. He assured President Polk in early 1847 that "the embarrassments of domestic affairs" in Europe would prevent the British and French from interfering in the war against Mexico. To Buchanan, Bancroft explained that widespread destitution and suffering in Ireland were draining England of revenue and power. The British government was spending more to feed its Irish subjects than the United States was spending on the Mexican War. Bancroft told editor William Cullen Bryant in late 1847 that the poverty in England was "appalling." "Here five are employed to do the work of two; because if not employed, the number supported by poor-rates would be still further increased," he noted. In Britain, unlike the United States, "*no hope* for the poor" existed.[10] Such reports prompted the expansionists to defy Britain. Time and again they asserted that the United States could pursue its ambitions without fear of European retaliation. Throughout the 1840s, they insisted that the Whigs who opposed expansion posed more of a threat to the country than any foreign power. The greatest menace to the United States was the domestic program championed by the Whigs and the agitation incited by their abolitionist allies—dangers more ominous than all the distracted empires of Europe combined.

Cognizant of the inherent hazards of imperial dominion demonstrated by Britain, the expansionists stressed that their territorial and commercial ambitions would not turn the United States into another Britain. On the contrary, they regarded as irrelevant all comparisons between their new empire and others, past or present. To help establish the uniqueness of their own empire, they returned to the writings of Madison and Hamilton. Just as Hamilton's repudiation of Montesquieu had supplied a rationale for the formation of the thirteen states into an extensive confederation under a more powerful central au-

10. New York *Herald,* February 24, March 1 and 26, and May 12 and 13, 1847; Bancroft to Polk, January 19, 1847, in M. A. DeWolfe Howe, *The Life and Letters of George Bancroft,* 2 vols. (New York, 1908), 2:8; Bancroft to Buchanan, February 3, 1847, James Buchanan Papers; Bancroft to Bryant, November 3, 1847, in Howe, *Life of Bancroft,* 2:26–27. See also the following: Bancroft to William H. Prescott, March 3, 1847, and Bancroft to Buchanan, October 18, 1847, in ibid., pp. 15, 23–24; Bancroft to Buchanan, May 18 and November 3, 1847, Buchanan Papers.

thority, so too did the ideas of Madison on territorial expansion help sanction the creation of a continental empire. While promoting a new American empire in the 1840s, the Democratic expansionists relied heavily on earlier theorists for concepts of representative government and American exceptionalism. In addition, they offered new insights into the favorable impact that recent technological advances in transportation and communication would exert on American social and political life. This new empire emerged as an empire without precedents or parallels. American political institutions and technological progress could make the United States a Greater Britain.

The novelty of American republicanism's separation of powers between the various states and the federal government seemed to the expansionists a crucial asset of empire. Hamilton had contended that a split sovereignty shared by the states and a new national government could secure to Americans the most attractive features of both monarchical and democratic rule. He thought that a confederation of states under the Constitution would best "suppress faction and . . . guard the internal tranquillity of states," as well as "increase their external force and security." Madison pushed this point a step further, speculating that an increase in the number of states comprising the confederation would multiply competing interest groups, disperse potential dissidents, and make it more difficult for members of factions to act in concert for selfish ends. Enlargement of the Republic, in other words, provided yet another set of checks and balances to protect the people from designing interest groups. As Madison had counseled in 1787, "Extend the sphere and you take in a greater variety of parties and interests; you make it less probable that a majority of the whole will have a common motive to invade the rights of other citizens; or if such a common motive exists, it will be more difficult for all who feel it to discover their own strength and to act in unison with each other."[11]

Neither Hamilton nor Madison formulated his ideas in the 1780s with the explicit intent of justifying territorial expansion, but certainly their abstractions could be used by others for that purpose. One who did so was James Monroe, an intellectual heir of Madison and an ardent expansionist. He utilized the ideas of Madison and Hamilton when he discussed the progress of the United States in his celebrated 1823 message to Congress. Looking back over the period since the adoption of the Constitution, Monroe observed, "By enlarging

11. Rossiter, *Federalist Papers,* no. 9, p. 73; no. 10, p. 83.

the basis of our system and increasing the number of states the system itself has been greatly strengthened in both its branches. Consolidation and disunion have thereby been rendered equally impracticable." Monroe heartily approved of the additions to the Union since 1789, concluding that the "expansion of our population and accession of new states to our Union has had the happiest effect on all its highest interests." Monroe's own administration demonstrated a persistent affinity for territorial expansion. Between 1817 and 1824, East Florida was acquired, Spain in response to heavy pressure relinquished its claim to the trans-Mississippi West north of the forty-second parallel, and Monroe and Secretary of War Calhoun revived the Jeffersonian dream of removing the eastern Indians to an isolated area of the Great Plains. Secretary of state John Quincy Adams negotiated tenaciously to undermine European colonialism on the North American continent as a preliminary to future American acquisitions.[12]

The expansionists of the 1840s invoked these earlier views as well as devising new ones apropos to their own time. When President Tyler submitted the Texas annexation treaty to the Senate in 1844, he emphasized how beneficial previous acquisitions had been to the Union. Since 1789, the number of states in the American confederation had doubled from thirteen to twenty-six, and these additions had "served to strengthen rather than to weaken the Union." He remarked that "the federative system is susceptible of the greatest extension compatible with the ability of the representation of the most distant state or territory to reach the seat of government in time to participate in the functions of legislation and to make known the wants of the constituent body."[13] Robert Walker agreed. "Of all the forms of government, our confederacy is most specially adapted for an extended territory, and might, without the least danger, but with increased security, and vastly augmented benefits, embrace a continent," he observed in his letter on Texas in 1844. Expansion across the entire continent was possible because of the Union's distinctive

12. See Samuel Flagg Bemis, *John Quincy Adams and the Foundations of American Foreign Policy* (New York, 1949), pp. 278–340, 482–536, 566–72; LaFeber, *Adams,* pp. 35–46, 69–95, 96–116.

13. James D. Richardson, ed., *A Compilation of the Messages and Papers of the Presidents,* 10 vols. (New York, 1897), 5 (April 22, 1844):2165–66. Madison had made the same point in *Federalist* no. 14: "The natural limit of a republic is that distance from the center which will barely allow the representatives of the people to meet as often as may be necessary for the administration of public affairs."

separation of powers. "Each state, within its own limits, controls all its local concerns," Walker explained, while the federal government confined its powers to matters "which appertain to commerce and . . . foreign relations." This dual sovereignty safeguarded the liberties of the people and also protected them from both domestic and foreign foes, because "as you augment the number of states, the bond of union is stronger; for the opposition of any one state is much less dangerous and formidable."[14] Each new state, then, whether slave or free, contributed to the country's security.

Previous expansionists such as John Quincy Adams had contemplated the likelihood of the United States gradually becoming coextensive with the entire North American continent over several generations, but the late Jacksonian Democrats demanded an immediate consummation of a continental empire. More impatient and pugnacious than Adams, they urged rapid expansion and a hastening of American destiny. Illinois senator Sidney Breese, for example, surmised in early 1844 that "our confederacy is peculiarly adapted to expansion, and any number of states can be added to it, strengthening it by their number, until its circumference shall embrace all the territory of this continent." Of one mind with Breese was Stephen Douglas. "Our federal system is admirably adapted to the whole continent," he assured legislators when he urged the annexation of Texas in early 1845. After helping guide the Texas resolution through the House, Douglas championed the All Oregon cause. Later he joined aggressive Democrats in supporting the Mexican War and demanding a vast territorial indemnity from the enemy. He advised his House colleagues to "exert all legal and honorable means to drive Great Britain . . . from the continent of North America, and [to] extend the limits of the republic from ocean to ocean." Annoyed by the boundary disputes with Britain earlier in the Northeast and now in the Oregon territory, Douglas declared, "I would make this an *ocean-bound republic,* and have no more disputes about boundaries or red lines upon the maps."[15]

O'Sullivan also coveted the entire continent. A close friend and

14. "Letter of Mr. Walker, of Mississippi, Relative to the Annexation of Texas" (Washington, D.C., January 8, 1844), p. 10. In this proannexation brief, Walker quoted Monroe's annual message of 1823 in which he had asserted that territorial expansion and the admission of new states had been crucial to the nation's progress.

15. *CG*, 28 Cong., 1 sess., App. 220 (February 27, 1844); *CG*, 28 Cong., 2 sess., App. 68 (January 6, 1845). See also Douglas to Polk, August 25, 1845, in Robert W. Johannsen, ed., *The Letters of Stephen A. Douglas* (Urbana, 1961), pp. 119–20.

supporter of Douglas, he shared Douglas's territorial ambitions, pre-
dicting as early as 1844 that the United States was "destined to
embrace within its wide sweep every habitable square inch of the
continent." Such extension posed no threat to Americans already
residing within the confederation, O'Sullivan argued, since the country's "representative system" was capable of "an indefinite extension
of territory, without weakening or impairing the political guaranties
of any of its inhabitants."[16]

Once the expansionists had demonstrated that previous acquisitions had not deprived the older states of any rights or privileges, the
next step was to convince skeptics that expansion had actually been
essential to American liberty and security. Most Democrats of the
1840s believed that westward expansion had not only enlarged the
sphere of liberty and prosperity, it had also fostered internal harmony among the states and their citizens. In addition, it had lifted the
United States into the ranks of a rising and respected power. Clearly,
territorial acquisitions brought good things to the country and its
people.

Many expansionists thought that the acquisition of land offered the
cheapest and most efficacious means of maintaining internal security.
New York congressman Chesselden Ellis argued in early 1845 that
expansion "augments the power against which the spirit of disunion
must contend whenever it awakes. It multiplies counteracting interests, and lessens the danger of its influence." Andrew Kennedy of
Indiana similarly maintained in the House that expansion diffused
discord, since new states showed greater loyalty to the nation than
older ones. New states "never have any desire to break off from us,
because they come in by their own consent," he declared in 1846.
Each new state "added another pillar to the temple of liberty."[17]

Even before implementing his strategy to acquire Mexico's northern provinces, President Polk, in his inaugural address, endorsed the
value of previous acquisitions. His enthusiastic approval of expansion
portended events to come. Reviewing the American past, Polk noted
that "as our population has expanded, the union has been cemented
and strengthened. As our boundaries have been enlarged and our

16. "The Texas Question," *Democratic Review*, 14 (April, 1844):429; "Territorial
Aggrandizement," *Democratic Review*, 17 (October, 1845):244. See also the revealing
editorial "European Views of American Extension," New York *Morning News*, October 13, 1845.
17. *CG*, 28 Cong., 2 sess., App. 138 (January 25, 1845); *CG*, 29 Cong., 1 sess., 180
(January 10, 1846).

agricultural population has been spread over a large surface, our federative system has acquired additional strength and security. It may well be doubted whether it would not be in greater danger of overthrow if our present population were confined to the comparatively narrow limits of the original thirteen states than it is now that they are sparsely settled over a more expanded territory."[18] Ritchie shared these sentiments. Calling for the acquisition of all of Oregon in early 1846, he claimed that the American people favored such expansion, since they "rightly judged that the more extended" the Republic became, "the stronger would be the necessity for mutual support and reliance, and, of course, the more secure and permanent the bonds of union."[19] Polk and his advisers believed that expansion would ensure domestic accord and increase national security.

The expansionists frequently compared their Whig opponents with the Hartford Convention Federalists of 1814 and stressed the dire consequences that would have ensued had the secessionist movement succeeded during the War of 1812. A disunionist conspiracy, added to the burdens of sustaining a major war, could have crippled the nation, hastened its defeat, and precipitated its rapid disintegration. Whereas the New England Federalists had afforded aid and comfort to the enemy through their separatist leanings, the more patriotic Jeffersonians had defeated Britain and its American quislings. In evaluating the past forty years, the Jacksonian Democrats perceived a pattern in which the party of Jefferson, Madison, Jackson, and Polk, the party of "the people," had consistently supported a rigorous assertion of national rights and territorial extension. The Federalists and Whigs, the party of "the privileged," on the other hand, had opposed both war and acquisitions. From this simplistic perspective the historical record suggested the wisdom of expansion and the foresight of those who had championed it. New acquisitions had minimized the threat of disunion by reducing the power of the New England states. Territorial additions had seemingly helped to diminish impulses toward separatism and secession. They had also contributed to individual mobility and freedom.

During the Mexican War the dispute over the extension of slavery increased the Whigs' reluctance to acquire more territory. They disapproved of acquisition by conquest and doubted whether the borderlands could be integrated into the Union. Daniel Webster spoke

18. Richardson, *Messages and Papers*, 5 (March 4, 1845): 2230
19. Washington *Daily Union*, January 1, 1846.

for most Whigs when he warned in 1847 that "the future is full of difficulties and full of dangers. We are suffering to pass the golden opportunity for securing harmony and the stability of the Constitution. We appear to me to be rushing upon perils headlong, and with our eyes all open." Alarmed by the political divisions over expansion and over the spread of slavery, Webster declared, "We want no extension of territory; we want no accession of new states. The country is already large enough."[20] More amenable to the expansion of trade, Webster welcomed the acquisition of valuable ports in California. But he feared that an extensive territorial indemnity from Mexico would complicate domestic disagreements over slavery and exacerbate sectional discord. Webster had good reason to be concerned, for the next thirteen years would be anxious ones for the United States as politicians, "rushing upon perils headlong," failed to avert sectionalism, disunion, and civil war. In 1847, however, ideas such as Webster's appeared preposterous to the expansionists. Too much territory was as nonsensical a notion as a square circle or water running uphill.

Seconding Webster's misgivings was Philip Hone. When Congress approved the annexation of Texas in early 1845, Hone grumbled in his diary that "the Goths are in possession of the Capitol, and if the Union can stand the shock it will only be another evidence that Divine Providence takes better care of us than we deserve." The campaign of conquest later carried on in New Mexico and California alarmed him even more. To Hone the reduction of the tariff had been an injury; the Mexican War seemed an added insult to Americans as well as Mexicans. It was "an unjust, unnecessary and expensive war," he lamented, the result of "the vilest cabal that ever was set on foot by corrupt demagogues."[21]

Ardent expansionists placed so much faith in their political system that they scoffed at all admonitions against extension. Unlike the Whigs, they regarded the war as a Heaven-sent opportunity to transform the United States into an impregnable continental empire. Here

20. *CG,* 29 Cong., 2 sess., 556 (March 1, 1847).
21. *The Diary of Philip Hone, 1828–1851,* Bayard Tuckerman, ed. (New York, 1889), 2 (March 1, 1845):243; (August 12, 1846):283; (March 13, 1848) :347. Hone described the Trist Treaty as one "negotiated by an unauthorized agent, with an unacknowledged government, submitted by an accidental president to a dissatisfied Senate." He complained of southern domination in American foreign and domestic policy, but he exaggerated the correlation between geography and political principles when he contended that the North and East were antiexpansionist and the South and West expansionist. Party affiliation was actually more influential than sectional loyalties.

was a chance to secure the nation against all foes, at home and abroad. Whenever Polk called upon Congress to appropriate funds for the war, Sidney Breese rallied behind the request. He believed that an investment in the war was an investment in additional land for the nation. "No imaginable bounds can be assigned to the proper extension of this Confederacy: it is peculiarly adapted to great enlargement and extension," he stressed in 1847. Breese recalled that many Americans in the 1780s had argued that democracy could flourish only if the thirteen states were divided into a number of separate republics. Later, during Jefferson's first term, the Federalists had opposed the purchase of Louisiana. But in retrospect these objections to expansion seemed groundless to Breese: "Since the adoption of the Constitution, fifteen states have been added to the Confederacy, six of them out of foreign territory, and against the same objections now urged, and all of them contributing new vigor to the system, and increased strength to the circle." The successful assimilation of these new states showed that the American system was "most admirably adapted to almost any degree of extension."[22]

Daniel Dickinson concurred. Defending the acquisition of California and New Mexico in the Senate in 1848, he maintained that the American form of government was "as powerful for good at the remotest limits as at the political centre" and for that reason was "admirably adapted to extended empire." To Dickinson, the nation's expansionist past seemed irresistible: "Cities and towns have sprung up upon the shores of the Pacific, and the river we essayed to fix as our western, now passes nearest to our eastern boundary. From three, our population has increased to twenty millions—from thirteen to twenty-nine states, with others in the process of formation and on their way to the union. Two great European powers have withdrawn from the continent, yielding us their possessions, and . . . numerous aboriginal nations have been displaced before the resistless tide of our prevailing arts, arms, and free principles."[23] France, Spain, and countless Indian tribes had surrendered their lands in North America to the United States; surely the British in Canada and the Mexicans in the Southwest would have to do the same. Dickinson spurned warnings that expansion would widen domestic rifts and encourage the dissolution of the Union. "Politicians could not dissolve it if they would, and would not if they could," he declared.[24]

22. *CG,* 29 Cong., 2 sess., App. 210 (February 23, 1847).
23. *CG,* 30 Cong., 1 sess., 157 (January 12, 1848).
24. *CG,* 29 Cong., 2 sess., App. 445 (March 1, 1847).

Other Democrats also argued that Polk's aggressive aggrandizement during the war conformed to a well-established tradition. Ingersoll
spoke with some authority on historical precedents, since he was the
author of a multivolume history of the War of 1812, the first install-
ment of which appeared propitiously in 1845. In early 1847 Ingersoll
advocated the use of greater force against Mexico and demanded a
vast territorial cession. An "extension of the territories of this republic" had been "the settled policy of every administration, since Washington began it by Indian conquests, which all his successors have
pursued to this moment," he recollected. Jefferson "signally developed it, by the acquisition of Louisiana; Madison, by part of what is
now Alabama, and an attempt to take all Canada; Monroe, by annexing Florida." John Quincy Adams had "conceived the wise plan of
acquiring Texas by purchase," and Jackson had continued efforts to
acquire Texas while also trying to obtain "a new boundary on the
Pacific . . . running through New Mexico to California." Ingersoll
praised Tyler as well, who had, like Adams, Jackson, and Van Buren,
"steadily and wisely pursued . . . the acquisition of more territory on
the Gulf of Mexico and the Pacific."[25]

Ingersoll not only defended expansionists and their policies; he
also led other Democrats in a sustained vendetta against critics such
as Adams and Webster. Late in 1844, Ingersoll complained to Jackson
that Adams, "after exhausting his malevolence on you has pledged
himself to make me his anvil." Ingersoll vowed to do battle against
Adams, and battle he did. Adams in turn despised Ingersoll, attribut-
ing his conduct to "a maggot in his brain."[26] Other prominent Democrats joined the attack. Richard M. Johnson described Adams as
"deranged" and "perfectly reckless." King referred to him as a "black
hearted old wretch" and an "old devil." Editor Jones called Adams
"the insane old man from Quincy" who had "infected others with his
monomaniac feelings." To discredit Adams further, Jones printed a
contemptuous toast presented at a party honoring Henry Wise. "John
Quincy Adams," someone had remarked, "once a man, twice a child,
and now a demon."[27]

25. *CG,* 29 Cong., 2 sess., App. 126–28 (January 19, 1847).
26. Ingersoll to Jackson, November 21, 1844, Andrew Jackson Papers; *Memoirs of
John Quincy Adams, Comprising Portions of His Diary from 1795 to 1848,* Charles Francis
Adams, ed., 12 vols. (Philadelphia, 1874–77), 11 (December 25, 1843):460.
27. Johnson to Buchanan, February 5, 1842; King to Buchanan, January 28, 1845,
Buchanan Papers; Washington *Daily Madisonian,* December 9, 1842, June 15, 1843.
Adams was aware of the southern Democrats' enmity. In early 1842, he observed,
"One hundred members of the House represent slaves; four-fifths of them would
crucify me if their votes could erect the cross" (*Memoirs,* 11 [February 6, 1842]:8).

Most Democrats prudently confined their attacks on Adams to private correspondence and conversations. One man who wished he had done so was Congressman Thomas Marshall of Kentucky, who never forgot the lashing he received from his cantankerous elder colleague. After a stinging rebuke on the House floor, Marshall confided to a friend, "I wish I were dead. I do. I would rather die a thousand deaths than again to encounter that old man."[28] Adam's abolitionist sentiments and his skepticism about adding more slave territory to the country made him anathema to slave-state Democrats and their northern cohorts, and his earlier contributions to the growth of the American continental empire went largely unacknowledged at this time. The "demon" was not to be given his due.

Webster received similar abuse from the expansionists. In 1845 and 1846, Ingersoll accused Webster of having misused secret service funds to buy the cooperation of persons in Maine and Massachusetts during his negotiations with Ashburton in 1842.[29] Severely denounced by many Whigs for his outbursts, Ingersoll, through Henry Hilliard of Alabama, made overtures to Webster for a reconciliation, but Webster, infuriated by Ingersoll's vicious attacks, refused to respond. After this rebuff, Hilliard noted, "Ingersoll, who seemed to be greatly angered, said to me that he would challenge Mr. Webster [to a duel], and that if he refused to meet him he would pursue him with pistols to Boston."[30] Ingersoll's pistols remained unfired, but he con-

28. Joshua R. Giddings, *History of the Rebellion: Its Authors and Causes* (New York, 1864), pp. 167–68. Giddings watched the encounter and described Marshall as "a standing corpse" that "exhibited no other sign of life than a nervous tremor which pervaded his system." Nathan Sargent reported that Marshall later admitted that other southern Democrats had persuaded him to denounce Adams. Marshall, according to Sargent, confessed that he had "suffered under that castigation little less than the torments of the damned" (Nathan Sargent, *Public Men and Events*, 2 vols. [Philadelphia, 1875], 2: 151). Mississippi's Henry S. Foote noted in his memoirs that Adam's "powers of sarcasm and denunciation were positively terrific, and no man ever dared to awaken his ire whom he did not speedily compel to regret his temerity" (*Casket of Reminiscences* [Washington, 1874], p. 6). See also John Wentworth, *Congressional Reminiscences: Adams, Benton, Calhoun, Clay and Webster* (Chicago, 1882), pp. 12–13.

29. Almost four years after the resolution of the northeastern boundary dispute, Ingersoll was still on the offensive against Webster: "It is [a] sickening, if not sad reality, that a man of fine abilities, as preposterously as profanely miscalled Godlike, should be exposed in his mean and paltry contrivances and associations with notoriously base fellows in palpably vile misuse of the public money" (*CG*, 29 Cong., 1 sess., 636 [April 9, 1846]). On the subject of Webster's use of the secret service fund to secure acceptance of the 1842 treaty, see Frederick Merk, *Fruits of Propaganda in the Tyler Administration* (Cambridge, Mass., 1971).

30. Henry W. Hilliard, *Politics and Pen Pictures at Home and Abroad* (New York, 1892), p. 161.

tinued his verbal sniping, as did other Democrats. Ritchie twice damned Webster, once for his earlier opposition to the War of 1812 and again for his opposition to the Mexican War. "He has involved himself in sophistries of the grossest description," Ritchie complained in late 1846.[31]

Personal animus and ideological differences sometimes provoked physical confrontations. In February 1843, John Dawson of Louisiana shoved Joshua Giddings of Ohio as they met in the aisle of the House, then partially bared his bowie knife from its scabbard while glaring at Giddings. Members whisked Dawson from the chamber to prevent bloodshed. In April 1844, angry House members exchanged punches during a melee on the floor, and a random pistol shot wounded a Capitol guard. Amid mounting tensions later that year, a ruffian assailed Adams in a corridor outside of the House chamber, but Adams warded him off until others subdued him. Adams escaped injury. During a particularly acrimonious exchange in early 1845, Edward Black of Georgia brandished his cane and threatened to beat Giddings. After friends ushered Black from the scene, Dawson then approached Giddings and cocked his pistol, muttering "I'll shoot him, by God, I'll shoot him." But when other armed men converged, Dawson desisted.[32] With each fracas, more and more members of Congress carried weapons into the chambers. When promoting expansion or protecting slavery, Democrats could be quite unscrupulous in their methods. Northern Whigs could also be less than genteel.

The expansionists sharply repudiated those who doubted the exceptionalism of American empire. To justify their nation's aggrandizement they argued that their system was superior to all others because it rested on consent rather than coercion; expansion was unimpeachable because the United States acquired and exploited

31. Washington *Daily Union*, December 7, 1846.
32. On the Dawson-Giddings encounter, see Giddings, *History of the Rebellion*, pp. 210–11; George W. Julian, *The Life of Joshua R. Giddings* (Chicago, 1892), pp. 145–46; *CG*, 27 Cong., 3 sess., 277 (February 13, 1843). Giddings was not easily intimidated. He reassured his daughter, "You need have no fears nor apprehensions for my safety. Dawson is a degraded drunken fellow, and is the same man who last session threatened to cut Arnold's throat" (Giddings to Lura Maria Giddings, July 12, 1844, Giddings Papers). The House melee of 1844 is noted in *Memoirs of Adams*, 12 (April 23, 1844):16; Ashtabula *Sentinel*, May 4, 1844; *CG*, 28 Cong., 1 sess., 551 (April 23, 1844). For the incident involving Adams, see *Memoirs*, 12 (December 18, 1844):126; Ashtabula *Sentinel*, December 27, 1844. The confrontation in early 1845 is described in Giddings, *History of the Rebellion*, pp. 238–41; Julian, *Life of Giddings*, pp. 173–74; Adams, *Memoirs*, 12 (February 6, 1845): 162–63; Ashtabula *Sentinel*, February 14, 1845; *CG*, 28 Cong., 2 sess., 255–56 (February 6, 1845).

land, not people. Again, the American past was projected through a rose-tinted lens, as expansionists often perpetuated the myth of an empty continent that had been dormant for centuries, awaiting the energizing presence of Anglo-Americans. Since the principles of this new empire of consent were so different from those of older empires of conquest, comparisons between them had no validity.

When pleading for Texas annexation in early 1844, editor John Jones admitted that former empires had collapsed because of overextension. Yet those empires had "violated every principle upon which we base the perpetuity of our institutions," he added. Because of this difference, "The union of these states is not to be judged by the history of any former nation." Dismissing European protests against American territorial expansion, O'Sullivan predicted in late 1845, "We are not merely to possess and occupy an unequalled extent of territory, or to extend our laws and institutions over a countless population, for the territory, though vast, will be compact, and what is of still greater value, the population will be homogeneous." Homogeneity, he explained, was an "element of power and stability" lacking in all former empires "composed of dissimilar and hostile materials." The American empire would prove superior because it would consist of politically equal units inhabited by a racially pure population. Andrew Kennedy stressed that other empires had not adhered to the principle of government by and through the consent of the governed, and this error had weakened them, because "what was acquired by the sword must be maintained by the sword." The United States, on the other hand, expanded through population dispersion and peaceful annexation, Kennedy told his fellow congressmen. Texas, of course, served as the ideal prototype of this process: Americans migrated to foreign territory, achieved their autonomy without interference from the United States, and then sought admission to the Union as equals. It worked so well. Prior to the outbreak of the Mexican War, for example, O'Sullivan and Bennett both predicted that California would follow the same pattern as Texas.[33]

At times expansionists predicted that restless pioneers would occupy the entire continent regardless of whether or not the national government provided protection and incentives to emigrants.[34] The

33. Washington *Daily Madisonian*, April 2, 1844; New York *Morning News*, October 13, 1845; *CG*, 29 Cong., 1 sess., 180 (January 10, 1846); New York *Morning News*, July 9, 1845; "Annexation," *Democratic Review*, 17 (July, 1845):9; "Territorial Aggrandizement," *Democratic Review*, 17 (October, 1845):244; New York *Herald*, September 30, 1845, May 2, 1846.

34. Western Democrats Lewis Linn and David Atchison of Missouri, Sidney Breese,

acquisition of an expansive confederation through such an immaculate process moved O'Sullivan to boast in late 1845, "No instance of aggrandizement or lust for territory has stained our annals. No nation has been despoiled by us, no country laid desolate, no people overrun." Bennett agreed. The United States was "the only power which has never sought and never seeks to acquire a foot of territory by force of arms," he argued. "Of all the vast domain of our great confederacy over which the star spangled banner waves, not one foot of it is the acquirement of force or bloodshed!" "Our government is not extended by the sword," Ritchie insisted when differentiating the United States from other expansionistic nations. "By its own merits it extends itself."[35] Such sweeping claims of exceptionalism and innocence must have raised eyebrows in Madrid, as officials there recalled United States actions in East and West Florida during the Madison and Monroe administrations. In London, leaders must have wondered how Americans had so quickly forgotton their two ambitious invasions of Canada. Nor would Native Americans preyed upon by individual squatters and removed at bayonet point by the United States army in the 1830s and early 1840s have agreed with these declarations of righteousness.

An Enterprising Empire: The Americans' "Higher Claim" to Dominion

With the campaign of conquest in the borderlands during 1846, a shift in emphasis necessarily occurred in the rationale behind American expansion. It was absurd to proclaim that the United States had never conquered any territory or despoiled another people when American troops were slaying Mexican troops on Mexican soil while taking possession of the northern provinces. The expansionists finessed the question of imperial plunder, insisting that regardless of the means employed to acquire territory, what mattered most was the long-range intentions of the United States. Since all acquisitions would eventually become integral parts of the Union, how they were obtained was secondary.

James Semple and John McClernand of Illinois, Robert Dale Owen of Indiana, and other expansionists expressed this view. O'Sullivan also emphasized acquisition through population dispersion when he coined the phrase *manifest destiny* in 1845. See "Annexation," *Democratic Review*, 17 (July, 1845):7; New York *Morning News*, July 9, October 13, and November 20, 1845.

35. New York *Morning News*, November 20, 1845; New York *Herald*, December 14, 1845; Washington *Daily Union*, October 27, 1845.

Expansionists asserted that Americans had a natural right to land not being fully utilized by its inhabitants. Congressman Timothy Pillsbury of Texas used his own state's history to demonstrate the dynamic that would strip Mexico of its borderland provinces and spread the American empire far beyond the Rio Grande. Anglo-Americans had made Texas progressive when it was still a part of Mexico, he argued in 1846. The Mexican government had encouraged American immigration into the province in the 1820s, but even if Mexico had not promoted settlement in Texas, "The citizens of the United States would have had the right to have occupied that soil on the ground of contiguity." According to Pillsbury, "A country kept vacant by the policy of a nation which claims the right of ownership over it, is common property, and reverts to the situation in which all land was before it became property, and is open to be occupied, subdued and cultivated by man—by those who will do so—as the Creator designed it should be."[36] On the basis of this principle, he hoped that the United States would obtain much, if not all, of Mexico as indemnity for the war. Only Anglo-Americans could convert Mexico's wastelands into prosperous farms and plantations.

Sam Houston expressed a similar view in 1847. In his opinion, settlers from the United States had redeemed Texas from a savage state. "They went there," he reflected, and "war succeeded war, and the Indian tribes were repelled. They reclaimed the wilderness, and it became cultivated fields, producing happiness and prosperity for civilized man." Houston expected a similar regeneration of the Mexican territory recently conquered by American forces. In early 1848 Houston vindicated the war and justified expansion on the basis of an inexorable trend: "Americans regard this continent as their birthright. . . . The pioneers who went forth into the wilderness poured out their heart's blood to prepare the country for their posterity; their scalps were taken by the Indians; they sacrificed their life's blood to acquire the possession[s] which we enjoy. If all these difficulties and sacrifices did not terrify the bold pioneers, the success of centuries only tends to confirm what they began, and nothing can prevent our mighty march." Just as Americans had wrested land from Indians for more progressive uses, so too would Americans dispossess Mexicans in order to produce "happiness and prosperity for civilized man."[37]

36. CG, 29 Cong., 1 sess., 980 (June 16, 1846).
37. CG, 29 Cong., 2 sess., App. 219 (February 19, 1847); "Houston's Address to the Democracy of New York," February 22, 1848, in The Writings of Sam Houston, Amelia W. Williams and Eugene Barker, eds., 8 vols. (Austin, 1938–43), 5:34–35.

Calhoun agreed with Houston that it was impossible to prevent American pioneers from occupying adjacent territory on the continent. In early 1847, he contended that the United States must obtain a substantial domain from Mexico. "It is impossible for us to prevent our growing population from passing into an uninhabited country, where the power of the owners is not sufficient to keep them out," he observed. Mexicans in California and New Mexico would have to relocate, just as the eastern Indians had done. The United States must "purchase their lands, and remove them to a greater distance," he advised. Only then could "an industrious and civilized race" redeem that "uninhabited and barren waste."[38] Calhoun stated frankly what other Democrats often implied: Mexicans would have to forfeit whatever lands they nominally held to more enterprising American pioneers.

Bennett repeatedly asserted that Americans had a right to expropriate Mexican territory, whether through population dispersion or military conquest. In the hands of nonwhite peoples Mexican territory was useless, and Americans had decided that these lands must be turned to advantage—American advantage. Texas had been the first domino; New Mexico and California must also fall to the United States. In 1848, Bennett, calling for the acquisition of all of Mexico, said that its population would never be able to utilize its rich resources. Were Mexico annexed and held as a territory by the United States, however, Americans could give "an entirely new character and new development to her resources and her population."[39]

Besides the bustling energy of the American people and the genius of their political institutions, technology too, the expansionists believed, could be made a servant of empire. The triumph of Yankee ingenuity over time and distance would permit the United States to integrate an entire continent into a cohesive Union. As historian John Higham has noted, Jacksonian America had "a culture with a very indistinct sense of limits, a culture characterized by a spirit of boundlessness."[40] Democrats of the 1840s expressed their sense of bound-

38. *CG*, 29 Cong., 2 sess., App. 325 (February 9, 1847). In early 1848, Senator John Dix of New York expressed a similar view: "If, in the progress of our people [migrating] westward, they shall occupy territories not our own, but to become ours by amicable arrangements with the governments to which they belong, which of the nations of the earth shall venture to stand forth, in the face of the civilized world, and call on us to pause in this great work of human improvement?" (*CG,* 30 Cong., 1 sess., App. 182 [January 26, 1848]).

39. New York *Herald,* July 28, 1844, June 5, 1846, and May 12, 1848.

40. John Higham, "From Boundlessness to Consolidation: The Transformation of American Culture, 1848-1860," Bobbs-Merrill reprint (Indianapolis, 1969), p. 6.

lessness primarily through their advocacy of territorial expansion. Hamilton and Madison had labored to refute the impression that liberty and extended dominion were incompatible; expansionists of the Tyler-Polk years went further and maintained that democracy and empire were actually inseparable. Dispersion of population over great distances inhibited rebellion and disunion, and revolutionary advances in transportation and communication linked the various parts of the empire together for their mutual protection and prosperity.[41] Here was another exceptional factor in the country's favor: the telegraph, the rotary press, railroads, and steamships had greatly altered previous notions of time and space and convinced the expansionists that administering a continental empire in the 1840s would prove easier than forming the original thirteen states into a single unified republic 60 years earlier.[42]

Impressive advances in technology gave Americans still another indication of their uniqueness and superiority. A *Herald* reporter suggested in 1844 that the telegraph "literally annihilated" distance and that the only task remaining for invention to achieve was "to discover news before it takes place." Bennett predicted in mid-1844 that the telegraph would "blend into one homogeneous mass . . . the whole population of the republic" and would make the entire continent "as consolidated and united" as New York City. No admirer of politicians, Bennett thought the telegraph would prove itself far more useful to the nation than its best statesmen. The telegraph could "do more to guard against disunion . . . than all the most experienced, the most sagacious, and the most patriotic government, could accomplish."[43] Bennett placed no limitations on American expansion: in addition to the acquisitions of the 1840s, he urged the occupation and eventual incorporation into the empire of all of Mexico, Cuba, and Canada as well.

Stephen Douglas denied that the American empire would become overextended if it expanded all the way to the Pacific. "The application of steam power to transportation and travel has brought the

41. The Democrats generally welcomed technological innovations in transportation and communication, but many also feared heavy industry and large corporations. The Jacksonians sought to integrate a vast empire, but they wished at the same time to protect the nation from industrialization and urbanization. The inconsistencies and incongruities in Jacksonian social and economic thought deserve an in-depth study.

42. The relationship between distance, time, technology, and westward expansion is discussed in Major L. Wilson, *Space, Time and Freedom: The Quest for Nationality and the Irrepressible Conflict, 1815–1861* (Westport, Conn., 1974).

43. New York *Herald*, May 3 and June 6, 1844.

remotest limits of the confederacy, now comprising twenty-six states
. . . much nearer to the centre than when there were but thirteen,"
he told the House in 1845. "The revolution is progressing, and the
facilities and rapidity of communication are increasing in a much
greater ratio than our territory or population." O'Sullivan saw the
situation in much the same way. The United States could "overspread" all of North America because its government was "organized
under that admirable federative principle which can govern equally
a continent or a county. . . . A vast skeleton framework of railroads,
and an infinitely ramified nervous system of magnetic telegraphs"
could furnish sinews to bind the empire together. The Mississippi
Valley and the Pacific Coast could be connected by rail, O'Sullivan
observed in mid-1845. This would allow "the conveyance of the
representatives from Oregon and California to Washington within
less time than a few years ago was devoted to a similar journey by
those from Ohio." His imperial imagination sprinted ahead of events:
the acquisition of Oregon and the conquest of California were still a
year away, and as yet there were no "representatives" to be conveyed
from the coast to the capital. But O'Sullivan was correct in anticipating Polk's efforts to plant the American flag over the Willamette
Valley and the harbor of San Francisco.[44]

The conquest of distance was as important to the Democrats as the
conquest of Indians and Mexicans. Cass hailed the occupation of the
borderlands and dismissed reservations about the country's rapid
enlargement. "As we increase in numbers and extend in space, our
power of communication is still more augmented," he declared in
1847. "The telegraph has come with its wonderful process to bind still
closer the portions of this empire, as they recede from its capital."
Speaking as chairman of the Senate Military Affairs Committee in
1848, Cass offered several justifications for a full-scale occupation of
Mexico that would modernize it under American auspices. Such an
extension of American rule posed no significant problems, since the
country possessed "a wonderful power of accommodating itself " to
extension. "Its double formation . . . of external and internal sover-
eignties, enables it to spread without weakness, and to preserve its
power of cohesion with its process of enlargement. And the progress
in the physical sciences comes in aid of our own political progress,"
Cass concluded.[45]

44. *CG*, 28 Cong., 2 sess., App. 68 (January 6, 1845); New York *Morning News*, July
9, 1845; "Annexation," *Democratic Review*, 17 (July, 1845):9.
45. *CG*, 29 Cong., 2 sess., App. 189–90 (February 10, 1847); *CG*, 30 Cong., 1 sess.,
App. 428 (March 17, 1848).

Ritchie agreed that distance should not impede expansion. Madison, he told his readers, had already demonstrated that the United States could expand indefinitely without harm, yet Madison in his time could not have anticipated "the immense improvements which were then concealed in embryo from the eyes of the most sagacious men. The railroad and the steamboat were then unknown. The magnetic telegraph had not entered into the dreams of the most enthusiastic philosophers." As far as Ritchie was concerned, "the problem of the practicability of an extended federal government" had been "solved by the art of man." Technological advances during the 1840s reoriented the Democrats' sense of time and distance. In the spring of 1846, for example, the telegraph linked New York City and Washington. Only eighteen months later Congressman James Bowlin of Missouri received in Washington a telegraphic message from St. Louis, the first of its kind transmitted from west of the Mississippi. In mid-1846 a *Herald* correspondent in the nation's capital reported that a single train had transported four hundred fifty passengers and their baggage out of the city after they had toured the national fair, itself an impressive display of American ingenuity. An express train carried Polk's third annual message to a Baltimore newspaper in only 53 minutes of running time, a feat that astounded Ritchie.[46] With such innovations at their disposal, the Democrats were confident that the United States could administer whatever it acquired.

When it became clear the United States would obtain land bordering on the Pacific, the expansionists began to consider connecting the Mississippi Valley with the West by rail. Foremost among Democrats urging a transcontinental railroad to promote commerce and to consolidate the empire was Sidney Breese. In early 1846 he presented to the Senate a petition from Asa Whitney requesting Congress to set aside a vast portion of the public domain to be used in financing the construction of a railway from Lake Michigan to Puget Sound. Breese recommended that Whitney's bold proposal be referred to the Committee on Public Lands, where it would receive favorable consideration, since Breese chaired the committee. He disagreed with Whigs who complained that the United States was losing its exceptional virtue and becoming like other empires. "Is there no difference of condition between us and them?" he challenged. "They had not the press, nor the compass, nor the steam-engine—none of those great

46. Washington *Daily Union,* August 19, 1847; New York *Herald,* May 25, 1846; Washington *Daily Union,* December 8 and 22, 1847.

instrumentalities which, wielded by freemen, are to revolutionize the world." He agreed with Douglas that the expansive empire of their time was actually more unified than the smaller republic of the 1780s. "By the agency of steam operating upon the boat, the railroad car, and the press," along with the telegraph, the United States would become "more compact, and in more constant and harmonious inter-course than the old thirteen states were at the period of the adoption of our Constitution," Breese observed.[47]

While Breese tried to gather adherents in the Senate for the rail-road scheme, Whitney appealed to Polk and his advisers to support his proposal. The explorer John Charles Frémont, Whitney wrote to Polk, had endorsed the feasibility of a railroad through the Rocky Mountains. What Whitney sought was a vast strip of land along the route that he would determine, a grant of territory sixty miles wide and some twenty-four hundred miles long that could be sold to help finance construction of the line. He estimated the cost of the project at twenty thousand dollars per mile, or about fifty million dollars all told. To lessen the shock of these staggering figures, he emphasized the impetus the rail line would give to commerce with Asia. Whitney had prospered as a merchant and an agent for China commerce in 1840–41, and he emphasized that a transcontinental railroad would cut six months off the time American and European merchantmen now devoted to a roundtrip expedition to China.[48] Moreover, a rail-road to the Pacific would allow the United States to direct the flow of European exports to Asia, since all merchants would utilize the faster rail service across the continent. American control over this new passageway to the Orient would eventually bring a virtual mo-nopoly over the entire trade with East Asia.

In contemplating the relationship between transportation, com-merce, and empire, Whitney saved his most candid comments for Secretary of the Treasury Walker. Walker, Whitney knew, had al-ready endorsed the construction of a railroad across the Isthmus of Tehuantepec, but Whitney doubted that a railroad through Central America would best serve the nation's interests. He suggested to Walker that it would be difficult for the United States to protect so distant a route. In addition, it was preferable that the environs of a major commercial thoroughfare be nearly, if not completely, self-

47. *CG,* 29 Cong., 1 sess., 414 (February 24, 1846); *CG,* 30 Cong., 1 sess., App. 350 (February 14, 1848).
48. Whitney to Polk, April 18, 1845, Polk Papers. See also Whitney to Buchanan, June 4, 1845, Buchanan Papers.

sufficient. This would be impossible in the isthmus because the region was not suited to American labor and would not attract permanent settlers. No such obstacles stood in the way of the projected route across the northern plains, however. Good land and a fine climate would soon entice masses of pioneers to the plains. "Reduce the cost of transit by means of [a transcontinental] railroad," Whitney advised, and "the surplus population will be induced to agriculture as the best reward for labor." Were the United States to build this vital trade route to the Orient, its economy would become "entirely independent of *all* the nations of the earth, and at the same time forcing tribute from them." A railroad from the settled East to the frontier West "would place us in a position to defy and if we please dictate to all the world," Whitney concluded in his appeal to Walker.[49]

Though Walker shared Whitney's ambitions for American commercial ascendancy, he doubted that this grandiose project offered the best means for attaining it. Other measures such as tariff reform, graduation and preemption legislation, and territorial and commercial expansion presented fewer problems and promised greater immediate rewards. As soon as the United States obtained formal possession of California in 1848, Walker urged Polk to authorize construction of a branch of the United States mint there. By making American currency abundant on the Pacific Coast, a branch mint would help to challenge Britain's advantage in the area. In addition, Walker suggested that more "first rate steam ships" flying the American flag in the Pacific would improve trade between the United States and Asia and Latin America. A railroad through the isthmus would have the same beneficial effect. After surveying the financial community in New York City during a brief visit in September 1848, Walker reported enthusiastically to Polk that "N[ew] York capital is *now ready* to make a railroad across the isthmus."[50]

Whitney failed with Walker, but he showed considerable acumen in stressing arguments of particular concern to him. Walker's neo-Jeffersonian fears of industrialization and urbanization and his preference for an agrarian society made him, as shown in Chapter 4, receptive to measures that would facilitate agricultural exports and promote farming and foreign trade. And Whitney's contention that the transcontinental railroad would increase American commerce

49. Whitney to Walker, April 7, 1847, Robert J. Walker Papers. Walker might have been more receptive to the railroad project if treasury funds had not been so badly depleted by the Mexican War.
50. Walker to Polk, September 21, 1848, Polk Papers.

and make the nation powerful enough to defy Europe undoubtedly impressed Walker. Had he, Polk, and other Democrats, especially Southerners, not been so imbued with the old Jacksonian prejudice against federal aid to such enterprise, Asa Whitney, not Leland Stanford, might have been the man to hammer in the golden spike somewhere between Chicago and San Francisco.

Bennett endorsed Whitney's arguments about future commercial dominion. With his customary zeal he predicted that construction of a transcontinental railroad would decide the struggle for commercial dominion in favor of the United States. "We would then have the pre-emption of all the markets in the Pacific," he noted in 1846. "Our manufactures would find an unlimited market—our agricultural interests would be spurred on—our commerce increase, and finally we would become master of the ocean, and the greatest nation in all creation." If Chicago were joined by rail with the Pacific, "the whole world" would become the "commercial tributary" of the United States. Before long the nation "would have a monopoly of the trade of the world," and Americans would "hold the rest of the world in the hollow of our hand."[51]

Though many expansionists found Whitney's ideas enticing, they were hesitant to repudiate the Jeffersonian-Jacksonian principle of equal rights for all and special privileges for none. The grant requested by Whitney violated a belief still sacred to many within the Democratic party, especially Polk and Walker. Even those more receptive to internal improvements balked at the proposal. Douglas informed Whitney in 1845, "Your scheme is too magnificent—the trust too great—the grant of lands too extensive—and the power over the rights and interests of the people, states, territories, and government, too monstrous to be confided to any citizen, no matter how virtuous, enlightened and patriotic." Saved earlier by Jackson from what the Democrats had labeled the "monster bank," the nation must not now call into existence a "monster railroad"—many Jacksonians might have used such imagery. Douglas at this time thought that settlement of the West should precede construction of the railroad and that the federal government should cede lands from the national domain to the individual states and territories in the West. The states and territories could then supervise this project. He

51. New York *Herald,* June 21, 1846; February 13 and November 18, 1846. Bennett printed a letter from Whitney stressing that a transcontinental railroad would render "the entire commerce of all the world tributary to and dependent upon us" (New York *Herald,* July 21, 1846).

did agree with Whitney that it would be advantageous to survey the route as quickly as possible, since such a step would attract settlers to the West. Bennett in 1848 reversed his earlier support of Whitney's plan and instead endorsed Walker's preference for an isthmian rail-way. He urged the Polk administration to demand from Mexico a right of way for a rail line across Tehuantepec. "Private American enterprise" could quickly construct a railroad across the isthmus that would bring the United States "command of the commerce of the world."[52]

Disagreements among Democrats on Whitney's railroad proposal reflected a broader division emerging over the role of the national government in internal improvement projects. As political historians have shown, sectional disputes about federally sponsored improve-ments contributed significantly to the decline in Democratic unity during the mid-1840s.[53] Increasingly, western Democrats sought fed-eral aid in promoting the West's economic development through river, harbor, road, and canal improvements. Southern Democrats, on the other hand, generally denied that the federal government had either explicit or implied powers to undertake such tasks. In vetoing the 1846 Rivers and Harbors Bill, for example, Polk emphasized that federal funds could be applied only to projects in which naval strategy or foreign commerce was the chief consideration.[54] Regional econom-

52. Douglas to Whitney, October 15, 1845, in Johannsen, *Letters of Douglas*, p. 129; New York *Herald*, June 19, 1848. In early 1849, after the discovery of gold in California and the beginning of a substantial migration there, Bennett switched back to the Whitney proposal (New York *Herald*, February 14, 1849). Benton ridiculed Whitney's plan. When Breese tried to present his committee's report to the Senate, Benton objected, insisting that "the idea of granting ninety millions of acres of land to individuals, for the purpose of constructing a road three or four thousand miles, through a wilderness and over a range of mountains double the height of the Alleghanies, [is] one of the most absurd and ridiculous that could be presented to Congress." Ironically, Frémont, who had suggested that the South Pass made such a railroad feasible, as noted earlier, was Benton's son-in-law (*CG*, 29 Cong., 1 sess., 1171 [July 30, 1846]).

53. The Senate, for example, passed the 1846 Rivers and Harbors Bill by a vote of 34 to 16, twenty-one Whigs being joined by thirteen Democrats (eight northern and five southern) in support of the bill. Opposing it were three Whigs and thirteen Democrats (eight southern and five northern). On the subject of internal improve-ments, see Charles G. Sellers, *James K. Polk, Continentalist, 1843–1846* (Princeton, 1966), pp. 473–77; Joel H. Silbey, *The Shrine of Party: Congressional Voting Behavior, 1841–1852* (Pittsburgh, 1967), pp. 56–58, 75–76, 172–82; Thomas B. Alexander, *Sectional Stress and Party Strength: A Study of Roll-Call Voting Patterns in the United States House of Representatives, 1836–1860* (Nashville, 1967), pp. 58, 64.

54. *CG*, 29 Cong., 1 sess., 1181–82 (August 3, 1846). See also *The Diary of James K. Polk during His Presidency, 1845–1849*, Milo M. Quaife, ed., 4 vols. (Chicago, 1910), 2 (July 27, 1846):51.

ic advancement was not a sufficient reason for federal intrusion. Douglas, however, rejected Polk's position on the 1846 improvements bill. "The West will never submit to an odious and unjust discrimination, which lavishes millions on the seaboard, and excludes the lakes and rivers from all participation," he complained.[55] Despite the opposition of dissidents such as Douglas, his Illinois colleague John Wentworth, and Jacob Brinkerhoff of Ohio, the Democratic-controlled House sustained Polk's veto because party discipline still remained strong. But disputes over federal sponsorship of internal improvements and northern dissatisfaction with the Walker Tariff demonstrated that however much the Democrats might agree on expansion, their conflicting notions about how to integrate and develop the empire would cause considerable strife in the future.

The Democrats did not recognize the incongruity between their party's domestic and foreign policies: they had obtained a 100-horsepower empire, yet they clung to a 10-horsepower engine of government to move it. The limitations they placed on federal power, whether desirable or undesirable in themselves, probably compounded many difficulties that arose during the Jacksonian period and shortly after. Earlier, for example, the Democrats' unwillingness to appropriate sufficient revenue for colonizing free blacks had closed off one possible avenue for solving or at least mitigating the racial crisis. Likewise, in the case of the Indians, the national government had failed to allocate the resources necessary to make the removal and reservation policies live up to the lofty promises of American officials. Though many mistakes and misunderstandings plagued Indian affairs, the failure of the central government to restrain the states and individual citizens from abusing Native Americans certainly undermined the stated objectives of federal policy. The Jackson, Van Buren, Tyler, and Polk administrations virtually had carte blanche when removing Indians, and Tyler and Polk exercised broad executive powers to expand the country. But when it came to consolidating territorial acquisitions, executive authority proved insufficient. The slavery extension controversy nearly incapacitated Congress during the late 1840s, and the Pierce and Buchanan administrations found it far more difficult to govern an expansive empire than the Democrats of the previous decade had anticipated.

The Whigs often chided the Democrats for their belligerence in

55. *CG*, 29 Cong., 1 sess., 1184 (August 3, 1846). See also Robert W. Johannsen, *Stephen A. Douglas* (New York, 1973), pp. 182–85.

foreign relations, but the expansionists were not bothered by warnings such as Senator Willie Mangum's that Americans had "a strong
predisposition to war" and that no other nation exhibited "so strong
a proclivity to pugnacity" as the United States. For a people supposedly isolationist and opposed to war, expansion-minded Americans
were uncharacteristically eager to spill blood in Mexico and to risk
war with England over Oregon in the mid-1840s. The Democrats
from the West, a *Herald* reporter observed during the debate on
Oregon, displayed "about as much respect and courtesy for old
England as a locomotive would to a bull upon a railroad track."[56] The
aggressiveness of many Democrats was another manifestation of
their assumptions about their exceptionalist empire: the uniqueness
of American political institutions, the compelling precedents of earlier acquisitions, the previous successes in tranforming acquired territories into new states, and the promise of technological advances in
communication and transportation were all critical components of a
developing imperial ideology. But one crucial prerogative of empire
remained to be established: the will and ability of the United States
to achieve its interests through the application of sustained military
power, perhaps even through war waged on foreign soil.

Even before Polk had informed Congress of the bloodshed on the
Rio Grande in 1846, a number of prominent Democrats had hinted
that a war would be beneficial to the United States. Urging Calhoun
to press for war with Mexico in 1844, Duff Green suggested that such
a war would force Mexico into "decent behavior" and prove that
Americans could avenge the wrongs done to them. The United States,
Green added, needed to send a message to European powers. "If you
could go abroad as I have done you would feel that we have lost caste
and that nothing but a war can regain the position we have lost. A
war with Mexico will cost us nothing," he advised, and would "rein-
state us in the estimation of other nations." Missouri's Bowlin agreed.
War is "no positive evil," he told his House colleagues in early 1846,
for it engendered in citizens a "self-relying confidence" and a sense
of "warm and patriotic devotion to their country." It also "secured
respect, by teaching others that we are not to be assailed with impunity." Breese, seemingly unalarmed by the Oregon crisis and Britain's
military preparations in early 1846, conceded to his colleagues that
war entailed suffering and certain dangers, but he denied that it was

56. *CG,* 29 Cong., 1 sess., 635 (April 19, 1846); New York *Herald,* January 10, 1844.

"barren of benefit." Americans had grown "too effeminate, luxuri-
ous, and extravagant." War would destroy these vices and "unite our
people more closely than they are now united, would increase their
energies, and, by calling into exercise the sterner virtues, lead, in the
end, to a vast increase of our power," he suggested.[57]

During the Congressional deliberations on Polk's war message,
several Democrats defined the crisis with Mexico as a welcome opportunity to impress Europe. "The present," Cass told the Senate, "is a
most important crisis in the history of this country—a crisis which is,
perhaps, to affect our character and our destiny for a long series of
years." More was at stake in the conflict than just those factors that
had precipitated it. "If we meet this act of aggression promptly,
vigorously, energetically, as becomes the representatives of a great
and spirited people, we shall furnish a lesson to the world, which will
be profitably remembered hereafter," he contended. Cass and many
other Democrats hoped that the conflict with Mexico could be used
to demonstrate the long dormant military capabilities of the American people.[58]

After the American victories at Palo Alto and Resaca de la Palma,
the expansionists began to suggest that the European nations would
have to reassess their own lingering territorial disputes with the
United States. Bennett, for example, hoped that a massive offensive
against Mexico would be launched so that the United States could
"teach foreign powers to dread the free people of this republic." The
Oregon question could be settled on American terms, he argued, "by
the energetic prosecution of the Mexican War." Ritchie felt that
American success on the battlefields in Mexico had greatly enhanced
the stature of the United States. "The military prowess of our people
and of our institutions has excited the astonishment and won the
admiration of the world," he wrote in 1847.[59]

The expansionists denied the notion that a powerful military and
a democratic government were incompatible. Foreign officials, the
expansionists contended, had erroneously assumed that the United

57. Green to Calhoun, November 12, 1844, in J. Franklin Jameson, ed., "Correspondence of John C. Calhoun," *Annual Report of the American Historical Association for
the Year 1899,* 2 vols. (Washington, 1900), 2:994; *CG,* 29 Cong., 1 sess., App. 79
(January 6, 1846); *CG,* 29 Cong., 1 sess., App. 386 (March 2, 1846).
58. *CG,* 29 Cong., 1 sess., App. 647 (May 12, 1846).
59. New York *Herald,* May 15 and 19, 1846. See also May 29, 1846, and October
25, 1847; Washington *Daily Union,* August 5, 1847. See also ibid., July 8 and November 3, 1846, and March 16, 1848.

States would acquiesce to European interests rather than resort to arms because of the American skepticism toward a large peacetime military establishment. The Mexican War, they trusted, had destroyed that illusion. Before the war, Cass recalled in 1847, the United States "had been at peace for a considerable portion of a century; our deeds of military prowess had been forgotten; our capacity, either to defend ourselves or to assert our rights and honor by arms, was almost unknown." The victories over Mexico, however, had "redeemed" the nation. "We take our station among the nations of the earth, willing to do right, and able to command it," he boasted. The triumphs in Mexico brought "character now, and security hereafter."[60]

Americans abroad similarly maintained that the war was altering attitudes towards the United States. Bancroft assured Polk in mid-1847 that the Europeans were startled by the prolonged American offensive against Mexico. He told Polk that he was trying to arrange for a Prussian officer to serve as a volunteer in the American army, a step that would "have a good effect in these quarters." Later that year Bancroft advised Polk that he could "annex all Mexico," since Britain would "not trouble herself much about it." The war had greatly elevated the reputation of the United States among European statesmen. As Polk's term drew to a close in late 1848, Bancroft reported that "these four years will be looked back upon . . . as full of glory." From his vantage point in London, he assured Buchanan, he could "testify how immensely our country has risen in the esteem of Europe during the period."[61]

Testimony from Bancroft, Donelson, and other diplomats reinforced the expansionists' belief that they had created a great empire. After Mexico and the United States had ratified the Trist treaty in mid-1848, Polk finally explained what he had meant by his war-time shibolleth, "Indemnity for the past and security for the future." The war had resolved an old dispute and would probably prevent new ones. Polk told Congress:

60. *CG*, 29 Cong., 2 sess., App. 195 (February 10, 1847).
61. Bancroft to Polk, June 3, 1847, Polk Papers; Bancroft to Polk, November 18, 1847, in Howe, *Life of Bancroft*, 2:28; Bancroft to Buchanan, November 3, 1848, Buchanan Papers. See also Bancroft to Polk, December 3, 1846, and May 18, 1847, Polk Papers; Bancroft to Buchanan, June 3, 1847, in William R. Manning, ed., *The Diplomatic Correspondence of the United States, Inter-American Affairs, 1831–1860*, 12 vols. (Washington, 1932–39), 7:291–92; Bancroft to Buchanan, May 18 and November 3, 1847, and February 8, 1849, Buchanan Papers.

The extensive and valuable territories ceded by Mexico to the United States constitute indemnity for the past, and the brilliant achievements and signal successes of our arms will be a guaranty of security for the future, by convincing all nations that our rights must be respected. The results of the war with Mexico have given to the United States a national character abroad which our country never before enjoyed. Our power and our resources have become known and are respected throughout the world, and we shall probably be saved from the necessity of engaging in another foreign war for a long series of years.

Five months later Polk used his final annual message to assess the war's significance. Before the war, he noted, "European and other foreign powers entertained imperfect and erroneous views of our physical strength as a nation and of our ability to prosecute war, and especially a war waged out of our own country." Under normal conditions the United States maintained an army of fewer than ten thousand men, while the European states supported "large standing armies for the protection of thrones against their own subjects, as well as against foreign enemies." Since the United States Army was spared from domestic duties, it could exert its full power in war. Polk also believed that the Europeans had underestimated the fighting potential of militia forces. But the successes in Mexico had shown "citizen soldiers" to be as effective as "veteran troops." It was now apparent that a republic could "prosecute successfully a just and necessary foreign war with all the vigor usually attributed to more arbitrary forms of government," Polk concluded.[62] The expansionists hoped to convince European leaders that whether a future dispute involved the status of Cuba or control over an isthmian canal, the United States would place its interests first and expect all other nations to do likewise.

62. Richardson, *Messages and Papers*, 5 (July 6, 1848): 2437–38; 5 (December 5, 1848): 2481–82. Polk thought that "our forces are the best troops in the world and will gain victories over superior forces of the enemy, [even] if there was not an officer among them" (*Diary*, 2 [April 30, 1847]: 492). Polk's positive assessment of the war is not entirely consistent with his complaints during the war, however. He filled his diary and correspondence with denunciations of Scott and Taylor, complaints about Congress's refusal to approve war taxes and appropriations, mutterings about war contracting procedures and wretched cost accounting methods in the quartermaster's department, criticisms of the federal mail service for its failure to deliver war news to Washington, and rebukes of Trist for negotiating a peace treaty after his recall. Polk's daily frustrations with waging the war should have led him to a more critical appraisal of American capabilities.

It was not by accident that the expansionist presidents of the 1840s assumed powers generally associated with "more arbitrary forms of government." Besides reminding Congress of his achievements in foreign relations, Polk used his final annual message to reaffirm his belief in bold executive leadership. Since only the president was elected by a national constituency, he and not Congress represented "the whole people of the United States." Moreover, Polk insisted, majority rule was justified only when that majority ruled in strict accordance with the Constitution. When Congress tried to block the president from pursuing policies that were in the public interest, or when Congress approved measures inimical to the states and the people, the executive as their agent had to resist the legislature.[63] Polk, as his diary repeatedly shows, did not doubt his ability to fathom the national will. "The people elected a majority of both Houses to sustain my policy, but their Representatives do not do so," he complained in early 1847. When Congress failed to comply fully with his requests for funds to make war and peace with Mexico, Polk suggested to Bancroft that public opinion was "far in advance" of Congress.[64] This presumption naturally led to forceful executive ac-tion in both domestic and foreign affairs. Like other Jacksonians, Polk believed that only a powerful president could protect the people from domestic and foreign dangers. While attacking and dismantling the remnants of the American System at home, Polk (and Tyler too) sought extensive territorial and commercial opportunities abroad. Though claiming to be strict constructionists of the Constitution, they interpreted their own powers broadly when land or markets were at stake. They often treated Congress as a troublesome obstacle to success rather than as a coordinate branch of the federal government, especially in the case of the annexation of Texas and relations with Mexico.[65]

---

63. Richardson, *Messages and Papers,* 6 (December 5, 1848): 2513–15.

64. Polk, *Diary,* 2 (February 25, 1847):392; Polk to Bancroft, "Private," January 30, 1847, Polk Papers.

65. Marvin Meyers refers to the twelve years of Jackson's and Van Buren's rule as "the veto era of the American presidency," but Tyler and Polk could also be included as part of a longer "veto era" from 1829 to 1849. The executive veto of congressional bills was similar to aggressive presidential initiatives in foreign policy: both were manifestations of a Jacksonian preference for an "imperial" presidency. The phrase quoted is from Meyers, *The Jacksonian Persuasion: Politics and Belief* (Stanford, 1957), p. 251.

The Legacy of Jacksonian Empire

The expansionists failed to discern the ironies in their course. Even as American troops penetrated into the heart of Mexico and then subdued and occupied Mexico City, Democrats continued to proclaim the exceptional virtue of the United States and to distinguish it from all other empires. More ironic, perhaps, was the expansionists' insistence that the sparsely settled lands acquired by conquest would relieve internal tensions and strengthen the Union. They had the opposite effect. The inability of most Democrats to sense the dangers in unprecedented expansion–especially in view of the increasingly severe sectional and political strains occasioned by the war and the proviso—was a graphic illustration of how powerful the ideology of exceptionalism and empire had become among the Jacksonians.

To assign ultimate responsibility for the Civil War to the expansionists of the late Jacksonian period would be misleading, however. Historians who have presented the 1840s primarily in terms of the rising sectionalism and political polarization of the decade have partly misrepresented its long-range significance—a significance that transcends the troubled period from 1848 to 1877.[66] However myopic the Democrats' expectations proved to be, the notion that territorial acquisitions might cause the country any harm or contribute significantly to its disintegration did not square with the Jacksonians' historical experience or ideology. They hoped that expansion would forestall discord and disunion, not produce them. That their actions eventually produced unanticipated problems indicates that they, like other leaders at other times and in other places, overestimated their ability to predict and control events. Previous territorial additions had obviously increased American power and security, as France, Spain, Britain, and numerous Indian tribes had ceded land to the United States. With Texas, half of Oregon, and New Mexico and California secured to the Union at the close of the Mexican War, the prospect must have seemed promising to the expansionists. The progress of the United States—the dramatic increase in its land, population,

66. Most historians look to the 1840s to find early signs of sectionalism and disunion. Such an approach has obscured the significance of the expansionism of the late Jacksonian period by placing an inordinate emphasis on sectional tensions and the fragmentation of the two major parties. Consequently, the concept of a new American empire and the motives for its acquisition have often been lost in the shadow of the issues of slavery and secession.

resources, wealth, and power—appeared to be inseparable from sixty years of territorial acquisitions.

It was ironic, too, that radical Free-Soil sentiment in the North and recurring allusions to secession in the South appeared simultaneously with the consummation of a continental empire. The acquisitions of the 1840s relieved some of the Democrats' anxieties about domestic and foreign threats to the nation, but new problems arose to prove that the Democrats had overestimated their potential to govern a continental empire. Their system did afford them some advantages: the Constitution had provided a means of avoiding the dangerous extremes of excessive federal authority, on the one hand, and disruptive state and regional supremacy, on the other. By the separation of powers between the states and the national government, the United States had avoided repressive consolidation and centrifugal fragmentation. Other assets of empire included the natural waterways, the turnpikes, and canals that had linked the states and sections; surely the railroad, the steamship, the rotary press, and the telegraph would bring the parts of the Union even closer together. An additional factor that gave the expansionists confidence was the previous success in checking threats to the Union. Though the slavery issue had menaced the country in 1819 and 1820, the Missouri Compromise had resolved the crisis. A decade later, Jackson had snuffed out the flames of nullification and secession in South Carolina, seeming to prove nationalism a stronger force than sectionalism. Polk, in orchestrated imitation of Jackson, denounced both southern and northern extremists who were threatening the viability of the confederation by their agitation of the slavery issue. Here, again, was a cruel irony: Polk, the self-proclaimed nationalist, was relying on the powerful presidency—a vital component of earlier Jacksonian success—to bring ominous divisive forces under control. But he could not duplicate Jackson's triumphs. The continental empire proved to be an unruly empire.

Rather than presenting the 1840s as the first major step toward secession and civil war, historians could instead couple the expansionists of the late Jacksonian period with the expansionists of the 1890s. Certainly the expansionists of the 1840s would have viewed the acquisition of an overseas empire in 1898 as a more predictable climax to their own efforts than the Civil War. The striking similarities between the two imperial decades need only be suggested here. Tyler, for example, scrutinized developments in Hawaii during his term and declared that the United States would look unfavorably upon any European interference there. In addition, he dispatched Cushing to

China to stick an American foot into what would be termed the Open Door fifty years later. Polk and Walker also looked beyond the continent during the late 1840s, anticipating some of the preoccupations of their expansionist heirs later in the century. Walker, for example, recognized the future commercial significance of a transportation route across Central America. As Polk noted in 1847, "Walker attached greater importance to [the administration's attaining] the free passage across . . . Tehuantepec than to the cession of New Mexico and the Californias," and he was willing to pay Mexico thirty million dollars for including that privilege along with the cession of the borderlands.[67] Walker, in fact, foreshadowed the position that President Rutherford B. Hayes adopted in 1880 when Hayes contended that any interoceanic canal across Central America would be "virtually a part of the coast-line of the United States." Since American commercial interests there were "greater than that of all other countries" and control over such a canal was vital to American "power and prosperity" as well as its "defense, . . . unity, peace, and safety," the question was one "of paramount concern to the people of the United States."[68] Those words might well have been Walker's or Polk's a generation earlier. Another striking similarity between the two imperial decades is the emphasis in each on increasing America's naval strength. In the 1840s, Upshur, Bancroft, Tyler, and Polk thought of naval policy in terms of the growing international trade of the United States. Fifty years later, theorists such as Alfred Thayer Mahan and Henry Cabot Lodge would also champion a reorientation in naval policy because of new interests and ambitions in American foreign affairs.

The Polk administration anticipated future United States policy in the Caribbean as well when it edged toward armed intervention in the racial war in Yucatán in1848. Ritchie explained that the administration sought "to prevent Yucatán from becoming a colony of any European power . . . and at the same time to rescue the white race from extermination or expulsion from their country." Bennett supported such intervention, emphasizing the danger of racial annihilation in Yucatán and the possibility of European encroachments there. He demanded that the United States assist the beleaguered whites. In imagery characteristic of the American frontier, Bennett cried, "Yucatán is in distress—her cities are burned up by hordes of savage

67. *Diary,* 2 (April 13, 1847): 473.
68. Quoted in Dexter Perkins, *A History of the Monroe Doctrine* (Boston, 1955), p. 163.

Indians—her people are driven from their homes to wander in naked-
ness and terror—a portion of civilization is threatened with savage
extinction!"[69] But with the army still entrenched in Mexico and stern
warnings against intervention emanating from Congress, Polk had to
give up on Yucatán and look elsewhere. He did not have to look
far.

Prodded by O'Sullivan and Douglas, Polk and Walker also decided
that the United States should add Cuba to its domain, and Polk
admitted to his cabinet that he would pay Spain as much as one
hundred million dollars for the island.[70] (Earlier, Polk had placed a
price tag of only twenty-five million dollars on California.) Rumors
to the effect that the administration had instructed its minister in
Spain to begin negotiations for the cession of Cuba spread through
Washington in late 1848. But Spain spurned all overtures, so this
effort to expand the empire into the Caribbean collapsed.[71]

Although Tyler and Polk did not intervene in Hawaii, Yucatán, or
Cuba, they anticipated the concerns of future leaders who did. Policy
makers such as McKinley, Hay, and Theodore Roosevelt moved beyond continentalism and sought a global empire for the United States,
but the transition is not as dramatic as is usually assumed. In retrospect, the objectives of the expansionists of the 1890s closely resembled those of their predecessors in the 1840s: each group hoped to
defuse a domestic malaise through expansionism and war; each sought
to enhance the country's commercial position, especially in Asia; and
each set out to show European powers that the United States could
and would employ force to secure its interests. Historians have until
recently accepted the view that the United States emerged as a world
power in 1898. Had the sectional crisis, the Civil War, and Reconstruction not directed American attention inward so extensively from
1848 to 1877, however, perhaps the Mexican War rather than the
Spanish-American War would be acknowledged as the most significant

69. Washington *Daily Union,* April 30, 1848; New York *Herald,* May 5, 1848. For
Polk's views on Yucatán, see *Diary,* 3 (April 25 and 27, 1848): 433–34, 436–37; (May
6, 1848), 444–45; Polk's message to Congress on Yucatán, April 29, 1848, in Richardson, *Messages and Papers,* 5:2431–33.
70. For the thoughts of Polk and his cabinet on Cuba, see *Diary,* 3 (May 10 and
30, 1848): 446, 469; (June 1, 2, 3, 6, 9, and 17, 1848), 475–79; 482–83, 485–88, 492–94.
For other relevant views, see O'Sullivan to Polk, May 10, 1848, Polk Papers; O'Sullivan to Buchanan, "Confidential," March 19, 1848, Buchanan Papers. Polk wrote in
his diary, "I am decidedly in favour of purchasing Cuba and making it one of the
states of [the] Union" (*Diary,* 3:446 [May 10, 1848]).
71. New York *Herald,* October 20 and December 16, 1848; January 7 and 26, 1849.

turning point in American foreign relations during the nineteenth century.[72]

Historical hindsight shows that the expansionists built not a castle of stone but a house of cards. The empire's flaws were not apparent to the Democrats, who branded as traitors and deserters those who did not share their optimism. Abolitionists warned that slavery would continue to haunt the Republic, and Whigs called for measures that would integrate and improve the Union, but the expansionists responded instead with additional pleas for new territory. Bennett expressed a common sentiment when he ridiculed the abolitionists as "the old women of both sexes, who are dissatisfied with all the exisiting arrangements of society, and are dreaming of vain reforms in the future." When Ritchie in 1848 considered the Polk administration's many tribulations, he grumbled, "The great difficulty which we have had to encounter, is not the enemy abroad, but the opposition at home."[73] This was a standard Democratic belief: republics rarely succumbed to defeat from without but usually crumbled because of discord and decay within.

By the close of the Mexican War, then, the United States possessed a continental empire as well as an elaborate ideology to sanction it. The victory over Mexico and the spectacle of American soldiers reveling in the Halls of Montezuma seemed a fitting climax to the quest for empire that had begun with the Revolution and independence. As devout anticolonialists, the policy makers of the United States had established a novel imperial arrangement whereby new territories entered the Union as equal states. After each successful

72. Even between the late 1840s and the 1880s, the impulse for aggrandizement persisted. From the Fort Laramie treaty of 1851 to the Wounded Knee massacre in 1890, the United States dispossessed the western Indians of hundreds of millions of acres that were then turned over to whites. The defeat and dispossession of western Indians from the 1850s through the 1880s fills in the misleadingly labeled "quiescent period" of American diplomacy. Historians of foreign relations have not adequately taken into account the expansionist principles behind American Indian policy from the 1780s through the 1880s. On the period after the Mexican War, see Robert A. Trennert, Jr., *Alternative to Extinction: Federal Indian Policy and the Beginnings of the Reservation System, 1846–1851* (Philadelphia, 1975); Loring B. Priest, *Uncle Sam's Stepchildren: The Reformation of United States Indian Policy* (New Brunswick, N.J., 1942); Robert W. Mardock, *The Reformers and the American Indian* (Columbia, Mo., 1971); Ralph K. Andrist, *The Long Death: The Last Days of the Plains Indians* (New York, 1964); Robert M. Utley, *The Last Days of the Sioux Nation* (New Haven, 1963); *Frontier Regulars: The United States Army and the Indian, 1866–1891* (New York, 1973); Richard N. Ellis, ed., *The Western American Indian: Case Studies in Tribal History* (Lincoln, Neb., 1972).

73. New York *Herald*, March 25, 1846; Washington *Daily Union*, March 16, 1848.

assimilation of new lands, Americans became increasingly convinced that their republican system with its separation of powers provided an ideal mechanism for transforming territorial acquisitions into semi-sovereign states, all of them adding wealth, security, power, and prestige to the nation. During the 1840s, the migration of Americans to Oregon and California and the startling advances in communication and transportation struck the Jacksonians as further evidence of American uniqueness: pioneers, not statesmen or soldiers, conquered land for the United States; technological innovation, not force, would bind the expansive empire into a cohesive whole.

The Tyler Whigs and Jacksonian Democrats, heirs to the Jeffersonian and Madisonian fears of Federalism, disunionist tendencies in older states, population growth and concentration, industrialism, and European hostility to the United States as a thriving repudiation of Old World ways, found in expansion the best means for maintaining American stability and security. American exceptionalism already defined the United States as a good nation. The expansionists fused that ideology of exceptionalism with concepts stressing the value of previous territorial acquisitions to the Union, thereby reconciling to their satisfaction the seemingly contradictory ideas of American virtue and American empire. Not entirely new to the 1840s, such a synthesis served the Democrats especially well in their efforts to portray American aggrandizement as unusually moral and humane. A good nation, they insisted, could also be a great nation.

CHAPTER 7

Divided They Fell: The Demise of Democratic Expansionism

For two decades fundamental Jacksonian preoccupations and principles found expression in territorial expansion. Beginning with Indian removal and climaxing with the conquest of California, the Democrats conducted a sustained campaign to obtain more land for the American people. The invasion of the borderlands during the Mexican War stands as both the most dramatic manifestation of this expansionism and its great culmination. It is often assumed that territorial expansion reached its apogee during Polk's term because the acquisition of Texas, Oregon, and California rounded out the nation's "natural" boundaries. Though there is some basis for that assumption, the Democrats of the late 1840s did not agree on just what the country's natural boundaries should be: some Democrats believed that parts (or all) of Canada should be brought into the Union, others hoped to acquire Mexico's provinces bordering the Rio Grande (some wanted all of Mexico), and still others insisted that the strategic locations of Cuba and Yucatán made their acquisition essential to the United States.

The inability of Democrats to secure any significant accessions to the Union between 1848 and 1861 ironically grew out of the party's striking successes in 1845 and 1846. Polk was able to marshal Democrats behind his administration during the first two years of his term, but his policies and his tactics inadvertently contributed to an unexpected paralysis in foreign and domestic affairs in 1847 and 1848.

Several factors contributed to the demise of Democratic expansionism: the circumstances of Polk's nomination; the way in which he handled the annexation of Texas, the Oregon question and relations with Mexico; his personal style; and—perhaps least expected and most ominous—the Free-Soil revolt, which Polk could neither comprehend nor contain.

With only three weeks remaining in his term, Polk in early 1849 reflected on his presidency: "They have been four years of incessant labour and anxiety and of great responsibility. I am heartily rejoiced that my term is so near its close."[1] What Polk omitted to say was that many other powerful Democrats were also "heartily rejoiced" to see his term end. Whatever solace Polk derived from his impressive policy achievements could not compensate for his frustrations during the second half of his term. Benton avoided him, Calhoun distanced himself from the administration, Dallas rarely spoke to Polk, and Buchanan, never very comfortable with Polk even early in the term, grew more aloof as time passed. Though an extremely private man, Polk needed affirmation that he had been Jackson's legitimate heir and had met the high standard of executive leadership established by his venerated predecessor.

Seldom had a president achieved so much so quickly; seldom had a president alienated so many men so completely. In 1837, Jackson had retired to spend his remaining eight years as the country's most revered public figure. In 1849, Polk retired, but he died only three months later, denied the satisfaction of seeing California admitted to the Union in 1850. Not only had times changed, but Polk was no Jackson. History had caught up with the Democrats: no longer could dynamic executive leadership control the forces threatening the nation.

Personal, geographical, and ideological differences splintered the Democratic party during Polk's term and ultimately raised the specter of secession and civil war. Temporarily but tenuously united by Polk's stunning victory in 1844, the Democrats could not maintain their harmony during the next four years. During Polk's first eighteen months in office, he accomplished all the goals he had set for his administration, yet each triumph brought troubles that weakened the party. In 1845 and 1846, the Democrats secured Texas, resolved the Oregon dispute, and conquered California and New Mexico. In

1. *The Diary of James K. Polk during His Presidency, 1845–1849,* Milo M. Quaife, ed., 4 vols. (Chicago, 1910), 4 (February 13, 1849): 331.

domestic affairs they enacted the Walker Tariff and established the Independent Treasury. To attain these measures the administration leaned heavily on congressmen who often resented the political pressure, even if they found the policies themselves acceptable. Many northern Democrats soon suspected that Polk's loyalties were sectional rather than national. Disapproval of Polk was not confined to the North, however. After the outbreak of the war with Mexico, faction after faction drifted away from the administration, inhibiting the interventionist and expansionistic tendencies of Polk and his advisers. By early 1848, dissension among Democrats forced the administration to accept a smaller territorial indemnity from Mexico than it wanted and blocked Polk from meddling in Yucatán's civil war. Though the impasse became obvious in 1848, it had actually begun to develop very early in Polk's term. In early 1845, Texas was one initial difficulty, patronage another.

The misgivings and misunderstandings among various Democratic factions concerning Texas made it a significant problem for the party. Certain that their advocacy of annexation would prove an advantage in 1844, a small but determined group of party strategists preempted the Texas issue in order to frustrate Tyler's ambitions for another term and to ensure that their party would nominate a dedicated expansionist to run against the antiterritory Whigs. Many northern Democrats, even those who favored annexation in the abstract, however, objected to the tactics of their party associates. In key northern states—especially New York—the Democrats feared the political power of the growing antislavery movement, and they did not want their party to become known as the party committed to the acquisition of slave territory. They favored territorial expansion and were not opposed to adding slave territory to the Union, but they wanted a judicious approach that would balance sectional preferences in the addition of territories to the nation. Moreover, whatever their personal feelings about slavery, they did not want the northern Whigs to be able to brand the Democratic party as a southern-dominated, proslavery party. These concerns made it imperative that the Democrats handle the Texas issue adroitly. They did not do so, and the party paid a dear price for its mistakes.

The loyal followers of Van Buren disliked the proceedings of the 1844 Democratic convention, and New York Democrats in particular warned that some compromise on slavery must be a part of any annexation bill. In late 1844 and early 1845, John O'Sullivan supported efforts to acquire Texas, but he urged that the territory be divided equitably between slave soil and free soil. He told Walker that he shared his desire "to consummate the annexation at this session," but he added that several northern Democrats would resist unless some restriction was put upon slavery. This concession to the North, he said, was "vitally indispensable." Congressman George Rathbun of New York agreed. In early 1845 he told his colleagues, "All the population of New York desire Texas if Texas can be had without slavery; and a large proportion—perhaps a majority—are willing to consent to a fair compromise on that subject." Throughout the entire state, however, only "a corporal's guard" composed of office seekers could be found "in favor of surrendering the whole territory to the South." Whig John Hardin of Illinois praised northern Democrats such as Rathbun for their skepticism and queried his House colleagues as to whether "the orders from the Hermitage" or the "expectation of office" from president-elect Polk would be "sufficient to drive or entice enough doubting Northern Democrats to its support to insure the adoption of the Southern plan of annexation." Premature in stressing sectional discord in the Democratic party at this point, both Rathbun and Hardin underestimated the northern Democrats' willingness to support the "Southern plan of annexation."[2]

To mollify hesitant northern Democrats, the House passed a "compromise" resolution of annexation on January 28, extending the Missouri Compromise line through Texas. All form and no substance—only a miniscule and desolate part of Texas lay north of that line—this meaningless gesture hardly assuaged the fears of wary Northerners, as southern Democrats well knew. Calhoun, for instance, privately admitted that the North received nothing from the measure.[3] O'Sullivan condemned the resolution as "mere mockery."

2. O'Sullivan to Walker, January 13, 1845, Robert J. Walker Papers; *Congressional Globe* (hereafter abbreviated *CG*), 28 Cong., 2 sess., App. 134 (January 22, 1845); App. 277 (January 15, 1845). For similar statements by O'Sullivan, see the New York *Morning News*, December 9, 1844, and "The General Issue and the Particular Issues," *Democratic Review*, 15 (December, 1844): 534–35. In the December 9 editorial, O'Sullivan complained, "This whole Texas business has been sadly mismanaged from beginning to end. A simple measure has been complicated, a straight one tangled, an easy one embarrassed, and a great one sadly belittled." A Whig journalist declared that "Southern blood-hounds are out full chase upon every one who does not go the length with them" (Ashtabula *Sentinel*, January 24, 1845). Democrats John Hale of New Hampshire and Jacob Brinkerhoff of Ohio also criticized the process of annexation. Polk was warned about the New York Democrats' reservations about annexation. See, for example, Henry Horn to Polk, November 16, 1844, James K. Polk Papers.

3. Calhoun had written to Robert M. T. Hunter, "The idea that Texas will afford

In 1844, O'Sullivan had vindicated the two New York senators who had voted against Tyler's annexation treaty; now, in early 1845, he defended the fourteen New York legislators who voted against this specious compromise.[4]

Benton, perhaps the most prominent Van Burenite who resisted the juggernaut of annexation throughout 1844, finally succumbed to the pressure exerted by Walker, Jackson, Polk, and Ingersoll. The Missouri legislature directed Benton to support annexation, and Jackson warned that further opposition to the acquisition of Texas would destroy his eminence in the party. In addition, political insiders close to Polk (probably Walker and Congressman Cave Johnson of Tennessee) made pledges to Benton concerning future patronage appointments and the incoming administration's intention to proceed cautiously on annexation.[5] On February 27, Whig senator Jacob Miller introduced a resolution calling upon the president to initiate negotiations with both Texas and Mexico to adjust the disputed border between them and to secure Mexico's assent to annexation. Miller reminded Benton that his resolution resembled one that Benton had proposed earlier in the session, and he implored him not to "destroy his own child." To the delight of the expansionists, Benton retorted, "I'll kill it stone dead." And kill it he did.[6]

Benton's infanticide and the passage of the annexation bill marked an end for the Democrats, but ironically it also marked a troubled beginning. Two weeks after approval of the Texas resolution, a Washington correspondent for the New York *Herald* reported that Polk had promised that he would delay annexation until a commission from

as many non-[slave]holding states, as slave-holding is perfectly idle. . . .The compromise line is the 36th latitude. The part of Texas north of it is a small zone of worthless land" (July 30, 1844, in J. Franklin Jameson, ed., "Correspondence of John C. Calhoun," *Annual Report of the American Historical Association for the Year 1899* (Washington, 1900), 2:602.

4. New York *Morning News*, January 27 and 28, 1845. See also "The *Democratic Review* and Mr. Calhoun,"*Democratic Review*, 16 (February, 1845):107–8.

5. Jackson to Blair, July 26 and August 13, 1844, Andrew Jackson Papers; Nathan Sargent, *Public Men and Events*, 2 vols. (Philadelphia, 1875), 2:262–63; Thomas Hart Benton, *Thirty Years' View; or, A History of the Working of the American Government for Thirty Years, from 1820 to 1850*, 2 vols. (New York, 1854–56), 2:636–37.

6. *CG*, 28 Cong., 2 sess., 362 (February 27, 1845). The Senate clerk described the response to Benton's remark: "General laughter, with an attempt at cheering, suppressed by the President." Benton's conversion also delighted Dallas. He chortled to Walker that Benton "has not only eaten all his own words" but also "in substance and spirit, chokes off Wright and outherods Herod" (Dallas to Walker, February 27, 1845, Walker Papers).

the United States could negotiate with Texas and Mexico to resolve all disputes between the three countries.[7] For three years this pledge concerning Polk's intentions faded from public consciousness, but in 1848 allegations resurfaced that in early 1845 Polk had promised Bentón, Benjamin Tappan, and Francis P. Blair of the Washington *Globe* that he would reopen talks with Mexico and Texas when he assumed office.[8] This pledge had secured proannexation votes in the Senate from Fairfield of Maine, Tappan of Ohio, Haywood of North Carolina, Dix of New York, and Benton.[9] All five soon found themselves at odds with Polk.

The manipulations and misrepresentations that surrounded annexation did not augur well for the Democrats. The method of annexation and the propaganda justifying it gave a significant but unintended boost to the Free-Soil movement in the North. Many Democrats who reluctantly supported annexation in early 1845 were instrumental in the formation of the Free-Soil party in 1848: King, Rathbun, and Dix of New York; Wilmot of Pennsylvania; Hamlin of Maine; and Tappan and Brinkerhoff of Ohio. The annexation of Texas alone, of course, did not drive these men from the Democratic party. But the conduct of Tyler, Calhoun, Polk, and Walker on Texas lent some credibility to the radical Whigs' accusation that a proslavery conspiracy dominated by southern sectionalists had captured the federal government for its own selfish ends. That belief was political dynamite, and it helped blow apart the second American party system.[10]

7. New York *Herald,* March 14, 1845. The correspondent repeated the allegation the next day. See ibid., March 15, 1845.

8. Benton, *Thirty Years' View,* 2: 636–37; Sargent, *Public Men and Events,* 2:262–63; *Memoirs of John Adams Dix,* Morgan Dix, ed. (New York, 1883), 1: 230. A Washington correspondent for the *Herald* reported a meeting on the Texas question between Polk and a congressional delegation (including Walker and Buchanan) at Coleman's Hotel on February 27 (New York *Herald,* March 1, 1845).

9. Benton noted that during the Senate's deliberations before Polk's inauguration, "Several senators and some citizens conversed with Mr. Polk, then in the city, and received his assurance that he would act on Mr. Benton's proposition, and in carrying it into effect would nominate for the negotiation a national commission, composed of safe and able men of both parties" *(Thirty Years' View,* 2: 636). Charles Sellers believes that Polk deliberately misled the Van Burenites (*James K. Polk, Continentalist, 1843–1846* [Princeton, 1966], pp. 213–20). Polk later denied making any commitment on his Texas policy. See Polk to Aaron V. Brown, "Private," September 6, 1848, and Polk to Bancroft, "Private and unofficial," September 7 and 15, 1848, Polk Papers.

10. During the debate on the Mexican War in mid-1846, Whig Caleb Smith of Indiana accused a prosouthern conspiracy of responsibility for both the ill-advised annexation of Texas and the outbreak of the war: "The [Polk] administration is a southern one. Its partiality for southern men and southern interests has already been so strongly manifested, as to excite loud and open murmers from many of its friends.

Texas was not the only immediate difficulty awaiting Polk. A dark horse who had triumphed through the prodigious efforts of many Democrats, Polk assumed office with numerous political debts to pay.[11] Patronage was his currency, but knowledgeable Democrats doubted that he could meet his many obligations. Shortly after the election, Van Buren maintained that "the rush of unsound men for the loaves and fishes" of patronage was "the natural consequence of . . . the way the nomination was produced, and the nature of portions of the support which it received." Polk, he predicted, would "have an oppressive time of it."[12] Politicians—factions of New York and Pennsylvania Democrats, in particular—sought positions for themselves while also trying to persuade Polk to deny appointments to their rivals.[13] Simultaneously disgusted and delighted with Polk's predica-

The acquisition of California is desired as a means of extending and perpetuating the power and influence of the South. The successful manner in which the iniquitous scheme of annexing Texas has been consummated, has but sharpened the appetite of those who desire the acquisition of southern territory" (*CG,* 29 Cong., 1 sess., App. 1118 [July 16, 1846]). Ohio's Joshua Giddings, a prime mover in the formation of the Free-Soil party in 1848, complained shortly after the declaration of war against Mexico, "For fifty years we have constantly changed and shifted our sails upon the ship of state in order to catch the changing southern breeze" (*CG,* 29 Cong., 1 sess., App. 826 [June 14, 1846]).

11. Between the election and the inauguration, Polk's correspondence was swelled substantially by recommendations and requests for appointments. The intensity of the rivalries must have given Polk pause. In New York the Barnburners (Wright, Dix, Butler, Cambreleng) were arrayed against the Hunkers (Marcy, Bouck, Dickinson, Ellis); in Pennsylvania Buchanan and Dallas struggled for supremacy; Benton and Calhoun were implacable enemies; and other ambitious Democrats such as Walker, Cass, and Allen sought to enhance their chances for the presidency in 1848. Polk's pledge to serve only a single term probably worsened the patronage scramble in early 1845.

12. Van Buren to Bancroft, November 28, 1844, in "Van Buren–Bancroft Correspondence, 1830–1845," Worthington C. Ford, ed., *Proceedings of the Massachusetts Historical Society,* 42 (Boston, 1908–09): 432. "In the opinion of many," Van Buren noted, Polk had been "prematurely called to the head of affairs" and would find it difficult "to meet the public expectation."

13. See John M. Belohlavek, *George Mifflin Dallas: Jacksonian Patrician* (University Park, Pa., 1977), pp. 79–118; Philip S. Klein, *President James Buchanan: A Biography* (University Park, Pa., 1962), pp. 142–74; Ivor D. Spencer, *The Victor and the Spoils: A Life of William L. Marcy* (Providence, 1959), pp. 123–36; Herbert D. Donovan, *The Barnburners* (New York, 1925), pp. 52–109; John A. Garraty, *Silas Wright* (New York, 1949), pp. 256–388. On Democratic politics at the national level, see Chaplain W. Morrison, *Democratic Politics and Sectionalism: The Wilmot Proviso Controversy* (Chapel Hill, N.C., 1967); Glyndon G. Van Deusen, *The Jacksonian Era,* 1828–1848 (New York, 1959); James Paul, *Rift in the Democracy* (Philadelphia, 1951); Joel H. Silbey, *The Shrine of Party: Congressional Voting Behavior in 1841–1852* (Pittsburgh, 1967); Edward Pessen, *Jacksonian America: Society, Personality and Politics* (Homewood, Illinois, 1969); Sellers, *James K. Polk, Continentalist.* Other useful biographies include Robert W. Johannsen,

ment, Philip Hone mused that Democrats seeking office would find "that the public swill-pail, capacious as it is, has not room for all their snouts."[14]

Democratic leaders recognized that political rivalries and personal enmities would complicate Polk's task. In late 1844, Buchanan told Pennsylvania's governor-elect Francis Shunk that the long-standing feud between Benton and Calhoun, Democratic divisions over the tariff, and disagreements on Texas would handicap Polk. "His path will be beset by many difficulties," Buchanan predicted, Calhoun being the first: "To remove him [as secretary of state] will give great offence to many of the Southern gentlemen, who were mainly influential in procuring the nomination of Mr. Polk—to maintain him, will exasperate Col[onel] Benton and that wing of the party." Buchanan recommended that Calhoun be exiled to London to serve as minister there. King also expected bitter internecine strife. In early 1845 he warned, "Twelve months will not pass over before the Democratic Party will be more divided, and the different sections more hostile to each other, than they were when the Baltimore Convention assembled." Jackson, like Buchanan, advised Polk to send Calhoun to England, as did Dallas. Dallas maintained that Calhoun had committed "some signal, if not fatal, mistakes" as Tyler's secretary of state, creating "an apprehension that . . . he is unfit for a post which requires profound caution, an habitual spirit of conciliation, and a total absence of what may be termed sectarian and sectional, in contradiction to universal and national politics." Calhoun, for his part, did not object to Polk's naming a new secretary of state. He acknowledged that an incoming president had an unimpaired right to select his own advisers.[15]

Stephen A. Douglas (New York, 1973); John A. Munroe, *Louis McLane, Federalist and Jacksonian* (New Brunswick, N.J., 1973); Frank B. Woodford, *Lewis Cass: The Last Jeffersonian* (New Brunswick, N.J., 1950); James P. Shenton, *Robert J. Walker: A Politician from Jackson to Lincoln* (New York, 1961); Charles M. Wiltse, *John C. Calhoun, Sectionalist, 1840–1850* (Indianapolis, 1951); William N. Chambers, *Old Bullion Benton, Senator from the New West* (Boston, 1956); Robert V. Remini, *Martin Van Buren and the Making of the Democratic Party* (New York, 1959).

14. *The Diary of Philip Hone, 1828-1851,* Bayard Tuckerman, ed., 2 vols. (New York, 1889), 2 (March 4, 1845):244.

15. Buchanan to Shunk, December 18, 1844; King to Buchanan, January 28, 1845; King to Buchanan, November 14, 1844; Buchanan Papers; Jackson to Polk, December 16, 1844, Polk Papers; Jackson to Blair, January 21, 1845, Jackson Papers; Dallas to Polk, December 15, 1844; Calhoun to Polk, February 27, 1845, Polk Papers. King complained that Polk and Dallas had been "bad selections." See also Calhoun to Mrs. Anna Clemson, March 11, 1845, in Jameson, "Calhoun Correspondence," 2:647–48, and Dallas to Mrs. Soph Dallas, February 22 and November 27, 1845, in Roy F. Nichols, "The Mystery of the Dallas Papers," *Pennsylvania Magazine of History and Biography,* 73 (1949):366.

Patronage problems were complicated by Polk's politically unsound notion of his executive role. He treated party members as if
they were merely his tools to move the nation's politics toward a
Jeffersonian-Jacksonian order based on rigid laissez-faire economics,
federal restraint and states' rights, agrarian predominance, and aggressive territorial and commercial expansion. Legislators, however,
viewed politics differently. Senators guarded their prerogatives in
evaluating treaties and executive nominations, and representatives
who faced frequent reelection expected favors for their support. Loyal
Democrats on all levels sought rewards for their fealty to the administration's policies. Polk never reconciled himself to these political realities. He considered his 1844 victory a mandate for his policies and
for whatever methods he chose to use to implement them. While
certain Democrats such as Cass and Sevier accepted Polk's broad
prerogative, others such as Calhoun, Dix, and Niles of Connecticut
rejected his view of the relationship between the executive and Congress.

Polk and his cabinet were continually besieged by supplicants for
office. Breese was particularly importunate, and Polk labeled him
"perhaps the most troublesome and inveterate seeker for office for
his friends in either House of Congress." Competition for that distinction was intense. A year into his term Polk marveled that "still the
pressure for office has not abated." "I most sincerely wish that I had
no offices to bestow," he sighed. "If I had not it would add much to
the happiness and comfort of my position." In late 1846, Polk grumbled that "there is more selfishness and less principle among members of Congress, as well as others, than I had any conception [of],
before I became president of the United States."[16]

Secretary of War Marcy also tired of incessant office grubbing. He
blamed Polk and his fellow cabinet members for continually referring
political fortune hunters to him: "Everyone who wants an office for
himself or a friend without knowing what office rushes to the War
Dep[artmen]t in the belief that I keep a variety store and that after
an hour's consultation with me he can find something to his fancy,
and if he cannot be supplied to his heart's content it is because I am
an unaccommodating old gentleman." Polk, Buchanan, Walker, and
Dallas, Marcy complained, sent office seekers to him, preferring that
he, not they, suffer the wrath of the parade of disappointed appli-
cants.[17]

16. Polk, *Diary*, 2 (March 17, 1847):426; 1 (March 4, 1846): 261; 2 (December 16,
1846):279.
17. Marcy to Wetmore, December 17, 1847, William L. Marcy Papers.

No president could have met every faction's expectations. Yet it was crucial to the party that the administration distribute favors as equitably as possible while placating those whom it refused. Northerners soon alleged that Polk looked too frequently to the South to fill coveted appointments. In late 1847, for example, a *Herald* reporter facetiously observed that Polk had nearly depopulated Tennessee by awarding so many jobs to residents of his home state—an exaggerated charge that suggests the increasing dissatisfaction in the North with Polk's course.[18] Polk did little to reassure wary Northerners of his fairness. By temperament and experience, he was ill suited to handle the patronage scramble. When resentment about executive appointments spilled over into the realm of policy, Polk and Ritchie responded severely, for they demanded absolute allegiance from Democrats, whatever their feelings about the distribution of offices.

Polk's selection of Ritchie as executive editor in 1845 probably exacerbated the administration's problems. Gall rather than ink seemed to flow from Ritchie's quill, and his vicious attacks on recusant Democrats irreparably damaged the party. Before entering office, Polk had decided to replace Francis P. Blair's *Globe* as his executive organ. Blair had served both Jackson and Van Buren, and during the Tyler interlude from 1841 through 1844 he had supported Van Buren's aspirations for a second term. When Van Buren declared against the immediate annexation of Texas in 1844, Blair followed suit, turning many expansionist Democrats against both men. In early 1845, Blair found himself in the anomalous position of being the most prominent Democratic editor in Washington, a member of the party that had triumphed in the fall elections—but whose preferred candidate had not been Polk. To Polk only one course seemed prudent, even if it meant repudiating Jackson's counsel that Blair be retained. Blair must go.

Soon after the inauguration Polk began to pressure Blair and his publisher John Rives to sell the *Globe* to someone more acceptable to the administration. Polk complained to Jackson that "there is at present no paper here which sustains my administration for its own sake" and compared his situation to Jackson's when he had substituted Blair's *Globe* for Duff Green's *Telegraph* during his first term. Polk hoped the *Globe*'s proprietors would "place it in the hands of a new editor," preferably Ritchie or Donelson. Polk implored Donelson to assume the post, promising him "a fine fortune" in the short term

18. New York *Herald,* October 30, 1847.

and preference in a presidential appointment later on. But Donelson expressed "great reluctance" to accept Polk's offer, denying that Blair was hostile to Polk. He urged that Blair be designated executive editor. Jackson seconded this recommendation.[19]

Polk persisted, reminding Jackson that Blair's stand on Texas had "made him unacceptable to a large portion of the ardent friends of that measure." Too much the puppet of Van Buren and Benton, Blair could not be trusted to be loyal to Polk. Jackson, however, reaffirmed his commitment to Blair and warned that any other editor would fragment the party. "If Polk does not look well to his course, the divisions in New York and Pennsylvania will destroy him," Jackson wrote to Blair in April. When Polk would not relent, Jackson finally acquiesced, but he still believed that Polk erred in replacing Blair with Ritchie.[20]

So Ritchie became executive editor of the Washington *Daily Union* in 1845, under circumstances yet to be explained or clarified in a satisfactory way. According to three reliable contemporary observ· ers, the Polk administration loaned federal funds to Ritchie so that he could purchase the *Globe*. The executive transferred fifty thousand dollars from the Treasury to a Pennsylvania bank, and three annual installments were paid on Ritchie's behalf to Blair and Rives. Not until the end of Polk's term did Treasury secretary Walker reclaim the money for the government.[21] In other words, the administration arranged an interest-free loan of public funds to Ritchie so that he could become its dutiful scribe. An additional political ploy probably lay behind these manipulations: Polk or his subordinates had vowed

19. Polk to Jackson, "Confidential," March 17, 1845, Jackson Papers; Polk to Donelson, "Private and unofficial," March 28, 1845; Donelson to Jackson, March 9, 1845, Donelson Papers; Jackson to Blair, March 18 and April 9, 1845, Jackson Papers.

20. Polk to Jackson, "Confidential," March 26, 1845, Jackson Papers; Jackson to Blair, April 4, 7, and 9, 1845, Jackson Papers. Polk justified his replacing Blair in a long conversation with Senator Allen, who "spoke strongly against Mr. Ritchie's course in conducting the *Union*" (see *Diary*, 1 [April 25, 1846]:356–59). Jackson had earlier complained to Blair that Ritchie "sometimes goes off at half cock, before he sees the whole ground, and does the party great injury before he sees his error; and then has great difficulty to get back into the right track again" (Jackson to Blair, "Private," December 14, 1844, Jackson Papers).

21. Benton, *Thirty Years' View*, 2: 650–55; Sargent, *Public Men and Events*, 2: 266–68; Poore, *Perley's Reminiscences*, 1: 336–37. See also Frederic Hudson, *Journalism in the United States from 1690–1872* (New York, 1873), p. 241; New York *Herald*, April 4, 1845. Ritchie later contended that he bought the *Globe* from Blair and Rives for thirty-five thousand dollars, but he did not specify how he financed the purchase (Washington *Daily Union*, June 13, 1848).

to dump Blair in order to placate Calhoun's anti–Van Buren faction.[22] These intrigues baffled Jackson, who admitted to Blair that he had "no information" as to who the "real proprietors" of the *Globe* were.[23]

Southern Democrats had again used Jackson for their own pur· poses. Walker, Polk, and Aaron V. Brown had earlier encouraged Jackson's pro-Texas (and anti–Van Buren) stance in 1844; they had urged him to try to muzzle Blair's criticism of the Tyler junto; and they had pushed him into advising Blair to sell the *Globe*. Benton pointed to Walker as "the prime contriver and zealous manager of the arrangements" that replaced Blair with Ritchie.[24] Walker again achieved his immediate objective, but another weight shifted that would kick the beam against the Democrats in 1848. In retaliation, Blair at that time refused to support Cass and instead backed the Free-Soil candidate, none other than Martin Van Buren. Within a decade Blair was one of scores of prominent former Jacksonians who had joined the new Republican party.[25]

Ritchie made personal vendetta a regular feature of the *Daily Union*. No Democrat who crossed the president or his advisers escaped Ritchie's pen unscathed. One of the first victims was William Hay· wood, a noteworthy victim because he and Polk had been friends for almost thirty years when political differences split the two men. Haywood angered the administration in mid-1846 when he opposed the Walker Tariff bill and rather than vote against it resigned his Senate seat. Fairfield sympathized with Haywood's dilemma. "Hay· wood . . . resigned, rather than vote upon the bill against his party one way or his conscience the other way," he noted. Far less charita· ble, Ritchie accused Haywood of "overweening vanity" and "feeble· ness of judgment," describing him as a man who had sacrificed the country's welfare "to his own conceits, eccentricities, and indeci· sion."[26]

22. Blair, encouraged by Benton, had repeatedly condemned the junto's Texas policy. In 1845, Calhoun still had presidential ambitions, and Blair's replacement by Ritchie was initially welcome to him. Calhoun, however, soon found himself at odds with Polk and his editor. The intense rivalry between Calhoun, on the one hand, and Van Buren and Benton on the other dated back to the struggle in 1829–30 to determine Jackson's heir.

23. Jackson to Blair, April 28, 1845, Jackson Papers.

24. *Thirty Years' View,* 2: 655.

25. See Eric Foner, *Free Soil, Free Labor, Free Men: The Ideology of the Republican Party before the Civil War* (New York, 1970), pp. 149–85.

26. John Fairfield to Mrs. Anna Fairfield, July 28, 1846, in Arthur G. Staples, ed., *The Letters of John Fairfield* (Lewiston, Maine, 1922), p. 414; Washington *Daily Union,* July 25, 1846. Polk was only slightly more charitable in his reaction. He acknowl· edged some admirable traits in Haywood but described him as "ambitious" and "a

This assault surprised Haywood, and for over two years he waited for Polk to vindicate him. In late 1848 he finally asked Polk for a public testimonial that the *Daily Union*'s attack upon him had not been initiated or sanctioned by the president. Polk privately responded that the articles in 1846 had been "the sole act of the editor." Ritchie alone, Polk pointed out, determined what went into the executive paper.[27] Even in a private letter Polk could not apologize or renew his former friendship. Unwilling to let the disagreement fade into the past, Polk pointedly reminded Haywood that his resignation had been "a fatal political error."[28]

Brinkerhoff aroused Ritchie's ire as well. In late June 1846, Brinkerhoff sharply criticized the administration for its handling of Oregon, its diplomacy with Mexico, and its patronage policy, contending that Polk consistently favored the South. Ignoring the substance of these complaints, Ritchie ascribed Brinkerhoff's course to frustrated personal ambition. He "would go to lick the hand that holds the office in its palm" but would then, "because he cannot obtain the spoils, try to strike at the administration which thinks it its duty to refuse him," Ritchie charged. Even if true, casting the dispute in such insulting terms was poor politics. Victims understandably responded in kind.[29]

man of great vanity . . . possessing a good deal of self-esteem" *(Diary*, 2 [July 25, 1846]:48). Senators representing both major parties objected to the gross attacks on Haywood. Willie Mangum, a North Carolina Whig, criticized Ritchie for assailing Haywood "with such . . . ferocity" and "so unjustly," while Democrat John Niles contended that the "severe castigation" heaped upon Haywood by the *Daily Union* and other party papers was intended to intimidate all independent-minded legislators and "to destroy the freedom of action of Congress." Benton and Dix told the Senate that they had conversed extensively with Haywood on the course he would follow on the tariff bill: Benton praised "the purity, the patriotism, and the elevation of sentiment" that had actuated Haywood's conduct, and Dix, who had tried to "dissuade him" from resigning, also conceded a "purity of . . . motives" to Haywood. Another Democrat, Senator Arthur Bagby of Alabama, told his colleagues that although he "differed totally from . . . the propriety of the course" taken by Haywood, it seemed that he had acted honorably "according to the dictates of his own conscience" *(CG*, 29 Cong., 1 sess., 1148–49 [July 28, 1846]).

27. Haywood to Polk, December 18, 1848; Polk to Haywood, January 17, 1849, Polk Papers. Polk's explanation was misleading, if not deceitful. In April 1846, Polk had noted in his diary that on two or three occasions he had "sketched an article for [Ritchie's] paper" *(Diary*, 1 [April 24, 1846]:352–53). Polk and his advisers often supplied material to the *Daily Union,* and Ritchie frequently sat in on cabinet meetings, taking his cues from the cabinet's proceedings.

28. Polk to Haywood, January 17, 1849, Polk Papers. See also *Diary,* 2 (July 26, 1846): 51; (July 27, 1846):52. To Polk's relief the Senate passed the tariff bill 28 to 27. Three Democrats, Pennsylvania's Cameron and Sturgeon and Connecticut's Niles, voted with the Whigs.

29. Washington *Daily Union,* July 1, 1846. See also the New York *Herald,* July 3,

Wilmot, who helped forge the Free-Soil coalition with Brinkerhoff, also alienated Ritchie. Polk and all his advisers resolutely condemned the Wilmot Proviso, an indication of the administration's growing political isolation and its inability to understand the Free-Soil movement. "It is calculated to divide our councils, to paralyze our exertions, and to animate the enemy by the prospect of our own divisions," Ritchie asserted in early 1847. The proviso might have had that effect, but such was not its intention. Ritchie impugned the Free-Soilers by accusing them of giving aid and comfort to Mexico through their untimely agitation of the slavery extension issue. He insisted that the proviso be abandoned and that the Missouri Compromise line be extended to the Pacific. In late 1847 and early 1848 Ritchie repeated that the proviso "was offered out of time and out of place" and "was calculated to embarrass the administration."[30] Polk also failed to fathom the dissidents' concerns. When first apprised of the proviso, Polk dismissed it as "a mischievous and foolish amendment," a view that he maintained throughout his term. In early 1847, he complained about the "mischievous and wicked agitation" throughout the country and the "worse than useless discussion about slavery" in Congress.[31] Seeing only a devious bid for political advantage in the Free-Soil movement, Polk and Ritchie could not understand that blocking slavery's expansion had become critical for a faction of Northern Democrats who had decided that their party consistently responded only to the needs of the South.

Wilmot's insurgency separated him from fellow Pennsylvanian Buchanan. Defending Buchanan, Ritchie labeled Wilmot a "young disorganizer" guilty of "foul-mouthed malignity" in his "gross and wanton assault" on Buchanan. Without provocation, Wilmot had "sought to stab in the back" the Polk administration, Ritchie asserted.[32] Though

---

1846. Polk noted that Brinkerhoff, "who had applied to be a paymaster in the army and been refused, attacked me." Though both Brinkerhoff and Tibbatts had been "elected as Democrats," they seemed to "think more of their own personal interests than they do of principle" (*Diary*, 1 [June 30, 1846]:497–98). In a similar manner the administration labeled John Wentworth of Illinois a "deserter" when he opposed a war tax on tea and coffee (see the Washington *Daily Union*, February 3 and 5, 1847). Polk observed that "the whole Federal party united with Mr. Wentworth and others" to defeat his tax bill (*Diary*, 2 [January 22, 1847]:347–48). Polk said that he had become "perfectly disgusted with the want of patriotism which seems to control the votes and course of a portion of the Democratic members."

30. Washington *Daily Union*, January 11, 1847, and January 25, 1848. Similar denunciations appear in these issues: February 19, March 12, 15, and 20, and October 18, 1847.

31. Polk, *Diary*, 2 (August 10, 1846):75; 2 (January 16, 1847):334.

32. Washington *Daily Union*, February 7, 1848.

Wilmot had backed the administration on every major policy question in 1845 and early 1846, his Free-Soil apostasy was more than Polk and Ritchie would tolerate. Because of Wilmot's disillusionment with Northerners such as Buchanan, Dallas, Cass, and Dickinson, who always deferred to southern slaveholders, Wilmot left the Democratic party and found a more congenial niche in the Free-Soil party in 1848. He later became a prominent Republican during the mid-1850s.

Senator Allen cautioned Polk in 1846 about Ritchie's negative effect on the party. Allen told Polk that Calhoun's faction particularly disliked Ritchie and that the administration could not carry the Senate if it lost the support of Calhoun and his followers. Allen advised that Blair be made an associate editor so that he could control Ritchie's impetuousness and promote party accord. Polk summarily rejected Allen's suggestion, insisting that Ritchie "had been labouring to keep the whole party united and harmonious." Though he had made mistakes, he "readily corrected them when he discovered them." Polk attributed Allen's recommendation to personal ambition. "Ritchie will not answer the purpose of aspiring politicians because he will not lend himself to any of the factions who look more to their own advancement than to the public good," Polk concluded. He decided to retain Ritchie as sole executive editor.[33]

Bennett criticized Ritchie for a different reason—his frequent unreliability. In mid-1846, Bennett complained that "in nearly one half of the important movements of the government," Ritchie had "misrepresented, falsified, deceived, cheated and humbugged the country." Scathing prose proving inadequate to convey his dissatisfaction, Bennett in 1848 resorted to doggerel verse:

> The big organ of state is quite out of repair;
> Its pipes are all leaky, it will not hold air;
> Old Ritchie in vain, with Jim Polk for an aid,
> Endeavors to prop up their wind-broken jade—
> The damage is great and all tune it defies—
> It's a worn-out organ, beyond all disguise.

Pennsylvania editor John Forney, a supporter of Buchanan, also thought Ritchie inept and labeled him "the unconscious harbinger of disunion." Forney noticed that Ritchie could not take a practical joke:

33. Polk, *Diary*, 1 (April 25, 1846):356–59. See also the entry for April 27, pp. 361–62.

"Every thing was serious to him; and it was amusing to note how the most trifling allusion to the president and his cabinet would quicken his facile pen, and how he would pour his almost unintelligible manuscript into the hands of the printer." Bennett's editorial assistant Frederic Hudson believed that Ritchie had been successful as a regional editor in Richmond but in Washington had served "without power, without vigor, and without influence." In late 1847, a *Herald* reporter ridiculed the notion that Polk would seek reelection. "The president is a shrewd politician," the reporter gibed, "and he is aware that one might as well attempt to cross the Atlantic in an eggshell, as to become president of the United States through the advocacy and support of the *Union.*"[34]

Even Polk occasionally expressed frustration with his editor. In late 1847, he complained of Ritchie's "passion to put everything he knows into his newspaper," a trait that made Polk more circumspect about what he confided to him. A year later Ritchie again angered Polk when he printed a preliminary summary of the forthcoming annual message. "It is an infirmity of Mr. Ritchie that he cannot keep a secret," Polk lamented. Buchanan questioned Ritchie's competence more frequently and, like other Democrats, encouraged Polk to select a coeditor who could counter Ritchie's rancorous partisanship.[35]

The Political Consequences of Aggressive Expansionism

Polk and Ritchie were poorly suited to the task of maintaining party unity, but their course was complicated by controversial issues such as the Oregon dispute and the Mexican War. Whatever notions Polk held about his leadership of the party were badly shaken by the protracted debate on the Oregon question. Considering the 1844 Democratic platform a promise to be kept and not propaganda to be forgotten, Polk declared in his inaugural address his intention to acquire Texas and all of Oregon for the United States. Southern Democrats favored the hasty annexation of Texas, but they hesitated to pursue an aggressive course on Oregon. Afraid that war with

34. New York *Herald,* June 4, 1846, May 5, 1848; John W. Forney, *Anecdotes of Public Men,* 2 vols. (New York, 1873), 1:107–8; Hudson, *Journalism in the United States,* p. 271; New York *Herald,* November 29, 1847. The verses are from the New York *Herald,* May 5, 1848.
35. Polk, *Diary,* 3 (December 3, 1847):238; 4 (November 29, 1848):214–15; 1 (April 24, 1846):351–53. For a more favorable assessment of Ritchie, see Charles H. Ambler, *Thomas Ritchie, A Study in Virginia Politics* (Richmond, 1913), pp. 246–72.

England over Oregon might lead to a disastrous slave insurrection and a termination of cotton exports, they preferred a compromise settlement at the forty-ninth parallel. During 1845, however, Polk became even more strident than he had been in his inaugural in pressing the American claim to the whole territory. As Polk and a corps of northwestern Democrats threatened hostilities with Britain, a number of slave-state Democrats reacted with alarm.

As early as May 1845, Calhoun had criticized Polk's stand on Oregon, contending that Polk had adopted "a false view of that important question." The inaugural address had "made it impossible to settle it by negotiation, unless he retracts, or explains away what he has said, which would be almost as embarrassing," he observed. Polk's impatience frightened Calhoun, who thought that the United States could eventually acquire all of Oregon "by standing still and letting time and emigration settle the question." Regardless of what Polk said or did, Calhoun added, southern leaders had to prevent war with England.[36]

Calhoun had cautioned Polk prior to the inauguration not to assert any claim to Oregon north of the forty-ninth parallel, but Polk had instead made the "imprudent declaration" that the United States had a right to the entire territory. Late in the summer of 1845, Calhoun warned that England would fight if pressed by the United States, and he stated again his dissatisfaction with the administration's conduct. "Polk made a profound blunder in alluding to it at all in his inaugural," Calhoun confided to a friend. He thought that no policy was the best policy, since both time and geographical proximity favored the United States. War would lose Oregon, not obtain it. Convinced that gradual possession through population dispersion was the safest means of acquiring the area, he returned to the Senate in late 1845 to oppose the partisans of All Oregon. That meant opposition to the Polk administration.[37]

Polk lost control of the Oregon dispute because he unnecessarily politicized it and helped make it a hobbyhorse for dogmatic northwestern Democrats. Determined to acquire all of Oregon regardless of the risks, these men demanded that the bargain struck in 1844 be

36. Calhoun to Francis W. Pickens, May 6, 1845, in Jameson, "Correspondence of Calhoun," 2:653.

37. Calhoun to Mrs. Anna Clemson, May 22, 1845; Calhoun to James H. Hammond, August 30, 1845, in Jameson, "Correspondence of Calhoun," 2:656, 671. See also Calhoun to John Y. Mason, May 30, 1845, and Calhoun to Thomas G. Clemson, September 18, 1845, in ibid., 2:660, 671–72.

honored. They had cooperated wholeheartedly in obtaining Texas; their southern colleagues must demonstrate equal resolve in acquiring every square inch of Oregon.

The growing belligerence of Polk and the northwestern Democrats worried Louis McLane, American minister to Britain, who hoped to preserve peace and to open British markets to more American exports. McLane accepted his appointment in mid-1845 under the assumption that the administration, whatever its rhetoric, favored a negotiated settlement of the Oregon dispute. His State Department instructions seemed to validate that impression, for in them Buchanan reviewed the American efforts since 1818 to settle the question and admitted that since the United States had earlier expressed a willingness to partition the territory at the forty-ninth parallel, "It is not now to be supposed that the British Government will now consent by negotiation to yield to us the whole territory up to 54°40'." The area north of the forty-ninth parallel was "with the exception of a few spots wholly unfit for agriculture and incapable of sustaining any considerable population," Buchanan noted. Furs, its only asset, were hardly significant. He indicated, however, that the administration offered to compromise only because of the constraints imposed by previous proposals. If Britain rejected the present offer, the administration would then press for all of Oregon, since Polk would then "be relieved from the embarrassments in which he has been involved by the acts, offers and declarations of his predecessors."[38]

McLane might have wondered why Polk had paid so little attention in his inaugural address to those previous "acts, offers and declarations," but he continued to believe that the administration desired a compromise. McLane maintained his attitude of accommodation even after British minister Richard Pakenham peremptorily rejected the administration's offer to divide the Oregon territory at the forty-ninth parallel and refused to forward the proposal to his government. Pakenham's foolish response incited the hard-liners in Congress and made Polk more truculent as well.

While McLane persisted in his conciliatory efforts, the administration sidled closer to the extremist bloc and summoned all Democrats to follow. In November 1845, Ritchie repeated Polk's claim of a "clear and unquestionable" American right to all of Oregon. "The democracy of this country will stand to its word," Ritchie affirmed. "It will not flinch." Several days later he called upon southern Democrats to

38. Buchanan to McLane, July 12, 1845, Buchanan Papers.

support efforts to acquire the entire territory. He reminded them that Walker had also called for the acquisition of all of Oregon in his famous letter on Texas, the letter that had "constituted the textbook" of the Democrats' 1844 campaign. Though Senators Calhoun, George McDuffie, and William Yancey called for mutual concessions, Ritchie exhorted all Democrats to close ranks behind the administration.[39]

McLane became more confused. His official dispatches sanctioned a fair division of the territory, yet rumors and newspaper reports suggested that Polk and many Democrats in Congress would choose war rather than permit Britain to obtain even one acre of Oregon. McLane suspected that domestic politics was behind the fierce agitation of the Oregon question: congressmen were slandering Britain and vaunting their willingness to go to war for partisan advantage. Fearing that this outpouring of aggressive nationalism was adversely influencing the administration, McLane grumbled to his son in late 1845 about his "painful and awkward" position caused by "the extraordinary change in the president's policy" on Oregon. "It is my duty to get back with as little delay as possible," he observed. Polk's provocative annual message in late 1845 and the increasingly shrill rhetoric in Congress increased McLane's worries. In May 1846, he complained that "Cass runs comparatively little risk in assuming a ground which, while it is not likely to make him responsible for war, may be calculated to recommend him to all who would really and at all hazards insist upon the whole." Denying that national honor could be maintained only if all of Oregon were acquired, McLane dismissed as useless the exhaustive congressional debates over discoveries, claims, and titles in the Pacific Northwest. He thought the issue of title should be dropped. Despite the increasing tension on both sides of the Atlantic, he and Lord Aberdeen arranged a compromise settlement in mid-1846.[40]

When rumors about McLane's disaffection circulated through Washington, Ritchie immediately discredited them. The administration and McLane, he wrote, were of one mind on Oregon. "That he wished to return, in a spirit of dissatisfaction and disgust, we learn from the best authority, ... is wholly gratuitous and untrue," he observed. Ritchie might have been unaware of McLane's actual sentiments, or perhaps Polk or Buchanan directed him to print the disavowal for their purposes. Denying any division over Oregon in the

39. Washington *Daily Union,* November 6, 18, and 22, 1845.
40. Louis McLane to Robert McLane, November 18, 1845 and May 3, 1846, Louis McLane Papers.

administration, Ritchie again called for the acquisition of the whole territory.[41]

McLane's anger increased after he sent his compromise proposal to the United States. The pact reached the administration on June 6, 1846. Rather than endorse the agreement and take responsibility for its terms, Polk instead submitted it to the Senate for advice without recommending approval. Finally realizing that the All Oregon move-ment comprised only a small faction in Congress and that the Senate especially would not support a policy that might lead to war with England, the administration tried to save face by turning the Oregon question over to the Senate. If the Senate endorsed the treaty, it could be blamed for the "surrender" of Oregon. This tactic fooled no one. Those who favored the compromise charged that the administration had played petty politics with Oregon and had been rescued from its folly by a more prudent Senate. The Fifty-four forties, on the other hand, condemned the administration for even submitting the dis-graceful treaty to the Senate. Polk could not appease both southern Democrats who generally preferred compromise to war and north-western Democrats who seemed to favor war over compromise.[42]

Polk's course incensed McLane. "What more could have been done here—what less at Washington?" he challenged from London. An-noyed by Polk's conduct, McLane admitted that he felt "not the slightest confidence in his truth or sincerity or manliness, or in the like qualities of anyone around him." Polk and Buchanan had "be-haved like scamps" on Oregon. McLane confided to his son that he would try to avoid "an open rupture" with the administration, but privately he encouraged others to present his side of the Oregon story to the public, instructing his friend Charles Davis to dispute Ritchie's explanation of the settlement by writing a second major article on Oregon for the influential New York *Journal of Commerce*. McLane also advised Davis to emphasize McLane's personal commitment to com-promise and his crucial role in resolving the crisis.[43] Clearly McLane did not trust Ritchie to present the issues accurately.

41. Washington *Daily Union,* November 14, 1845. See also the issues of November 17, 18, and 22, 1845. O'Sullivan was also confident that the administration would insist on 54° 40'. When Horace Greeley suggested that the dispute would be settled at the forty-ninth parallel, O'Sullivan dismissed his remark as an "insult" to the administration and a "miserable supposition" (New York *Morning News,* April 8, 1846).

42. Bennett recognized Polk's predicament: "Settled or unsettled, the Oregon question demolishes . . . Polk with his own party" (New York *Herald,* April 25, 1846).

43. Louis McLane to Robert McLane, July 3, 1846; Louis McLane to C[harles] A[ugustus] D[avis], "Confidential," June 28, 1846, McLane Papers.

After the Senate approved the treaty, McLane took Buchanan to task for releasing to Congress selective (and deceptive) excerpts from his dispatches that made him appear to be a proponent of acquiring all of Oregon. The administration well knew his preference for compromise, McLane explained, but as Polk's voice in London he had tried to present the best case for the American claim to 54° 40'. Having established a cordial working relationship with Aberdeen, McLane was concerned to preserve it and asked Buchanan to clarify that he had always advocated a fair division of the territory, regardless of the administration's policy. The devious editing of his dispatches made him appear hypocritical, suggesting that he had reassured Aberdeen that he favored a fair adjustment of the dispute while actually supporting the extreme American claim. McLane seemed more worried about Aberdeen's opinion of him than Polk's and Buchanan's.[44]

McLane did not allow his anger to interfere with his political advancement, however. After Polk accepted Buchanan's request for an appointment to the Supreme Court, he offered the soon to be vacated office of secretary of state to McLane. Conveniently letting bygones be bygones (and recent bygones at that), McLane in July eagerly accepted Polk's offer.[45] But Buchanan changed his mind and remained in the cabinet, so McLane returned from London in the autumn of 1846 to private business pursuits in Maryland.

Many other southern Democrats shared McLane's desire for an equitable adjustment on Oregon. McDuffie sparred with Breese in the Senate in April 1846 when Breese implied that Oregon was a veritable Garden of Eden that must belong to the United States. McDuffie countered that "a great deal of the country, for purposes of agriculture, was not worth a fig." Haywood contended that certain Democrats were agitating the Oregon issue "for the sake of putting great men down, and exalting little men to high places, more than . . . for the purpose of securing our national rights." Also urging restraint at this time, Donelson counseled Polk to resolve the Oregon question before undertaking more crucial issues such as tariff reform and the acquisition of California. From Paris, King repeatedly advised that a division of the territory at the forty-ninth parallel would be an honorable settlement. "Cass, Allen and Company will find that no political

44. McLane to Buchanan, "Private and Personal, not for the file," July 15, 1846, McLane Papers.
45. Polk to McLane, "Private and Confidential," June 22, 1846, Polk Papers; McLane to Polk, July 17, 1846, McLane Papers.

capital can be made by arraying themselves against an arrangement which makes the forty-ninth parallel the boundary," he argued in March of 1846. Governor Aaron V. Brown of Tennessee similarly encouraged Polk to resolve the dispute by settling for half the territory.[46]

With the Whigs and Southern Democrats virtually unanimous in their support for a compromise, there was little that Polk and the All Oregon faction could do. The Senate repudiated Polk's pretension that the United States possessed a "clear and unquestionable" right to Oregon. Backing the compromise were forty-one senators—all twenty-four Whigs plus seventeen Democrats—while fourteen Democrats opposed it. Of those in opposition, only two were Southerners: James Westcott of Florida and David Atchison of Missouri.[47] Northern Democrats, especially those from the northwestern states, condemned the compromise—Cass of Michigan, Allen of Ohio, Hannegan and Bright of Indiana, and Breese and Semple of Illinois were joined by Cameron and Sturgeon of Pennsylvania, Dickinson of New York, Atherton and Jenness of New Hampshire, and Fairfield of Maine. So, as matters stood in the summer of 1846, the United States had successfully *reannexed* Texas but had failed to *reoccupy* Oregon. In the scramble for territorial spoils, the South had received the "bigger half."

Northwestern Democrats sharply denounced the administration. Even before the treaty's adoption, extremists had warned against any concessions to Britain. Hannegan, for example, lashed out against the moderates in March, proclaiming that if Polk retreated from 54° 40',

46. *CG*, 29 Cong., 1 sess., 608 (April 4, 1846); *CG*, 29 Cong., 1 sess., App. 377 (March 4-5, 1846); Donelson to Polk, February 20, 1846, Polk Papers; King to Buchanan, June 30 and November 28, 1845, and January 27, February 28, March 28, and April 30, 1846, Buchanan Papers; Brown to Polk, June 10, 1846, Polk Papers. Ritchie denied that Haywood spoke for the administration, but Benton maintained that "Haywood spoke with a knowledge of the president's sentiments, and according to his wishes." Benton, like Haywood, believed that Polk would accept a compromise settlement at the forty-ninth parallel. Benton found the administration's course an anomalous one, noting that he was "attacked in the morning [by Ritchie's *Daily Union*] for what the president was hurrying him to do the night before" (Washington *Daily Union*, March 8 and 9, 1846; Benton, *Thirty Years' View*, 2:662-67).

47. Polk had misread Congress. In a spirited exchange in late 1845, Polk had insisted to Buchanan that only one of every ten men in Congress would support a compromise at the forty-ninth parallel. Buchanan disagreed, believing that a majority would endorse such a solution (Polk, *Diary*, 1 [November 29, 1845]:106-8). On the Senate vote, see Benton, *Thirty Years' View*, 2:674-77; *CG*, 29 Cong., 1 sess., 1223-24 (June 18, 1846); Polk, *Diary*, 1 (June 18, 1846):479.

his "irretrievable disgrace" and "abasement" would send "him and his name together to an infamy so profound, a damnation so deep, that the hand of resurrection will never be able to drag him forth." Allen, chairman of the Senate Foreign Relations Committee, advised Cass and the other Democrats on his committee to resign in protest against the treaty. They did not do so, but Allen gave up his chairmanship on June 15 to show his dissatisfaction.[48]

Polk and his advisers feared that Allen would retaliate against the administration. Worried about Allen's anger at Polk, Ritchie approached Allen's friend William Medill during a presidential reception in late August and asked if Allen intended to attack the administration during the fall campaign. Ritchie had heard rumors that Allen had threatened to "take to the stump" across Ohio to condemn Polk's course on Oregon and had said that if there were too few stumps to speak from he would see to it that enough were cut to meet his oratorical needs. Medill reassured Ritchie that these rumors were unfounded. Congressman James Faran of Ohio shared Allen's disdain for the treaty and believed that the Oregon compromise had hurt the Democrats in the fall elections in several northern states, especially New York, Pennsylvania, Maine, and Iowa. "In losing Oregon we lost a rallying point not easily made up," Faran complained to Medill. "The South acted with so much apparent treachery on the Oregon matter, that the mass of the Democrats in the free states have lost all confidence in Southern Democrats." Douglas, though less disparaging of the southern wing of his party, also denounced the treaty.[49]

O'Sullivan expressed a view common among northern Democrats when he stated in July that an "implied contract that the South would stand by the West for Oregon up to 54° 40' " had been breached. Cheated once by the meaningless slavery compromise on Texas, the North had again been betrayed on Oregon. Marcy anticipated a severe reaction against Polk's course. In a letter to his friend Prosper Wetmore he urged him to try to discourage antiadministration rallies

48. On Hannegan, see *CG*, 29 Cong., 1 sess., 460 (March 5, 1846); Benton, *Thirty Years' View*, 2:665; and New York *Morning News*, March 9, 1846. For Allen's protest, see *CG*, 29 Cong., 1 sess., 972 (June 15, 1846); Polk, *Diary*, 1 (June 15, 1846):471–72; New York *Herald*, June 16, 1846; and William Allen to Mrs. William (Effie) Allen, June 28, 1846, William Allen Papers.

49. Medill to Allen "Private," September 1, 1846, Allen Papers; Faran to Medill, November 10, 1846, William Medill Papers; Stephen A. Douglas to John J. Hardin, June 16, 1846, in Robert W. Johannsen, ed., *The Letters of Stephen A. Douglas* (Urbana, 1961), p. 139.

in New York. Polk had done all he could, he wrote, and any protest would be "wrong and unjust towards the president." Not all northern Democrats proved so magnanimous.[50]

Though Polk partly mollified the All Oregon men with another nationalistic crusade—the war against Mexico and the conquest of the borderlands—his handling of the Oregon question alienated many northern Democrats and made them more suspicious of their southern counterparts. Like so many other developments after the Baltimore convention, the Oregon settlement seemed a manifestation of a strong prosouthern orientation in the Jacksonian party. The disaffection is difficult to quantify because it seldom surfaced in congressional voting. In subtle but significant ways, however, factions of Democrats were beginning to evaluate issues in terms of North against South, as well as Democrats against Whigs.

Whigs recognized the predicament that Oregon presented to the Democrats. A Whig reporter, for example, claimed that Polk had dissembled in his call for the acquisition of all of Oregon: the administration favored the South and had no real desire to add free territory to the Union. Whigs such as Joshua Giddings, the reporter noted, recognized that Polk could not escape his uncompromising rhetoric on Oregon, so they had "seized an opportunity, in the early part of the debate, to tear the lion skin from the ass, and to place him before the country in his true character." Jacob Miller observed the vacillation and confusion on Oregon among the Democrats, noting that at one time 54° 40' seemed to be their goal and at others the forty-ninth parallel. The border preferred by the Democrats, he told the Senate, "seemed to fall and rise according to the temperature of gentlemen who advocated it. Like the mercury in the thermometer, it varied according to who had his thumb upon the bulb."[51]

50. New York *Morning News,* July 3, 1846; Marcy to Wetmore, June 14, 1846, Marcy Papers. In February, Orlando Ficklin had noted, " 'Texas and Oregon' were cradled together in the Baltimore Convention, were inscribed on our banners, and were flung to the breeze in every portion of the Union." Hannegan and Wentworth also paired Texas and Oregon. See *CG,* 29 Cong., 1 sess., App. 171 (February 6, 1846); *CG,* 29 Cong., 1 sess., 110 (December 30, 1845); *CG,* 29 Cong., 1 sess., 206 (January 14, 1846). In commenting on the Twenty-Ninth Congress, Joel Silbey contends that "Western bitterness was not justified; the South and the West had not been operating together." That is true in terms of domestic policy, but it is misleading when applied to the Texas-Oregon question (see Silbey, *Shrine of Party,* p. 141).

51. Ashtabula *Sentinel,* February 13, 1846; Joshua R. Giddings, *History of the Rebellion: Its Authors and Causes* (New York, 1864), pp. 249–50; George W. Julian, *The Life of Joshua Giddings* (Chicago, 1892), pp. 185–89; *CG,* 29 Cong., 1 sess., App. 568 (March 26, 1846).

The disparity between the administration's assertions and its actions proved useful grist for the partisan mill. Certain that Polk desired a compromise, regardless of his posturing on Oregon, Whig Congressman Milton Brown emphasized the irony in the Whigs' "sustain[ing] *what the president has done;* the Democracy *what he has said."* When Polk *"abandoned* the extravagant pretensions of the Baltimore Convention and his own inaugural . . . we said he did right; and we still say so," Brown declared.[52] How anomalous this situation was—the Whigs welcoming Polk's final decision on Oregon, and a significant bloc of Democrats condemning it. Shortly after the Oregon settlement, dissident Senate Democrats acted to frustrate Polk's effort to have his faithful supporter Sevier succeed Allen as chairman of the Foreign Relations Committee. Bewildered and angered by the snub, Polk excused himself of all blame for the dissension. "They can find no just cause of complaint against me," he insisted.[53]

Polk's immediate political prospects in mid-1846 might have been worse had he not goaded Mexico into war at the very time when the Oregon crisis was coming to a climax. With American troops engaged in battle in the Rio Grande Valley, Democrats rallied behind the flag and the administration. Polk expected to chastise Mexico and acquire California within a few months, but the war lasted far longer than he had anticipated. Though California and New Mexico were eventually obtained, the war brought little advantage to the Democratic party. Contrary to the administration's expectations, the war complicated problems within the party and fragmented it more than any previous event or issue.

While Calhoun challenged the military strategy of the administration, several northern Democrats, as noted earlier, demanded that slavery be excluded from any acquired territory. Democrats such as Cass, Dickinson, and Douglas joined the administration in condemning the Free-Soil movement, but other Democrats insisted that the moment had come to redress the North's accumulated grievances. Already fragmented when Congress declared war in May, the party split into several irreconcilable factions during the next two years.

Even before the outbreak of the war, Calhoun had learned that the administration had directed Taylor and his troops to occupy the

52. *CG,* 29 Cong., 1 sess., App. 695 (April 15, 1846).
53. *Diary,* 1 (June 24, 1846):487. Only ten days earlier, the Senate had rejected Polk's nomination of Henry Horn to be collector of the port of Philadelphia. Referring to the several Democrats who had voted against the appointment, Polk fumed, "Their course is that of spoiled children" (*Diary,* 1 [June 14, 1846]:485–87).

contested region between the Nueces and Rio Grande rivers. Distressed by this provocative maneuver, Calhoun had privately urged
a few Whig senators to inquire into Polk's conduct in order to arrest
his course before it led to hostilities. No one heeded his suggestion.[54]

Mexico's attack on Taylor's forces confirmed Calhoun's premoni-
tion, and on May 11 Polk presented Congress with a de facto state
of war. The House responded by passing a war appropriation bill
within hours of receiving Polk's urgent message. The Senate debated
for two days before approving a declaration stating that Mexico was
solely responsible for the war. Calhoun objected. "Never was so
momentous a measure adopted, with so much precipitancy; so little
thought; or forced through by such objectionable means," he wrote
to his son.[55] As the months passed, Calhoun refused to accept Polk's
view that the United States was totally blameless for the war. Calhoun
knew better.

Calhoun saw no reason to send Americans to fight and die in
Mexico. Amenable to the acquisition of California and New Mexico
but fearful of a long and divisive war, Calhoun in early 1847 urged
the administration to withdraw American forces to a cordon along
the Rio Grande and the thirty-second parallel. Senator Andrew Butler
agreed with his fellow South Carolinian's reservations about the invasion of Mexico. "We are certainly in a difficult position," he admitted
to his colleagues. "If we quit the war, it will be apparently with
dishonor. If we go on it must end in mischief. The truth is, we are
like the shepherd who has got the wolf by the ears! It is hazardous
to let go—it is worse to hold on."[56]

Because of the Democrats' fragile majority in the Senate and the
need to keep Calhoun's faction in the fold, the administration hesitated to antagonize Calhoun. Though opposed to his recommendation for withdrawal, Ritchie initially treated Calhoun's ideas with
respect, probably because James Barbour had warned him that "a
rupture" between Calhoun and the administration would harm the
party and the nation and "do no one good." Ritchie wrote in early
1847 that Calhoun's suggested indemnity line was "certainly recommended by strong considerations," but he rejected the idea of with-

54. Calhoun to Andrew P. Calhoun, May 14, 1846; Calhoun to James Edward
Calhoun, May 29, 1846, in Jameson, "Correspondence of Calhoun," 2:690, 693.

55. Calhoun to Andrew P. Calhoun, May 14, 1846, in Jameson, "Correspondence
of Calhoun," 2:690.

56. *CG*, 29 Cong., 2 sess., App. 323-27 (February 9, 1847); *CG*, 29 Cong., 2 sess.,
450 (February 18, 1847).

drawing American forces to the Rio Grande, arguing that such a retreat would only lead to an interminable border war with Mexico. Nothing but a decisive military victory, Ritchie claimed, would secure a lasting peace.[57]

Ritchie reacted more vindictively when Calhoun objected to the administration's call for ten additional regiments to prosecute the war. After Ritchie harshly scolded the Senate in early 1847 for delay-ing the bill, Calhoun and his followers voted with the Whigs to expel Ritchie from his privileged press seat in the chamber. Ritchie blamed Calhoun for his humiliating expulsion. "We were afraid to see him in the Senate," Ritchie confessed after the rebuke. "His fiery and restless spirit seeks its gratification in the possession of power. He must rule in our public councils. He must sweep on to the great object of his political life."[58] Calhoun had now crossed the administration three times: he had stymied its All Oregon crusade; he had criticized its military strategy in Mexico; and now he had helped disgrace its editor.

Polk agreed that political ambition drove Calhoun. During the Oregon debate Polk complained that many senators, especially Cal-houn, were not chiefly concerned with the question of 49° or 54° 40' but rather were preoccupied with the question of '48—that is, the next presidential election.[59] Calhoun had "embarrassed the adminis-tration" on Oregon by "playing a game to make himself president, and his motives of action are wholly selfish," Polk charged. Labeling Calhoun "the most mischievous man in the Senate," Polk attributed Calhoun's opposition to his having been denied a cabinet appoint-ment in early 1845. There is no evidence to confirm that suspicion, however, for Calhoun had generally approved of the administration's program up to mid-1846.[60]

57. Barbour to Ritchie, June 13, 1846, Thomas Ritchie Papers; Washington *Daily Union,* February 10, 1847.

58. Washington *Daily Union,* February 13, 15, 16, and 18, 1847; New York *Herald,* February 18, 1847.

59. Polk to William Polk, "Private," March 27, 1846; Polk to Louis McLane, "Private and confidential," April 29, 1846; Polk to William Polk, April 29, 1846; Polk to Brown, "Private," July 7, 1846, Polk Papers; Polk, *Diary,* 1 (December 24, 1845):141–42; (March 4, 1846):265; (March 8, 1846):280; (April 21, 1846):344; (April 22, 1846):345; (May 25, 1846):426–27.

60. Polk, *Diary,* 1 (April 21, 1846):344; 2 (February 8, 1847):371; Calhoun to Thomas G. Clemson, July 11, 1846, in Jameson, "Correspondence of Calhoun," 2:701. Cal-houn concluded: "With the exception of the Mexican War, the course of events thus far this session has been more in conformity to my views, than what they have been for many years."

By early 1847, Polk was complaining in his diary that his party was "in truth in a minority in each House" because of "the disappoint-ments about office among the members, and the premature contest which they are waging in favor of their favorites for the presidency in 1848."[61] With Calhoun growing more outspoken in his criticism, Ritchie stepped up his attacks on the rebellious Democrats.[62] The administration's claim that the dissident Democrats in Congress were simply making political capital out of their opposition was not very convincing, though, since Polk repeatedly stressed that the people overwhelmingly supported his Oregon policy and his conduct of the war. If the public so clearly supported the administration's measures, as Polk and Ritchie maintained, it was not apparent, then, how Cal-houn and others could gain politically by opposing those popular policies.

There were legitimate reasons for Calhoun to be concerned about the consequences of the administration's foreign policy, and, as some of his friends realized, he could not win favor by opposing the war. Troubled by Calhoun's inexpedient course, Senator Dixon H. Lewis of Alabama told a mutual friend in 1848, "He reminds me of a great general—who wins great battles and then throws his life away in a street fracas." His "self-sacrificing course, particularly on the Mexican War," had diminished his stature and his popularity.[63] Denunciation of a war provided no ladder to the presidency, as Calhoun undoubt-edly knew. An ardent nationalist and war hawk in 1812, Calhoun had witnessed the political demise of the antiwar Federalists. There was no reason to expect that those who condemned "Mr. Polk's War" would fare any better than those who had condemned "Mr. Madi-son's War." Moreover, Calhoun recognized that his own principles were at odds with those of most Americans. "Our people have under-gone a great change," he observed in late 1847. "Their inclination is for conquest and empire, regardless of their institutions and liberty; or rather, they think they hold their liberty by a divine tenure, which

61. *Diary*, 2 (January 22, 1847):347. As early as April 1846, Polk observed to Louis McLane, "With a nominal majority of eight (including the Texas senators) in the Senate—I cannot with any certainty calculate on carrying any measure in that body" (Polk to McLane, "Private and confidential," April 29, 1846, Polk Papers).

62. Polk *Diary*, 2 (April 6, 1847):459; Washington *Daily Union*, March 1, 15, 16, and 27, 1847.

63. Lewis to R. K. Crallé, May 11, 1848, in Frederick W. Moore, ed., "Calhoun as Seen by His Political Friends: Letters of Duff Green, Dixon H. Lewis, and Richard K. Crallé during the Period from 1831 to 1848," *Publications of the Southern History Association*, vol. 7, nos. 3–6 (Washington, D.C., 1903):425.

no imprudence, or folly on their part, can defeat."[64] These were not the views of a man who expected his party's next presidential nomination.

Calhoun turned the tables on Polk and assigned him chief responsibility for the Democrats' woes. In late 1846, Calhoun suggested that Polk's mistakes on Oregon, his policy toward Mexico, and his executive appointments had "distracted and divided and disheartened and alienated the party to an extent unknown heretofore." Six months later he remarked that Polk had "sought by the Mexican War to perpetuate the power of the party" but instead he would find it "the means of his and their overthrow."[65] Just as Calhoun believed the United States might have eventually obtained all of Oregon without effort, so too he thought that California might have been acquired without a divisive war of conquest.[66] When the war ended in early 1848, Calhoun expressed relief, but he maintained that the terms of the treaty were "not such as to confer any eclat on the war, or the administration."[67]

A Paralysis in Policy: Political Divisions and Sectional Strains

Polk's conduct of the war and his reaction to the slavery extension controversy especially alienated the New York Barnburners and other Democrats who supported Free Soil principles. When the Oregon territory was partitioned with England, many Northerners interpreted the settlement as proof that the administration was more

64. Calhoun to Mrs. Anna Clemson, December 26, 1847, in Jameson, "Correspondence of Calhoun," 2:742.
65. Calhoun to Lewis S. Coryell, November 7, 1846; Calhoun to Thomas G. Clemson, May 6, 1847, in Jameson, "Correspondence of Calhoun," 2:709–10, 728.
66. Though Benton and Calhoun despised each other and disagreed on many issues, they agreed that the United States could have obtained California without war. See Benton, *Thirty Years' View,* 2:710. Benton thought that "with the claims [of Americans against Mexico] assumed, the amount paid for the territories, and the expenses of the war, the acquisitions were made at a dear rate." He called the war with Mexico "the great blot" upon the Polk administration (pp. 710, 738). On the day Polk submitted his war message to Congress, he conversed with Benton about the skirmish on the Rio Grande and Benton said that "he was willing to vote men and money for defence of our territory, but was not prepared to make aggressive war on Mexico. He disapproved [of] the marching of the army from Corpus Christi to the left bank of the Del Norte, but . . . never said so to the public" (Polk, *Diary,* 1 [May 11, 1846]:390).
67. Calhoun to Thomas G. Clemson, March 7, 1848, in Jameson, "Correspondence of Calhoun," 2:746.

eager to obtain slave territory than free territory. These suspicions increased when American forces crossed the Rio Grande and occu-pied Mexico's northern provinces in mid-1846. The likelihood of slavery's extension westward and the additional political power it would bring the South concerned several northern Democrats, among them Senator Dix of New York. His anxiety about expansionism surfaced during a critical conversation he had with Polk on July 10.

Polk told Dix that he would nominate him to be McLane's succes-sor in London if he desired the post.[68] Dix later declined, but pressed for clarification of a rumor circulating in Washington and reported by the New York *Herald,* that Colonel J. D. Stevenson, a political crony of Marcy's, was recruiting and training a regiment of volunteer emigrants to fight in California and take possession of it for the United States. The volunteers, it was said, would receive federal land grants to encourage their permanent settlement in California when their service ended.[69] Bennett applauded this scheme, but Dix and others, increasingly sensitive about the expansion of slavery, disap-proved of it. Aware that the acquisition of territory west of Texas would involve the question of slavery, Dix sought reassurance that the rumors about the Stevenson regiment were unfounded. Polk disavowed any intention of conquest, a relief to Dix, who immediate-ly reported the disclaimer to his friend Silas Wright, governor of New York:

> The president desired me to say to you . . . that he had no schemes of conquest in view in respect to Mexico, no intention to take posses-sion of any portion of her territory with a view to hold it, and that his only object was to push military operations so vigorously that she should be made willing to adjust the matters in dispute between her and us on fair terms. As to the regiment designed for California, the intention was to have it discharged there, and it was, therefore, deemed wise to have it composed of persons who would be willing to remain and become citizens of our own territory on the Pacific—i.e. Oregon.[70]

68. Polk, *Diary,* 2 (July 10, 1846):19.

69. On the Stevenson regiment, see Polk, *Diary,* 1 (June 16, 1846):473; 2 (July 6, 1846):13–14; (August 15, 1846):83–84; (August 29, 1846):103–4; (September 5, 1846):117; (September 20, 1846):146–47; (November 2, 1846):214–15; Buchanan to Polk, Sep-tember 10, 1846, Polk Papers; Marcy to Wetmore, September 6, 1846; Marcy to Wetmore, "Private," September 14, 1846; Stevenson to Polk, May 17 and 18, 1847; Marcy to Wetmore, September 24, 1847, Marcy Papers; New York *Herald,* June 28, 1846, September 6, 17, 23, and 26, 1846; New York *Morning News,* June 29, 1846. Ritchie and the *Daily Union* did not comment upon the rumors about the administra-tion's territorial designs.

70. Dix to Wright, July 10, 1846, in *Memoirs of John Adams Dix,* Morgan Dix, ed., pp. 202–3.

Unless Dix misconstrued or totally misunderstood what was said, Polk's explanation was a blatant lie. As early as May 30, six weeks before his conference with Dix, Polk had announced to his cabinet that he intended "to acquire . . . California, New Mexico, and perhaps some others of the Northern Provinces of Mexico whenever a peace was made." Again on June 30, Polk's cabinet had discussed the issue of territorial indemnity in detail: at that meeting Polk and Walker had argued that Mexico should be compelled to cede all its land north of the twenty-sixth parallel to the United States. Buchanan opposed such a vast cession, arguing that only California and New Mexico should be acquired. After an "animated" exchange between Walker and Buchanan, Polk terminated the meeting by concluding that the United States must at the very least "obtain Upper California and New Mexico in any treaty of peace we would make." And just three days before conferring with Dix, Polk reiterated his desire for California and New Mexico, but added that he also wished to acquire most of Coahuila, Chihuahua, and Sonora.[71]

Polk intentionally misled Congress about his imperial ambitions. Proceeding with a strategy of secrecy and deception, he decided in early July to ignore the Senate's request for information on the Stevenson expedition. Determined to acquire the borderlands, Polk did not want a European power or his own Congress to impede him.[72]

---

71. Polk, *Diary*, 1 (May 30, 1846):438; (June 30, 1846):495–97; 2 (July 7, 1846):15–16.

72. Polk, *Diary*, 2 (July 6, 1846):13–14. Polk argued that the release of any correspondence concerning the regiment "would be proclaiming to Mexico and the world our plans of conducting the war, and particularly in regard to California." See also Polk to William Polk, "Private," October 2, 1846, Polk Papers. Polk also worried about congressional opposition. As early as May 12, Giddings had proclaimed that the army had been ordered to the Rio Grande "for the purpose and with the full intention of bringing on a war with Mexico without consulting Congress." The administration planned to seize California and New Mexico, Giddings warned (*CG*, 29 Cong., 1 sess., App. 642–43 [May 12, 1846]). Since Democrats had insisted in May that territory was not the object of the war, Polk could not admit that a huge territorial indemnity had been part of his plan since the very beginning. Such a plan, however, had its perils. Van Buren cautioned in early 1845 that Northerners would perceive a war against Mexico as a plot to extend slavery: "Too much care cannot be taken to save us from a war, in respect to which the opposition shall be able to charge with plausibility if not truth, that it is waged for the extension of slavery." Such a war would drive northern Democrats "to the sad alternative of turning their backs upon their [southern] friends, or of encountering political suicide with their eyes open" (Van Buren to Bancroft, February 15, 1845, in Ford, "Van-Buren–Bancroft Correspondence," p. 439).

United States troops occupied the borderlands in 1846, but simultaneously another war commenced in which Polk could not function
as commander-in-chief—this one on the floors of Congress over the
Wilmot Proviso. The next session of Congress accomplished virtually
nothing because of the daily wrangling over aggrandizement and
slavery. Dismayed by the factionalism, King complained that "the
conduct of a large portion of the Democratic Party in this Congress
would disgrace the tenants of a lunatic asylum."[73]

The Senate had saved Polk from an impasse on Oregon in 1846.
Now, in early 1848, Nicholas Trist, whose authorization to negotiate
a treaty had been revoked by the administration, delivered a peace
proposal ending the war with Mexico. The treaty's auspicious appearance lessened the tension provoked by the proviso and extricated
Polk from another crisis.[74] But Polk's serious difficulties with Congress
did not end with the close of the war.

The entire trans-Mississippi West now belonged to the United
States, but how Congress would proceed on the territorial question
remained to be seen. During the first half of 1848, Congress failed to
provide territorial governments for Oregon or the borderlands. To
make matters worse, Indians attacked whites in Oregon during a
spring uprising, prompting Ritchie to castigate Congress for leaving
Oregon's inhabitants at the mercy of hostile Indians. "No arms have
been sent them," he complained, "and they had scarcely powder
sufficient to fire a national salute on the last anniversary of Washington's birth."[75] In August, Congress finally approved a territorial bill
for Oregon, but it contained a slavery exclusion amendment, an
indication of the growing influence of Free-Soil sentiment in the
North. Polk signed the bill, but only because all of Oregon lay north
of 36° 30'. He warned Congress that he would veto any territorial bill
for California and New Mexico that included an absolute prohibition
of slavery.[76]

73. King to Buchanan, February 10, 1847, Buchanan Papers.

74. Polk sharply condemned Trist for continuing his negotiations after his recall.
Trist, Polk complained, was "destitute of honor or principle, and . . . a very base
man" who had "proved himself to be an impudent and unqualified scoundrel" (Diary,
3 [January 15, 1848]:301, 3 [February 24, 1848]:358). Polk feared that the Senate
would reject the treaty because Trist's authorization had been withdrawn and because both the "no territory" and the All Mexico extremists would oppose it (ibid.
[February 28, 1848]:363–66).

75. Washington Daily Union, June 2, 1848.

76. Polk's message on the Oregon bill, in James D. Richardson, ed., A Compilation
of the Messages and Papers of the Presidents, 10 vols. (New York, 1897), 5 (August 14,
1848):2458–59; Washington Daily Union, August 15, 1848. Polk explained to Calhoun
his reasons for signing the bill: "The first reason would be the urgent necessity for

Congress had not yet passed territorial bills for the borderlands when Polk retired in early 1849. Despite the Gold Rush, which brought a mass of new pioneers to California in 1848 and 1849, Congress could not resolve the territorial crisis. When Cass and the Democrats met defeat at the hands of Taylor and the Whigs in the 1848 election, Polk was alarmed. "California may be lost to the Union," he fretted to Bancroft in early 1849. Because of "the recently discovered mineral wealth" and the province's "vast commercial advantages," immigration there would be "rapid beyond any former example," he predicted. With such bright commercial prospects, California might opt for independence, and the incoming Whig administration might permit, even encourage, the separation of California from the United States in order to evade the slavery issue. Polk could do little but worry.[77]

The administration's inability to control the party became apparent gradually, almost imperceptibly, but the dispute over Yucatán in the spring of 1848 demonstrated the shift in Democratic politics. In late April, Polk had informed Congress that he favored armed intervention in Yucatán's civil war, "if we had troops to spare for this purpose," in order to prevent its becoming "a colony of any European power" and "to defend the white inhabitants against the incursions of the Indians."[78] After Polk suggested that American forces be dispatched to occupy the Mexican province, a small but outspoken faction of Democrats began to urge the acquisition of the troubled peninsula. Cass deemed Yucatán "a case of crying necessity" and described the conflict as "precisely one of those wars in which a nation ought to engage on the side of humanity." Hannegan warned that Yucatán was vital to American interests because Britain held possession "of various points along the gulf coast of the Isthmus. . . .

a Government in Oregon, and the second that the whole territory of Oregon lay north of the Missouri Compromise line." Calhoun strenuously opposed any slavery exclusion amendment, fearing that it would serve as precedent for later bills dealing with the borderlands (Polk, *Diary,* 4 [August 13, 1848]:72–74).

77. Polk to Bancroft, January 5, 1849, Polk Papers. See also Polk to Cass, "Private," December 15, 1848, and Polk to Brown, "Private," January 9, 1849, Polk Papers. Whig senator John H. Clarke of Rhode Island suggested to Polk that eastern merchants "would derive as much advantage" from California, whether it were independent or incorporated into the Union (Polk, *Diary,* 4 [January 18, 1849]:293–4).

78. Richardson, *Messages and Papers,* 5 (April 29, 1848):2432; Washington *Daily Union,* April 30, 1848. See also Polk, *Diary,* 3 (March 7, 1848):373–75; (April 25, 1848):433–34; (May 6, 1848):444–45. Polk said that Walker favored Yucatán's "ultimate annexation to the United States"—a prospect that Polk also favored, "rather than see it fall into the hands of England" (ibid.).

Cuba has been called the key of the Gulf," he noted. "Yucatán and Cuba combined are the lock and key." He urged intervention and eventual annexation. Senator Henry Foote of Mississippi also sup-ported the acquisition of Yucatán and advised his colleagues to take control of Cuba as well: "We will have complete control of the Gulf of Mexico, and of all the commerce that floats over its surface; we will have it in our power to establish at once a direct communication between the Pacific and Atlantic oceans; we will be able to secure to ourselves the rich monopoly of the East India trade; we will be safe in every direction from foreign assailment." Both compassion and calculation, then, necessitated American intervention.[79]

But the Senate had grown wary of Polk. Democrat John Niles of Connecticut cautioned, "There certainly should be some deliberation before we interfere with a civil war in any other country." Calhoun told the Senate to oppose any meddling in Yucatán and drew an explicit parallel to Polk's earlier manipulation of Congress in 1846: "I did hope that the experience of the Mexican War—that precipitate and rash measure which has cost the country so dearly in blood and treasure—would have taught the administration moderation and cau-tion, and induced them to shun any course of policy calculated to plunge the country in[to] a similar cost and sacrifice." The administra-tion apparently had not learned the lessons Calhoun wished, but Congress had. With so many vital questions at home demanding resolution, Polk could not obtain cooperation for intervention in Yucatán.[80]

Polk could no longer call the tune. His policies had estranged many people, his personality many others. A dogmatic, ill-humored man, he was not well liked even by those who shared his rigid Jacksonian principles. Ingersoll complained in mid-1847 that Polk would "not take advice" and added, "It is amazing how many of those who shout his support whisper their dislike of him." Polk dreaded social gather-ings, and in one of his first acts as president banished dancing from the White House. He maintained a strained cordiality during his ceremonial duties, but people were a distant second to politics in his affections. In early 1846, Senator Fairfield admitted to his wife, "To-

79. *CG,* 30 Cong., 1 sess., App. 591 (May 4, 1848); App. 596–97 (May 5, 1848), and App. 602 (May 5, 1848).
80. *CG,* 30 Cong., 1 sess., App. 596 (May 4, 1848) and App. 590 (April 29, 1848). Calhoun privately referred to Polk's request for intervention in Yucatán as "one of the wildest and most absurd measures ever proposed by the Executive" (Calhoun to James E. Calhoun, May 22, 1848, in Jameson, "Correspondence of Calhoun," 2:756).

night the president has his first levee. I had rather be whipped than go, but circumstances render it unavoidable. There will be no dancing and no refreshment of any kind." Polk's sense of virtue blinded him to the importance of cakes and ale in antebellum politics. His charac-ter discouraged conviviality and friendship, impairing his effective-ness as a party leader.[81]

Polk's demeanor was better suited to a pulpit than a smoke-filled room.[82] However laudable his private character and however sincere his professions of nationalistic pride, exhortation alone could not alleviate the perils facing the country or restore the prewar harmony of the Democrats. By late 1846 and early 1847, many Northerners had found the notion that a proslavery conspiracy was in command of the government more plausible, and many Southerners were becom-ing convinced of a growing abolitionist conspiracy determined to emancipate the slaves whatever the costs. It was not the absence of sharp differences but the increasingly symbolic nature of disagree-ments that undermined the stability of the second American party system.[83] Resolving substantive disputes was one thing; coping with delusions quite another.

New York Democrat Graham Worth responded to the crisis with grim humor. In late 1848, he advised his friend Marcy to begin farming a patch of swampy land near Albany. There he could culti-vate rice and hemp—rice to make up for shortages when South Carolina rebelled against the Union, and hemp for rope the govern-ment would need to hang southern traitors. Though a loyal Demo-

81. Ingersoll to Buchanan, June 11, 1847, Buchanan Papers; John Fairfield to Mrs. Anna Fairfield, January 21, 1846, in Staples, *Letters of Fairfield*, p. 380. Dallas com-plained that Polk "has the faculty of making mountains out of mole-hills" (George Dallas to Mrs. Soph Dallas, November 27, 1845, in Nichols, "Dallas Papers," p. 363).

82. Sarah Mytton Maury described Polk as "habitually grave and thoughtful," a man who smiled but "never . . . indulge[d] in laughter" (*The Statesmen of America in 1846* [London, 1847], p. 5). A revealing episode was Polk's reaction to a juggler and magician who performed at the White House. "Mr. Alexander exhibited his art greatly to their wonder and amusement," Polk noted, "but . . . not much to their edification or profit." He described the entertainment as "innocent in itself," though it took "time unprofitably spent" (*Diary*, 1 [February 6, 1846]:213). Naval explorer Charles Wilkes observed of Polk, "Out of politics he had little to converse about and he never appeared to advantage in his intercourse with those who had . . . inclination for other matters, and his social habits were confined to a very small circle"; he lacked "the tact and manners to please" (*Autobiography of Rear Admiral Charles Wilkes, U.S. Navy, 1798–1877*, William James Morgan et al., eds. (Washington, D.C., 1978), p. 591.

83. For a different interpretation, see Michael F. Holt, *The Political Crisis of the 1850s* (New York, 1978).

crat, Worth did not regret Cass's defeat in the presidential contest of
1848. Cass was "always ultra," Worth complained, "always ready to
adopt the wildest popular doctrines and projects of the day—ready
for war with England on any occasion, and for any object—one of
your 54° 40' men—the whole or nothing," willing to "annex Canada,
Cuba, the whole of Mexico and Kamtschatka besides."[84] Cass commanded little respect in Washington. Reporter Oliver Dyer described
him as "a dull, phlegmatic, lymphatic, lazy man," and Free-Soiler
George Julian believed that Cass had secured the Democratic nomination in 1848 "by multiplied acts of the most obsequious and crouch-
ing servility to his southern overseers."[85]

Polk could not stem the rising tide of antisouthern sentiment in the
free states. Polk, a *Herald* correspondent argued in 1848, had "never
done anything" for the North: "The subjects in which a majority of
the people were most interested, [such as] . . . river and harbor improvements, a protective tariff, and all of Oregon, as an offset to an
increase of slavery territory, he sacrificed for the South."[86] Though
exaggerated, the charge was not without substance. Even if the complaint had been entirely unwarranted, a growing number of Northerners were becoming disposed to believe it anyway.

The mounting sectional animosity surfaced during an exchange in
the Senate between Hale of New Hampshire and Foote of Mississippi
in April 1848. Harsh words had often marked encounters between
members of the two major parties, but both Hale and Foote were
Democrats. Foote warned Hale that if he ever preached abolitionism
in Mississippi the way he did in the Senate, he would find himself

84. Worth to Marcy, November 23 and November 12, 1848, Marcy Papers. Marcy
did not have to be reminded of the political crisis. In early 1848 he wrote, "We are
approaching the end of our money means—our forces can at best be kept where they
are as to numerical strength—and Congress are at a standstill, and, if perchance they
should move, will probably go in the wrong direction." Marcy later admitted that
it was "more difficult and perplexing to get an army out of the field than into it"
(Marcy to Wetmore, January 28 and August 20, 1848, Marcy Papers).

85. Oliver Dyer, *Great Senators of the United States Forty Years Ago* (New York, 1889),
p. 45; Julian, *Political Recollections*, p. 51. Even more heavy-handed than Dyer and
Julian was James Russell Lowell, who in "The Biglow Papers" had Calhoun address-
ing Cass: "Gen'nle Cass, Sir, you need n't be twitchin' your collar,/Your merit's quite
clear by the dut on your knees,/At the North we don't make no distinctions o'
color;/You can all take a lick at our shoes wen you please." See *The Complete Poetical
Works of James Russell Lowell*, Cambridge ed. (Boston, 1896), p. 199. A campaign
broadside ridiculed Cass as "another goose, a downright Michi-GANDER" and a
"northern dough-faced booby" (E. M. P. Rose, *The Poetry of Locofocoism* [Wellsburgh,
Va., 1848], pp. 22, 32).

86. New York *Herald*, April 27, 1848.

suspended from a tall tree—Foote himself offering to serve as hang-man. Hale retorted that if Foote visited New Hampshire he would be treated kindly and provided with a forum in which to present his proslavery doctrines; he would be given just enough rope to hang himself.[87] Disputes over slavery's expansion and the territorial ques-tion were paralyzing American politics, the selection of a House Speaker in late 1848 dramatizing the deadlock. Three weeks and sixty-two ballots after convening, the House finally chose Democrat Howell Cobb of Georgia for the post. But the stormy second session of the Thirtieth Congress accomplished even less than its predecessor. Bennett called the session "one of the most unprofitable that has ever been held."[88]

Polk, discouraged and emaciated, returned to Tennessee in early 1849 to a short retirement and a premature death.[89] His own failing health and deterioration during the last half of his term coincided with the decline of aggressive aggrandizement as one of the most persistent and powerful strains in Jacksonian policy. Polk had arrived in Washington during the final phase of the debate on Texas, and he had enlarged the United States by unprecedented proportions. Nei-ther the Treaty of Paris in 1783, Jefferson's purchase of Louisiana in 1803, Monroe's acquisition of East Florida in 1819, or Jackson's and Van Buren's acquisitions of Indian lands could compare with Polk's territorial achievements.

But neither had the previous acquisitions raised such a furor among the American people and their representatives. By the late 1840s, the

87. *CG*, 30 Cong., 1 sess., App. 502-3 (April 20, 1848); Henry S. Foote, *Casket of Reminiscences* (Washington, 1874), pp. 74-76; Dyer, *Great Senators*, pp. 127-28. On Hale, see Richard H. Sewell, *John P. Hale and the Politics of Abolition* (Cambridge, Mass., 1965).

88. For a summary of the contest for the speakership, see Julian, *Political Recollec-tions*, pp. 74-78. Julian had just entered the House as a Free-Soil congressman from Indiana. Bennett's dismay with Congress is expressed in the New York *Herald*, March 3, 1849. At this time Calhoun wrote to Donelson, "I fear the slavery question has gone so far, that it will be very difficult if not impossible to adjust it" (Calhoun to Donelson, March 23, 1849, Donelson Papers).

89. Ritchie noted that Polk, during his final night in office, summoned him three times for advice. Polk feared that Congress would pass a slavery exclusion bill for California and New Mexico, and he also worried that a general appropriation bill essential to the continued operation of the government would not be brought up and approved. "He was almost distracted by his anxiety," Ritchie recalled. Polk, Buchan-an wrote to Donelson, "was the most laborious [hard-working] man I have ever known, and in the brief period of four years had assumed the appearance of an old man" (Thomas Ritchie to George Ritchie, March 12, 1849, Ritchie Papers; Buchanan to Donelson, June 29, 1849, Donelson Papers).

Jeffersonian notion of measuring the progress of the country in terms of territorial extension was becoming obsolete. Every American step into the wilderness no longer symbolized advancement, for Americans now contested whether that step should be taken by a white laborer, a slaveholder, a chattel, or a free black. Slaveholders often viewed advancement and security in terms of the expansion of slavery; a growing number of Free-Soilers, on the other hand, envisioned progress in terms of confining slavery to its existing limits. As the two irreconcilable camps attracted recruits who had earlier been satisfied to acquire land regardless of its ultimate use, the obstacles to further expansion increased substantially.[90]

Ironically, the imperial thrust of the Jacksonian persuasion was blunted at the very moment it reached its culmination with the expansion to the Pacific in 1846. The dissension over the Oregon question and the Mexican War, further complicated by disagreements over the tariff and internal improvements legislation, prompted a rising number of northern Democrats to support restrictions on expansion that had not been so strenuously advanced before. Many southern Democrats (and some southern Whigs), on the other hand, opposed all federal restrictions on slavery in the territories. Many Whigs saw no escape from the impasse other than to prohibit all further territorial acquisitions. The controversy involved far more than the relative rights and wrongs of slavery: the two parties and the sections were contesting the future development of three-fifths of the entire American empire. The magnitude of that process, the impact it would eventually have on the eastern states, and its ultimate significance for the entire nation were questions that the Democrats could not address with outmoded Jeffersonian and Jacksonian nostrums.

The expansionists became victims of their own propaganda. Expansionism, touted as the panacea for several perils threatening the nation, actually created as many problems as it solved. The annexation of Texas did not siphon off large numbers of southern slaves, nor did it alleviate the North's racial difficulties—one of the worst disappointments for the extreme Negrophobes across the nation. The Asian market never met the Democrats' high expectations. The acquisition of the continental empire failed to prevent rapid industrializa-

90. Benton had predicted that moderates would be forced into the extremist camps. "Truly the abolitionists and the nullifiers were necessary to each other—the two halves of a pair of shears, neither of which could cut until joined together," Benton concluded (*Thirty Years' View*, 2:695).

tion and urbanization in the East. After the Civil War, congestion increased in northern cities as a distinct working class crowded into the rapidly growing number of shops and factories, and hardship and economic dislocations became a recurring reality of both city and country life during the closing decades of the century. The expansion-ists did not attain a homogeneous nation, either: blacks remained in the United States after emancipation, Native Americans survived, and immigration from central and southern Europe further diversified the population. Most incongruous for the Democrats themselves, expan-sionism helped splinter their party. In a sense the party molded by Jackson and Van Buren perished alongside American soldiers who died in battle in Mexico.[91] It was fortunate for the Democrats that disagreements over expansion and slavery divided the Whigs as well. Events seemed to have their own momentum, and there was no returning to the more tranquil past.

Not just the policies themselves but also the pace at which they were pursued divided the Democrats. The annexation of Texas could have been delayed until Mexico assented and the boundary dispute was resolved. Had Polk appointed a Senate commission to negotiate differences between the United States and Mexico, Congress might well have proved more cooperative on other issues as well. The administration should have kept Oregon in the realm of private diplomacy rather than embroiling the dispute in domestic politics, since Polk's gasconading worked against the long-term interests of his administration and his party. On domestic issues, the administration might have worked out a compromise on internal improvements that would have appeased northern Democrats without alienating their colleagues who opposed such projects. The Walker Tariff might have been handled more adroitly: various protective duties could have been retained in order to placate Pennsylvania Democrats and other protectionists, and the lower duties might have been phased in more gradually. While the tariff reductions were being phased in, Ritchie probably should have been phased out. Finally, with a political pro-

91. The period from 1848 to 1861 was one of drift and indecision in national policy. Partly a result of the complexity of the problems facing the country, the period's political malaise also stemmed from a repudiation of the strong executive leadership characteristic of the Jacksonian period. Taylor, Fillmore, Pierce, and Buchanan never wielded the kind of power exercised by Jackson, Van Buren, Tyler, or Polk. Expansionism could not thrive in the late 1840s and 1850s in large part because aggressive executive leadership was essential to territorial acquisitions. An imperial nation required an imperial presidency.

gram that seemed to favor the South, Polk could have awarded appointments more generously to the North.

In the final analysis it is difficult to determine the extent to which Polk's personality, vital political differences, or larger historical forces initiated the Democratic defeat of 1848, the dissolution of the second party system, and the drift toward civil war.[92] For a quarter of a century the Jacksonians successfully kept slavery out of national politics, but the Free-Soilers broke the moratorium in 1846. Within eighteen months during 1845 and 1846, the United States attained its continental breadth, launched its first sustained foreign war, and confronted again the dilemma of equality and inequality, freedom and slavery. The issues rekindled by this rapid expansion could not be resolved by American political institutions, since history refused to conform to the pretensions of exceptionalism and superiority so sacrosanct to the Jacksonians. The Polk administration achieved much, but its illusions of mastery and its inability to transcend the minutiae of partisan politics served the country badly. The unprecedented expansion of the mid-1840s unleashed forces that defied direction and control. Ralph Waldo Emerson, a keen observer made uneasy by the whirl of events at this time, with greater insight compared successful aggrandizement to the taking of arsenic: the nation would swallow the territory, but the territory would inevitably consume the nation.[93]

92. Major Jack Downing, the political savant and adviser created by Maine editor Seba Smith, held Polk primarily responsible for the chaos and turmoil of 1848. After the election of Taylor, Major Downing advised Polk to linger in Washington while the new administration took shape. "I see they are looking round all over the country for men to make up a Cabinet for Gineral Taylor; and they seem to be going upon the rule that them that did the most toward electing him must have the first chance in the Cabinet," Downing told Polk. "Now, going upon that rule, the first chance belongs to you, of course; for there isn't no other man in the country that did a quarter so much toward electing him as you did" ([Seba Smith], *My Thirty Years Out of the Senate* [New York: 1859], pp. 320–21).

93. *Journals of Ralph Waldo Emerson*, Edward Waldo Emerson and Waldo Emerson Forbes, eds., 10 vols. (Boston, 1909–14), 7 (1912):206.

CHAPTER 8

The Myths of Manifest Destiny

When John O'Sullivan coined the felicitous phrase "manifest destiny" in mid-1845, he provided Americans then and since with an invaluable legitimizing myth of empire. During the final phase of the Texas annexation crisis, he accused the European nations of "hostile interference" in American affairs, "for the avowed object of thwarting our policy and hampering our power, limiting our greatness and checking the fulfillment of our manifest destiny to overspread the continent allotted by Providence for the free development of our yearly multiplying millions." In his justification for American expansion, O'Sullivan reconciled democracy with empire while he implicitly sanctioned the dispossession of all non-Anglo peoples on the continent. During the mid-1840s, he repeatedly stressed that the United States must acquire abundant land for "the free development" of its "yearly multiplying millions"; without territorial expansion the novel experiment in free government and free enterprise might collapse.[1]

---

1. "Annexation," *Democratic Review,* 17 (July, 1845):5. O'Sullivan repeatedly absolved the United States of blame for the removal of Indians or the dispossession of Mexicans. Ironically, though, O'Sullivan's original concept of manifest destiny differs significantly from the way in which it has been used to describe the expansion to the Pacific. In his article coining the phrase *manifest destiny,* O'Sullivan predicted that pioneers would acquire the entire continent for the United States peacefully by settling in remote regions (including Oregon and California), forming their own autonomous governments, and then seeking annexation to the United States. Texas served as his prototype for this unique method of empire building in North America. In 1846, however, O'Sullivan abandoned his gradualism and supported Polk's strategy for wresting the borderlands from Mexico.

The recurring emphasis on material factors in the Democrats' speculations about the need for expansion raises some important questions about the purported idealism of both "Jacksonian Democracy" and manifest destiny. To O'Sullivan and other Democrats, previous territorial acquisitions had been indispensable to the success of the American political and economic system. And though the Jacksonians were convinced of the superiority of popular government, they were much less certain about its viability. Their ambitions for a continental empire represented much more than simple romantic nationalism: they demanded land because they regarded it as the primary prerequisite for republican government and for an economy and society based upon individual acquisitiveness, geographical and social mobility, and a fluid class structure. These beliefs—best expressed by O'Sullivan but articulated by other Democrats as well— were crucial to most Jacksonian policies, especially those promoting territorial and commercial expansion. To consider manifest destiny in the context of such principles of political economy is a way of making more comprehensible the sustained drive for empire in the 1840s.

Misconceptions about manifest destiny still influence Americans' impressions about their nation's history. Although the civil rights struggle and the Vietnam War have led many Americans to question several of the prevailing orthodoxies of United States history, popular attitudes about the country's past—the self-concept of Americans and their definition of their nation's role in world affairs—have shown a remarkable resiliency, despite the challenges of revisionist scholars. Prevailing ideas about westward expansion are inextricably linked to the values associated with American exceptionalism and mission, fundamental components of the Jacksonian creed. The persistence of manifest destiny ideology under radically different political, economic, and military realities since the 1840s attests to the significant impact these legitimizing myths of empire have had on popular beliefs about United States history. Since continental expansion gave birth to and nurtured so many nationalistic myths, a reevaluation of the historical circumstances that spawned them is an essential exercise in the reassessment of the American past.

Complicating any separation of historical myth from historical actuality is the confusion surrounding the concept of territorial expansion as a policy implemented by national leaders and the concept of the frontier experience as a spontaneous process initiated by pioneers. Long before Frederick Jackson Turner began studying the evolution of a frontier area from "savagery" to "civilization," Americans speculated about the significance of westward expansion upon their institutions and character as well as about its effects upon the world at large. In their own minds, Americans believed that their progress provided a beacon light to a world in darkness. Moreover, though the ever-expanding frontier represented a process quintessentially American, it was also a process with ramifications for people across the Atlantic. From the very beginning of British settlement in North America, the expanding frontier and its pioneer inhabitants were as influential in historical development as were the seat of empire and its imperial officials. This preoccupation with the frontier and its impact on American character and destiny became even more pronounced after the Revolution, then reached new heights during the Jacksonian era. Images of mountain men, freedom fighters at the Alamo, wagon caravans, and prospectors rushing to California appeal more to romantic sensibilities than Calhoun's dispatches, Walker's propaganda, or Polk's devious manipulations to gain title to the Spanish borderlands. The frontiersmen deserve the pages of print that have been devoted to them, though theirs is but half the story. The epic quality of the pioneers' adventures lends sanctity to American expansion and obscures the actual dynamics of empire building. Pioneers alone did not take possession of the continent, nor did policy makers alone acquire it. Two complementary assaults by national leaders and individual pioneers achieved a continental empire during the mid-1840s.

Jacksonians exalted the pioneer as the epitome of the common man, and they celebrated American expansion as an integral part of their mission to obtain a better nation and a better world based on individual freedom, liberalized international trade, and peaceful coexistence. The Democrats equated American progress with global progress and repeatedly argued that European oligarchs were actually opposing the interests of their own people by trying to discourage the expansion of the United States. Geographically and ideologically separated from Europe, the United States, under Jacksonian direction, tried to improve its democratic institutions, utilize the land's rich resources, and demonstrate to the world the superiority of a system allowing free men to compete in a dynamic society. Consequently, the impact of the pioneering process transcended the concerns of the frontiersmen. In forming "a more perfect union" on a continually expanding frontier, Americans thought that they were actually serving the cause of all mankind.

Such a melding of exceptionalism and empire permitted the Jacksonians the luxury of righteous denunciation of their critics at home and abroad. Their domestic foes could be paired with European monarchs as spokesmen for an old order of aristocracy, privilege, and proscription; American expansionism and the Jacksonian domestic program, on the other hand, represented the antithesis of traditional systems. Since territorial acquisitions and Democratic policies fostered opportunity and democracy, they liberated men from oppressive social and economic relationships. The Jacksonians' program promised so much for so little; no wonder messianic imagery appeared so frequently in their rhetoric.

Skeptical Whigs often challenged the Democrats' sincerity, however, sensing that the Jacksonians' motives for aggrandizement were more selfish than they usually admitted.[2] The Democrats' rhetoric proved more resilient than the Whigs' trenchant criticisms of "manifest destiny," however, and so subsequent generations of Americans have underestimated the extent and the intensity of opposition to the policies behind expansionism in the 1840s, especially the Mexican War. Enduring misconceptions about the period have not only obscured the complexities of territorial and commercial expansion during the late Jacksonian era; they have also contributed to an erroneous impression of American history during the entire century from the close of the War of 1812 to the entry of the United States into World War I. A reassessment of these misconceptions shows a greater continuity between nineteenth- and twentieth-century foreign policy than is customarily supposed. The myths of manifest destiny perpetuate an unwarranted nostalgia for times past and conceal some of the striking similarities between the past and the present. The splendid half-century of American isolation and expansion had a darker side, too.

Since the advent of the atomic age, many historians have looked wistfully back to the nineteenth century as a simpler, more secure, and more innocent era in American history. During the national

2. Congressman William Duer of New York, for example, protested in early 1848: "Away with this wretched cant! ... Away with this mawkish morality, with this desecration of religion, with this cant about 'manifest destiny,' a *divine mission,* a warrant from the Most High, to civilize, christianize, and democratize our sister republic at the mouth of the cannon!" (*Congressional Globe* [hereafter abbreviated *CG*], 30 Cong., 1 sess., 347 [February 14, 1848]). James Russell Lowell thought that "all this big talk of our destinies" was "half of it ign[or]ance, an' t' other half rum" (*The Complete Poetical Works of James Russell Lowell,* Cambridge ed. [Boston, 1896], p. 189).

debate on the purported missile gap in 1960, for example, C. Vann Woodward observed that "throughout most of its history the United States has enjoyed a remarkable degree of military security, physical security from hostile attack and invasion. This security was not only remarkably effective, but it was relatively free." Woodward and many of his contemporaries stressed discontinuity in the relative security of the United States before and after its rise to world power. Before the twentieth century, the Atlantic and Pacific Oceans, a weak Mexico and Canada, and European distractions that diverted attention from American affairs gave the United States peace without onerous military expenditures, complicated diplomacy, or devastating wars. But free security disappeared with the quantum leaps in weapons technology in the twentieth century. No longer could the United States repose in the comforting knowledge that its sphere was insulated from the vicissitudes of the shrinking globe.[3]

For most historians who wrote during the two decades following the Second World War, American security in the nineteenth century had not only been free; it had been innocent as well. Samuel Flagg Bemis observed in 1965 that "American expansion across a practically empty continent despoiled no nation unjustly." Whereas European empires had exploited and oppressed their colonial subjects, the United States had adhered to nonintervention, free trade, amicable diplomacy, and self-determination for all peoples. American leaders between the War of 1812 and the Spanish-American War based their foreign policy on what Bemis labeled the "two pole-stars" of United States foreign relations, "anti-imperialism and isolation." Noted diplomat and scholar George F. Kennan likewise viewed the nineteenth century as an era of detachment and naive innocence in American affairs. Kennan believed that American leaders during this period failed to recognize "the global framework" that buttressed the security of the United States. According to Kennan and others troubled by the exigencies of global conflict in their time, the United States during most of the nineteenth century had experienced the rare blessings of isolation and effortless security, an insularity and immunity from international strife that enabled Americans to devote virtually all their attention to domestic development. Spared from the wiles of

3. See C. Vann Woodward, "The Age of Reinterpretation," *American Historical Review,* 66 (October, 1960):1–19. For similar views of nineteenth-century security, see Ralph Henry Gabriel, *The Course of American Democratic Thought,* 2d ed. (New York, 1956), p. 11; Thomas A. Bailey, *A Diplomatic History of the American People,* 8th ed. (New York, 1969), pp. 4–6.

European statecraft and war during much of its history, the United States seemed to Kennan ill prepaped to deal with the new age of superpowers and superweapons after 1945.[4]

American history books, including diplomatic history texts, rein-force the idea that the United States became concerned with consider-ations of national security only in the twentieth century. Historians of foreign relations usually cover the century from the winning of independence to the outward thrust of the 1890s only cursorily. After the American Revolution little of major importance is said to have occurred in American diplomacy except the proclamation of the Monroe Doctrine: the United States had seemed to lack anything resembling a foreign policy during that century of dramatic internal growth. Because 1898 represents for many scholars a sharp transition in the national experience, earlier continental expansion appears irrelevant to the global power politics of the twentieth century. The acquisition of Hawaii and the Philippines in 1898, for example, has received far more careful study than the annexation of Texas in 1845. Such neglect of the first century of American diplomacy and such inordinate emphasis on the period since the Spanish-American War conveys the impression that continental expansion was a foregone conclusion, a long but somewhat uneventful rehearsal for the emer-gence of the United States as a world power in the twentieth century.[5]

Scholarly journals and monographs in American foreign relations repeat this pattern. An overwhelming proportion of recent articles and books on American diplomacy cover the period since World War I. By its virtual absence in both scholarly and popular publications, the pre-1898 era is rendered irrelevant by default, a mere antecedent to the more exciting and more perilous twentieth century. Scholars of American foreign relations have not carefully reexamined the territorial expansion of the United States in the late Jacksonian era and its relative importance in American history, though the fact that the United States doubled its domain in only three short years and fought its first sustained foreign war during the same period suggests that the period deserves some reconsideration.[6]

4. Samuel Flagg Bemis, A Diplomatic History of the United States, 5th ed. (New York, 1965), pp. 216, 244, 1004; The Latin American Policy of the United States: An Historical Interpretation (New York, 1943), pp. 91–92; George F. Kennan, American Diplomacy, 1900–1950 (New York, 1951), pp. 9–11.

5. Two diplomatic history texts that demonstrate this disproportionate emphasis on the second century of American foreign relations are Robert H. Ferrell, American Diplomacy: A History, rev. ed. (New York, 1969), and Richard Leopold, The Growth of American Foreign Policy: A History (New York, 1962).

6. Recently a few scholars have pointed out the neglect of the pre-Wilsonian period

The expansionism of the 1840s acquires a new significance, however, when it is considered within the context of the cultural, social, and political factors that motivated the Jacksonians to pursue a continental empire. In promoting the acquisition of new lands and new markets, the Democrats greatly exaggerated the extent of European hostility to the United States and refused to admit the duplicity and brutality behind their own efforts to expand their nation's territory and trade. By joining their concepts of exceptionalism and empire, the expansionists found a rationale for denying to all other nations and peoples, whether strong or weak, any right to any portion of the entire North American continent. If a rival was strong, it posed a threat to American security and had to be removed; if a rival was weak, it proved its inferiority and lent sanction to whatever actions were taken by pioneers or policy makers to make the territory a part of the United States.

The confusion surrounding expansion results in part from the ambivalence of the Jacksonians themselves, who demonstrated both compassion and contempt in their policies, depending on the racial and ethnic identities of the peoples to be affected by Democratic measures. Generous and humane toward impoverished Americans and poor immigrants from Europe, the Democrats showed far less concern for nonwhites whom they dispossessed or exploited in the process of westward expansion and national development. Removal, eclipse, or extermination—not acculturation and assimilation—awaited the Indians, blacks, and mixed-blood Mexicans on the continent. Despite occasional statements to the contrary, the expansionists regarded the incorporation of nonwhite peoples into the country as both unlikely and undesirable. Without hint of hypocrisy the Jacksonians sought lenient naturalization laws and opportunities for newcomers while strenuously defending policies to separate Indians and Mexicans from their lands and programs to relocate blacks to Africa and Central America.

When expansionists did express concern for nonwhites, they did not question the basic assumptions behind racial proscription and dispossession. They trusted masters to treat their slaves humanely; they urged that the federal government compensate Indians adequately for their territorial cessions. Few expansionists, however,

---

of American foreign relations and have called for a new look at this material. See the comments by Michael Hunt and Walter LaFeber in response to Charles S. Maier's article "Marking Time: The Historiography of International Relations," *Diplomatic History*, 5 (Fall, 1981):354–58, 362–64.

could see any alternative to the removal or extermination of Indians or the enslavement or proscription of blacks. Indians had no legitimate claim to land; blacks no legitimate claim to freedom. Even Free-Soilers who opposed the extension of slavery had little sympathy for the slave, arguing, in essence, that black freedom was detrimental to white status. The racism in Washington was matched by racism on the frontier: pioneers in both Oregon and California adopted restrictive measures in the late 1840s to discourage or prohibit the migration of free blacks to the far West.

The expansion to the Pacific was not primarily an expression of American confidence. Anxiety, not optimism, generally lay behind the quest for land, ports, and markets. A powerful combination of fears led the neo-Jeffersonians of the 1840s to embrace territorial and commercial expansionism as the best means of warding off both domestic and foreign threats to the United States. The Jacksonians were proponents of laissez-faire only in a limited sense, and their sustained efforts to acquire land and markets were their equivalents for what they saw as the Whigs' dangerous propensity to meddle in the domestic economy. Rather than give an "artificial" stimulus to the economy through protective duties or privileged charters, the Democrats preferred to assist American producers by means of territorial acquisitions, reciprocity treaties, improvements in the navy, and a liberal land policy. Frightened by rapid modernization in the United States, the Democrats warned that both European monarchs and the Whig opposition were threatening the Republic—the Europeans by their attempts to contain American expansion, the Whigs by their resistance to Jacksonian foreign policy and their support of legislation that would hasten industrialization, urbanization, and class polarization in the United States.

Jeffersonian ideology, especially its romantic agrarianism, its fear of industrialization, and its conviction that the United States had a natural right to free trade, contributed significantly to the ideology of manifest destiny. To the Jeffersonians and Jacksonians, American farms raised good republican citizens as well as corn, cotton, and wheat: cultivated fields produced virtuous, cultivated people. Whatever the realities of the late Jacksonian period, the expansionists insisted that agricultural societies fostered opportunity and political equality, the essential features of American uniqueness. Moreover, the neo-Jeffersonians contended that only industrial nations became international predators; agricultural countries were self-contained and did not need colonies or privileged markets. These misconceptions cloak some of the more unflattering aspects of antebellum economy and society: slavemasters, not sturdy yeomen, dominated the social and political life of the South; the country's most important export crops, cotton and tobacco, were produced by forced labor; Indians were cruelly dispossessed of their lands and often their culture to make room for American producers; "go-ahead" Americans frequently seemed more interested in land speculation schemes than in patient tilling of the soil; and the United States, like other empires, did prey upon other peoples and nations to augment its wealth, power, and security.

The fact that the United States acquired contiguous rather than noncontiguous territory makes American aggrandizement no less imperial than that of other empires of the mid–nineteenth century. The United States enjoyed several advantages that facilitated its enlargement and made it more antiseptic. Mexico's weakness, the inability of Indian tribes to unite and resist dispossession, the decline of France and Spain as colonizing powers in the New World, and geographical isolation from Europe all served the interests of the United States as it spread across the continent. In addition, the preference for an anticolonial empire embodied in the concept of a confederated Union also contributed to American success. But many Democrats wanted to venture beyond the continent, and had the party not become so divided during and after the Mexican War, the Polk administration probably would have taken steps to add Yucatán and Cuba to the United States, thereby extending the empire into the Caribbean.

The urge to expand beyond the continent was diminished by the fact that the continent itself was incredibly rich in resources. Those abundant resources provided the basis for unparalleled economic growth at home and power in relations with countries abroad. The expansionists regarded the nation's productivity as an irresistible weapon that could counterbalance the military strength of Europe. Here, again, an old Jeffersonian perception dating back to the 1790s came into play: the world desperately needed American commerce and would sacrifice a great deal to obtain it. Although the expansionists never had cause to drive the masses of Europe to starvation and revolution through an embargo on grain and cotton, their speculations on the subject showed them to be far more imperial than philanthropic in their attitudes toward their nation's wealth.

Distressed by many trends in American life, the Democrats formulated their domestic and foreign policies to safeguard themselves and their progeny from a potentially dismal future. They hoped to pre-vent domestic disturbances by acquiring additional territory and mar-kets. Other measures were also devised to protect the country from various perils: the Democrats discouraged the growth of manufactur-ing and monopolistic banking, attempted to minimize the conflict over slavery, encouraged the sale and settlement of the national domain, and tried to discredit the efforts of dissidents to form third parties that might jeopardize the two-party system.

During the 1840s, then, national security was not "free," nor was it attained without constant effort. The expansionists utilized propa-ganda, personal vendetta, legislative legerdemain, confidential agents, covert military pressure, and offensive war to achieve their goals. The Jacksonians, in fact, felt as insecure in their world as their heirs felt in the 1940s, when the Soviet threat called forth a policy of ambitious containment. The insecurity of the 1840s prompted attempts to en-large the United States; the insecurity of the Cold War prompted policies to hem in the Soviet Union. In both cases, anxiety was a major factor behind American actions.

Another myth of manifest destiny concerns the role of military power in American expansion. On May 11, 1846, President Polk informed Congress that "after reiterated menaces, Mexico has passed the boundary of the United States, has invaded our territory and shed American blood upon the American soil." War had begun, Polk observed, in spite of "all our efforts to avoid it."[7] Much evidence, however, raises doubts about just how hard Polk tried to prevent war. Six weeks before Polk's war message, for example, Captain William S. Henry, a subordinate commander in Taylor's army en route to the city of Matamoras, noted in his journal, "Our situation is truly ex-traordinary: right in the enemy's country (to all appearance), actually occupying their corn and cotton fields, the people of the soil leaving their homes, and we, with a small handful of men, marching with colors flying and drums beating, right under the very guns of one of

---

7. James D. Richardson, ed., *A Compilation of the Messages and Papers of the Presidents,* 10 vols. (New York, 1897), 5:2292. Senator John Davis of Massachusetts immediately pointed out the inescapable inconsistency in Polk's message: "We are told in that document that the blood of American citizens has been spilt on our soil. This may be so. It may be true. But in the same message we are told that there is a question of boundary between us and Mexico, and an unsettled question; and that the Minister [Slidell] was sent there from here for the purpose of negotiating that very question" (*CG,* 29 Cong., 1 sess., 786 [May 11, 1846]).

their principal cities, displaying the star-spangled banner, as if in defiance, under their very nose."[8] This army's purpose was not limited to the defense of Texas. It is true that the United States claimed the Rio Grande as the border; it is also true that the United States, in the person of James K. Polk, claimed that the nation had a "clear and unquestionable" title to Oregon up to 54° 40'. But the issue for the Polk administration was not the validity of various boundary claims, but rather the issue of whether military pressure could force Mexico to relinquish the disputed territory between the Nueces and Rio Grande, and the undisputed territories of New Mexico and California besides. The Democrats chose war to defend an unclear and questionable title in the Southwest but retreated from a supposedly clear and unquestionable title in the Northwest. The hypocrisy did not escape the Whigs.[9]

The war promised other benefits as well. Slidell encouraged the Polk administration to prosecute the war with vigor. "The navy should have an opportunity to distinguish itself," Slidell counseled after Taylor's army had already won its laurels. "The people *must* have something to huzza about."[10] Americans rushed by the thousands to fight in Mexico, and several congressmen begged Polk for commissions to command them. The bloodshed elevated to prominence the next two elected presidents, Taylor and Pierce, as well as the future president of the Confederacy, Jefferson Davis. In Senator Benton's words, "gunpowder popularity" often served as "the passport to the presidency" at this time.[11] Benton himself urged Polk to name him supreme commander in Mexico: the precedent of Jackson's meteoric rise to eminence through the killing of redcoats and redskins was not lost on ambitious Democrats. Benton did not become supreme com-

8. William S. Henry, *Campaign Sketches of the War with Mexico* (New York, 1847), p. 70. Congressman Solomon Foot of Vermont told the House of Representatives on July 16, "The President might have said with more propriety that the United States had passed the boundary of Mexico and invaded her territory. This territory had always been in her exclusive possession. She had her military posts there, she had her custom-house and collectors there, she had her resident citizens there, and these citizens were represented in the Mexican Congress" (*CG*, 29 Cong., 1 sess., App. 1100 [July 16, 1846]).

9. Polk, Congressman Joshua Bell of Kentucky noted, had yielded half of Oregon to Britain but had pushed Mexico to war over the Texas boundary. "This, to some extent," he observed, "looks like cringing to the strong and oppressing the weak" (*CG*, 29 Cong., 2 sess., App. 249 [January 19, 1847]).

10. Slidell to Buchanan, November 5, 1846, James Buchanan Papers.

11. *Thirty Years' View; or, A History of the Working of the American Government for Thirty Years, from 1820 to 1850*, 2 vols. (New York, 1854–56), 2:613.

mander and he never attained the presidency. To Polk's chagrin, the war's two most celebrated generals, Taylor and Winfield Scott, turned out to be Whigs. Contrary to the Democrats' expectations, the war did not help their party at the polls.

In contrast to the turmoil of the 1850s and the ordeal of the Civil War and Reconstruction, the 1840s appear in history books as years of stunning success. Within a thousand days the United States ac-quired its continental empire, adding vast territories at an unprece-dented rate. After World War II, several historians who studied westward expansion depicted the 1840s as a golden age in American diplomacy, a time when enlightened self-interest and adequate power and resolve to attain it guided United States foreign policy. Norman Graebner so assessed the decade, contending in 1955 that expansion to the Pacific "was a unified, purposeful, precise movement that was ever limited to specific maritime objectives. . . .It was . . . through clearly conceived policies relentlessly pursued that the United States achieved its empire on the Pacific," he concluded. Another prominent postwar scholar, Arthur M. Schlesinger, described Polk as "undeser-vedly one of the forgotten men of American history." Polk declared "certain definite objectives" for his term and achieved them all: a reduced tariff, an Independent Treasury, and the acquisition of Ore-gon and California. "By carrying the flag to the Pacific he gave America her continental breadth and ensured her future significance in the world," Schlesinger noted. Many postwar scholars who had witnessed the rise and fall of fascism only to face another menace in Cold War communism understandably assessed manifest destiny chiefly in terms of how the acquisitions had increased the wealth and power of the United States, equipping it to counter totalitarian regimes a century later. This perspective enhanced the reputations of the ex-pansionists.[12]

12. Norman A. Graebner, *Empire on the Pacific: A Study in American Continental Expansion* (New York, 1955), pp. vi, 228; Arthur M. Schlesinger, *Paths to the Present* (New York, 1949), pp. 97–98. Up until the late 1940s, the "Whiggish" view of late Jacksonian expansion generally prevailed. That view held that Tyler and Polk had been proslavery sectionalists who had subverted the Constitution and despoiled Mexico in order to gain additional slave territory. During the height of the Cold War, however, many scholars tended to interpret expansion in terms of how powerful (and how great a force for good) territorial acquisitions had made the United States. Since the Civil Rights movement, the interventions abroad in the 1960s, and the Vietnam War, another generation of scholars have increasingly seen the policies of the 1840s as striking manifestations of a recurring arrogance of power in American relations with nonwhite peoples in weaker nations.

The Cold War view of manifest destiny is instructive not only for what it asserts but also for what it neglects or ignores. American policy makers in the 1840s did define the national interest in terms of acquiring land and markets, and they did find various ways to attain their ambitions. In fact, rarely have two presidents acted as audaciously as Tyler and Polk to overcome foreign and domestic opposition to their policies. The cavalier methods of the expansionists during the mid-1840s often appalled contemporaries such as the poet Emerson. "The name of Washington City in the newspapers is every day a blacker shade," he lamented in 1847, "all the news from that quarter being of a sadder type, more malignant. It seems to be settled that no act of honour or benevolence or justice is to be expected from the American government, but only this, that they will be as wicked as they dare."[13] Cold War scholars, however, were often no more squeamish about the methods of aggrandizement than the expansionists themselves had been. Unlike Emerson and the anti-war Whigs, they seemed to accept the idea that the end justified the means.

A more detached analysis of the history of the 1840s—one less influenced by Cold War assumptions about the positive effects of nineteenth-century expansion—demonstrates how high a price was paid for the acquisitions. The expansionists' shortcomings and mistakes were as historically significant as their much touted strengths and accomplishments, for even when they attained their immediate goal, it seldom lived up to their long-term expectations. They acquired a continental empire but could not govern it. Too certain that their political institutions could resolve fundamental internal divisions and too complacent about the mounting sectional rancor over the expansion of slavery, the Democrats failed to integrate the new acquisitions into the Union and failed to keep the Union itself intact. No triumphs of technology—no quantity of railroads, steamships, telegraphs, and rotary presses—could sustain the expansive confederation. Limitations on expansion did exist, though the Democrats seemed incapable of discerning them during the 1840s. Their perceptions of the past and their fears for the future blinded them to perils in the realignment of sections and politics.

The expansionists' far-fetched notions about nonwhites precluded their thinking constructively about racial questions. By denying the likelihood of a permanent black and Indian population on the conti-

13. *Journals of Ralph Waldo Emerson*, Edward W. Emerson and Waldo E. Forbes, eds., 10 vols. (Boston, 1909–14), 7:253–54.

nent, antebellum Americans had difficulty preparing themselves and their descendants for racial heterogeneity in the United States. The acceptance of racial diversity as a reality of national life came largely through necessity, not choice. As most European visitors realized, racial prejudice permeated the country and transcended the sectional dispute over slavery. Americans, however, hardly seemed to question the intense racial animus across the nation; it was such a common-place of life that it drew only isolated comment or criticism. There were many gradations of racial feeling among Americans, of course, and a small corps of radical abolitionists indicted the North for its failure to practice racial egalitarianism in the free states. But there is no denying that racial prejudice was a basic determinant of American domestic and foreign policy during the Jacksonian period.

The expansionists' ethnocentrism also sowed the seeds of future discord between the United States and the peoples of Latin America. The annexation of Texas and the Mexican War created a legacy of suspicion and anger toward the United States among peoples south of the Rio Grande. However much the United States professed to be a "good neighbor" to other countries in the hemisphere, those coun-tries often held more ambivalent views. This tension has complicated United States relations with Latin America for well over a century and persists to the present. During much of its history the United States has reserved its diplomacy for European countries. Usually a distinct lack of diplomacy has characterized relations with Indians, Asians, and Latin Americans.

American arrogance was not confined to the Western Hemisphere. The swashbuckling demeanor with which Caleb Cushing and his crew confronted the Chinese in 1844 demonstrated that Americans were, much like the British, self-interested, presumptuous, and bound to create problems for the unreceptive and understandably frightened Chinese. Americans stressed their uniqueness and benevolence, but the Chinese tended to see greater similarities than differences be-tween the various Western intruders. The persistent pattern of Amer-ican condescension toward nonwhite peoples has made it difficult for twentieth-century leaders to adapt to the challenges of a shrinking globe and the recent dispersion of wealth and power away from Europe and America toward East Asia, the Middle East, and Africa. In their zeal to bring "the American way of life" to other peoples, several generations of United States policy makers have overlooked the fact that racism, aggressiveness, and self-righteousness have often been part of that way of life. The paradox of American benevolence coupled with awesome military power found expression more than a century before the United States intervened in Vietnam. During the Mexican War, for example, James Russell Lowell lampooned American pretensions in his "Pious Editor's Creed":

> I du believe wutever trash
>   'll keep the people in blindness,
> Thet we the Mexicuns can thrash
>   Right inter brotherly kindness,
> Thet bombshells, grape, an' powder 'n' ball
>   Air good-will's strongest magnets,
> Thet peace, to make it stick at all,
>   Must be druv in with bagnets.[14]

Bayonet diplomacy (or "big stick" diplomacy) did not originate with Theodore Roosevelt and his interventionism in Latin America. Though not usually so described, the war against Mexico was the first instance of gunboat diplomacy. When a writer for the *Democratic Review* justified the invasion and occupation of Mexico in 1847, for example, he anticipated Roosevelt's 1904 corollary to the Monroe Doctrine. "It is an acknowledged law of nations," the *Review* writer maintained, "that when a country sinks into a state of anarchy, unable to govern itself, and dangerous to its neighbors, it becomes the *duty* of the most powerful of those neighbors to interfere and settle its affairs."[15] Acting upon such assumptions, the United States has been doing its "duty" in Latin America for almost 140 years.

In many respects the expansionists' outlook turned out to be strikingly unrealistic. The United States was hardly overcrowded in the early 1840s: millions of acres within the existing national domain remained to be occupied and cultivated. Racial fears were also exag-

14. In *Complete Poetical Works*, p. 202.
15. "The War," *Democratic Review*, 20 (February, 1847):101. The similarity between this view and Roosevelt's later statement says a great deal about the continuity in American perceptions of and policies toward Latin America. In his annual message of 1904, Roosevelt explained his meddling in Latin America: "Chronic wrongdoing, or an impotence which results in a general loosening of ties of civilized societies, may in America, as elsewhere, ultimately require intervention by some civilized nation, and in the Western Hemisphere the adherence of the United States to the Monroe Doctrine may force the United States, however reluctantly, in flagrant cases of such wrongdoing or impotence, to the exercise of an international police power." Roosevelt intervened in Latin America as "reluctantly" as Polk did in Mexico.

gerated. When southern slaves attained their freedom in 1865, no war between blacks and whites ensued. After the Civil War, scores of large cities and hundreds of factories and corporations spread across the country, yet democratic institutions and capitalism survived the transformation. Despite the undeniable hardships and radical adjustments precipitated by rapid industrialization, few Americans would argue that manufacturing weakened rather than strengthened the United States. The Democrats also overestimated the hostility of Britain. The British ministry acquiesced in the annexation of Texas; it did not incite Mexico to make war upon the United States; and it did not try to acquire California before the United States seized it in 1846. Several major premises behind the expansion of the late Jacksonian period proved erroneous.

The decade of the 1840s should be placed in a different historical context: United States policy in this crucial decade prepared the way for both late-nineteenth-century and twentieth-century imperialism. The expansion of the Tyler-Polk years, like that of the 1890s, grew largely out of a recurring domestic malaise that found expression in American aggrandizement. During both decades, ambitious and anxious policy makers welcomed war and expansion as alternatives to basic structural changes in American economics and politics. The methods of American foreign policy also suggest continuities over time. The tactics employed by Tyler and Polk to expand the empire suggest that the label "imperial presidency" should not be confined to presidents of the Cold War era: Polk, especially, acted as imperially as any of his twentieth-century successors. Democratic process and an aggressive foreign policy were as incompatible in the mid-nineteenth century as in the twentieth, as congressional critics frequently noted. In late 1846, for example, Whig Garrett Davis pointed out that the founding fathers had "entrusted to the president the national shield," but they had intentionally given the national sword and "the entire war power" to Congress. "To make war is the most fearful power exerted by human government," Davis warned, a power too momentous to be placed in any one man's hands.[16] That admonition was out of fashion for two decades after World War II, but Vietnam gave it new meaning. In the 1840s and in the 1960s, Congress was remiss in its responsibility to scrutinize how American military power was used, for what purposes, and under what pretenses. In both cases a scheming president misled Congress into sanctioning a wider war

16. *CG,* 29 Cong., 2 sess., App. 104 (December 22, 1846).

than anticipated. Though Congress does delay while it deliberates, there are also drawbacks in granting the president the nation's sword as well as its shield: the skirmish on the Rio Grande, the attack in the Gulf of Tonkin, and, more recently, the meddling in Nicaragua, El Salvador, and Lebanon attest to that.[17]

Orthodox historical "truths" possess considerable resiliency. By extolling the virtues and achievements of a self-conscious people, they appeal to nationalistic feeling, and through constant repetition they acquire an aura of unquestioned certainty over time. The idealism of westward expansion embodied in the concept of manifest destiny persists because it helps to reconcile American imperialism with an extremely favorable national image. The assumed benevolence and the supposedly accidental nature of American expansion are conve-nient evasions of the complexities of the past. In accepting the rheto-ric of American mission and destiny, apologists for the expansionists of the 1840s have had to minimize or ignore much historical evidence. Perhaps more to the point, defenders of American exceptionalism and innocence have actually had to slight other crucial motives for expansion that the Democrats themselves often candidly admitted.

Though the phrase *manifest destiny* appears repeatedly in the litera-ture of American foreign relations, it does not accurately describe the expansionism of the 1840s. It is one of many euphemisms that have allowed several generations of Americans to maintain an unwarrant-ed complacency in regard to their nation's past, a complacency that has contributed in a fundamental way to the persistent quandary the United States has faced in trying to define a realistic role for itself in a world that seldom acts according to American precepts. Geographi-cal isolation and a powerful exceptionalist ideology have insulated the United States from the complexities of culture and historical experience affecting other peoples, leaving Americans susceptible to myths and misconceptions at home and abroad. Often unaware of their own history, Americans frequently misunderstand foreign cul-tures and experiences as well. Myths and misconceptions often fill the void created by ignorance of history.

The expansionists of the 1840s should not be permitted to expro-

17. The ill-defined and untenable United States military mission in Lebanon, so strenuously supported by the Reagan administration, is a striking example of the way in which American policy makers frequently miscalculate how much can be lost and how little gained by committing United States military power abroad. Americans apparently cannot understand that military intervention by a major power some-times provokes rather than deters aggression.

priate many of the best Americans ideals for their own purposes. Just
as they manipulated the Census of 1840, the Democratic convention
of 1844, and the Mexican-Texas border dispute for their own ends,
so too did they exploit American exceptionalist ideology to ennoble
their ambitions for riches and dominion. But rhetoric could not hide
the chauvinism, aggressiveness, and design that were essential components of continental expansion. The United States used many
tactics to expand its domain, and like other empires it created legitimizing myths to sanction that expansion. Some Americans, however, challenged the validity of those myths and condemned the conduct
they excused. But critics of national policy seldom reach generations
other than their own, for history—especially American history—
often records only the dominant voices of the past. That the United
States has changed dramatically since attaining its continental empire
is obvious. That the American people have reassessed their basic
assumptions about themselves, their national experience, and their
approach to other nations is not so obvious.

Since impressions about the past affect consciousness in the present
and help define possibilities for the future, the way in which historical
events are interpreted significantly influences the ongoing process of
defining national identity, national character, and national purpose.
Because history involves both continuity and change over time, a
historical work serves two crucial purposes: it provides a window to
the past, and it furnishes a mirror to the present. However striking
the changes in American life since the Jacksonian era, the persistence
of certain principles and biases—the consistency of much of American political and diplomatic "culture" over several generations—ties
the present to the past, and links both to the future. For that reason
the legacy of the 1840s should be of concern to all Americans—not
just historians.

A Note on Sources

The footnotes accompanying the preceding chapters provide the principal bibliographical guide to both the primary and secondary sources utilized in this study. What follows is a brief overview of materials that are particularly important for understanding American territorial and commercial expansionism within its political and cultural context during the late Jacksonian period.

Public leaders usually confined their most candid remarks to private correspondence. Many letters cited in this study bear notations such as "confidential," "private," or "not for the file." Not coincidentally, those letters often proved to be particularly revealing in their commentary on events and individuals. Though several manuscript collections contributed to my sense of the 1840s, the following were most instructive: for the Tyler years, the papers of Duff Green and Andrew Jackson, and for the Polk years the papers of James Buchanan, Louis McLane, William Marcy, and James K. Polk. Andrew Jackson Donelson's collection also contains valuable material for the entire period. All of the manuscript collections cited are in the Library of Congress, with the exception of the letters of Robert J. Walker, which are in the National Archives.

A number of published collections of letters are more readily available than the unpublished collections, and they complement the private papers mentioned. Two works of value on Calhoun are J. Franklin Jameson's edition of the "Correspondence of John C. Calhoun," *Annual Report of the American Historical Association for the Year 1899,* vol. 2 (Washington D.C., Government Printing Office, 1900), and Frederick W. Moore, ed., "Calhoun as Seen by His Political Friends: Letters of Duff Green, Dixon H. Lewis and Richard K. Crallé during the Period from 1831 to 1848," *Publications of the Southern History Association,* vol. 7, nos. 3–6 (Washington, D.C.: Southern History Association, 1903). John Tyler's private papers are few and disappointing, but the void is partly filled by Lyon G. Tyler, ed., *The Letters and Times of the Tylers,* 3 vols. (Richmond: Whittet & Shepperson, 1884–85). For letters of less prominent but important leaders of the time, see George P. Hammond, ed., *The Larkin Papers: Personal, Business, and Official Correspondence of Thomas Oliver Larkin, Merchant and United States Consul in California,* 10 vols. (Berkeley: University of California Press, 1951–1964); Roy F. Nichols, "The Mystery of the Dallas Papers," *Pennsylvania Magazine of History and Biography,* vol. 73 (Philadelphia: Historical Society of Pennsylvania, 1949); M. A. DeWolfe Howe, ed., *The Life and Letters of George Bancroft,* 2 vols. (New York: Charles Scribner's Sons, 1908); Arthur G. Staples, ed., *The Letters of John Fairfield* (Lewiston: Lewiston Journal Co., 1922); Amelia W. Williams and Eugene C. Barker, ed., *The Writings of Sam Houston, 1813– 1863,* 8 vols. (Austin: University of Texas Press, 1938–1943); Worthington C. Ford, ed., "Van Buren–Bancroft Correspondence, 1830– 1845," *Proceedings of the Massachusetts Historical Society,* vol. 42 (Boston, 1908–09).

Antebellum politicians were not shy about writing detailed memoirs, probably because they did not want their partisan rivals to have the last word, even after death. These diaries and reminiscenses frequently present contradictory views of people and events. Often self-serving and purposely selective, such autobiographical sources are no less valuable to the historian for that, since the biases themselves help demonstrate the intensity of political passions at this time. Of particular value because of their comprehensive scope are Thomas Hart Benton, *Thirty Years' View; or, A History of the Working of the American Government for Thirty Years, from 1820 to 1850,* 2 vols. (New York: D. Appleton, 1854–56), and *Memoirs of John Quincy Adams, Comprising Portions of His Diary from 1795 to 1848,* Charles F. Adams, ed., 12 vols. (Philadelphia: J. B. Lippincott, 1874–77). Besides the Adams diary, two other diaries are indispensable: *The Diary of James K. Polk during His Presidency, 1845–1849,* Milo M. Quaife, ed., 4 vols. (Chicago: A. C. McClurg, 1910), and *The Diary of Philip Hone, 1828–1851,* Bayard Tuckerman, ed., 2 vols. (New York: Dodd, Mead, 1889). Other valuable memoirs and reflections include Nathan Sargent, *Public Men and Events, from the Commencement of Mr. Monroe's Administration, in 1817, to the Close of Mr. Fillmore's Administration, in 1853,* 2 vols. (Philadelphia: J. B. Lippincott, 1875); Duff Green, *Facts and Suggestions, Biographical, Historical, Financial, and Political* (New York: C. S. Westcott, 1866); Benjamin Perley Poore, *Perley's Reminiscences of Sixty Years in the National Metropolis,* 2 vols. (Boston: E. R. Curtis, 1886); Anson Jones, *Memoranda and Official Correspondence Relating to the Republic of Texas, Its History and Annexation,* reprint ed. (Chicago: University of Chicago Press, 1966); John W. Forney, *Anecdotes of Public Men* (New York: Harper and Brothers, 1873); Henry S. Wise, *Seven Decades of the Union* (Philadelphia: J. B. Lippincott, 1881); Joshua R. Giddings, *A History of the Rebellion: Its Authors and Causes* (New York: Follett, Foster, 1864); George W. Julian, *Political Recollections, 1840 to 1872* (Chicago: Jansen, McClurg, 1884). One point should be made about several of the memoirs cited in this study. Many of them were published near the end of Reconstruction or shortly afterward, and several, especially those by Southerners, tend to stress national harmony and reunification rather than sectional discord and secession. Their retrospective conciliatory tone masks some of the animosity and viciousness that so frequently characterized the late 1840s and 1850s.

Various government documents are valuable sources on the politics and diplomacy of the Tyler-Polk years. Though both voluminous and tedious, the congressional debates on Texas, Oregon, and the Mexican War define the partisan disagreements on issues and indicate as well the intensity of party conflict. For these debates see the *Congressional Globe,* vols. 82–90 (Washington: Blair & Rives, 1842–1849). For presidential addresses by Tyler and Polk, see James D. Richardson, ed., *A Compilation of the Messages and Papers of the Presidents,* vols. 5–6 (Washington: Government Printing Office, 1897). Vital foreign relations documents appear in William R Manning, ed., *The Diplomatic Correspondence of the United States, Inter-American Affairs, 1831–1860,* 12 vols. (Washington: Carnegie Endowment for International Peace, 1929–1939). The diplomacy of Texas before annexation can be followed in George P. Garrison, ed., "Diplomatic Correspondence of the Republic of Texas," *Annual Report of the American Historical Association for the Year 1908,* 2 vols. (Washington: Government Printing Office, 1911). The series *Senate Documents* and *House Documents* also contain useful material, especially the annual reports by cabinet members. Particularly instructive in terms of the concerns that gave impetus to the expansionism of the Tyler-Polk years are the reports of the secretaries of war, the navy, and the treasury. The yearly assessments by the commissioners of Indian affairs also proved valuable.

A study oriented more toward popular opinion would have relied more heavily on newspapers and periodicals. The few cited here, however, provided relatively complete and reliable accounts of the day-to-day activities of the Tyler and Polk administrations. The two executive papers, John B. Jones's *Daily Madisonian* and Thomas Ritchie's *Daily Union* are essential for understanding the politics and diplomacy of the 1840s. Since James Gordon Bennett maintained several correspondents in Washington while Congress was in session, his New York *Herald* is an excellent source on the daily whirligig in Washington. The *Herald* correspondents often disagreed with each other, so they present a wide disparity of views rather than a single party line. John L. O'Sullivan's journal, The *Democratic Review,* and his short-lived paper, the New York *Morning News,* were especially helpful on Jacksonian ideology and Democratic party politics. Political historians could use the *Democratic Review* far more than they have in recent years.

European visitors' accounts presented striking insights into American politics and culture as well as providing enjoyable reading. Most instructive were Alexander Mackay, *The Western World, or, Travels in the United States in 1846–47,* 2 vols. (Philadelphia: Lea & Blanchard, 1849); Thomas Colley Grattan, *Civilized America,* 2 vols. (London: Bradbury & Evans, 1859); John Robert Godley, *Letters from America,* 2 vols. (London: J. Murray, 1844); and Frederick Marryat, *A Diary in America, with Remarks on Its Institutions,* 3 vols. (London: Longman, Orme, 1839).

Citing the most significant primary sources is much easier than singling out the most significant secondary sources. Perhaps each generation does write its own history, but each generation also benefits from the contributions of its predecessors. The following works probably influenced this study more than the footnotes suggest: Albert K. Weinberg, *Manifest Destiny: A Study of Nationalist Expansionism in American History* (Baltimore: Johns Hopkins University Press, 1935); Henry Nash Smith, *Virgin Land: The American West as Symbol and Myth* (Cambridge, Mass.: Harvard University Press, 1950); Norman A. Graebner, *Empire on the Pacific: A Study in American Continental Expansion* (New York: Ronald Press, 1955); Leon Litwack, *North of Slavery: The Negro in the Free States, 1790–1860* (Chicago: University of Chicago Press, 1961); Walter LaFeber, *The New Empire: An Interpretation of American Expansion, 1860–1898* (Ithaca: Cornell University Press, 1963); Charles G. Sellers, *James K. Polk, Continentalist, 1843–1846* (Princeton: Princeton

University Press, 1966); George M. Fredrickson, *The Black Image in the White Mind: The Debate on Afro-American Character and Destiny, 1817– 1914* (New York: Harper & Row, 1971); Robert F. Berkhofer, Jr., *The White Man's Indian: Images of the American Indian from Columbus to the Present* (New York: Alfred A. Knopf, 1978). Though my focus and interpretation are often different from theirs, these scholars (many of whom raise issues and ideas not generally addressed by historians of American foreign relations) provided insights and suggestions that helped guide me to my own questions and conclusions.

Index